ASPECTS OF
EUROPEAN HISTORY
1789–1980

STEPHEN J. LEE

ASPECTS OF EUROPEAN HISTORY 1789–1980

METHUEN

LONDON & NEW YORK

Again, for Margaret

First published in 1982 by Methuen & Co. Ltd
11 New Fetter Lane, London EC4P 4EE

Published in the USA by Methuen & Co.
in association with Methuen, Inc.
733 Third Avenue, New York, NY 10017

Printed in Great Britain by
Richard Clay (The Chaucer Press) Ltd
Bungay, Suffolk

British Library Cataloguing in Publication Data
Lee, Stephen J.
  Aspects of European history 1789–1980.
  1. Europe – History – 1789–1900
  2. Europe – History – 20th century
  I. Title
  940.2'8   D299

  ISBN 0–416–73170–8
  ISBN 0–416–73180–5 Pbk (University paperback 764)
Library of Congress Cataloging in Publication Data
Lee, Stephen J.
  Aspects of European history, 1789–1980.

  Bibliography: p.
  1. Europe – History – 1789–1900.   2. Europe –
  History – 20th century.   I. Title.
  D299.L39   940.2'8   82-6310
  ISBN 0-416-73170-8   AACR2
  ISBN 0-416-73180-5 (pbk.)

Contents

List of illustrations

MAPS

FIGURE

Introduction

This book is a sequel to *Aspects of European History 1494–1789*. It is based on an interpretative approach to some of the topics most commonly encountered in modern European history and is designed to be used in addition to specialist works and standard textbooks. The main intention is to stimulate thought and to assist in the preparation of essays and seminar papers by encouraging the student to develop an angle or an argument, whether in agreement with the chapters or in opposition to them. It is also hoped that the topics and the approach to them will be of interest to the general reader who seeks to understand the background to some of the problems of the modern world.

This volume contains a larger number of contemporary quotations than the first and, in some chapters, more direct reference to recent views of and major controversies among historians.

The chapters suggest a variety of methods by which a theme or argument may be presented.

1 Chapters 6, 9 and 21 stress the ideas, policies and problems of individual statesmen.
2 Chapters 20 and 31 examine an issue from two opposite viewpoints; in Chapter 20 the arguments are separated, in Chapter 31 they are integrated.
3 Chapters 4 and 12 present one viewpoint only and use only carefully selected factual material.
4 Some chapters use the analogy of 'forces' ('internal' and 'external', 'centrifugal' and 'centripetal'); examples are Chapters 1 and 17. Others, like Chapters 4, 18 and 28, emphasize 'contradictions' and 'paradoxes'.
5 Comparisons and contrasts are sometimes drawn; Chapter 9, for example, deals with the ideas and policies of two statesmen.
6 Chapters 33, 34, 35 and 36 provide a survey of four major themes affecting Europe as a whole and other parts of the world.

All the chapters are designed for extensive note-taking. They were built up step by step and the sections and paragraphs of each chapter are each intended to represent a stage in the argument. It should, therefore, be possible to break all the chapters down into their

Aspects of European History 1789–1980

constituent parts. It is hoped that this will ease the task of essay preparation and examination revision.

Because of the problem of compressing such a wide period into a book of this size, the coverage, as in Volume 1, is for the most part political. There is, however, an attempt in many chapters to include economic, social and intellectual trends. Chapters 22, 29 and 32 deal specifically with economic history. Finally, the period since 1945 is dealt with more generally. It is so complex and eventful that detailed analysis would require an entire volume.

1

The Origins of the French Revolution

The purpose of this opening chapter is to provide a synthesis of some of the more important interpretations of the outbreak of the French Revolution.

The 1770s and 1780s brought with them a serious economic depression. This seemed the worse because it followed a long period of mounting prosperity and it caused a sense of resentment and bitterness as all classes faced a decline in their status. The fabric of society was now threatened with rupture by the exertion of two internal forces. These had existed for much of the eighteenth century but were now greatly accentuated by the economic crisis. The first force was the hostility between the Second Estate (aristocracy) and the Third Estate (bourgeoisie, peasantry and urban proletariat) as they pulled further apart from each other. The second force was the simultaneous attempt of both Estates to pull away from the policies of the monarchy and the implications of absolutism. For a while the Estates formed an unnatural alliance against the central power of the monarchy, and so the second force was the stronger. The king, finding himself in serious difficulties, yielded to the combined demands of the different classes, and agreed to summon the Estates General. Now that the central authority seemed to have collapsed, the original antagonism between the Estates reasserted itself so violently that the first force tore through the fabric of the *ancien régime*. The influence of the nobility was now overwhelmed by successive waves of the Third Estate as the bourgeoisie, peasantry

Aspects of European History 1789–1980

and proletariat each pressed for the achievement of their aspirations.

*

It is a common assumption that revolution is caused by misery; Marx certainly believed that worsening conditions create a situation favourable to revolution. In the mid-nineteenth century, however, Alexis de Tocqueville advanced the theory that the French Revolution broke out when conditions were improving. He observed: 'It is not always by going from bad to worse that a country falls into a revolution.' Moreover: 'the state of things destroyed by a revolution is almost always somewhat better than that which immediately precedes it.'[1] In 1962, J. C. Davies used a slightly different approach, but complemented de Tocqueville's view. He suggested that 'revolutions are most likely to occur when a prolonged period of objective economic and social development is followed by a short period of sharp reversal'.[2] This seems to be borne out by the general economic trends of the eighteenth century.

Between 1741 and 1746 France experienced a high overall economic growth rate. Large sections of the bourgeoisie benefited from the threefold increase in trade and the fivefold increase of overseas trade, together with the revived prosperity of ports like Dunkirk, Le Havre, La Rochelle, Bordeaux, Nantes and Marseilles. The increase in prices (estimated at 65 per cent between 1741 and 1765) drove up the value of farm produce and greatly improved the living conditions of the tenant farmers. Although famines did occur, for example in 1725, 1740, 1759 and 1766–8, there was nothing in the 1780s to compare with the catastrophic levels of starvation during the years 1693–4 and 1709–10. In the general upsurge of prosperity, the French bourgeoisie and peasantry seemed distinctly better off than their counterparts in Central and Eastern Europe.

When it came, during the 1770s and 1780s, the slump had a profound effect. France experienced a recession similar to that suffered by other countries; this was probably no more than a temporary dip in a lengthy economic cycle, possibly precipitated by a shortage of bullion from the New World. French industry and commerce were, however, badly affected because of the inadequate nature of French credit facilities. Production therefore declined, unemployment increased and the recession soon spread to agriculture. To make matters worse, there was a severe drought in 1785,

The Origins of the French Revolution

and in the following years the peasants were unable to afford the usual quantity of seed, the inevitable result being short yields. The 1788 harvest was ruined by an abnormally wet summer and the position was even worse in 1789. The degree of starvation was lower than it had been at various stages during the reign of Louis XIV, but the suddenness of the decline in the fortunes of each class in the 1770s and 1780s had a far more dangerous psychological impact. The bourgeoisie and the peasantry, in particular, saw the gap between their aspirations and their achievements growing ever wider, while the nobility struggled desperately to hold what they had. The result was deep resentment and growing bitterness, both of them more inflammable revolutionary material than suffering by itself. The social classes looked with increasing suspicion at each other and at the régime itself, trying desperately to recapture their former share of the national wealth and to continue their previous quest for material advancement.

*

The eighteenth century had seen a gradual deterioration in relations between the Second and Third Estates. Each had improved its position economically compared to its own past, but each came to regard the other as a serious threat to its security and well-being. This resentment greatly increased after 1776.

The nobility managed to reassert its influence over the administration and local government by the alliance between the *noblesse d'epée* and the *noblesse de robe*, while positions of authority within the Church had, in the words of Talleyrand, become the preserve '*presque exclusif de la classe noble*'.[3] On the other hand, the nobility feared the ambitions of the wealthy sections of the bourgeoisie and resisted fiercely any attempts by the latter to break the monopoly of the *noblesse de robe* over the administrative offices and the *parlements*. The bourgeoisie regarded their ultimate aim as passage into the Second Estate through the traditional method of ennoblement. Increasingly, however, this form of upward mobility was blocked and with it any chance of gaining political power. Two future leaders of the Revolution showed the effects that disillusionment with this state of affairs could produce. Carnot's radical views followed his unsuccessful attempts to gain ennoblement, while Danton claimed that 'The Old Régime drove us to [revolution] by giving us a good education, without opening any opportunity for our talents'.[4] The peasantry, although lacking the education and economic power of the bourgeoisie, had their own aspirations which were challenged by the rural nobility. Seigneurial rights and dues were extracted to the full, and the peasantry had to suffer the inconveniences and hardships produced by the *banalité du moulin, banalité du four, banalité du pressoir, droit de chasse* and *droit de bauvin*. And, according to one of the *cahiers* of the peasantry in 1789, 'the contempt of the nobility for the commonality is beyond belief".[5] The nobility therefore came to be regarded as a parasitic element, enjoying seigneurial privileges without carrying out the functions which had once accompanied them.

The rift between the Second and Third Estates widened during the 1770s and 1780s. Under the impact of the recession, the peasantry found the seigneurial dues particularly onerous, while the nobility increasingly tightened up their exactions in order to solve their own difficulties. The burden of the depression was therefore passed downwards to the section of society least able to bear it. The bourgeois complaint about the nobility was more indirect but nevertheless significant for the future. They accused the nobility of resisting any rationalization of the economic and financial structure and of perpetuating anachronistic institutions at a time when reform was most urgently needed.

Yet tensions between the social classes did not result in immediate conflict. For a while they were partially restrained by a temporary and basically artificial coalition against a common target, the absolute power of the monarch.

*

The motives of each class in establishing this common front against the central government differed widely, but each had a fixed idea that the régime in its present form could no longer serve its interests or guarantee it from exploitation. The government had, therefore, to be modified. Precisely how remained a matter of vague speculation until the monarchy actually collapsed under the combined pressure.

The nobility feared absolutism more profoundly in the 1770s and 1780s than ever before. The banning of the *parlements* seemed to be an attack on the most cherished power of the nobility, gained after a long struggle since 1715, namely the questioning of royal legislation. When the *parlements* were restored in 1774 the nobility returned to the offensive, only to be confronted by the appalling

The Origins of the French Revolution

spectre of a reforming monarch who, to make matters worse, was served by ministers who openly expressed reservations about the existing fiscal system and the exemptions from taxation. Louis XVI seemed a greater menace than Louis XV because he appeared to be more willing to embark upon an extensive remodelling programme which would reduce the social status of the nobility in a way never even considered before. The nobility therefore used every device available; they fought the reform programme in the *parlements*, in the Court and in the Assembly of Notables. As the financial crisis worsened after 1787, they demanded the convocation of the Estates General. This was merely an appeal to an early precedent, one which the nobility knew the monarch could not ignore. The Estates General would naturally confirm the powers of the nobility, since on the traditional method of voting the First and Second Estates would outnumber the Third.

The bourgeoisie saw matters differently but went along with the tactics of the nobility. To them, the Estates General offered the prospect of fundamental constitutional reform, which would enable the bourgeoisie to exert more control over the political institutions and to redesign the economic structure. After the brief experiments of the Regency with *laissez-faire*, France had seen the return of the mercantilist policies of Colbert from 1726 onwards, and the restoration of the oppressive guild system and internal customs barriers. Then, during the reign of Louis XVI, government policy seemed to lose all sense of overall direction. At the very depth of the economic depression the government seemed prepared to unleash the market forces of Great Britain; by the free trade treaty of 1786 it exposed the struggling French industries to *laissez-faire* at the very time that protection was most needed. If the chaotic economic and fiscal system were to be reorganized, the bourgeoisie would have to play an active role. This could no longer be done by hoping for a special relationship with the monarchy as had existed in the reign of Louis XIV; the nobility had long since blocked the access to political positions. The solution, therefore, had to be found in representative institutions – in a parliamentary monarchy. Much as the bourgeoisie resented the nobility, they therefore resented the latter's demands for the calling of the Estates General.

The peasantry regarded the meeting of the Estates General as a panacea. It would be the means whereby the unequal distribution of taxation would be remedied. The *taille, capitation, vingtième, gabelle*

5

and *aides* would be reassessed or possibly replaced by a graduated land or income tax. The institution of monarchy still commanded respect, but it was felt increasingly that its powers should be limited. The peasantry suspected that the government had been making profits from fluctuations in the price of grain; this and other grievances could now be articulated openly, with greater hope of redress.

In expressing its opposition to the policies of the régime each class made use of the ideas of the leading French *philosophes*. It is often assumed that Montesquieu, Voltaire and Rousseau exerted direct influence on the growth of revolutionary feeling and thereby precipitated the events of 1789. In reality, the growth of dissent was not actually stimulated by the *philosophes*; rather, dissent was expressed with the help of quotations taken liberally from their writings. The Paris *parlement*, for example, used Montesquieu's theories of the balance of power. Sometimes the phrases used closely resembled the American constitution which, in turn, borrowed from the *philosophes*. The *parlement* of Rennes, for example, declared in 1788: 'That man is born free, that originally men are equal, these are truths that have no need of proof',[6] an obvious mixture of Jefferson and Rousseau. The *cahiers* of each social group in 1789 contained examples of an unusually lucid statement of general grievances. It appears, therefore, that Montesquieu and Rousseau had more influence on the expression of opposition than on its actual formation.

*

Such a distinction would have offered little comfort to Louis XVI. During his reign the monarchy not only reached its lowest ebb for two centuries; it eventually proved incapable of presiding over the normal process of government. The main problem was that the monarchy could no longer maintain a careful balance between the divergent social forces for the simple reason that it had no consistent basis of support. Louis XIV had promoted the image of absolutism by elevating the monarchy into a lofty position of isolation. But he had taken care to maintain the support of the bourgeoisie in order to counter the hostility which his policies often invoked from the nobility. After 1851 Napoleon III was to depend on the backing of the peasantry to counterbalance the opposition of the workers. The French monarchy could survive only if it was able to rely upon a

The Origins of the French Revolution

politically significant section of the population, or to pursue the more difficult policy of 'divide and rule'.

The vulnerability of Louis XVI was all the greater because of the financial crisis which lasted throughout his reign, and which proved that he could not maintain his authority without the goodwill, or at least indifference, of his subjects. Intolerable strains had been imposed on the financial structure by the Seven Years' War and the War of American Independence, and he was forced to consider changes in the methods and assessment of taxation. The situation was not without precedent: Louis XIV had had to agree to the introduction of the *dixième* and *capitation* during the War of the League of Augsburg (1688–97) and the War of the Spanish Succession (1701–14). But Louis XVI had to deal only with a relatively docile nobility, and with an impoverished and not yet articulate peasantry. Louis XIV encountered much more widespread opposition, and in particular a concerted demand, from 1787, for the convocation of the Estates General. In finally giving way in 1788, he acknowledged the collapse of absolutism and the existence of a political vacuum at the centre.

*

Freed from the necessity of having to co-operate against the régime, the Second and Third Estates now expressed their fears of each other more openly, and the crisis became revolution.

The nobility showed their determination to maintain the traditional voting procedures once the Estates General had convened. This brought out into the open their differences with the Third Estate, which proceeded to reconstitute itself as the National Assembly. This was the first sign of institutional revolution, as it was an open defiance of the authority and procedure of a traditional body. From this stage onwards, as G. Lefebvre argues, the momentum was increased by the participation of all the conflicting, rival, disparate elements within the Third Estate. The bourgeoisie appeared to have accepted the new political situation of July 1789 as permanent. The peasantry, however, hastened the destruction of feudal and seigneurial rights in August by a series of riots in the provinces. The artisans and proletariat of Paris pushed the Revolution into the more violent phase of 1791–4, providing solid support for the sweeping changes made by the National Convention.

It is often stated that the Revolution broke out in 1787 as a result of the pressure exerted by the Paris *parlement*. It is possible, however, to put this a different way. For a revolution to begin, a certain momentum is needed. In the nineteenth century, France possessed a large repository of revolutionary experience which exerted the vital push on several occasions (1830, 1848, 1871). During the 1780s there was no such knowledge or leadership; but the nobility, from their position of strength, and as part of their reactionary stance, delivered the first blow. The momentum of this act of political defiance was enough to encourage the different sections of the Third Estate to bring about the destruction of the *ancien régime*, and with it the Second Estate. This seems to confirm the view put forward by Montaigne as far back as 1580 that 'Those who give the first shock to a state are the first overwhelmed in its ruin'.

*

Recent research, particularly by R. R. Palmer and J. Godechot, has placed France in a more general context of revolutionary change which also affected Geneva (1768 and 1792), Ireland (1778 and 1798), the Netherlands (1784–7), Poland (1788–92), the Austrian Netherlands (1787–90) and Hungary (1790), as well as the North American colonies (from 1775). There certainly appear to have been major common problems affecting Europe as a whole. One was a rapid growth of population (100 million to 200 million between 1700 and 1800). Another was a sharp depression in the 1770s and 1780s, following a long period of economic growth. The overall result was increased competition for existing land resources, a huge rise in unemployment, and serious financial problems which confronted virtually every government in Europe and forced a re-examination of the traditional forms of revenue. Given the inability of most governments to deal with a major recession, it is hardly surprising that unrest should have been so widespread.

The majority of the revolutions, however, ended in failure. Palmer emphasizes the importance of a strong bourgeoisie (lacking in Poland and Hungary) and of close co-operation between the different social classes. In Poland and Hungary the huge peasantry remained largely indifferent, while in the Netherlands they backed the forces of counter-revolution. Ultimately, the country which possessed the largest bourgeoisie and the most extensive dissatisfaction within each class was the most likely to experience fundamental change.

The Origins of the French Revolution

That is why, despite the widespread incidence of unrest in the late eighteenth century, it was France which underwent the most violent upheaval and experienced the most advanced political, social and economic reforms.

2

The Course of the French Revolution

The opening years of the French Revolution (1789–92) can be regarded as a period of rapid social and institutional change during which the whole structure of the *ancien régime* was dismantled. This was, however, also the 'moderate' phase, as leaders of the National and Constituent Assemblies endeavoured to control the radicals, and to create a 'balanced' constitution.

The speed with which the changes occurred during the year 1789 was the result of a pendulum reaction between the king's government and the people of Paris. Louis XVI attempted to win back some of the ground he had lost to the recently formed National Assembly by dismissing his most progressive minister, Necker, and reconstituting his government. This provoked demonstrations and riots which culminated, on 14 June, in the fall of the Bastille – an event which symbolized the bankruptcy of royal authority. The king, nevertheless, tried to maintain his powers by rejecting some of the reforming legislation of the National Assembly. The result was the March of the Women (5 October) and the forcible removal of the king from Versailles, the seat of royal power since the 1680s, to Paris. Here the city's populace could exert more continuous and direct pressure on both the king and the National Assembly. Popular participation spread to other areas; as R. R. Palmer states, 'Plain people took part in continuing revolutionary activity at the bottom, while the Constituent Assembly and its successors governed at the top'.[1]

If events in and around Paris resembled the action of a pendulum, the relationship between the capital and the provinces could be described as 'tidal'. Rural unrest and the threat of peasant revolt put considerable pressure on Versailles and Paris to introduce legislation to alter the social structure. Hence the Constituent Assembly abolished feudalism, ended personal obligations and the tithe, formulated the Declaration of the Rights of Man and, in November, put up most of the Church lands for sale. The reverse flow, meanwhile, brought the influence of Paris to the rest of France, resulting in the dismissal of *intendants*, the suspension of *parlements* and the removal of other institutions of the *ancien régime*.

Every effort, however, was made to control the direction of this hectic activity. The 1791 Constitution, for example, reflected the desire for political balance and social harmony. One of its principles was decentralization, which allowed the newly formed *départements* considerable autonomy. Another was the separation, at the centre, of the legislature (in the form of the Constituent Assembly) from the executive (or the king and his ministers). This was in line with the widely accepted theories of Montesquieu and with the proven, if brief, experience of the United States. As a further safeguard against radicalism, the Assembly restricted the franchise to 'active' citizens, who numbered about 4.3 million taxpayers and property owners. The overall intention, therefore, was to reform, but also to hold back; Mirabeau, for example, called himself 'a partisan of order, but not of the old order'.

How long could this harmony and balance be maintained? The 1791 Constitution opened up, in the words of J. Roberts, a 'Pandora's box',[2] from which emerged unforeseen conflicts and complications. Between 1791 and 1792 all prospects of consensus disappeared and France split between Right and Left.

The Right was, of course, based on the king, who had become increasingly disillusioned with the restraints on his authority. He strongly opposed the Assembly's legislation concerning émigrés and non-juring clergy and, in his powerlessness to prevent it, complained: 'What remains to the king other than a vague semblance of royalty?'[3] The Left, meanwhile, had begun to press for a republic, arguing that, as long as France was a monarchy, the legislature and executive would be antagonistic as well as separate. Some deputies were also extremely concerned about the limits placed on reforming legislation; Marat, for example, found his blood 'boiling at the sight of so many decrees . . . which derogate from the Declaration of the Rights of Man and which are mortal to liberty'.[4] Others, like

Robespierre, condemned the limited franchise and 'the monstrous distinction' which makes a citizen 'active or passive'.[5] The conflict between Right and Left was aggravated by the changeover, in 1791, from the Constituent to the Legislative Assembly. A 'self-denying ordinance' ensured that the Legislative Assembly contained none of the deputies of the Constituent, thereby ending the continuity of personnel which had contributed to the political stability of the period 1789–91. Of the new members, 250 were Feuillants, or staunch loyalists, and the rest were radicals, comprising the Girondins and the more extreme Montagnards, of whom the Jacobins were the core. The Feuillants were soon to be pushed aside and the radicals eventually fought among themselves to capture and redirect the Revolution.

*

During its second phase (1792–4) the Revolution became more violent and doctrinaire. The Swiss historian Burckhardt commented that, as the Revolution accelerated, the representatives of the previous stages were cut down as 'moderates'; hence *'La révolution dévore ses enfants'*.

The catalyst for this change was the war. Most sections of the Assembly were enthusiastic about the prospect of taking on France's neighbours; the Feuillants assumed that a national struggle could only strengthen the authority of the king, while the Girondins reasoned that a 'people's war' would destroy the monarchy altogether. Events proved the Girondins correct as, in the words of D. I. Wright, the war 'revolutionized the revolution'.[6] A wave of terror was caused by the impending Prussian invasion, and the search for internal enemies resulted in the notorious massacres of September 1792. In the same month, the right-wing Feuillants were virtually eliminated in the elections for the new National Convention, and power was now shared between 165 Girondins and 145 Montagnards. The Girondins pressed for the indictment of the king, arguing that he was now a rallying point for counter-revolutionaries and that, while he remained on the throne, Austria and Russia would be unlikely to relax their efforts to restore him to his former power. Hence, as a result of the war, a republic was proclaimed on 25 September 1792, and Louis XVI was executed the following January.

By 1793 the Girondins had accomplished their basic aims – a

The Course of the French Revolution

people's war and a people's republic. It was now time to call a halt and consolidate. After all, asked Brissot, one of the Girondin leaders: 'What more could they [the people] want?'[7] In effect, the Girondins now came to regard themselves as conservatives and they bitterly opposed the attempts of the Left, or Montagnards, to increase the momentum of the Revolution. Brissot and Louvet feared that the Montagnards would open up the National Convention to the influence of the Paris 'mob'; the Girondins would be helpless against this type of popular pressure since their own support came from the *départements* of south-western France. Above all, the Girondins were appalled by the prospects of a Montagnard dictatorship, directed by the tightly-knit Jacobin clubs of Paris. Unfortunately, they lacked the strength to resist the Montagnards or apply a brake to the Revolution. As a party, they were far less cohesive than the Montagnards and they lacked popular support where it really mattered – in the capital. Hence, by June 1793, their position was hopeless. The leading Girondin deputies were dragged from the Convention by a crowd of 20,000 Montagnard supporters and were subsequently tried and executed.

The Montagnards now had the field to themselves, and introduced the phase of the Revolution usually referred to as the 'Terror' (1793–4). This was undoubtedly the most complex period, and it threw up a series of contradictions. For example, the Montagnards made much use of the demonstrations of the *sans-culottes*, particularly the Paris tradesmen, shopkeepers, artisans and wine merchants. And yet they gradually narrowed the actual power-base of their régime by giving all executive powers to a few committees of the Convention. They showed that they were committed to democracy by extending the franchise and removing the distinction between 'active' and 'passive' citizenship. And yet the men who ruled France through the Committees of Public Safety and General Security were less accountable to the electorate than at any other period in the Revolution. There was also an ideological paradox. The Jacobin leaders, especially Marat and Robespierre, explicitly upheld liberty as a key doctrine of the Revolution. But it was the type of liberty which existed only collectively and not in an individual sense. According to Robespierre the will of the people as a whole was 'the natural bulwark of liberty'.[8] Individuals, therefore, could find their freedom only by conforming to the 'general interest'. Robespierre was clearly influenced by the famous argument in Rousseau's *Social Contract* that dissidents, in their very act of disagreeing with the 'general will', were enslaving themselves and that 'it may be necessary to compel a man to be free'.[9]

The principle that freedom could be achieved through compulsion was applied during the course of 1794 by the Committees and the Revolutionary Tribunal. The result was the Terror, a revolutionary device which was justified by the Jacobins provided that the motives were 'pure'. Robespierre, for example, argued that 'virtue' without 'terror' was 'impotent', and Marat urged that 'liberty must be established by violence'.[10] This violence, previously the spontaneous demonstration of mob frustration, was now institutionalized and became the monopoly of the government; hence the guillotine of the Tribunal replaced the butchers' knives of the *sans-culottes*. Terror, however, came to feed upon itself and was used by the Robespierrists to eliminate rival Jacobin factions. The Hébertists, for example, were executed in March 1794, and the Dantonists a month later. Robespierre narrowed the base of power so much that eventually he regarded himself as the personification of the Republic: 'Je suis peuple moi-même'. For this reason, Robespierre has been the subject of greater controversy than any other revolutionary figure.[11] The traditional view is that the Terror perverted the aims of the Revolution and allowed Robespierre to set up a particularly odious dictatorship. To use the analogy of several historians, the French Revolution was a fever, the crisis of which was the Terror; before the patient, or France, could recover, Robespierre had to be cast off. Two French historians have adopted a more positive view of Robespierre: Lefebvre called him 'the resolute and faithful representative of that revolutionary mentality',[12] while Mathiez considered him 'the incarnation of Revolutionary France in its most noble, most generous and most sincere aspects'.[13]

It is also possible to depict the Terror as a period of constructive achievement. The measures taken by the Convention to mobilize the nation and to control the supply of food did more than anything else to turn the tide of the war and therefore to save the Revolution from destruction by foreign armies. Carnot's *levée en masse* created an entirely new approach to warfare and made possible the victories of Bonaparte a few years later. The Montagnards also reinterpreted the objectives of the first phase of the Revolution. Some of the reforms of the Constituent Assembly were reversed; the best example was the end of decentralization, which had brought two

The Course of the French Revolution

years of administrative chaos. Others however were confirmed and extended; these included the Declaration of the Rights of Man, the Civil Constitution of the Clergy and the sale of Church lands. It is often pointed out, however, that the Convention achieved little outside the context of the war or beyond the modification of previous reforms. Of its main innovations, the attempt to introduce the worship of the Supreme Being was a total failure, and the Revolutionary Calendar lasted less than twenty years. The only long lasting non-military reform which originated specifically in the Convention was the metric system of weights and measures.

*

The third period of the Revolution (1794–9) has been extensively reinterpreted. The traditional picture was that the Revolution reached a climax with the overthrow of Robespierre on 9 Thermidor 1794 and that a sharp turn to the right followed, preparing the way for Bonaparte's takeover in 1799. Historians used to dismiss the period 1795–9 as being outside the scope of the Revolution, thus placing it in limbo between two periods which were considered more important and certainly more interesting. Recent works, however, have restored the Thermidorians and the Directory fully to the context of the Revolution. C. Church, for example, called the Directory 'a board of executors for the revolutionary settlement', [14] while 1799, rather than 1794, is now generally taken as the terminal date of the Revolution.

Other assumptions have been challenged as well. There used to be agreement that the *coup d'état* of Thermidor was a right-wing reaction against the radical policies of Robespierre. M. Lyons, however, has argued that some of the plotters, like Tallien, Barras and Fouché, were left-wing Montagnards who considered Robespierre's ideas too moderate. There was also considerable opposition from the atheists within the Committee of General Security to Robespierre's introduction of the Cult of the Supreme Being. For a while, the Thermidorians were even joined by Babeuf and other socialists. 'In a sense, therefore,' says Lyons, 'the *coup* of 9 Thermidor was a revolution of the Left.' [15] There was also a wave of panic among the deputies of the Convention that they would be included in the next batch of Robespierre's victims. The events of 9 Thermidor, therefore, were also a 'revolution in self-defence against impending proscription'. [15] In one respect, Robespierre had only himself to blame; he had narrowed the base of his authority so far that no attempts were made to save him from his fate. It is ironical that the man who claimed to personify the people of Paris was reviled by them on his way to the guillotine.

Thermidor may have been inspired by the Left, but it was the Right which ultimately benefited. Large numbers of moderates resurfaced in the Convention after the overthrow of Robespierre and proceeded to dismantle the institutions of the Terror which had held them, and the Convention itself, in subjection. They also put the Revolution back on the course originally charted between 1789 and 1791 by the Constituent Assembly while, at the same time, retaining Robespierre's policy of central government control over the *départements*. Determined to prevent, in the future, any other Jacobin groups in the Convention from seizing control of the administration, the Jacobins resolved to reintroduce the strict separation of the legislature and executive and also to reduce the influence of the Paris mob by tightening the suffrage. The result was the Constitution of the Year III (1795) which established, as the executive, a Directory of five, and, as the legislature, a bicameral *corps*, comprising the Council of Five Hundred and the Council of Elders. The domestic record of this new régime was not unimpressive. The severely inflated *assignats*, introduced in 1789, were replaced by a new paper currency, the *mandats territoriaux*, and then by the first coin-based currency since the days of the *ancien régime*. From 1797 there were also extensive fiscal reforms, directed by de Nogaret, the minister of finance. Meanwhile, communications were generally improved and attention given at central and local levels to the reorganization of poor relief.

Whatever its achievements, the Directory proved more vulnerable than any of the other revolutionary régimes to military takeover and the emergence of the cult of personality. The success of Bonaparte's *coup d'état* of Brumaire (1799) showed that the Directory had never itself experienced the sort of stability it had brought to the Revolution. For one thing, the separation of the legislature and executive by the 1795 Constitution had ensured that no deputies elected to the Council of Five Hundred would ever serve on the Directory or as a government minister. Since executive posts were not, therefore, allocated on the basis of majorities in the legislature, there was no incentive to organize political parties. This was a serious deficiency in a constitution which otherwise had many of the hallmarks of a liberal democracy. Indeed, the Directors made the mistake of assuming that parties would undermine the régime. La Revellière Lépeaux, for example, argued that it would be preferable 'to die with honour defending the republic and its established government than to . . . live in the muck of parties'.[16] It was because of this obsession with 'faction' that the Directory virtually threw away its authority. By 1799 Siéyès and Ducos had become so alarmed by the prospect of a Jacobin revival that they intrigued with Bonaparte for a revision of the constitution. The result was a further swing to the Right and the beginning of the period known as the Consulate.

3
The Reforms of Napoleon I

Napoleon Bonaparte ruled France as First Consul between 1799 and 1804, and as Emperor between 1804 and 1814–15. He has always been one of the more difficult statesmen to identify with a particular era; indeed, his rule showed aspects of three different phases in European history.

For one thing, he has been called the 'child of the Revolution'. Certainly, he owed his rapid rise from obscurity to political power to the events of the Revolution and to the opportunities which the *ancien régime* could not have provided. His success in the Revolutionary War coincided with the political vulnerability of the Directory, enabling him to seize power by a *coup* which had the tacit support of several ministers. Once installed as First Consul (1799) he proceeded to build on the domestic achievements of the Directory. He stressed that he was the heir to the Revolution, which he had 'stabilized on the principles which began it'.[1]

At the same time, he renounced his own Jacobin connections and cut France off from the doctrinaire period of the Revolution. He rejected the ideology of Rousseau and the attempts made by Robespierre to apply it. In this sense, he considered that his task was 'to close the Romance of the Revolution'.[2] He returned for much of his intellectual inspiration to the earlier philosophers of the Enlightenment – writers like Montesquieu and Voltaire. This gave him much in common with the enlightened despots of Russia, Austria and Prussia; he shared their gloomy view of the 'credulous and criminal' nature of humanity and their belief that the only way to

The Reforms of Napoleon I

prevent chaos was the firm and authoritarian enforcement of humane and enlightened policies. Napoleon, therefore, looked back beyond 1779 and some of his measures show the hallmarks of the *ancien régime*. Surveying his career while in exile on St. Helena, he claimed that he had been 'the natural mediator in this struggle of the past against the Revolution'.[3]

He was not, however, merely a revolutionary or merely an enlightened despot; nor was he simply a combination of the two. He fused the Revolution and the *ancien régime* in such a way as to produce an entirely new element. This could be described as 'democratic' or 'plebiscitary' 'dictatorship', achieved by the energies of a self-made man, upheld by a broad base of popular support, sustained by all the trappings of the personality cult, and dedicated to military glory. Bonapartism, therefore, has links with the twentieth century as well as the eighteenth.

The rest of this chapter will elaborate on these three characteristics of Bonapartism in a survey of Napoleon's political, economic and social reforms.

*

The Revolution provided the vital background to Napoleon's political and constitutional changes. It cleared away the obstacles of the *ancien régime*, including the *parlements*, corporations and other vested interests. Napoleon incorporated some of the Revolution's achievements directly into his system. At local government level he kept the *départements* which had been established in 1790 by the Constituent Assembly, and continued the centralizing policies of the National Convention and the Directory. He also built on the Directory's Ministry of the Interior, finding the Ministry's Commissioners particularly useful as government agents in the *départements*. This centralization and uniformity of administration were the basis of Napoleon's authority and, because of the groundwork provided by the Revolution, he possessed more effective powers than had belonged to any of the Bourbon monarchs. The security which his position thus attained enabled him to take liberties with the legislature and executive, although he always claimed that he was, in fact, continuing and rationalizing revolutionary practice. The Constitution of the Year VIII (1799) continued the trend, started by the Constitution of 1795, towards legislatures with more than a single chamber. It should be emphasized, however, that Napoleon went further than the later revolutionaries had ever envisaged; he not only established three chambers instead of two, but also ensured that each had precise and strictly limited powers. The executive, by contrast, was narrowed down, but with the same aim in mind: the quest for personal power. It had originally consisted of the various committees of the National Convention, but had been narrowed down in 1795 to five Directors; Napoleon continued the process by entrusting power to three Consuls. But, even when he made himself First Consul for Life, in 1802, and crowned himself in 1804, he stressed that he was still linked to the Revolution, claiming that 'The government of the Republic is confided to an Emperor'.[4] He was also careful to maintain the appearance of democracy by means of a wide franchise, even if he did elaborate and refine the Directory's formula for making democracy indirect by means of a multiple list system which operated in elections for the legislature.

Napoleon also introduced features which would be more commonly associated with the *ancien régime* and the era of enlightened despotism. He was careful, for example, to avoid any explicit statement of ideology in his constitutions; hence there was no reference to the *liberté, égalité, fraternité* of the Revolution. Like Catherine the Great and Frederick the Great, he considered that a declaration of rights would merely hamstring the authority of the executive. Also, he had a pragmatic approach to constitutional reform which allowed him to use eighteenth-century devices, and hence to blend the Revolution with Bourbon France and Frederician Prussia. Hence he introduced a senate, adapted the old *conseil d'état* and, in local government, resurrected the *intendant* in the form of the prefect and sub-prefect. Above all, he succeeded in combining the power base which he had inherited from the Revolution with the traditional authority of royalty. Like Louis XIV, he was upheld by the concept of Divine Right. An extract from a catechism used by the French Church after 1804 reads: 'God has established him as our sovereign and has made him the minister of His power and His image on earth'.[5] He also adopted, in 1807, the title *le Grand*, thus following the example previously set by eighteenth-century rulers like Peter I, Frederick II and Catherine II.

The title 'Emperor' was not entirely a throwback to the *ancien régime*. It had certain connotations which sound familiar to the twentieth century as well. Napoleon's military success enabled him to maintain a dictatorship based cn massive popular support but

The Reforms of Napoleon I

stripped of the party politics which characterize parliamentary democracies. Refusing to be 'a man of a party', he aimed to depoliticize the régime by destroying 'the spirit of faction' which was 'hurling the nation into an abyss'. Mussolini later developed this approach, claiming that he was cutting the 'Gordian knot' which 'enmeshed' Italian politics, and that he was the focal point for his country's 'most vital forces'. Like Mussolini, Napoleon strengthened his position through the most effective use of the personality cult that Europe had yet seen. He manipulated public opinion by publishing only favourable material and by extensive use of what Hitler later called 'the Big Lie'. Confident in the image created by a carefully controlled press and by the paintings of David and Géricault, Napoleon was able to appeal directly to the people for their support. To do this he used a device which became particularly popular in the Second Empire (1852–70): the plebiscite. This proved a very effective means of seeking popular support for specific issues rather than for a wider range of policies. In 1804, for example, the establishment of the Empire was approved by a vote of 3.57 million to only 2569. As a result, Napoleon made the claim of the type much used by future dictators: 'I did not usurp the crown; I found it in the gutter and the French people put it on my head.'

*

Napoleon openly acknowledged the influence of the Revolution on his economic policies. He intensified the Directory's efforts to bring the *départements* under more effective financial supervision by the central government and maintained the *agence des contributions directes*, set up by the Directory to assess taxes throughout France. He extended this principle of centralization by insisting on the appointment of tax collectors by the Paris administration rather than by the *départements*. To reduce the incidence of tax evasion, he undertook a nationwide survey of capital assets and property, a scheme which had been proposed by the National Convention in 1793 but subsequently shelved. The currency was re-established on a metallic base, along the lines put forward in 1797 by the Directory, and credit was given a more systematic outlet in the Bank of France (1800), again an institution envisaged between 1795 and 1799. The reformed currency was valued in accordance with the decimal system, which had been introduced during the Terror but only sporadically enforced before 1799. Napoleon also promoted and encouraged industry by means of fairs and exhibitions, a practice initiated by the Directory. In general, he made full use of the more constructive policies of the Revolution to ensure that there would be no return to the economic chaos and financial maladministration of the Bourbon era.

In some respects, however, Napoleon's economic thinking was more in tune with eighteenth-century ideas. Although he was popular with the bourgeoisie and relied upon their support, he remained unconverted to the middle-class creed of *laissez-faire* and, like the enlightened despots, preferred the system of mercantilism, with its scope for government intervention. He also retained the eighteenth-century notion that agriculture, rather than industry, was the base of the economy: 'Agriculture is the soul, the foundation of the kingdom; industry ministers to the comfort and happiness of the population. Foreign trade is the superabundance.'[6] Further-more, the basic principles of his Commercial Code (1808) are reminiscent of the Commercial Ordinance (1673) and the Marine Ordinance (1681) of Colbert. Napoleon also restored some of the financial institutions of the *ancien régime*: the chambers of commerce, suspended in 1791, were reinstated; by 1803 there were twenty-two of these, one allocated to each *département*, to assist in the formulation of policy. Perhaps the most obvious return to the practices of the *ancien régime*, however, was Napoleon's preference for indirect taxation at the expense of direct. He established an Excise Bureau in 1804 and subsequently imposed heavy duties on beer, alcohol, wine and salt. By 1810 he had reversed the Revolution's emphasis on direct taxes and had, apparently, adopted a series of measures similar to those of eighteenth-century Prussia.

Napoleon's dictatorial powers depended, as we have seen, on his military success and personal prestige. This meant that he had to focus his economic policies on providing for a massive war machine which could guarantee his supremacy in Europe. He established several particularly important precedents for the future. The first was the Grand Empire, an economic entity which would feed the French system with tribute and recruits. The second was the Continental System, established by the Berlin and Milan Decrees (1806 and 1807) to seal Europe off from British commerce. These ideas later influenced the ambitious plan, drawn up by Chancellor Bethmann Hollweg during the First World War, for German domination of the whole continent. Hollweg hoped to create a

The Reforms of Napoleon I

Greater Germany through the annexation of neighbouring states, and also an extensive trade area and customs union which would exclude Britain and thereby destroy her commercial base. Thirdly, Napoleon established over industry tighter controls than had ever been achieved before. Mussolini was eventually to take these to their logical conclusion in his 'Corporate State'.

*

The Revolution had made substantial changes to the social structure. These, by and large, Napoleon retained. The power of the bourgeoisie, always latent during the *ancien régime*, was released by a revolution which, according to A. Soboul, established the general principles of bourgeois society and the liberal state.[7] Napoleon continued to elicit the support of the bourgeoisie, who saw in the Consulate an improved and more stable version of the Directory. The peasantry also found Napoleon willing to maintain some of the major achievements of the Revolution like the destruction of feudalism and the sale of Church lands; they were therefore content to support a régime which confirmed their possession of small-holdings. The urban workers were less fortunate; Napoleon expressed little concern about harsh working conditions and frequently legislated in favour of employers. But this was not necessarily out of step with the Revolution; his policy was entirely consistent with, for example, the Chapelier laws of June 1791 which had banned combination and strikes. Besides, the revolutionary leaders had always opposed the more radical elements of the working class, as was shown by the summary treatment of Babeuf and his followers.

The Revolution had also outlined a policy and structure for education and a legal code, but had been too preoccupied with the struggle for survival to carry them through. The National Convention had divided the educational structure into primary, secondary and higher levels. These were confirmed by Napoleon and integrated into the Imperial University after 1808. The Constituent Assembly had, in 1791, resolved to draw up 'A code of civil laws common to the whole kingdom'.[8] The legislation which followed was incomplete, but provided the basic outline for Napoleon's reforms, particularly in the areas of marriage, divorce, property and inheritance. According to J. Godechot, B. Hyslop and D. Dowd,

Aspects of European History 1789–1980

Napoleon's Civil Code 'expressed the great social upheavals of the Revolution and consolidated its great conquests'.[9]

Napoleon was, however, prepared to return to some of the practices of the *ancien régime*, particularly in his re-creation of a French nobility. The *noblesse* had been abolished as a class in June 1790, and even the Directory had introduced laws removing any remaining nobles from administrative posts. From the foundation of the Empire in 1804, Napoleon moved towards the re-establishment of a social élite. He began to confer hereditary fiefs in 1806 and, in 1808, created a new hereditary aristocracy comprising, in descending order, princes, dukes, counts, barons and knights. To some extent, this was a compromise: it retained the career open to talent which had been made possible by the Revolution while, at the same time, reverting to the enlightened despots' emphasis on 'service nobility'. It could also be argued that Napoleon restored the upward mobility between the bourgeoisie and the *noblesse* which had existed during the reign of Louis XIV but ended in the eighteenth century.

There was also compromise over the legal codes and religion. The Civil Code, for example, stressed equality before the law, but also restored, in almost tyrannical form, the authority of the head of the family. There was also a partial return to eighteenth-century property law. The Revolution had banned primogeniture, intending that a will should benefit all children equally. The Civil Code retained this ban but, as a concession, allowed the testator to dispose of 25 per cent of his property as he wished. Napoleon's attitude to women marked a complete departure from the liberalizing tendencies of the Revolution; he insisted on a complete return to Roman Law, and the subjection of wives to their husbands. He also took a backward step with the Code of Criminal Procedure (1808) which virtually revived the notorious *lettres de cachet* of the *ancien régime*, and the Penal Code (1810) which reintroduced branding.

Napoleon's attitude to religion was very similar to that of the enlightened despots. He considered it useful as a social cement, but wished to avoid the dangers of religious controversy. Hence 'I don't see in religion the mystery of the incarnation, but the mystery of the social order'.[5] Concerned with upholding the hierarchy which he had established, Napoleon reasoned: 'Society cannot exist without inequality of fortunes, and inequality of fortunes cannot exist without religion. When a man is dying of hunger alongside another

24

The Reforms of Napoleon I

who stuffs himself, it is impossible to make him accede to the difference unless there is an authority which says to him, "God wishes it thus" '.[5] Since religion fulfilled a social function, it had to be carefully directed, which meant that it 'must be in the hands of the government'.[10] The Concordat, formed with the Pope in 1801, ensured government control over the appointment of clergy and minimized papal interference in France. In this respect it also represented the final triumph of Gallicanism in its prolonged conflict, during the seventeenth and eighteenth centuries, with Ultramontanism.

Napoleon's own contribution to the French social structure was a more conscious and deliberate moulding of society than had ever been attempted before. He tried to create a pyramid, a hierarchy of classes, each bound by its own interests to the régime, and each aware of its place. The authority of the emperor would permeate all levels by means of the administrative reorganization and the legal changes, while the people would be committed to the régime emotionally through effective propaganda and military success. The secret police, under the efficient direction of Fouché, could be relied upon to eliminate opposition and discourage dissension. Indeed, this was to be a particularly important precedent. As M. Latey writes, 'the absolute monarchs, who re-established themselves after his fall, learned from Napoleon's techniques and in doing so helped to lay the groundwork of modern totalitarian rule'.[11]

*

Napoleon's achievements represent a synthesis of ideas and influences so complex that they are bound to attract an enormous range of historical interpretation. At one extreme, Napoleon appeared as a manifestation of Revolution, especially in those parts of Europe which had not previously been affected by revolutionary upheaval. At the other, the Napoleonic Empire was seen as a perversion of the revolutionary ideal; Trotsky, for example, later used Bonapartism as a term of abuse to describe the capture of a revolution by military reactionaries.

The Napoleonic era was also bound to throw up contradictions. The most important of these was the struggle of the heir to the Revolution, a monarch who had literally made himself, to coexist with rulers whose powers and prerogatives extended far back into the *ancien régime*. This theme will be explored in the next chapter.

4

The Fall of Napoleon I

While in exile on St. Helena, Napoleon composed a memorandum which illuminated his main policies as Emperor between 1804 and 1815. One was 'to reconcile the old France and the new', another 'to reconcile France with Europe'.[1] The implications of the first are dealt with in Chapter 3; this chapter, in examining the reasons for the fall of his régime, explores the meaning of the second.

Throughout his reign Napoleon remained an outcast in Europe. Other rulers declined to accept him as a dynastic equal. The European peoples, whether the middle classes of Italy and Germany, or the peasants of Spain and Russia, came to fear him as a tyrant worse than any lumbering out of the *ancien régime*. Above all, he was despised by Britain and, in his attempts to overcome British opposition, he resorted to devices which eventually unleashed the accumulated resentment of an entire continent.

This resentment was given increasingly effective military expression. Although he possessed clear initial advantages over the rest of Europe, Napoleon gradually lost the initiative as Britain and the powers of the European *anciens régimes* adjusted to the French methods of conscription, learned how to deal with Napoleon's strategy, or took advantage of a series of blunders caused by over-confidence and arrogance.

*

The ruling classes of Europe detested Napoleon because he was a product of the France of the 1790s. Metternich, for example, referred

The Fall of Napoleon I

to him as 'the Revolution incarnate'[2] and told Napoleon in 1813 that, between Europe and the latter's aims 'there is an absolute contradiction'.[3] Anna Pavlovna, sister of Tsar Alexander I, spoke of the 'hydra of revolution' and 'this murderer and villain',[4] while Queen Louisa, wife of Frederick William III of Prussia, scorned Napoleon as 'the scum from Hell'.[4]

Napoleon was certainly conscious of his humble origins and the absence of aristocratic pedigree in his genealogy. He was intensely irritated by descriptions like 'the Corsican', 'the usurper' and – the ultimate of insults – the title given to him by the King of Sweden: 'Monsieur Napoleon Bonaparte'. One solution was to establish his own dynasty, and to claim indirect connection with the Bourbons; hence he referred to Louis XIV, curiously, as *mon oncle*, while denying that he was really 'the successor to Robespierre'. Another was to cultivate the Napoleonic Legend, emphasizing the twin virtues of glory and success and disregarding the taunts of the old Europe. In his relations with other states, therefore, he sought to gain permanent acceptance through military victory and a position of diplomatic strength.

There emerged, however, a fundamental contradiction in his attitude to the other European rulers which meant that he and they were ultimately irreconcilable.

On the one hand, it seems that Napoleon did have a genuine desire for acceptance; after meeting the Tsar at Tilsit in 1807 he wrote: 'I like Alexander and he ought to like me'.[5] He also sought permanent links with European royalty to provide a sanction for his power which would transcend mere military conquest. On being refused the Tsar's sister, he married Marie-Louise, daughter of the Emperor Francis of Austria in 1809. The latter regarded this as a 'Sacrifice' necessary to placate Napoleon after the recent French victories in the Austrian War of 1810. Several French marshals, particularly Murat, criticized the marriage on the grounds that Napoleon was betraying the heritage of the Revolution. 'When France raised you to the throne, it believed it had found in you a popular chief, with a title that put you above all the sovereigns of Europe . . . But today you are doing homage to claims of sovereignty which are not yours and which are opposed to your own.' Napoleon remained unmoved. 'You don't like this marriage? I do. I regard it as a great success on a level with the victory of Austerlitz.'[6] He hoped, moreover, that full acceptance by European royalty would follow the birth of his son who was, after all, half Habsburg. He had already taken care to extend the range of his dynasty by installing members of the Bonaparte family on thrones within the Grand Empire; these included Holland, Westphalia, Spain and Naples. 'I am,' he said 'creating a family of kings, or rather of vice-kings.'[7] He also introduced all the outward trappings of kingship, believing that 'sovereigns must always be on show'.[1] Accordingly, on 25 May 1812, he presided over an elaborate ceremony in Dresden in which all his vassal princes, the King of Prussia and the Emperor of Austria, participated. This type of gathering, of which Dresden was the last and the greatest, seemed to imply that Napoleon had gained the recognition which he had sought. Could he keep this permanently?

He never had the opportunity to find out, for another and more destructive element intruded into his diplomacy.

Although he sought acceptance, Napoleon was not prepared to confer partnership. Because he put so much trust in military conquest he never learned how to draw up lasting diplomatic settlements and he frequently had to use further force to overcome resistance to his treaties. He failed to realize that if conquest were to be permanently effective, it must be followed by reconciliation, necessitating concessions by the victor as well as the vanquished. This was later understood by Bismarck and was a course urged upon Napoleon by the astute Talleyrand. In dealing with his three major continental rivals, however, Napoleon drew up a succession of unbalanced settlements which created only resentment, and therefore the incentive for future revolt against him.

He had to subdue Austria five times. The first two wars were a continuation of the struggle between Austria and Revolutionary France, but the other three were the product of insupportable treaties. The Treaty of Lunéville (1801) was forced upon Austria by an extended military campaign to hurry along negotiations. The Emperor Francis' efforts to reverse this in 1805 resulted in military defeat and the still heavier Treaty of Pressburg, by which Austria ceded all her Italian lands to France, and substantial German possessions to Napoleon's satellite states – Bavaria, Baden and Württemberg. Talleyrand urged caution and clemency and his warning was vindicated by another Austrian revolt in 1809. The Treaty of Schonbrünn extracted further territory from Austria, including Illyria and Galicia, and imposed a war indemnity. According to Francis, these terms were 'fatal to the existence of

The Fall of Napoleon I

Austria'.[6] Furthermore, 'From the day when peace is signed we must confine our system to tacking and turning and flattering. Thus alone may we possibly preserve our existence, till the day of general deliverence.'[8] The King of Prussia had even greater grievances. Despite his admiration for Frederick the Great (1740–86), Napoleon considered that Prussia was not rightfully one of Europe's major powers, especially since she had grown effete under Frederick William II and Frederick William III. His victory over Prussia in 1806 was followed, in the Treaty of Tilsit (1807), by exceptionally severe terms. Prussia lost half her territory, her western provinces being given to the Kingdom of Westphalia and her Polish lands to the Grand Duchy of Warsaw; her army was limited to an insignificant 42,000 men, and an indemnity was imposed. The King of Prussia played no actual part in the settlement as Napoleon considered that his presence at Tilsit would be superfluous. Even Russia, the power for which Napoleon had most respect, claimed grounds for resentment. The Treaty of Tilsit, negotiated between Alexander I and Napoleon, was intended to divide Europe into two main spheres of influence, confirming French dominance over Western and Central Europe, and give Russian interests an outlet in the East. Between 1807 and 1812, however, Napoleon removed the basis of genuine partnership by refusing to countenance Russian claims to Constantinople. Alexander also reacted with intense hostility to Napoleon's efforts to make Russia adhere to the continental blockade against Britain, and rapidly came to the conclusion that the Tilsit agreement was 'ignominious'.[9]

All this resentment was fully appreciated by Talleyrand, who now began to negotiate secretly with Napoleon's enemies; in 1808, for example, he urged the Tsar to make haste to save Europe from Napoleon. Before 1812, however, Austria and Prussia remained, for the time being, submissive. Then Russian success in the war of 1812 brought about yet another Coalition in 1813, which eventually defeated Napoleon at Leipzig. The powers were, by this time, prepared to overlook the very substantial differences between themselves in their efforts to overthrow the settlements which Napoleon had imposed upon them.

Napoleon's disillusionment became evident in 1814. He had always known that 'between old monarchies and a young republic hostility must always exist'.[10] He had therefore transformed the republic into a monarchy, only to find that this was even more unacceptable. To Napoleon the rulers of Europe had, by 1813, become the revolutionaries. Hence he complained: 'I have behaved to the kings as a sovereign; they have behaved to me like Jacobins'.[3]

Napoleon became no less intensely disliked by the European peoples. He should have possessed some basis of popular appeal as, after all, he claimed that monarchy must be justified by 'l'intérêt des peuples'.[11] Despite his dynastic interests he did continue the work of the Revolution by reforming institutions throughout the Grand Empire. His positive achievements included the abolition of serfdom where it still existed in Germany and Italy, and the introduction of the Civil Code, which had already been applied in France. At the same time, however, he strongly resisted any move towards 'popular sovereignty',[12] which he associated with the 'principle of rebellion'. He therefore came to be regarded as the heir to enlightened despotism quite as much as the product of the Revolution and, as the war spread after 1808, he came to be seen as a tyrant. Popular movements arose in Spain, where peasants actually co-operated with the nobility against Joseph Bonaparte. The latter said despairingly: 'I haven't a single supporter here.'[13] Napoleon failed to improve the lot of the peasantry in Eastern Europe. Kosciuszko, the leader of the Polish revolt against foreign domination in the early 1790s, complained, 'He thinks of nothing but himself'.[14] Napoleon actually turned his back on the prospect of liberating the Russian serfs, and he condemned 'the brutal nature of this large class of Russian people'.[9] The serfs' opposition to the French was one of the key factors in the failure of Napoleon's 1812 invasion, bringing with it the unexpected and irresistible element of guerrilla warfare. Popular discontent was also widespread in Germany and Italy, where the rigours of the continental blockade alienated the large middle class, and the numerous levies led to growing opposition from men who objected, in the words of an Italian poet, to being 'killed by the enemies of another people'.[15] The sentiment of German and Italian nationalism stirred in opposition to French rule. It is easy to exaggerate the impact of this nationalism, for Napoleon was eventually brought down by kings, not peoples. But the peoples did contribute to the campaigns of 1812 and 1813 and seemed to give some credibility to the kings' claims to be liberating Europe.

The most formidable and consistent of Napoleon's enemies was Britain, the only power to maintain the struggle without compromise between 1803 and 1814. Bonapartism was even more

The Fall of Napoleon I

abhorrent to the English establishment than to the absolute monarchs on the Continent. It seemed to represent the worst threat imaginable to the evolutionary course of British constitutional development so tenaciously upheld in the speeches and writings of Edmund Burke. Few statesmen acknowledged the need for any reform or change in Britain, most agreeing with Lord Braxfield that 'the British constitution is the best that ever was since the beginning of the world, and it is not possible to make it better'.[16] To British leaders like Pitt, Napoleon was the inevitable result of the upheaval of the 1790s, a combination of Terror and Tyranny. Britain could coexist with the absolutism of the *ancien régime*, but not with military absolutism born of revolution.

Napoleon faced enormous difficulties in trying to wear Britain down. He was fully aware of British naval power and relied initially on the invasion scheme of 1803–04. This prospect, however, was destroyed at the Battle of Trafalgar (1805) and the disparity in the naval resources of the two countries grew steadily wider. By 1813, for example, France possessed only seventy-one ships of the line (most of them blockaded in port) to Britain's 235. The implications of this were enormous. Britain maintained and increased her normal commercial links with other continents and was able to land and supply expeditionary forces under Wellington in the Iberian Peninsula.

Eventually, Napoleon had to resort to desperate measures but, in the process, he precipitated more intense opposition from all parts of the Continent. Britain's life-blood was her trade and, in Caulaincourt's words, 'since their trade had ramifications everywhere, he had to pursue them everywhere'.[17] The purpose of the Berlin Decree (1806) and the Milan Decree (1807) was to close the European Continent to British exports; the result would be a crisis of overproduction in Britain, followed by unemployment and rampant inflation. At times the Continental System seemed to come close to success. 1808 and 1811 saw a significant drop in the value of British exports (from £48.8 millions in 1810, to £32.4 millions in 1811). Eventually, however, Napoleon had to admit failure. Two factors were responsible for this: the first was the resilience of British traders, who sought and obtained new outlets in South America and managed, from wartime distribution centres like Heligoland and Malta, to keep illicit commercial contacts with Prussia, Holland, Spain, Naples and other states subject to Napoleon. The second was the inconsistency of Napoleon himself. He seemed to alternate between harsh application of the System, which undoubtedly caused difficulties in Britain, and the granting of special concessions. After 1807, for example, he occupied most of Europe in order to enforce the System. Yet, in 1811, he adopted a more moderate policy. In a year which brought for Britain a chronic shortage of grain and the most unfavourable trade figures of the entire war, he allowed selected imports from Britain on licence, together with the export of grain supplies from France. Napoleon's reasoning was understandable. French commercial interests were also suffering and the selective re-establishment of contacts with Britain would bring relief to French traders and farmers. Hence, 'undoubtedly we must harm our foes, but above all we must live'.[18]

The Continental System had a devastating effect on Napoleon's power and reputation in Europe. In enforcing the blockade, Napoleon over-extended the borders of his influence. The occupation of Spain in 1808 to compel the Iberian Peninsula to close its ports to Britain was a serious mistake: it created, in the Peninsular War, a constant drain on French resources. 'Those devilish Spanish affairs',[19] compounded as they were by guerrilla warfare and the first signs of British military success, kept several hundred thousand troops occupied. These were increasingly needed elsewhere in Europe, for Alexander began to express dissatisfaction with the Tilsit settlement by flouting Napoleon's Continental System. This form of pressure incensed Napoleon to the point of open war with Russia in 1812 – a catastrophic blunder which encouraged other monarchs to rise against him in 1813.

*

Napoleon's military measures against the continental powers at first met with considerable success. The nature of warfare had already been radically altered by the French Revolution, which gave Napoleon an immediate advantage over his rivals. The size of his armies, for example, owed much to Carnot's *levée en masse* (1793), which had produced some 750,000 troops by 1794. This had been modified by Jourdan's Law of 1798 and was finally codified by Napoleon in 1811. Between 1800 and 1812, it has been estimated, 1,100,000 soldiers were mobilized for the Grand Army, or two million between 1800 and 1815. The resulting armies were massive when compared with any raised in the eighteenth century; whereas

The Fall of Napoleon I

Frederick the Great had commanded about 40,000 men at Leuthen (1757) and Kunersdorf (1759), Napoleon led some 190,000 in his Ulm and Jena campaigns. Eventually, however, Napoleon was confronted by two overwhelming problems. One was the growth of mammoth armies in other continental countries, despite the restrictions imposed by the Treaties of Tilsit and Schönbrunn. By 1813, for example, Prussia had introduced conscription for all men between seventeen and forty, mobilizing a total of 300,000 men, while Austria and Russia had the capacity to exceed this figure. The other problem was the resentment caused by Napoleon's conscription of foreigners into the French army, particularly from the vassal states of the Grand Empire. By 1814 only 40 per cent of Napoleon's army consisted of Frenchmen, the rest being drawn from Italy, Germany, Poland and Spain. The result was that the French army became more disunited and less homogeneous at the very time that it was being outnumbered by the forces of the Allies. At the Battle of Leipzig (1813) Russia, Prussia and Austria overwhelmed Napoleon with the colossal figure of 365,000 against 195,000. In 1815, the Allies were able to muster over 600,000 troops for the invasion of France herself. As the Grand Empire contracted, of course, the supply of recruits to the French army dwindled.

Larger armies had originally been introduced in the name of the people. By Carnot's *levée en masse*, for example, 'All Frenchmen are called by their country to defend liberty'.[20] The justification for size was necessarily ideological, and the combination of the two elements revived the practice of destructive warfare after a comparative lull between 1648 and 1792. Again, Napoleon had the early advantage. He took much of Europe by storm and, in his initial success, he came to regard war as a solution for all diplomatic problems, without the impediment of rules. War became virtually self-generating or, in Napoleon's own words, 'war must support war'.[21] France did not, however, retain the monopoly of total war, and there were two notable examples of its use by her enemies. The first was the Russian reaction to the invasion of 1812 – the so-called 'Great Patriotic War' – while the second was the great campaign of 1813. The Battle of Leipzig has been called 'the Battle of Nations'; this aptly describes the extent of European involvement in what was, in terms of numbers, the greatest single pitched battle in the history of mankind.

Napoleon's strategy at first inflicted a series of shocks on the continental powers. He emphasized the importance of forced marches and precisely timed manoeuvres on the battlefield. Everything depended on mobility. As Thiers put it: 'Our Emperor has found out a new way of making war; he no longer makes it with our arms but with our legs.'[22] In many ways he was continuing the policy of the Revolution that armies should be self-sufficient and unimpeded by the type of heavy baggage trains which had accompanied eighteenth-century armies. French troops were expected to supply themselves by foraging in enemy territory. This worked well in the Italian campaigns (1796–7 and 1800), as well as against Austria (1805) and Prussia (1806). The Peninsular War and the Russian Campaign, however, showed the defects of this policy. Despite careful preparations for the 1812 campaign, Napoleon's troops were held up by the dreadful state of Russian roads which slowed down the passage of essential equipment, and by the low standard of Russian agriculture which made foraging much more difficult. Napoleon therefore found himself under severe pressure, and had to seek military confrontation without his usual finesse. The result was the Battle of Borodino, a narrow victory for the French, marred by appalling losses. Worse was to come: the burning of Moscow and the constant harrying of the French army during its retreat. Another paradox emerged. Napoleon, for all his military genius, was entirely unable to comprehend guerrilla warfare, tuned as he was to decisive pitched battles in conditions of his own choosing. He could only, in his own words, 'make war offensively'.[17] What happened in Moscow shocked him profoundly. 'They themselves are setting it afire . . . The barbarians! What a terrible spectacle!'[23] The French performance against guerrillas in Spain was equally ineffectual. Soult and other marshals were also out-manoeuvred by Wellington, who solved the supply problem by using light carts and maintaining continuous contact with the British navy at the mouth of the Tagus. By 1813 the Allies had also learned how to deal with Napoleon's surprise attacks on the battlefield and worked on the principle of evading action until a decisive numerical superiority in the order of two to one could be brought to bear against the French.

Napoleon's battle tactics, in fact, showed the same vulnerability as his campaign strategy. During the late eighteenth century most powers made use of the *ordre mince* (the advance of extended lines), although there was some support for the *ordre profond* (a more

The Fall of Napoleon I

concentrated attack in columns). Napoleon succeeded in confusing the Austrians and Prussians by resorting to a highly effective combination of the two, carried out in such a way as to encourage the enemy to commit itself while, at the same time, concealing his own intentions. The subsequent confusion and the crushing pursuits ensured overwhelming French victories. But Napoleon's mastery of battle formations came to be matched by Wellington, who reintroduced the *ordre mince* in the form of disciplined lines and squares. One British observer, J. W. Croker, had already said of the French strategy, 'I think it is a false one against steady troops'.[24] This assessment was vindicated at the Battles of Vittoria (1813) and Waterloo (1815). Napoleon felt that the Allies had improved their battle tactics, but that he had made no corresponding progress. On St. Helena he remarked, 'I have fought sixty battles and I have learned nothing which I did not know in the beginning'.

Before Tilsit France's greatest military asset was the personal leadership of Napoleon. After Tilsit, however, this became an increasing liability. He succeeded initially because he dared do what others would have feared. He failed eventually because he lost all sense of caution, regarding impossibility as 'a word found only in the dictionary of fools'.[25] After Tilsit he seemed to believe his own officially sponsored legend and told his brother Lucien: 'I can do everything now.'[9] Certainly his ambition increased until, according to Alexander, it knew 'no bounds'. He continued to act on the assumption that military solutions were always attainable. Consequently, as his diplomatic problems increased, his military campaigns became ever more ambitious, stretching French resources to breaking point. His attitude during the Russian campaign is particularly revealing. After the Russian armies had begun to retreat, Napoleon insisted on moving towards Moscow, at whose gates, he was convinced, 'the conclusion of peace awaits me'.[26] His marshals thought otherwise and attempted, unsuccessfully, to dissuade him. Murat warned: 'Moscow will destroy us.'[26] Reminded of the failure of Charles XII and the Swedish army in similar circumstances in 1709, Napoleon revealed an insight into his basic philosophy. 'It is not the rule that creates success, but success that creates the rule, and if I should achieve success by further marches, my new success will create new principles.' Hitler made similar comments in 1941 when reminded of the fate of Napoleon.

Another shortcoming of Napoleon as a leader was his inability to delegate authority effectively. He never seriously considered training a successor and rarely attempted to impart the underlying principles of his military success to his marshals. Thus a huge gap opened between his own strategy and its tactical execution by his subordinates. One result was Ney's failure to turn the advantage created by Napoleon in the Battle of Bautzen into a decisive victory. Another was a series of French disasters in Spain as inexperienced marshals struggled to apply elusive and only partly known Napoleonic rules of warfare. It is ironical that one of the powers which eventually defeated Napoleon had itself been a victim of the same problem. Under Frederick the Great (1740–86) Prussia had been excessively centralized and had become totally dependent on the personality and policies of the king. Frederick's death in 1786 had thrown Prussia into chaos, making possible Napoleon's spectacular victory in 1806. But there then occurred a metamorphosis. Prussian revival was effected by collective leadership and planning, which was followed by deep suspicion for the next fifty years of anything resembling a personality cult. It was France who now became addicted to personal leadership, and even the defeats of 1814 and 1815 were not enough to destroy the Napoleonic Legend. The struggle between Prussia and France was renewed in 1870 and Bonapartism's real Waterloo was the Battle of Sedan.

5

The Concert of Europe 1815–48

The Concert of Europe is the term used to describe various attempts made by the major powers to co-operate, after 1815, in settling possible causes of conflict between themselves in order to prevent the possibility of another large-scale war. At first the European statesmen favoured a conciliar system; according to Article VI of the Quadruple Alliance (1815) 'the High Contracting Powers have agreed to renew at fixed intervals . . . meetings consecrated to great common objects and the examination of such measures as at each one of these epochs shall be judged most salutary for the peace and prosperity of the nations and for the maintenance of the peace of Europe.'[1] This provided the basis for the four further congresses which followed the Congress of Vienna itself, namely Aix-la-Chapelle (1818), Troppau (1820), Laibach (1821) and Verona (1822). By 1823, however, the attempt had broken down, and the idea of relating diplomacy to regular councils had to be abandoned.

A major reason for this was that a gap opened between Britain and the continental autocracies of Austria, Russia and Prussia, caused largely by different policies over the question of intervention against revolutionary movements. Britain's foreign secretaries, Castlereagh and Canning took their stand on a narrow and legalistic interpretation of the Quadruple Alliance, while the absolutist powers held to the Troppau Protocol of 1820 which was, in essence, a reinterpretation of the Holy Alliance of 1815. This conflict ended the possibility of a general conciliar system consisting of both constitutional and autocratic powers. It does not, however, explain why the autocratic powers failed to substitute a regular system of their own, either before or after 1823. The reason for this is twofold. On the one hand, the absolute monarchies had their own rivalries which prevented concerted action at several crucial stages. On the other, there was considerable diplomatic accord between Britain and each of these monarchies at different times and on specific issues. There existed, therefore, no real motive for permanent and concerted opposition to Britain from Russia, Prussia and Austria.

The 1830 revolutions helped inject more unity into the absolutist powers, while there was also some ideological sympathy between Britain and France. But the period between 1830 and 1853 saw much the same general trend as that between 1815 and 1830: ideological formations continued to be undermined by individual interests. After 1830, therefore, no attempt was made to revive conciliarism as a regular device, although concert was still possible over specific issues and at specially convened conferences.

*

The fundamental division in the 'Congress System' had become apparent by 1820; Britain had become increasingly cut off from Russia, Austria and Prussia, while France had contacts with both sides of the divide. The major issue was undoubtedly the use to which the System was to be put in dealing with constitutional movements and revolutions in the various sensitive areas of Europe. This preoccupation was inevitable, partly because all statesmen feared that the French Revolution was still a powerful influence, and partly because the 1815 Vienna Settlement had failed to satisfy widespread aspirations of nationalism and constitutionalism. Metternich, in particular, regarded revolution as a 'terrible social catastrophe' and believed that 'only order produces equilibrium'.[2] Such a balance could be maintained only by the most careful vigilance. Hence, he observed in 1817, 'You see in me the chief Minister of Police in Europe. I keep my eye on everything. My contacts are such that nothing escapes me.'[3] In his *Profession of Political Faith* (1820), Metternich argued that all monarchs should be prepared to take common action. At the Congress of Troppau he was able to make common cause with Alexander I of Russia who, repenting of his earlier liberal views, was now talking of radicalism as 'satanic genius', progressing by 'occult methods' to establish a 'reign of evil'.[4] The Prussian position was less obvious, but Frederick

The Concert of Europe 1815–48

William III had nothing to gain by holding out against the policies of Metternich and Alexander. The overall result, therefore, was the conversion of Alexander's Holy Alliance (1815) with its nebulous and idealistic principles, into the Troppau Protocol of 1820. The latter specifically allowed for the intervention of the major powers in the internal affairs of any state undergoing a constitutional change not sponsored by its ruler.

The British government remained constantly suspicious of this interpretation of the role of the congresses. Castlereagh expressed his contempt for the Tsar's ideal of a mystical union and tried, without success, to get him and his ministers 'to descend from their abstractions'.[5] Profoundly suspicious of the Holy Alliance, Castlereagh took his stand on the Quadruple Alliance (1815), giving it a limited and juridical emphasis by insisting that the only valid purpose of congress diplomacy was to uphold treaty obligations between the powers, and thereby prevent unilateral action by any state to change agreed boundaries. Intervention for any other reason would be a perversion of the Quadruple Alliance. In fact, 'nothing would be more immoral or more prejudicial to the character of government generally than the idea that their force was collectively to be prostituted to the support of established power, without any consideration of the extent to which it was abused'.[6] This argument was used by Lord Stewart, sent to the Congress of Troppau as an observer rather than as a plenipotentiary, to condemn the 1820 Protocol. Stewart added that the policy propounded by the continental powers was 'destructive of all correct notions of internal sovereign authority'.[5] After Castlereagh's death in 1822 and his replacement as Foreign Secretary by Canning, the gap between Britain and the continental autocracies widened. Canning reaffirmed Castlereagh's hostility to collective intervention in equally categorical terms: 'England is under no obligation to interfere, or assist in interfering, in the internal affairs of independent states.' But, whereas Castlereagh had merely distanced Britain from the policies of the continental powers, Canning was entirely happy to break the System altogether by recognizing the new republics in Latin America, and refusing to consider any scheme by which Spanish colonial rule might be restored. He must have had in mind the imminent collapse of congress diplomacy when he justified his American policy with the famous words: 'I called the New World into existence to redress the balance of the Old.'[7]

Aspects of European History 1789–1980

*

The collapse of the Congress System was followed by neither a purely continental conciliar movement, nor by the return to the diplomatic free-for-all of the eighteenth century. The reason was the extraordinary complexity of international diplomacy after 1815, producing unexpected cross currents of rivalry and co-operation. This process can be illustrated by a brief examination of the relations before 1827 between Austria and Russia, Britain and Austria, Britain and Russia, and Britain and France.

For two powers with similar interests in preventing revolution, Austria and Russia had a surprisingly stormy relationship. This was caused, in part, by Metternich's deep suspicion of Alexander's liberal pretensions between 1813 and 1818. Suspicion turned to alarm when Alexander spoke of the 'absurd pretensions of absolute power'.[8] Eventually, Metternich succeeded in restoring Alexander to autocratic principles, aided by the Tsar's revulsion against the assassination of Kotzebue in Germany (1819), the Riego Revolt in Spain (1820), the murder of the duc de Berri in France (1820) and the revolt of the Semyonovski Regiment in St. Petersburg. In October 1820, Alexander renounced his progressive views and confessed to Metternich: 'You have correctly judged the state of affairs. I deplore the waste of time, which we must try to regain.'[8] Metternich said with considerable relief: 'If ever anyone turned from black to white, he has.'[9] Alexander's conversion brought the two countries closer together ideologically at the very time that British policy was at its most obstructive, but it did not eliminate Austro-Russian rivalries altogether. Alexander had always pressed for a more sweeping view than Metternich's of the role of the Congress System and now wanted joint action to suppress the revolutions in Spain and Naples. Metternich, on the other hand, feared the prospect of Europe being inundated with Russian troops and preferred punitive action to be taken unilaterally by the major power most affected. The Greek revolt posed an even more difficult problem, as Alexander had a natural sympathy towards the Balkan Christians which went against Metternich's principle of upholding all authority, including Turkish. Between 1822 and 1825 Metternich succeeded in restraining Russian policy, but the death of Alexander in 1825 meant that this task became more difficult. Nicholas I, anxious to rescue Russia from Austrian tutelage, prepared for measures against

The Concert of Europe 1815–48

Turkey which Metternich considered thoroughly dangerous. The disagreements between the two countries between 1825 and 1830 therefore go a long way towards explaining the absence of any Austro-Russian conciliar system to replace the broader pattern of Congresses.

In theory, it would be difficult to conceive two more contrasting powers than Britain and Austria. Yet several points of limited contact between them did exist. Castlereagh, for example, considered the existence of a strong power in Central Europe essential to restrain France and Russia; in his view the Habsburg Empire was 'the great hinge upon which the fate of Europe must ultimately depend'.[10] Metternich, in turn, greatly respected Castlereagh's emphasis on the 'balance of power' of European states as being the most effective means of preventing the outbreak of future wars. Britain and Austria did, in fact, co-operate in 1815 to try to dissuade Russia from annexing Poland and Prussia from claiming Saxony. Furthermore, Castlereagh did not object to *all* cases of intervention against revolution. He disliked the extent of Metternich's conservatism and opposed the Troppau Protocol, but was also prepared to concede that Austrian intervention in Naples (1821) had a juridical basis, since the Neapolitan revolt destroyed a treaty previously drawn up with the Habsburgs. What really separated Castlereagh from Metternich was the latter's temporary reconciliation with Alexander, and the adoption of a more united ideological stance by the autocratic powers. Even so, there was always the prospect of further contact until Castlereagh's death in 1822. The latter was a disaster for Metternich, since Canning was in no way prepared to compromise with Austria. Metternich's views of the new Foreign Secretary were unequivocal: 'He knocked down and undermined a great deal, but finished nothing.' His views were occasioned partly by Canning's open contempt for the Austrian Chancellor and partly by the more openly opportunist base of British foreign policy which prompted Canning's remark: 'Each country for itself and God for us all.'[4] Yet even Canning did not destroy Britain's links with Austria. Palmerston, although in many aspects of foreign policy a pupil of Canning, was later to revive Castlereagh's concept of the Austrian bulwark against Russia.

The rivalry between Britain and Russia was the deepest and most consistent of all, as might be expected from the world's greatest naval power and the Continent's strongest military state. There was

Aspects of European History 1789–1980

intense mutual mistrust over the operation of the Congress System, and considerable resentment over Castlereagh's contacts with Metternich. Alexander, indeed, tried to create his own balance of power by encouraging the revival of French and Spanish maritime strength to 'group' Britain on the world scene, just as Castlereagh had 'grouped' Russia in Europe. But even Anglo-Russian relations went through more positive periods of co-operation. The accession of Nicholas I in 1825 saw a simultaneous *rapprochement* between Britain and Russia, and alienation between Russia and Austria. In 1826, Canning secured from the Tsar a Protocol which provided the basis of agreed Anglo-Russian action in support of the liberation of Greece from Turkey. The Treaty of London followed in 1827, together with the destruction of the Turkish fleet by Britain, Russia and France at Navarino. The period 1825–7 showed a definite, if temporary, withdrawal from what must have appeared to be en-trenched positions on foreign policy. As a result, Russia would have had little motive to construct a rival system of councils with Britain as the target, even assuming that she could have attained the necessary agreement with Austria.

It seemed, in 1820, that Britain and France had much in common. Neither approved of the proposals for intervention and neither sent official representatives to the Congress of Troppau. Could not the two constitutional monarchies of Europe have attempted to establish their own device for regular meetings? Apparently not, for other issues cut across any possibility of close co-operation. France aimed at re-establishing the Bourbon *Pact Famille* with Spain as a prelude to becoming a world power. Naturally, this caused appre-hension in the British cabinet, since it might revive the great Anglo-French conflicts of the eighteenth century. Furthermore, Canning was deeply suspicious of French intrigues in the newly independent states of Latin America, one of which was an attempt to instal a Bourbon nominee as King of Buenos Aires in 1820. France, in turn, suspected Britain of trying to monopolize trade with the new republics. French intervention against the Spanish revolutionaries in 1823, despite earlier pronouncements against such a policy, was yet another reason for British reluctance to see in France a permanent ally against Austria, Russia and Prussia.

*

The revolutions which occurred in many parts of Europe in 1830

The Concert of Europe 1815–48

stimulated a brief revival of ideological unity between Austria, Russia and Prussia. Nicholas I's immediate reaction to these was to prepare for an invasion of Central and Western Europe, until his attention was diverted by the Polish Revolt. Metternich considered 1830 a catastrophe, and the three East European monarchs felt impelled through common fears to revive the Holy Alliance and Troppau Protocol by a series of treaties in 1833. At Teplitz, for example, Metternich and Frederick William III agreed to take measures to combat liberalism in the German Confederation. The Münchengrätz Agreement was intended mainly to prevent Austro-Russian misunderstanding over the Eastern Question, but it had an important by-product – the Triple Declaration, which was signed in Berlin in October. This bound Russia, Prussia and Austria to assist any ruler who requested aid in overcoming revolutionary forces. The most successful application of this Treaty was the Russian invasion of Hungary in 1849, following Francis Joseph II's request for help against the Magyar uprising.

Britain, by contrast, sympathized with some of the aspirations of the revolutionaries. Palmerston, in fact, considered 'constitutional states' to be the 'natural allies of this country',[11] and he revived the traditional policy of 'non-interference by force of arms in the affairs of any other country'.[11] The overthrow of the Bourbon monarchy in 1830 gave France a vested interest in liberalism, so that Louis Philippe moved closer to the general principles of Palmerston. Anglo-French co-operation was evident over the Belgian issue (1830) and in the formation of the Quadruple Alliance with Spain and Portugal, in 1834. Metternich and Nicholas regarded these developments with foreboding, emphasizing that the Quadruple Alliance had been set up to counter the Treaties of Münchengrätz.

But once again individual rivalries prevented this ideological gap from becoming permanent. The main irritant during the 1830s was the Eastern Question. Metternich, for example, was always concerned about the prospect of further Russian expansion into Eastern and possibly Central Europe. Relations between Britain and France deteriorated rapidly when Louis Philippe supported the Egyptian Khedive, Mehemet Ali, against the Ottoman Sultan in 1839; this directly challenged British intentions of propping up Turkey as a barrier against Russian expansion into the Eastern Mediterranean. As a result, the Anglo-French understanding, brought about by the Quadruple Alliance, disintegrated into intense mutual suspicion.

Aspects of European History 1789–1980

The 1840s and 1850s saw further disagreements between supposedly friendly powers. Louis Philippe again annoyed Palmerston, this time over the Spanish marriages question (1846), while Austria and Prussia came close to war over Frederick William IV's proposal, in 1850, to establish the Erfurt Union between Prussia and the north German states. Even Russia's assistance to Austria in 1849 brought problems. There were open disagreements between the two armies as they campaigned in Hungary, while the new Austrian Chancellor, Schwarzenberg, was apprehensive about the concessions which he expected Russia to extract in return for her intervention. Indeed, he stated quite openly that 'Austria will surprise the world with her ingratitude'.[12]

Rivalries like these certainly prevented any further experimentation with a regular Congress System. At the same time, however, they gave diplomacy sufficient fluidity to allow for the settlement of the most contentious issues of the day by means of several *ad hoc* conferences in London. In 1830, for example, the three absolutist powers co-operated with Britain and France to secure the separation of Belgium from the Netherlands. Nicholas had little choice because of his preoccupation with the Polish Revolt, while Metternich probably hoped that agreement on Belgium would remove the possibility of Russian troops invading Western Europe. In 1841, Britain, Austria, Russia and Prussia put diplomatic pressure on Louis Philippe to abandon his support for Mehemet Ali, and this co-operation culminated in the Straits Convention, by which all the powers upheld the territorial integrity of the Ottoman Empire, and agreed that the Straits should be closed to warships of all nations. This treaty was among the major diplomatic achievements of the first half of the nineteenth century and gives substance to the view that the Concert of Europe survived long after the collapse of the Congress System.

6

Metternich and the Austrian Empire 1815–48

Clement von Metternich, Minister of Foreign Affairs (1809–48) and Austrian State Chancellor (1821–48), was the most significant conservative statesman in Europe during the period 1815–48. As well as dominating affairs within the Austrian Empire, he often dictated policies within the German Confederation and the Italian peninsula, and directly influenced the pattern of international relations through the medium of the Concert of Europe.

He was regarded, by admirers and opponents alike, as the major spokesman of the first half of the nineteenth century against all forms of revolution. An important theorist of the continental variety of conservatism, Metternich insisted that full monarchical powers should be retained. He returned frequently to his cardinal fear: that the proper restraints imposed on humanity by 'pure and eternal law' were being threatened by the growing presumptions of a dangerous minority who deliberately encouraged violent change rather than a well-ordered evolutionary social and political development. He also seems to have had reservations about man's ability to deal sensibly with technical progress. In his *Political Testament*, written in 1820, he affirmed that the range of human knowledge had widened considerably in recent centuries, but without a corresponding development in human wisdom. Innovations had, therefore, produced unsettling side-effects. Printing, for example, furthered the spread of false and seditious doctrines and ideologies, while the discovery of America had destroyed the traditional notion of landed property as the true source of value, and substituted a more volatile attitude to commercial wealth based on bullion. The ultimate human folly had been the French Revolution, a 'terrible social catastrophe'[1] and an inevitable result of unchecked human presumption.

Although influenced by several theorists of the eighteenth-century Enlightenment, Metternich was in no way an advocate of 'progress'. For him the cosmic principle was equilibrium, whether in politics, society or international relations. He had, after all, lived through an era when equilibrium had been dramatically overturned; he therefore placed particular emphasis after 1815 on order, for 'only order produces equilibrium'.[2] In a time of crisis 'it is above all necessary that something, no matter what, remain steadfast, so that the lost can find a connection and the strayed a refuge'.[3] Despite the restoration settlements of 1815, the danger of revolution in Europe was still considerable. The new menace emanated from liberalism, especially from demands for constitutions and for the recognition of basic rights. He warned of the peril facing any rulers who compromised in any way with such demands by providing written guarantees. 'Parlez d'un contrat social, et la révolution est faite.'[4] What was most needed was action by monarchs to reimpose equilibrium – internally by responsible policies, and externally by joint action on the basis of treaties like the Troppau Protocol (1820) and the Münchengrätz Agreement (1833).

Metternich's conservatism did not entirely preclude change. After all, 'stability is not immobility'.[5] He did have a positive goal – the gradual and very cautious improvement of the condition of the people, and of the functioning of the administration. Unfortunately, he felt negative measures, like the extension of police powers and the imposition of censorship, had to be used to clear the way. Throughout his period of office, Metternich's negative measures so outweighed any positive achievements that it would be difficult to think of a statesman who had in him less of the reformer.

Two main reasons will be advanced in this chapter for such lack of achievement: the shortcomings of his own analysis on the one hand and, on the other, the serious obstacles impeding those changes which he did propose. He was blind to the former, and vociferously aware of the latter. As the negative policies predominated and the internal problems of the Austrian Empire remained unsolved, Metternich became increasingly disillusioned and full of pessimism about the future.

Metternich and the Austrian Empire 1815–48

*

What measures did Metternich adopt for the administration of the Austrian Empire and its dependent territories? How did these reflect the more negative features of his political philosophy? The major problem within the Habsburg empire was undoubtedly the existence of a dozen major racial groups within its frontiers; these included Germans, Magyars, Italians, Romanians and Slavs (who were further subdivided into Czechs, Slovaks, Poles, Ruthenes, Serbs, Croats and Slovenes). The main political units of the Empire were the Austrian Hereditary Lands (including Austria, Styria, Carinthia, Carniola and Tyrol), the Bohemian Lands (Bohemia, Moravia and Upper Silesia), Hungary (which also dominated Galicia, Transylvania and Croatia) and the Italian acquisitions of 1815 (Lombardy and Venetia). Metternich was convinced that the variety of aspirations which inevitably result from this diverse make-up presented a constant threat of disruption. He considered that the only means of controlling the centrifugal forces of nationalism was by upholding the one centripetal power, the traditional authority of the Habsburg dynasty. Unfortunately, his measures lacked vision and consistency, while he appeared, at times, profoundly ignorant of the psychological power of nationalism in Central Europe.

Metternich had a particular suspicion of the one possible remedy of the internal problem of competing nationalities – federalism. It is true that he had a true conservative's respect for local traditions and that he favoured the full use of existing provincial institutions, but he instinctively opposed anything which suggested liberalism or political and social reform. This meant that there were occasions on which he lost the opportunity to work with moderate reformers like Andrian-Werburg, a widely respected Austrian, and Count Széchenyi. The latter led a large group in the Hungarian Diet which stood between the two extremes of the pro-Austrian conservatives and the radical secessionists. At several stages during the 1820s and 1830s Széchenyi sought Metternich's support for a series of moderate social and political reforms, but received nothing but open discouragement. Indeed, from 1837 Metternich followed a policy which he described as 'salutary terror' designed to 'enlighten' the people of Hungary. Although he decided to abandon this after 1841, enormous damage was done as moderates like Széchenyi lost ground to the extremists. One of the outspoken and anti-Austrian Magyars of the 1840s was Kossuth who described Metternich's influence in vivid and violent terms: 'From the charnel house of the Viennese system a pestilential breath steals over us which paralyzes our nerves and deadens our national spirit.' In 1848 resentment against the unreformed link between Vienna and the provinces erupted openly in Hungary, Bohemia and the Italian states of Lombardy and Venetia. The separatist movement in Hungary was so powerful that Russian troops were needed to restore Habsburg rule. Although Metternich cannot be blamed for not finding an overall solution to the Empire's regional antipathies, he can certainly be accused of shortsightedness in missing opportunities for compromise.

Instead, he followed his own instinctive views on nationalism. Within the Empire he alternated between promoting provincial identities and following a crude version of the principle of 'divide and rule' by encouraging antagonism between the different races. The Emperor Francis gave this policy his full approval, adding: 'From their antipathy will be born order and from their mutual hatred general peace'.[6] Any short-term strategic gains made by such a course were outweighed, in 1848, by the explosion of resentment of Slav against German, Magyar against German, and Slav against Magyar. Outside, and on the periphery of the Empire, Metternich underestimated the capacity of the Germans and Italians to develop closer national links. The Germans, he concluded, were unlikely to develop anything beyond 'provincial patriotism', while the Italians would have to concede that only Austria could maintain public peace and prevent the disintegration of law and order. The inaccuracy and, indeed, complacency of these views was shown by the eventual ejection of Austria from Italy in 1859, and from the German Confederation in 1866.

Metternich opposed federalism largely because he felt that it would have to be accompanied by constitutional concessions in the form of greatly strengthened representative bodies. He never willingly surrendered political powers, believing that the really efficient and successful statesman governs 'so as to avoid a situation in which concessions become necessary'.[3] More fundamentally, he detested the ideological role played by liberalism in sponsoring parliamentarianism; liberalism, in fact, was merely the 'accomplice of demagogy' and invariably prepared the way for popular violence. The section of society most responsible for the spread of 'this moral

Metternich and the Austrian Empire 1815–48

gangrene' was the middle class, for this promoted political parties which, in turn, prepared demands and applied pressure for constitutional change. The ultimate source of evil was the universities, which taught openly 'the most subversive maxims' and made a virtue of defying authority and undermining tradition. It is hardly surprising, therefore, that Metternich should have been convinced of the necessity for repressive measures. He controlled his own secret police force, which was smaller and more efficient than the official corps of Count Sedlnitzky. He reacted swiftly to internal disturbances within the German Confederation by imposing the Carlsbad Decrees in 1819 and the Six Articles in 1832. Above all, he refused to compromise over censorship. There were, he argued, only two possibilities: either severe censorship or total freedom of the press. Austria would not repeat the mistake made in France of tolerating something between them. After Russia, Austria was the most intransigent autocracy in Europe and seemed unable to follow the periodic examples of Prussia in accommodating to political changes and even experimenting with representative institutions.

Austria lagged behind Prussia also in the treatment of her social problems. Joseph II had been the first of the continental autocrats to abolish serfdom, but his successors in Austria had allowed it to creep back so that, between 1815 and 1848 Austria and Russia were the only major European powers to tolerate feudalism. Metternich refused to follow the example of Stein and Hardenberg, who had ensured its abolition in Prussia after 1807, even though it was becoming increasingly clear that serfdom was counter-productive economically, and unpopular even with some sections of the land-owning nobility. Metternich feared that fundamental social reforms would upset the internal equilibrium of the class structure and prepare the way for destructive revolutionary forces. He did alleviate peasant burdens in Galicia, but this was a tactic designed to alienate them from the Polish nobility who had organized themselves into anti-Austrian nationalist groups in 1846. Elsewhere, peasant grievances mounted; conditions were exacerbated by the depression and the bad harvests of the mid-1840s. It is probable that widespread peasant revolts within the Empire were forestalled only by the outbreak of a wider pattern of revolutions in 1848.

To Metternich, the Austrian Empire was the repository of the only type of conservatism which was likely to succeed in Europe – one which avoided the French pattern of compromise with

Germans

Magyars

Czechs

Slovaks

Poles

Ruthenes

Slovenes

Serbs and Croats

Romanians

Italians

Slavs

The peoples of the Habsburg Monarchy 1815–1908

Metternich and the Austrian Empire 1815–48

constitutionalism and also the more brutal Russian model. Consequently, he projected his ideas and policies beyond a limited domestic scale, hoping to provide a European formula for equilibrium; one of his most celebrated assertions was that Austria was Europe's House of Lords. Even here, however, there were serious defects in his policy; his foreign commitments were not commensurate with Austria's military and economic resources. In part, he adopted this wider scope through desperation, hoping for greater success on the diplomatic level than had proved possible on the domestic. This would explain his confession: 'I have sometimes held Europe in my hands, never Austria.'[1]

*

It could be argued in Metternich's defence that he was confronted with intolerable difficulties which impeded any progressive elements of his political programme. Certainly he was not slow to draw attention to these. Referring to the cumbersome operation of the whole government system, he complained of the obstacles with which he had to contend in the bureaucracy, especially the 'lack of energy'.

He was fortunate in having the support of the Emperor Francis, whose confidence was evident in his Political Will (1835). This urged Ferdinand I to bestow on Metternich the same degree of trust and to take no decision 'on public affairs, or respecting persons, without first hearing him.' Unfortunately, Ferdinand's accession marked the end of any special relationship between Chancellor and Emperor. Ferdinand proved totally incompetent, a mere shell of a ruler. In one minister's words, Austria now had 'an absolute monarchy without a monarch'.[7] The Empire was actually governed by the Conference of State under the chairmanship of the Archduke Ludwig, the rest of the authority being divided between the Archduke Francis Charles, Kolowrat and Metternich. It was a notoriously touchy team, prone to frequent conflict and rarely managing to achieve consensus.

Particularly damaging was the rivalry between Metternich and Kolowrat. The latter had risen to power rapidly during the 1820s and, in the 1830s, headed a series of committees dealing with financial affairs. Metternich complained bitterly that all internal matters were referred to Kolowrat and that his own sphere of responsibility as Chancellor was being steadily reduced. This suspicion was combined with a deep personal animosity and a basic clash of national policies: Kolowrat, a Czech, was strongly inclined to uphold the interests of Bohemia, while Metternich claimed to have a broader and less provincial viewpoint. Metternich found two clashes particularly irksome. The first was Kolowrat's insistence that Austria's military estimates should be reduced; this, of course, would weaken Metternich's position in Europe. The second was provoked by Kolowrat's demands that the Empire's first railway lines should be built within Bohemia; Metternich fought this proposal on the grounds that priority should be given to connecting the Austrian High Command with the vulnerable provinces of Northern Italy. Overall, Metternich accused Kolowrat of being the archetypal bureaucrat, lacking in foresight and imagination and, what was worse, devoting his limited energies to disrupting Metternich's own plans.

These schemes had, in fact, seemed ill-fated throughout his administration. Although he was not renowned as a reformer, Metternich did consider certain constitutional changes necessary to sharpen the Austrian bureaucracy. In 1814, for example, he proposed the replacement of the traditional colleges by modern ministries. The scheme was largely shelved, as Francis had little taste for innovation. In 1816, Metternich set up a *Kommerz-direktorium* to co-ordinate economic planning, but this faded out in 1824. He submitted to Francis several lengthy memoranda on reform concerning the State Council, the State Conference and a series of new regional chancelleries. Francis took no action and, when pressed after 1830, he pointed to the revolutions which had recently affected Western and Central Europe. 'I want no change,' he insisted. 'This is no time for reforms. The people are like men who have been badly wounded. One must not keep touching and irrit-ating their wounds.'[8] This obstruction was maintained by the other members of the State Conference after the death of Francis in 1835, and showed itself increasingly in economic as well as con-stitutional terms. During the late 1830s Metternich endeavoured to secure Austrian membership of the *Zollverein*, but the necessary step of lowering the Empire's tariff barriers were fiercely resisted by Kolowrat and the archdukes who acted as the Emperor Leopold's spokesmen. Metternich was reminded, somewhat curtly, that economic matters were not within his competence. It is not difficult to see, therefore, why Metternich attached most of the blame for growing political problems and economic stagnation to the rigid and stubborn leadership of an unreformed administration. He might well have agreed with the opinion of a socialist leader, three-quarters of a century later, that the basis of Habsburg authority was 'absolutism tempered by slovenliness'.

*

The collapse of the old order as a result of the French Revolution and the conquests of Napoleon created in Metternich a profound pessimism about human affairs. As his own failures became more apparent and resistance to his policies ever stronger, he became increasingly outspoken. His third wife described him in 1843 as a Jeremiah, but added, 'no one listens to him'.[9] He appeared convinced that 'our society is on the downward slope,' and that he was devoting his energies to 'underpinning buildings which are mouldering into decay'.[4] Most revealing of all, he believed that the world in which he lived was in a terrible hiatus. After the 1830 revolutions he observed: 'Old Europe is at the beginning of the end . . . New Europe, however, has not yet even begun its existence, and between the end and the beginning there will be chaos.'[10]

It could be argued that Metternich's failures were due generally to the incompatibility between his variety of conservatism and the changing conditions of Europe. He frequently used the metaphor of a house which was threatening to collapse; in 1825, for example, he denounced Szechenyi's scheme for reforms in Hungary with the warning 'No, no! Take one stone out of the vaulting and the whole thing collapses.' The description is particularly apt. Austrian conservatism had become totally lifeless and had to be propped up against the forces challenging it from without. By contrast, English conservatism was thriving, strengthened by the theoretical base given to it by the ideas of Burke before the turn of the eighteenth century. Burke had preferred to associate the development of a nation, its society and institutions with the metaphor of a living organism. This being could certainly be damaged by a major up-heaval like the French Revolution which, 'like a palsy, has attacked the fountain of life itself'.[11] But it was also capable of sustained growth and needed the occasional sharp corrective to the system like, for example, the Revolution of 1689, which had guaranteed the permanent supremacy of Parliament. 'An irregular, convulsive movement may be necessary to throw off an irregular, convulsive disease. But the course of succession is the healthy habit of the

British constitution.' French conservatism, as expressed by Guizot during the reign of Louis Philippe, also possessed vitality, recognizing the social achievements of the French revolution. Both English and French forms managed to adjust to, and secure the support of, the more constructive sections of their societies. Austrian conservatism possessed no such positive spirit.

Metternich's own explanation for his failures was naturally somewhat different. He would never admit to an error of judgement. 'There is a wide sweep about my mind. I am always above and beyond the preoccupations of most public men; I cover a ground much vaster than they can see, or wish to see. I cannot keep myself from saying about twenty times a day, "How right I am and how wrong they are."'[5] The only possible explanation, therefore, was that the rest of the world was wrong or, to put it another way, that he was born into the wrong era. Indeed, he openly wished that he had lived in either the eighteenth century or the twentieth. It is ironical that the man who was most widely regarded as typifying the establishment should have seen himself as an anachronism.

7

The Revolutions of 1848–9

The 1848 revolutions were the most widespread popular disturbances of the nineteenth century; they had a direct impact on France, the German Confederation, Prussia, the Habsburg Empire (especially Austria, Bohemia and Hungary), the Italian states, Wallachia and Moldavia. Other areas were peripherally influenced, including Switzerland, Belgium, Denmark and Spain. Only Russia remained totally unaffected. Yet 1849 was a year of disappointment and anticlimax. The revolutions collapsed in Central Europe, and reactionary régimes recovered their authority and confidence in a way which would have seemed impossible in 1848.

This chapter will deal with two main issues. First, who were the revolutionaries? What drove and inspired them? And why were they at first so successful? Second, why did the Revolutions collapse in 1849? And what enabled the forces of authority to recover so rapidly?

*

The 1848 revolutions were the result of extensive disillusionment within a broad area of society in many continental countries, and of a temporary co-operation between members of different social classes and occupations. Workers, artisans and students provided the activists and the street fighters who manned the barricades in Paris, Berlin and Vienna, and brought fresh intervention when the original impetus began to slow down. The wealthier and more influential elements of society, especially businessmen and lawyers, found themselves in sympathy with the spontaneous rioting of the activists, but soon sought to control what they regarded as dangerously irrational forces and to divert the Revolutions towards achieving more limited and specific objectives. They were ideally placed to do this since they were articulate and influenced the composition of the various provisional governments formed in 1848.

By far the most militant of the revolutionaries of 1848 were the artisans, especially metalworkers in Paris, and weavers in Berlin. They had been a volatile element of the population for several decades because everywhere they were confronted by the problems brought about by economic changes. Increased production in every major European state reduced the emphasis on skilled labour and opened a wide gap between masters and journeymen. A potent revolutionary factor has always been the deterioration of once acceptable conditions and the removal of a long-established means of upward social and economic mobility (see Chapter 1); this was becoming increasingly common by the mid-nineteenth century as industrialization made the progression from journeyman to master more difficult, and threatened to depress the skilled worker to the level of labourer. To make matters worse, the artisans faced increased pressure from below as the population growth in most countries induced migration from the countryside to the towns. Governments were reluctant to consider the interests of the artisans. Indeed, they tried to legislate against them, and the protection provided by the guilds in France, Northern Italy and the western parts of the German Confederation was removed. A rash of artisan disturbances in the 1840s in several German cities, as well as in Paris, Lyons and Marseilles, showed that this section of the population had become sufficiently desperate to resort to direct action. 1848 was a culmination of these activities. The artisans took to the streets of Paris on 22 February, of Vienna and Prague from 11 March, and Berlin from 17 March. They also challenged the policies of the provisional government in Paris, and the recommendations of the Frankfurt Parliament.

Of the rest of the activists, the role of the factory worker should not be exaggerated. After all, mechanization was still very limited outside the textile industry and affected major cities like Paris, Vienna and Berlin less than the medium-sized towns. It could be said, however, that once the revolutions had broken out, the factory workers provided support for the artisans in the western states of

The Revolutions of 1848–9

Germany. Of greater importance were the very poor and unemployed; although they were too downtrodden and disorganized to take a revolutionary initiative, they had nothing to lose by swelling the numbers behind the barricades at crucial moments in March 1848. More purposeful were the small groups of university students who joined in – and sometimes led – the demonstrations and riots in Vienna, Prague, Munich and the northern Italian cities, articulating the social grievances of the workers and unemployed, and feeding the artisans with radical, sometimes socialist, ideas. The part played in the revolutions by the peasantry provides more contrast and variety. This group certainly had reason to be militant; they were under severe pressure as a result of the population growth and the spread of capital-intensive farming which discriminated against the vast majority of small farmers. In some areas, like southern Italy and Bavaria, the peasantry took direct action, attacking landed proprietors and seizing land. In others, however, they remained passive. In France, for example, they feared the radicalism of the Paris workers more than they resented exploitation by landlords; while in Austria they were bought off by the régime's promise of total emancipation from serfdom.

Meanwhile, the professional and financial sectors of the middle classes had also accumulated their store of resentment against the various governments; it was they who gave the riots a political purpose and who gained most from the embarrassment of the rulers. Their most apparent grievance was political. They were excluded from power in every leading state; even in the France of the so-called 'bourgeois monarchy', high property qualifications restricted the electorate to a mere 240,000. Landed property owners, mostly aristocrats, still dominated the political processes. It is hardly surprising, therefore, that more widely representative institutions should have been the most immediate objective of middle-class leaders in 1848. Behind the political programme, however, lay a series of social and economic grievances. Again, the prospect of upward mobility had been blocked, especially in the bureaucracy. Too few posts were available for the ever-increasing numbers of highly educated lawyers; with luck, constitutional reform would greatly extend the scope of the state apparatus and therefore eliminate this bottleneck. Accompanying legal reforms, including guarantees of *habeas corpus*, would further enhance the role of lawyers by increasing the need for defence attorneys. In Central Europe a change of régime would also help realize some of the economic aspirations of German businessmen. The existing policy of the Prussian government favoured agriculture rather than industry, while even the *Zollverein* proved inadequate commercially. Much more appealing than the existing system would be a constitutional democracy, operating a revised economic policy within the context of a single German state. Writers, professors and teachers formed the final dissident group within the middle class. For some time they had been kicking against the censorship imposed in Austria and in the German Confederation as a result of Metternich's Carlsbad Decrees (1819). All these different groups gradually coalesced, giving a wider purpose to the street fighting by winning constitutions and guarantees of individual rights.

Three powerful forces transformed dissent into revolutionary action. The first was the economic depression of the 1840s. The potato crop of 1845 was ruined, while those between 1846 and 1847 showed little improvement. Similar losses in grain harvests forced prices upwards, creating widespread hardship and misery among the lower classes. The middle classes were affected by a business depression caused by a fall in the population's spending capacity. The different manifestations of the slump provoked revolt or open defiance of authority. The second influence was a widespread feeling of disillusionment following the restored old régime that held sway over much of Europe after 1815. Had the overthrow of Napoleon benefited the majority of Europeans? Byron asked of the Duke of Wellington in *Don Juan*:

> And I shall be delighted to learn who,
> Save you and yours, have gained by Waterloo?

He also maintained that 1815 had served only to 'repair legitimacy's crutch'. The antidote to Metternich and his policies was, of course, the ideals of the French Revolution. Even the mild Lamartine confessed to the power of these: 'France is revolutionary or it is nothing. The Revolution of 1789 is her political religion.'[1] The way in which France could influence the rest of Europe can be seen in the declaration of the people of Wiesbaden in Nassau in March 1848: 'The latest French Revolution . . . has shaken Europe. It is knocking on the doors of Germany.'[2] The third force was confined to Central Europe: the desire for national unification, as in Italy and Germany, or for national self-determination, as in the Habsburg Empire.

The Revolutions of 1848–9

Most of the revolutions of 1848 were disorganized, even haphazard in their immediate origin. The Paris risings, for example, were a spontaneous response to the government's decision to ban the great reform banquet meeting on 22 February. France, in turn, provided the example for movements elsewhere. On 3 March Kossuth demanded in Pressburg constitutions for the whole Habsburg Empire; while, on 12 March, Vienna was the scene of student demonstrations which, in the succeeding weeks, expanded into popular uprisings. By 17 March Berlin was similarly affected and the barricades went up in April. The Italian states had also erupted: Sicily the first area in Europe, in January, and Piedmont, Rome, Venice and Milan in March. Everywhere, authority gave way with remarkably little show of resistance. According to Louis Blanc, Louis Philippe 'let the sceptre slip voluntarily from his hand'.[3] De Tocqueville came to a similar conclusion: 'The government was not overthrown, it was allowed to fall.'[4] Other régimes hastened to make concessions in a manner which would have seemed incredible a year earlier. The Habsburg monarchy promised a constitution for Hungary in March and, in April, for Austria, Bohemia, Moravia and Galicia. Frederick William IV gave a similar guarantee to Prussia, and an Assembly eventually convened in Berlin in May. Rulers of the smaller German and Italian states also seemed to vie with each other in liberalizing their régimes.

Why did this almost unseemly abdication of authority take place? The most immediate reason was the element of shock. Metternich, it is true, had warned the monarchs to expect trouble from the bourgeoisie. But, since the latter had been relatively quiet during the 1840s, many rulers assumed that the danger had passed. No one, apparently, saw any immediate danger from the lower orders. Thus complacency affected all the régimes, and this turned to paralysis under the combined and unexpected onslaught of the different social classes in February and March 1848. Metternich observed that the monarchies had 'lost confidence in themselves'. Certainly there were divided counsels in response to street violence. Metternich and Windischgrätz, for example, urged immediate military action, but Emperor Ferdinand I was persuaded, instead, to grant concessions and dismiss Metternich. Frederick William IV of Prussia, on being asked for permission for the army to storm the barricades in Berlin, said: 'Yes, but don't fire!' and followed up with an emotionally worded appeal to 'my dear Berliners'.[5] The immediate result of the absence of clear orders was demoralization, affecting the armies and para-military defence guards in all the major capitals of Western and Central Europe. The Habsburgs had the additional problem of trying to appeal to over a dozen different races, and the initial success of the insurgents owed much to the confusion in Vienna. This was evident in the Proclamation to the Italian people made by the provisional government of Milan after the eviction of the Austrians in March: 'Fellow citizens, we have conquered. We have compelled the enemy to fly, oppressed by his own shame as much as by our valour.'[6] Was there, perhaps, a warning here that the victory was incomplete and that shame can generate revival?

*

By the end of 1848 the revolutions were in disarray and the period 1849–51 brought the hardening of reaction. The Habsburg recovery started with the bombardment by Windischgrätz of Prague in June 1848, and Vienna in October. Franz Joseph, who succeeded Ferdinand as Emperor in December, continued the offensive, closing the Austrian Assembly in March 1849, while General Radetzky subdued the Northern Italian provinces of Lombardy and Venetia between March and August. The final threat, Hungarian separatism, was disposed of with the assistance of Russian troops. Meanwhile, Frederick William IV had recovered his nerve sufficiently to apply the brake to constitutional developments in Prussia, to reject liberal schemes for German unification, and to send Prussian troops against the dissidents in Dresden (May 1849) and Baden (July 1849). France, it is true, did not see the restoration of the previous régime, but she did undergo her own form of reaction. The franchise was restricted in May 1849, and in September censorship was reimposed on the press. There was also a powerful wave against republicanism, beginning with the use of French troops to destroy Garibaldi's Roman Republic in July 1849 and culminating with Louis Napoleon's *coup d'état* of 1851 and the proclamation of the Second Empire in 1852. The dramatic transformation in all these states can be explained by the growing weakness of the revolutionaries and the revival of strong executive powers in the various European capitals.

The initial advantages of the revolutionaries had been the unexpectedness and simultaneity of the uprisings. But these were not accompanied by clarity of purpose and planned action. Mazzini had

Europe 1815–48

Legend:

- Russian Empire
- Austrian Empire
- Prussia
- Kingdom of Sardinia
- Kingdom of Naples

Italian States
- P = Parma
- M = Modena
- L = Lucca (to 1847)

German States
- H = Holstein
- Ba = Baden
- W = Württemberg
- Sa = Saxony
- Me = Mecklenburg

E = Boundary of German Confederation

laid down in 1831 the basic requirements for a successful conspiracy: 'The security, efficacity and rapid progress of an association, are always in proportion to the determination, clearness and precision of its aims.' Equally important was the 'homogeneity' of the revolutionary elements and the 'perfect concordance ... as to the path to be followed'.[7] He had also warned that the apparent harmony which existed 'during the work of destruction' might subsequently be undermined by dangerous 'discords'. Mazzini was to have his worst fears confirmed as the revolutionary movements of 1848 split along two lines of cleavage – those of social confrontations and nationalist rivalries.

Referring to the former, E. J. Hobsbawm asserts that 1848 failed because the decisive confrontation was not between the old régime and the united forces of progress, but between order and social revolution.[8] Others have argued that the bourgeoisie aimed at a constitution, with the accompanying liberal requisites of a free press, legal equality and favourable conditions for industrial and commercial progress. The rest of the urban populations, by contrast, wanted more sweeping social changes; on March 26, for example, the workers of Berlin produced demands for universal suffrage, a ministry of labour, a ten-hour working day and a minimum wage. At first the liberal provisional governments deferred to some of the workers' needs. National workshops were set up in Paris, and a road-grading scheme in Vienna guaranteed employment for the destitute. But eventually a conflict developed, revealing two fundamentally different philosophies: *laissez-faire* and state intervention. The former regarded social policies as irreconcilable with economic growth, while the latter argued for certain constraints upon that growth. Everywhere the middle-class liberals gained the greatest representation in the new legislatures. In the French Assembly the April elections returned only eighty-five socialists and radicals (including only thirty workers) out of a total of 876 deputies. The Frankfurt Parliament comprised four journeymen and one peasant, as against thirteen businessmen, ninety-two lawyers, 104 professors and teachers, and one hundred judicial officers.

The previous alliance between the middle and lower classes was now to be torn apart by mutual fear and recrimination. Businessmen and lawyers, who had once welcomed the revolutionary impetus at the barricades, soon came to recognize it as a hostile force. One delegate at the Frankfurt Parliament warned of the consequences of

The Revolutions of 1848–9

radicalism which 'seeks to do away with all natural differences in intellectual and physical endowment and to neutralize their consequences in employment and in the acquisition of wealth'.[9] Dumas, the novelist, used even more emotive words to convey the fears which many members of the French bourgeoisie possessed: 'The terrorists are out to destroy the country, the socialists are out to destroy the family and the communists are out to destroy property.'[10] These words were provoked by the June insurrection in which the workers of Paris defied a government decree closing the National Workshops. Similar fears arose in Vienna in August over protests against the cancellation of the road-grading schemes. In both instances the professional classes welcomed the use of troops against the radicals who, in the meantime, could not even console themselves with the knowledge that the peasantry were behind them. The French peasantry had been largely responsible for the conservative composition of the Assembly, and volunteered in their thousands to join the National Guard to 'put an end to the intolerable dictation of the chronically insurgent Parisian workers'.[11] The key to their behaviour is probably that they were now small landowners and gave priority to defending their property against strange and alarming ideologies. The Austrian peasantry remained totally passive, probably the result of the politic abolition of serfdom by the authorities. Everywhere in Central Europe the tide of opinion ran against radicalism, while, in France, the Second Republic was irreparably damaged; indeed, Lamenais mourned the death of the Republic after the June Days and spoke bitterly of the 'saturnalia of reaction around its bloodstained tomb'.[12]

One reason for the collapse of the revolutions, therefore, was the swift discovery that temporary co-operation between different social groups did not automatically mean a long-term convergence of interest. Another was the confrontation between different nationalities. These can be categorized as external and internal.

External disputes developed between Germans and Slavs (especially Czechs and Poles) and between Magyars and Slavs (especially Serbs and Croats). Among the proposals for a united Germany put forward in the Frankfurt Parliament in 1848 was a scheme whereby the German and Czech areas of Austria would be joined to Prussia and the smaller German states within the German Confederation. This, however, was strongly resisted by the Czechs, and their leader, Palácky, declined an invitation to attend the proceedings. Some Germans preferred a formula which would exclude all Austrian territory, but they came into conflict with another Slav group – the Poles. Delegates at the Frankfurt Parliament justified the inclusion of the Polish-speaking areas in the East by Prussia's 'right of conquest'. The sole Polish member of the parliament, however, warned: 'The Poles have been swallowed up but, by God, it will not be possible to digest them.'[13] Meanwhile, the Magyars, in their attempt to destroy the Habsburg Empire and establish an autonomous Hungary, had fallen foul of the Slavs. Palácky recognized in this Empire a useful means of counterbalancing the pretensions of both the Germans and the Magyars. In a famous defence of the principle of federation he maintained that 'If Austria did not already exist it would be necessary to invent it.'[8] The policy of Austro-Slavism, which saw the future in a reformed and balanced Empire, was also accepted by the Croats, Slovenes and Serbs of the South; they feared and detested the Magyars' contemptuous attitude towards the other races of Hungary. The Magyar reformer, Széchenyi, had warned his compatriots of this as far back as 1847: 'Incite every nationality against the Magyars and you fill to the brim the cup of vengeance with your poison.'[13] Much to the relief of the Emperor, the demands of the Slavs and Magyars were so incompatible that they brought about civil war, in which the Habsburgs were able to enlist the support of one side to defeat the other.

Internal clashes developed among the Germans, Italians and Slavs. The Frankfurt Parliament was divided between pan-Germanism, which aimed at incorporating the whole of German-speaking Europe into the new nation state, and the *Kleindeutsch* movement, which confined itself to the formula of Prussia plus the smaller states of the German Confederation. The Parliament took so long to work out the boundaries of the new state that the revolutionary impetus had dissipated by the time that the leadership was offered to the King of Prussia. The latter killed the whole scheme, in any case. Realizing that his authority would derive from the people rather than from fellow rulers, he bluntly declined to pick the crown of Germany 'from the gutter'. The Italians fared no better in *their* endeavours to create a larger political unit. Charles Albert of Piedmont merely wanted to expand the territories of the House of Savoy, while in the South, Sicily sought separation from mainland Naples; and in the East, the city of Venice remained at odds with

The Revolutions of 1848–9

mainland Venetia. Even the Slavs, obdurate in their resistance to the claims of the Germans and Magyars, found a common constitutional programme impossible to attain. Slovaks feared the prospect of being overshadowed by Czechs, while Serbs and Croats possessed deep religious and cultural differences.

While these divisions were growing ever wider, the régimes of Central Europe were recovering their confidence, and France was moving towards Bonapartism in a desperate search for order. The Habsburgs and Hohenzollerns owed much to the twin pillars of *vormarz* absolutism, the bureaucracy and the army, neither of which was ever threatened or infiltrated by the revolutionaries. Indeed, the army often took the initiative and, during the course of 1848 and 1849, the Austrian commanders, Jellačič, Windischgrätz and Radetzky were usually a step ahead of the Emperor and his cabinet in their campaigns against the main troublespots. As they recovered their nerve, the governments of Vienna and Berlin followed a more systematic policy, combining well-timed concessions to the middle classes and peasantry with a more determined use of the army against the remaining radicals. Thus, although the initial response of the rulers to the disturbances had been weak and indecisive, their recovery was complete; according to Küdlich, 'Because of a lack of grapeshot they lost their absolute, untouchable position in March, and they won it back in October . . . because of the power of their cannon.'[14]

Since the armies were so much in control in 1848, the revolutionaries, with the possible exception of the Hungarians, never stood much chance of success. The radicals had placed too much confidence in the 'Bastille' tradition and had assumed that a massive turnout in the streets over a short period would be enough to overturn the hated régimes. But the continental powers, although badly shaken, were not sufficiently effete to be toppled by spontaneous demonstrations. It gradually became apparent that a far more effective agency of change was the damage which these powers could inflict on each other; war, rather than revolution, brought some of the desired reforms during the 1860s. Austria, for example, experimented with constitutionalism after her defeat in Italy in 1859, and, by the *Ausgleich*, gave Hungary autonomy as a direct consequence of military defeat by Prussia in 1866. France rejected the Empire in 1870 after the disaster at Sedan. It took the devastation of the First World War to bring down the Habsburgs and Hohenzollerns, while

Russia, also in defeat, eventually succumbed to a revolution which, although it began much as the 1848 revolutions had begun, overthrew an old régime helpless because it had no army left to defend it.

There is one instance of a régime which actually strengthened itself by absorbing some of the influences of 1848 and then using them as antibodies against future revolution. Prussia abandoned the type of reaction which had been upheld by Metternich in favour of a compromise between an authoritarian executive and a broadly based legislature. The shadow of parliamentarianism passed into the 1871 Imperial Constitution while, all the time, Bismarck sought to 'eliminate the liberal and democratic ideas of 1848' (B. E. Schmitt). The Prussian establishment also captured German nationalism, transforming its original association with liberal democracy into a close alliance with conservatism and militarism. In Bismarck's own words, German nationalism was to become 'the moral force with which to expand and buttress the power of the Hohenzollern monarchy'.[15]

8

The Impact of the Crimean War on European Diplomacy

The impact of the Crimean War on Europe was deceptive. At first, it appeared that the Treaty of Paris (1856) might actually revive the prospect of international co-operation, especially since the erring state, Russia, had been brought back into line by Anglo-French policing action, and Turkey was no longer excluded from the diplomatic scene. In addition, the powers seemed to be extending the range of their collective responsibility. Article XV of the Treaty of Paris, for example, provided an international guarantee for freedom of navigation along the Danube; this reaffirmed, in more specific form, the principle laid down in the Treaty of Vienna (1815).

Despite these auspicious signs, it soon became apparent that the Crimean War had brought disruption, not continuity, to nineteenth-century diplomacy wrecking the Concert of Europe, which had existed since 1815, and making possible the extensive territorial changes of the 1860s. The Treaty of Paris did not even solve the problems associated more specifically with the Near East; indeed, for the rest of the century these remained an irritant to diplomacy between the major powers.

*

There is a considerable difference between the periods 1815–54 and 1856–71. The first was the longest period in modern history in which none of the major powers fought a war in Europe. There had, it is true, been numerous rivalries and diplomatic cross-currents which had brought about the collapse of the Congress System. But the common interest which all the powers had in preserving the Vienna Settlement meant that the Congress System was survived by a looser consensus generally known as the Concert of Europe. A delicate diplomatic balance had been maintained, resting on the unstated principle that no one power could be permitted by the others to upset the Settlement. In the general quest for a lasting European peace, all statesmen had seen it in their interest to accept the occasional check and to impose the occasional self-restraint. In complete contrast, the second period saw an explosion of armed conflict as Prussia and Austria each fought three wars and France two.

The reason for this transition was that the Crimean War severely weakened the two traditional guarantors of the *status quo* in Europe, Austria and Russia. The vacuum which resulted gave a unique opportunity to a new generation of statesmen with revisionist aims and a willingness to use force to achieve them: Napoleon III, Cavour and Bismarck.

Despite their many differences and rivalries, Austria and Russia had possessed the same basic interests: the preservation of autocracy, the prevention of territorial change in Central Europe and the suppression of revolution. Metternich had seen Austria as the pivot of European equilibrium, but there were times when Russian diplomatic, even military support had proved essential to enable Austria to fulfil her role as 'Europe's chamber of peers'. Although misunderstandings and diplomatic clashes had prevented a permanent military alliance, there were two particularly important examples of Russian assistance to Austria. The first was Nicholas I's intervention in Hungary in 1849 to put down the Magyar revolt and thereby restore Habsburg authority to Central Europe. The second was Russian diplomatic support for the Austrian Chancellor, Schwarzenberg, against Frederick William IV of Prussia. The latter attempted, by means of the Erfurt Union, to integrate Prussia more closely with some of the smaller German states, but was forced, by the Punctuation of Olmütz (1850) to drop the scheme and agree to the revival of the German Confederation under Austria's presidency. It seemed that as long as Russia was prepared to adhere to the Vienna Settlement and to commit herself ideologically and, if necessary, militarily to its defence, there was little chance of the mould of 1815 being destroyed.

The Crimean War, however, cut the link between Russia and

The Crimean War and European Diplomacy

Austria. Nicholas I had expected Austria to show some gratitude for Russia's military assistance in 1849 by remaining neutral and unresponsive to overtures from Russia's enemies. Instead, Austria proved hostile to Russia throughout the War. In 1854, for example, she joined an alliance with Britain and France (even though this did not actually involve military commitments against Russia), while, in 1855, she demanded the immediate Russian acceptance of the Vienna Four Points. After the War it became clear that the longstanding *entente* between Austria and Russia was over; this was confirmed in Russia by the replacement of an Austrophile foreign minister, Nesselrode, by Gorchakov, an Austrophobe. For the rest of the 1850s and the whole of the 1860s Austria remained in isolation. She now faced the impossible task of preventing political and territorial changes in Central Europe without Russian aid, and with an economic and industrial base which was far smaller than those of Prussia and France.

Austria's difficulties were compounded by another effect of the Crimean War, the destruction of the balance of power which had allowed her ascendancy over Central Europe. This balance had been upheld partly by the peripheral powers of Britain and Russia; indeed, it was the shadow of Russia over Central Europe, just as much as any direct intervention, which had guaranteed the *status quo*. The situation was very different after 1856. Quite apart from her deep alienation from Austria, Russia now had neither the means nor the inclination to revert to her former role. (A. J. P. Taylor argues that the Crimean War destroyed both the myth and the reality of Russian military power, ensuring that Russia would carry less weight in European affairs after 1856 than at any other time since 1721.[1]) Even if she had not been so seriously affected militarily, Russia would no longer have gained anything from upholding the existing system. She could feel no attachment to the Treaty of Paris, the terms of which she found deeply humiliating. From being one of the pillars of the Vienna Settlement, Russia joined the ranks of revisionist powers. She was now prepared to co-operate with any government which appeared willing to lend diplomatic support to her main objective: the repudiation of the Black Sea clauses of the Treaty of Paris.

The contraction of Russia was accompanied by a reduction in the continental role of her great rival, Britain. Although a victor in the Crimean War, Britain drifted through two decades of uncertainty, and her handling of European issues like Italian unification, the Polish uprising (1863) and the Schleswig Holstein dispute (1864) was either indecisive or failed through lack of co-operation from other governments. The more fluid diplomatic conditions which resulted from the weaker roles of the peripheral powers benefited, instead, those states which had not previously been able to dominate the international scene. The way was now open for France, Piedmont and Prussia to attack the one remaining guardian of the 1815 settlement – Austria.

The immediate beneficiary was Napoleon III, who was a revisionist in two ways. First, he aimed at ending the debilitating restraint which the Vienna Settlement imposed on any active French policy. He was even prepared, until the Polish revolt of 1863, to make common cause with Russia, and he observed to Alexander II in 1858: 'You wish to change in part the Treaty of Paris: I would change in part the treaties of 1815'.[2] He hoped that Paris would become the focal point of European diplomacy and that he would be the arbiter of a new network of alignments. Second, he expressed certain sympathies with the nationalist aspirations of the fragmented areas of Central Europe; indeed, he had already published a pamphlet entitled *The New Map of Europe* (1854). The disintegration of the Concert of Europe after the Crimean War gave Napoleon his chance. In 1858, for example, he co-operated with Russia to assist the Romanian independence movement and, in 1859, sent French troops to assist Piedmont to eject the Austrians from Lombardy and, he hoped, set up an independent Northern Italy which would become a French satellite.

Meanwhile, Cavour had also exploited the opportunities offered by both the Crimean War and the Treaty of Paris. It has been argued that he deliberately committed Piedmont to the War as part of a long-term plan to gain international recognition of the Italian cause and to prepare the way for some major power to assist Piedmont. Most historians, however, see Cavour's policy as short-term and opportunist, based on the general hope that an allied victory would bring territorial gain to Piedmont or, at least, a willingness to modify the Vienna Settlement in Italy. To this end he used the forum offered by the Congress of Paris to put Piedmont's case against the Austrian presence in Lombardy. This did not, it is true, produce immediate results; neither the British nor the French governments were prepared to support Piedmont at this stage. But Cavour's

The Crimean War and European Diplomacy

contacts were significant in that they opened up options for the future. By 1858 French and Piedmontese policies had clearly converged, the result partly of Cavour's insistent diplomacy and partly of Napoleon III's growing receptiveness. The latter had by this time come to realize that the Crimean War had effectively isolated Austria and removed the psychological barrier imposed by the Vienna Settlement against territorial revision in Europe. This was the ideal moment for quick and decisive military action, provided, of course, the blame for the outbreak of war could be made to rest with Austria. Hence, by the Pact of Plombières, Napoleon III committed France to the first of the post-Crimea struggles.

By far the most single-minded and effective of the new revisionists, however, was Bismarck, minister president of Prussia from 1862. He rejected the Vienna formula for Germany – a loose confederation under Austria's presidency – and pursued, instead, a policy of Prussian expansion. He made skilful use of the anarchic state of international relations in the 1860s, which proved ideally suited to his pursuit of *Realpolitik* and of the 'strategy of alternatives' (see Chapter 10). Three examples can be given of the way in which he exploited the legacy of the Crimean War. First, he worked on the weakness and isolation of Austria, eventually reversing the Prussian humiliation of Olmütz (1850) by victory at Sadowa (1866). Second, he ensured Russia's neutrality throughout the crucial period of German unification by offering Prussian diplomatic support for the abrogation of the hated Black Sea clauses of the Treaty of Paris. Third, he exploited the diplomatic blunders made by Napoleon III, who had been emboldened by the opportunities offered by the realignment of powers after 1856 but, by the 1860s, had shown that his policies lacked caution and perspective. The Franco–Prussian War (1870–71) destroyed whatever advantages Napoleon had gained in 1856 and showed that Prussia, not France, was the long-term beneficiary of the Crimean War.

This was partly because the international scene after 1856 was uniquely favourable to the short war with specific objectives, a device much more appropriate to Prussia than to France. The Crimean War, for all its blunders and casualties, had been successfully localized and had disproved the fears of those who had drafted the Vienna Settlement that any conflict between major powers must inevitably lead to a general European war. Thus a number of governments came to see warfare not as the penalty for the failure of diplomacy but rather as a device to ensure eventual diplomatic success; the famous dictum of Clausewitz that war is the continuation of diplomacy by other means proved to be more applicable to the 1850s and 1860s than to any other period since the middle of the eighteenth century. This approach, however, favoured the state with the greatest potential for military efficiency as well as the strongest industrial base. It was, therefore, fortunate for Bismarck that Prussia's economic growth had been the most rapid in Europe and that her industrial infrastructure was, by the 1860s, second only to that of Britain. Prussia was also armed with justification for aggression. The fulfilment of German unification, one of the motive forces behind the 1848 revolutions, could now be used as a slogan by dynasts on behalf of their subjects, rather than as a means of peoples trying to persuade dynasts. In this sense, the Crimean War made possible the transformation which had eluded the revolutionaries of 1848.

*

In a wider sense the Crimean War marks, in the words of J. A. S. Grenville, a 'point of transition in the history of Europe'.[3] The same cannot, however, be said of its impact on the Balkans and the Near East, the area which had spawned the conflict.

The Treaty of Paris was intended primarily as a solution to the two main problems affecting the Ottoman Empire and its relations with the rest of Europe. The first was the external pressure and the attempts made by Russia to gain control over the Black Sea and uncontested naval access to the Eastern Mediterranean. The Treaty of Paris therefore imposed certain restraints. The Russian land frontier was pulled back in Bessarabia, while Article XI declared: 'The Black Sea is Neutralized'. Consequently, according to Article XIII, 'the maintenance or establishment upon its Coast of Military–Maritime Arsenals becomes alike unnecessary and purposeless'. The second problem was the danger of internal upheaval and the possibility of total disintegration. The British and French delegates assumed that this could be dealt with by extensive internal reforms designed to satisfy the subject peoples of the Balkans. Hence Article IX recorded with approval 'the generous intentions' of His Imperial Majesty the Sultan 'towards the Christian population of his Empire', while Articles XXI, XXII, XXIII, XXVIII and XXIX provided for

The Crimean War and European Diplomacy

greater autonomy within Moldavia, Wallachia and Serbia, although under the sovereignty of the 'Sublime Porte'.

These solutions, however, proved illusory for, in the long term, the Treaty of Paris settled very little. The constraints on Russia could not be enforced; Alexander II succeeded in 1870 in repudiating the Black Sea clauses, while his reconstituted armies were strong enough by 1877 if not perhaps to play a European role then at least to defeat the Turks. Hopes for reform within the Ottoman Empire were also disappointed. Sultan Abdul Aziz (1861–76) assumed that the preservation of his Empire against Russian encroachment would always be a vital strategic consideration for the other powers, and that future assistance would not be made to depend on the degree of progress made towards liberating the subject peoples. He therefore felt that there was a strong case for doing nothing. Moldavia and Wallachia largely escaped Ottoman misrule when, in 1862, they were reconstituted as the autonomous state of Romania. But the other areas of the Empire continued to experience maladministration and neglect. Discontent eventually boiled over, between 1875 and 1876, in a series of revolts in Bosnia, Herzegovina, Bulgaria, Serbia and Montenegro, while the Turkish massacres in Bulgaria demonstrated that the régime was still prepared to resort to brutality. The powers were even hampered by the Treaty of Paris in their attempts to put pressure on Sultan Abdul Hamid II at the 1877 Constantinople Conference. Refusing to accept an international commission to ensure that reforms were implemented, the Sultan took his stand on Article IX, which expressly stated that the powers had no right 'to interfere, either collectively or separately, in the relations of His Majesty the Sultan with his subjects, nor in the Internal Administration of his Empire'. This deadlock precipitated unilateral action by Russia against Turkey and, in 1878, the Congress of Berlin, like the Congress of Paris before it, produced another series of temporary solutions.

During the period 1856–1914 the Eastern Question persistently eluded any lasting settlement. Between 1856 and 1871 it appeared insignificant beside the momentous changes which were taking place in Central Europe. But, by 1871, these changes had worked their way through. Napoleon III had been overthrown in the process, Cavour was dead, and Bismarck was now seeking his objectives by diplomacy rather than by warfare. It was at this stage that the Eastern Question became a constant irritant, inflaming relations between Austria–Hungary and Russia and throwing up major threats to European peace, like the Russo–Turkish War (1877), the Bulgarian Crisis (1885–7), the Bosnian Crisis (1908–9), the Balkan Wars (1912–13) and the Sarajevo assassination (1914).

9

Cavour, Garibaldi and the Unification of Italy

Italy had, for some centuries, been regarded as the part of Europe least likely to be united, and seemed to merit Metternich's observation that it was merely a 'geographical expression'. Yet undercurrents of national sentiment did exist, as did a willingness in all parts to rise against foreign rule or local oppression. There were also theoretical schemes for unification, including the federal scheme of Gioberti and the unitary republicanism of Mazzini. The failure of the 1848 revolutions, however, proved that the expulsion of the foreigner and the reduction of the number of political units required consummate diplomatic and military skills as well.

These were provided by Count Camillo di Cavour (1810–61) and Giuseppe Garibaldi (1807–82) who, between them, succeeded where others had failed. It would be difficult, however, to imagine two more different statesmen. Cavour was an aristocrat, while Garibaldi was the son of a merchant seaman. Cavour's early commitments were to farming and journalism before he became a politician in the 1850s, and he possessed an extensive knowledge of economic and political theory and institutions. Garibaldi spent his early career in the merchant navy. After his hasty withdrawal from Piedmont in 1834, he devoted his attention to guerrilla warfare in South America before returning to Italy in 1848. He was a military leader rather than a politician, with little education and even less pretension to theoretical knowledge.

This chapter will explore three main contrasts in the ideas and activities of Cavour and Garibaldi: their concepts of 'Italy', the base of their power and influence, and their practical contributions to Italian unification.

*

The Kingdom of Italy, which was established in 1860, conformed to the original vision of neither Cavour nor Garibaldi. Indeed, both found it necessary to change their initial conception of 'Italy' and to compromise – Cavour on Italy's geographical extent, and Garibaldi on the type of political structure.

During the 1850s Cavour considered unification of the entire peninsula neither possible nor desirable; he therefore differed fundamentally from Garibaldi, who argued that '*a single Italy* must be our first goal',[1] and who hoped to incorporate the existing states of Piedmont, Sardinia, Lombardy, Venetia, Parma, Modena, Tuscany, the Papal States and Naples. Such was the scope of his vision that Garibaldi was prepared to fight anywhere – in Lombardy against the Austrians in 1848 and 1849, in Rome against the French in 1849, and in Sicily and Naples against Bourbon rule in 1860. Cavour, however, envisaged only an enlarged Piedmont, which would include Lombardy and Venetia. At its most ambitious, his scheme was for an Italian Confederation; this was explicitly stated in a confidential memorandum to Victor Emmanuel explaining the contents of the secret Pact of Plombières with Napoleon III in 1858. Mazzini, fully aware of Cavour's caution, described him as 'the ministerial liberator who taught his master how to prevent the union of Italy'.[2] It does, indeed, appear that Cavour was willing to halt the growth of the Italian nation at a stage already reached by Germany in the loosely structured Confederation.

Between 1859 and 1860, however, Cavour was pushed along irresistibly by the sequence of events and had to adapt his former proposals. His original dislike of total unification had been due largely to his fear of the radical republicans who had made it their ultimate aim. But when Napoleon III withdrew France prematurely from the war with Austria by the Treaty of Villafranca in 1859, Cavour threatened to 'turn revolutionary and conspirator' himself and he resigned his office of prime minister. Until his recall a few months later, Cavour now found himself approving and depending on the activities of Ricasoli, Farini and Azeglio to gain popular acceptance for the incorporation of Tuscany, Modena and Romagna into Piedmont in defiance of the Villafranca settlement. Once

Cavour, Garibaldi and the Unification of Italy

reinstalled as prime minister, this time of a greatly enlarged kingdom in Northern Italy, Cavour was again carried forward by the momentum of change. He was seriously concerned about the activities of Garibaldi and the 'Thousand' in Sicily and Naples (1860) and their threat to the Papal States in Central Italy. He realized that to oppose Garibaldi directly would incur the wrath of Italian patriots everywhere, including Piedmont. To take no action would enable Garibaldi to establish a rival state in the south or, at best, give him the credit for the unification of Italy. Cavour found this prospect abhorrent and was quite adamant that 'The King cannot accept the crown of Italy at the hands of Garibaldi'.[3] The only solution to this dilemma was to take direct military and diplomatic action: to annex the Papal States and to outmanoeuvre Garibaldi into relinquishing his hold on the south. The overall result would have to be a kingdom covering the entire peninsula.

If Cavour's ideas about the extent of Italy underwent a major change, so, too, did Garibaldi's views on the most suitable form of government. Garibaldi had originally agreed with Mazzini's dictum that 'our Italian tradition is essentially republican'.[4] Cavour, on the other hand, opposed republicanism as a dangerous form of radicalism and refused to consider anything but a constitutional monarchy which, in his view, was 'the only type of government which can reconcile liberty with order'.[5] This time the change was made by Garibaldi. As early as 1855 he stated that the main priority must be unification and that all the elements of Italy 'must amalgamate and join whoever is strongest among them'.[1] He applauded the formation of the National Society in 1857, and the decision of many republicans to seek the leadership of the King of Piedmont. His slogan was now: 'Unite yourselves to our programme – *Italy and Victor Emmanuel* – indissolubly.'[6] He also remained on excellent personal terms with the King, affirming in 1860: 'I am truly his friend for life.'[7]

Inevitably both Cavour and Garibaldi had feelings of uneasiness about their changes of plan. Cavour died suddenly and unexpectedly in 1861, before the Kingdom of Italy was more than a few months old; but he had already encountered serious problems over the local administration of the new nation, caused largely by the last-minute inclusion of Naples and the Papal States. He must, therefore, have regretted being pushed by Garibaldi into extending the kingdom in Northern Italy to the Kingdom of Italy. For his part, Garibaldi looked back with some distaste on his surrender of Naples.

> We drove the Bourbon out and took that other,
> Dethroned a corpse, and set up its sick brother.[8]

Indeed, Garibaldi went further, complaining that the Kingdom of Italy was, in the 1870s, corrupt, backward and disunited. Towards the end of his life, therefore, he reaffirmed the ardent republicanism of his youth, and in 1872 declared: 'I am a republican, since I believe this the best kind of government for honest people, the one most generally desired and least dependent on violence or imposture.'[9]

*

Perhaps the greatest contrast between Cavour and Garibaldi lay in the basis of their power and their concept of authority. Cavour was a parliamentarian with an inherent suspicion of mass participation. Garibaldi, on the other hand, was a populist, prepared to appeal directly to the support of the masses. Cavour opposed revolution and radicalism, adopting a stance of conservative liberalism which was similar to the philosophy of Guizot and of the French Orléanist monarchy (1830–48). Garibaldi was one of the great radicals of the nineteenth century, considering himself an ideological descendant of the first French Revolution.

It is hardly surprising that Cavour should have put his faith in parliamentary institutions, since they had shaped his political career. He was elected to the Piedmontese Assembly in 1848, rising in rapid succession to the positions of Minister of Marine and Commerce (1850), and Prime Minister (1852). He owed his power and influence to complex parliamentary manoeuvres. In 1852, for example, he engineered the downfall of Prime Minister Azeglio by building a large centrist *bloc* known as the *connubio* and, for the rest of his life, skilfully maintained a majority for himself. He made full use of his power to take the initiative when dealing with political opponents and this parliamentary *Realpolitik* earned him the grudging acclaim of Gattina (a backbencher): 'Count Cavour is a cross between Sir Robert Peel and Machiavelli.'[10]

Garibaldi, too, had experience of politics in Uruguay before 1847, Rome in 1849, and Turin from 1860. On one famous occasion he clashed with Cavour in the Italian parliament and lost: Cavour was able to drum up a majority against Garibaldi's censure of his

(a) Italy before 1848

Provinces of the Austrian Empire

Ruled by members of the Habsburg family

Kingdom of Piedmont/Sardinia

Kingdom of the Two Sicilies (Naples)

(Lucca ended 1847)

(b) The stages of unification

Kingdom of Sardinia in 1858 (plus Savoy and Nice)

Added to Sardinia after conquest from Austria 1859

Added to Sardinia after plebiscites 1860

Conquered by Garibaldi Added to Sardinia 1860

Garibaldi's route 1860

Conquered by Sardinia 1860

Added to Kingdom of Italy 1866

Added to Kingdom of Italy 1870

Nice and Savoy (ceded to France 1860)

Kingdom of Italy 1861

The unification of Italy

recent conduct of the war. The two men presented a strange contrast in their powers of oratory. Gattinara observed that Cavour was a speaker in the English parliamentary style; his arguments were reasoned but his delivery not particularly impressive. Garibaldi, by contrast, possessed a voice which was renowned throughout Europe and he was at his best when delivering a spontaneous address which appealed to the emotions. For this reason, he found parliamentary debate sterile, and preferred more direct contact with the masses, amongst whom he was known as *il padre dell'Italia*. He had no aspirations to ministerial office and frequently questioned the need for parliamentary sovereignty at all. He went so far as to suggest that dictatorship might be more appropriate to Italy's needs.

This, in fact, was the point of greatest disagreement between Cavour and Garibaldi. Cavour was uncompromising in his hostility to the idea of dictatorship, whether popular or monarchical, revolutionary or reactionary. Besides, Cavour realized, 'parliament enables me to do many things which would be impossible for an absolute ruler'.[11] He found Garibaldi's attachment to dictatorship sinister and alarming; his fear of what Garibaldi might do with this power in Southern Italy induced him, in 1860, to take the extraordinary measures described in the next section. It could be argued, however, that Cavour sometimes misunderstood Garibaldi's motives; the latter was not tempted by power for its own sake, but rather as a means of taking direct action on behalf of the people, thereby reducing the possibility of obstruction and delay which he considered the inherent defects of parliamentarianism. He advocated a return to the constitutional device of Ancient Rome whereby a single leader could assume total authority in times of emergency. He advanced this as a solution to Italy's problems on three occasions. The first was in Rome in 1849, but his path was blocked by the followers of Mazzini. The second was after the conquest of Sicily and Naples in 1860, when Garibaldi ousted the Bourbon administration and ruled by decree, although, according to Crispi, 'by love not by force'.[12] A few months earlier he had urged Victor Emmanuel to take more active measures to complete Italian unification: 'Sire, Italy does not need elections or liberty, but battles; assume the dictatorship!'[13] Victor Emmanuel was not averse to this prospect, but nothing came of it. Cavour had already side-stepped a somewhat clumsy royal attempt to weaken parliament in 1855, and his ministerial position was invulnerable.

Cavour, Garibaldi and the Unification of Italy

Italy's parliamentary institutions were therefore upheld by a conservative, whose contact with the people was indirect and limited, against a radical, whose personal appeal and popularity were unquestioned. Ultimately the traditional concept of legislative checks and balances prevailed over the demand for the personification of the masses by an unfettered executive.

*

What, in practical terms, did Cavour and Garibaldi contribute to the unification of Italy?

The role of Cavour was entirely diplomatic, his fundamental aim being to secure further territory for Piedmont by the expulsion of the Austrians from Northern Italy. Like Bismarck, with whom he is often compared, he showed an uncanny ability to realize his objectives, even if it meant adopting a devious approach and bending to circumstances. Hence his cousin, de la Rive, described him as 'a bar of iron painted like a reed'.[10] Indeed, he was so well versed in the art of diplomacy that Mazzini called him the 'pale ghost of Machiavelli'.[14] Two examples can be used to illustrate this. The first was the provocation of war with Austria in 1859. Cavour was realistic enough to consider French assistance essential if Austria were to be excluded from Northern Italy. Napoleon III, in his own words, was anxious 'to do something for Italy', but, naturally enough, wanted Austria to appear the aggressor. Consequently, the secret Pact of Plombières, drawn up between France and Piedmont in 1858, made French assistance conditional on Austrian aggression. Cavour devoted himself to preparing for war and finding a devious way of stinging Austria into delivering an ultimatum; in his jubilance he said, in a famous mixed metaphor: 'We have Austria in a cleft stick and she cannot get out of it without firing a cannon.' The second example of Cavour's diplomatic art was his invasion of the Papal States in 1860. Although his motive was undoubtedly to prevent Garibaldi from making an attempt on Rome, Cavour manufactured a more appealing excuse. The inhabitants of the Marches were secretly encouraged to rise against the 'brutal oppression' of foreign troops employed by the Pope and to appeal to Piedmont for protection. When the Papacy failed to respond to an ultimatum delivered by Piedmont for the dismissal of foreigners, Cavour sent an army to annex the whole area (with the exception of Rome and the adjacent Patrimony). A frank observation once made by Cavour seems especially appropriate to this sequence of events: 'If we did for ourselves what we do for our country, what rascals we should be!'[2]

Garibaldi, too, had some experience of foreign dealings, his particular ability being to gain the moral backing of other leading statesmen for the cause of Italian unity, but he lacked the unscrupulous element which brought Cavour success. Oliphant called him, in 1860: 'The most amiable, innocent, honest nature possible, and a first rate guerilla chief, but in council a child.'[15] In fact, his real strength was as a soldier. He harassed the Austrians in Northern Lombardy in 1848 and 1859, achieving far greater successes than the regular armies of Piedmont, and bringing to Italy the techniques of guerrilla warfare which he had learned and perfected during his long exile in South America. His campaigns against the Bourbons in Sicily and Naples (1860) were especially important. They enlarged the original plans for unification to embrace the entire peninsula, and also saved Italians from the charge that national unity had been accomplished only by Cavour's manipulation of foreign aid. Garibaldi showed the rest of Europe that Italians could be aroused into sustaining a series of popular campaigns against disciplined armies.

What, in retrospect, appear to be complementary roles, were, at the time, very much in conflict. By 1860 each statesman had developed a profound mistrust of the other. Cavour observed of Garibaldi: 'He is a soldier of fortune, and behind his outward petulance there lies the profound dissimulation of a savage',[16] while Garibaldi described Cavour as 'a low intriguer'. Cavour's attitude to Garibaldi can best be illustrated by his policies towards the Thousand's conquest of Sicily and Naples. He was fundamentally opposed to the expedition because of possible diplomatic complications with France and other powers. But he could not be seen to be too obstructive, as Garibaldi had become enormously popular in Piedmont, as well as in other parts of Italy. Consequently, he allowed the Thousand to sail from Piedmont, but was also determined to keep his options open. 'If the insurrection is put down,' he observed in private, 'we shall say nothing; if it is successful we shall intervene in the name of order and authority.'[3] Garibaldi, however, proved unwilling to hand over Sicily to Piedmont, preferring to proclaim himself temporary dictator and use it as a base from which to conquer mainland Naples. Cavour was now seriously

Cavour, Garibaldi and the Unification of Italy

concerned that Garibaldi's conquest of the whole of Southern Italy would threaten 'the national and monarchical character of the Italian movement'.[17] Characteristically, therefore, Cavour now engaged in secret conspiracy to overthrow the Bourbons before Garibaldi's arrival. But the speed of Garibaldi's advance from the Strait of Messina to the city of Naples took Cavour by surprise and negated all his efforts. Fortunately, Garibaldi was prepared, by November, to hand over his conquests to Victor Emmanuel, thus allaying Cavour's fears.

Garibaldi was embittered by the whole episode and subsequently attacked Cavour for his delaying tactics: 'Every possible obstacle was raised in our path between the time we left Genoa and when we arrived at Naples.'[18] Yet he accomplished his victories largely by ignoring Cavour and trusting to the goodwill and support of Victor Emmanuel. Thus, when La Farina was sent by Cavour to Sicily to dissuade the Thousand from crossing to the mainland, Garibaldi ordered his immediate deportation. Throughout his 1860 campaigns, Garibaldi refused to compromise with Cavour, determined that the southern half of the peninsula should be incorporated into a united Italy by his efforts alone. It was an arrogance which Cavour detested but also misunderstood; for Garibaldi was actually working for the extension of Victor Emmanuel's authority and not, as Cavour feared, for the realization of Mazzinian republicanism.

*

Victor Emmanuel's predecessor, Charles Albert, had once maintained *'Italia farà da sè'* ('Italy will make herself'). Cavour always worked on the assumption that this was totally inappropriate and therefore secured outside help to expel the foreigner. It was Garibaldi, however, who extended the process of unification well beyond the original projections of an enlarged Piedmont. In this sense, it could be argued that Italy *completed* herself.

10

The Unification of Germany

In September 1862 Otto von Bismarck, Prussia's newly appointed
Minister President, addressed the Budget Commission of the
Prussian *Landtag*. The delegates had recently rejected overwhelmingly an Army Bill, introduced by von Roon, to increase the
number of cavalry and infantry regiments. Bismarck now reminded
them that if Prussia were to play a dominant role in German affairs,
this role must be underpinned by military security. 'Germany', he
concluded, 'looks not to Prussia's Liberalism, but to her power . . .
The questions of the day will not be decided by speeches and majority
decisions . . . but by blood and iron.'[1]

The 'blood and iron' speech passed into mythology as well as
history, becoming the phrase most commonly used to describe the
method by which a united Germany was eventually created. Until,
that is, the British economist John Maynard Keynes challenged the
long-held assumption that diplomatic and military factors alone
created Germany. Instead, he argued, the long period of economic
and industrial preparation must be taken into account, for without
this the German nation would have been a mere shell. Hence 'The
German Empire was created more by coal and iron than by blood and
iron.'[2]

This chapter will weigh up the relative importance in German
unification of both influences: diplomatic-military and economic-
industrial. It will also look at another controversy. Was the German
Empire which emerged in 1871 the model which Bismarck had in

The Unification of Germany

mind from the very start? Or was it the outcome of a series of fortuitous developments?

*

Before unification Germany was a triad, consisting of a group of smaller states and two major powers, Austria and Prussia.

Until 1806 the smaller states had numbered over 2000, but Napoleon I had, in destroying the Holy Roman Empire and substituting his own Confederation of the Rhine, reduced them to sixteen. In 1815, these were incorporated into the German Confederation, which was established by the Congress of Vienna. The opening decades of the nineteenth century were of vital importance for the development of nationalism in these smaller states. In the first place, Napoleon's constitutional consolidation removed the tiny splinter states and free cities which had, for centuries, impeded any form of unity. Secondly, Germans in Hanover, Mecklenburg, Bavaria, Baden, Württemberg, Saxony and other states were conscious of a common role in ejecting French rule. Whether, in fact, Napoleon had been defeated by traditional powers rather than by incipient nationalism, did not really matter. The myth of the patriotic war blended with the common cultural heritage which German Romanticism had given a powerful boost. The result was that 'Germany' exerted, for the first time, a strong emotional and intellectual appeal among liberals, students and a wide cross-section of the middle classes.

The other two components of the triad, Austria and Prussia, each had territory inside and outside the Confederation. Between 1815 and 1848 the two powers remained wary of any manifestations of German nationalism, especially those accompanied by liberal programmes, because these seemed to threaten their more traditional dynastic foundations. There was, therefore, considerable co-operation between the two governments of Berlin and Vienna over policy towards the rest of the Confederation. This period of 'peaceful dualism'[3] was in sharp contrast to the bitter Austro-Prussian rivalries of the eighteenth century. The 1848 revolutions, however, brought dualism to an end and altered the whole nature of the German question. The smaller states had, through their representatives in the Frankfurt parliament, taken the initiative in devising a scheme for a united Germany. Although this was not implemented, it was clear that the clock could not be turned back to 1815 and that

Aspects of European History 1789–1980

extensive revision of the existing German Confederation would be only a matter of time.

The question now arising was: which of the two powers would be able to take charge of and direct this aspiration towards unity? At first sight, Austria might seem the more appropriate. Since she was, herself, a multi-racial and heterogeneous empire, she would be more likely than Prussia to respect the individualism of the smaller German states within a federation. Austrian leadership of Germany would also be in accord with historical evolution. After all, she had dominated the Holy Roman Empire for the second half of its thousand years' existence. Yet it was to Prussia that the majority of German nationalists looked in 1848. Many had deep misgivings about the militarist tradition which Prussia had acquired from Frederick William I (1713–40) and Frederick the Great (1740–86). But the doubters were outnumbered by the *Kleindeutsch* supporters, who saw in Prussia a more cohesive state which was less archaic than Austria in its policies and, above all, more progressive economically. Austrian leadership might be safer, but Prussian leadership would be more in tune with the type of economic progress which the majority of the middle class considered the main priority for the future.

*

Prussia's economy grew steadily between 1815 and 1848 and then, during the 1850s and 1860s, experienced the first industrial revolution on the Continent.

During the earlier period, Prussia had three major advantages. First, she had a tradition of economic reform. Following Prussia's military defeat by Napoleon, ministers like Stein and Hardenberg overhauled the financial system and modified the social structure by abolishing serfdom. What Hardenberg called 'timely reforms from above'[4] gave a vital shove to private enterprise which an unchanged system still held back in Austria. Second, the Congress of Vienna (1815) gave Prussia the coal- and iron-producing areas of the Rhineland in compensation for the Polish provinces annexed by Russia. The Ruhr and Saar regions complemented Silesia in transforming Prussia from a state with relatively few natural resources, to one with the richest mineral deposits in Central and Western Europe. Third, Prussia was able to extend her influence over fellow

The Unification of Germany

German states, from 1834 onwards, by means of the *Zollverein* customs union, which brought together the Prussian-Hessian, the South German and the Central German Customs Unions. By 1834 many of the smaller German states were linked commercially to Prussia, and were becoming increasingly cut off from Austria (which, of course, was not a member of the *Zollverein*). The middle-class liberals within these states responded enthusiastically to the opportunities offered, and began to think in terms of political unity with Prussia as a means of preserving a larger market and developing Germany as a more powerful economic entity.

During the 1850s the Prussian economy took off, encouraged by the progressive policies of Manteuffel (Minister President), von der Heydt (Minister for Trade) and, above all, Delbrück (an Under-Secretary in the Ministry of Trade). The railway network in Prussia increased from 3869 kilometres in 1850, to 7169 by 1860 and 11,523 by 1870. Coal production in the Saar mines increased from 700,000 tons in 1850 to 2.2 million in 1860 and, in the Ruhr during the same period, from 2 million to 4.3 million. The steel industry, which took full advantage of the Bessemer process (developed in 1856), was further enhanced by the existence of the most highly developed chemical industry in the world. Credit for industrial growth was widely available, whether in the form of investment from abroad or of German joint stock banks like *Disconto-Gesellschaft* (1851), *Darmstädter Bank* (1853) and *Berlin Handelsgeselschaft* (1856). Prussia's economic growth pulled the rest of Germany behind it. The total value of the *Zollverein's* exports, for example, increased between 1853 and 1856 from 356.9 million to 456.1 million thaler, while Germany's combined coal production expanded from 3.2 million tons in 1846 to 12.3 million in 1860.

Meanwhile, Austria had become more and more concerned about the influence being exercised by her rival over the smaller states. To make matters worse, her own economic position was extremely precarious. Between 1853 and 1856, for example, Austrian exports fell from 184.3 million thaler to 150.3 million, while the continental depression which followed the Crimean War had a particularly serious effect on Austria in 1857. The Vienna government awoke, belatedly, to the commercial isolation imposed on Austria by the *Zollverein*. During the 1850s, therefore, Austrian ministers sought to transform the *Zollverein* into a wider customs union covering the whole of Central Europe. Bruck, Minister of Commerce from 1848, hoped eventually to fit Austria into a huge free trade area covering the whole Continent between the Rhine and the Black Sea, with the centre of gravity in Vienna rather than Berlin. Such proposals were, however, doomed to failure. Prussia neatly evaded and side-stepped all proposals to reform the *Zollverein* and, from 1859, Austria became involved in more urgent issues like the Italian War. Austria came out the worse from a further round of negotiations with Prussia in the early 1860s. By 1864 the *Zollverein* was still firmly dominated by Prussia, and Austria had been effectively denied even a treaty of limited accession.

There can be no doubt that Prussia's economic domination of the smaller states was a vital factor in her eventual success in uniting Germany. It was not, however, sufficient. By the early 1860s it had become apparent that the political framework of the German Confederation was acting as an obstacle to any further progress towards unity. By the Olmütz Punctuation (1850) the institutions of the Confederation were restored in full, and Prussia's brief experiment with the Erfurt Union was summarily ended. The Confederation might not be the perfect arrangement for Germany but, to Austria, it was preferable to a closer form of political unity or to allowing the smaller German states to revolve around Prussia. Despite its defects, therefore, the Confederation was the only type of Germany which Austria would tolerate. In the words of Schwarzenberg, Austria's Minister President, 'a threadbare and torn coat is better than no coat at all'.[5] Thus, although Prussia had succeeded by 1860 in preventing Austria from modifying the economic arrangements of the *Zollverein*, Austria had managed, equally effectively, to veto any constitutional change in the Confederation. The progress towards a united Germany had, therefore, reached a political impasse which would have to be resolved by political means.

*

This was to be the achievement of Otto von Bismarck, appointed Minister President by William I in 1862. During the next nine years Prussia found herself at war for the first time since 1815, and against no fewer than three enemies. The first war, against Denmark in 1864, released the Duchies of Schleswig and Holstein for the German Confederation; the second expelled Austria from Germany in 1866, and united the north; while the third resulted, by 1871, in the defeat of France and the incorporation of the south German

The Unification of Germany

states into the new German Empire. By a combination of subtle diplomacy and naked militarism Bismarck appeared to have fulfilled his 1862 prediction that Prussia would unite Germany by 'blood and iron'.

Was this sequence of events carefully engineered by a master strategist of *Realpolitik*? Bismarck himself tried to create the impression that it was. After his retirement in 1890 he stressed the importance of Prussian militarism in German unification and his own role in bringing about the right circumstances. Hence he remarked: 'The Gordian Knot of German circumstances was not to be untied by the gentle methods of dual policy [but] could only be cut by the sword.' Furthermore, 'In order that German patriotism should be active and effective, it needs as a rule to hang on the peg of dependence upon a dynasty.'[6] As for his own role, he provided Disraeli, in 1862, with a much quoted outline of his future intentions. 'When the army has been brought to such a state as to command respect, then I shall take the first opportunity to declare war with Austria, burst asunder the German Confederation, bring the middle and smaller states into subjection, and give Germany a national union under the leadership of Prussia.'[7] Such apparent confidence in his ability to redirect events was clearly intended for the notice of historians and fellow statesmen. Bismarck showed more concern than most about the judgement of posterity and clearly hoped to hang on to his reputation as the most successful, if the most ruthless, diplomat of the entire century.

In fact, most historians present a considerably modified picture of Bismarck's methods. It is important to realize that Bismarck was appointed Minister President in an age of growing uncertainty: the map of Europe could change within the near future in several different ways. No statesman could have complete confidence in dictating the course of this change. On the other hand, there was more scope than usual for a brilliant opportunist who was not afraid of experimentation and, as a last resort, conflict. The key to Bismarck's diplomacy was one of his most moderate assertions that events were part of an irresistible 'time stream' of history. He observed on one occasion: 'One cannot make history.' Nevertheless, it was possible, through an intuitive understanding of the issues involved and decisive action, to achieve certain broad objectives by becoming part of the 'time stream'. In other words, 'Man cannot create the current of events. He can only float with it and steer'.[8] The essential thing,

The unification of Germany

however, was to pursue several alternative policies simultaneously and for as long as possible; 'always have two irons in the fire'.[9] Eventually, one of these would emerge as the only possible course and the others would be eliminated. Where most statesmen erred was in committing themselves too soon to a plan which eventually turned out to be inappropriate. Bismarck's diplomacy, by contrast, was aggressive and devoid of moral restraint but, at the same time, the capacity to defer the vital decision to the last possible moment enabled him to move with history into one of the channels which he had foreseen. In so doing, he gave the impression that he had directed, even diverted, the flow of events. His dealings with Austria and France provide ample evidence of his 'strategy of alternatives'.[9]

Austria had been seen by Bismarck as an obstacle to German unity ever since the Olmütz Punctuation of 1850. There were, however, several methods of dealing with the problem. One was to come to an arrangement between Prussia and Austria, partitioning Germany at the River Main. Another was to aim for Prussian dominance over all the smaller German states, and thereby eject Austria from Germany altogether. Bismarck probably had, in the early 1860s, no clear concept of 'Germany' beyond the enlargement of Prussia at the expense of her immediate neighbours; he therefore followed several policies simultaneously. Between 1864 and 1865, for example, he promoted an alliance with Austria, reasoning that this would allay the fears of the southern German states, who were more naturally inclined towards Vienna than Berlin. This co-operation seemed to reach a climax in 1864 with the joint Austro-Prussian intervention against Denmark and the occupation of Schleswig and Holstein. The 1865 Convention of Gastein between Austria and Prussia was described by Bismarck as 'papering over the cracks' between the two powers. Yet this statement reveals another motive behind Bismarck's diplomacy. He hoped that Austria would concede to Prussia the lion's share of political influence in Northern Germany. If, however, Austria should resist this development, the situation in Schleswig-Holstein could be used to precipitate, at a time of Prussia's own choice, a conflict which would have become inevitable. Meanwhile Bismarck was also hedging his bets in his international diplomacy. His negotiations with France in 1865 and vague hints of territorial gain kept Napoleon III favourably disposed towards Prussia, while Bismarck's moral support for the Russian government over the Polish Revolt won the gratitude of Alexander II. These two powers could, therefore, be relied upon to support Prussia against Austria in any constitutional alterations within the German Confederation. Should Prussia find herself at war with Austria, her two neighbours could be expected to remain neutral. Bismarck's master-stroke was the Italian alliance of 1866. This put Austria under intense diplomatic pressure, outflanked her in the event of war, and gave Bismarck the appearance of taking over from Napoleon III as the benefactor of Italian nationalism. Bismarck's position by 1866 was, therefore, unassailable, for whatever Austria might attempt, he could apply an immediate antidote. As events turned out, he chose to bring on a war from which Prussia forged the North German Confederation.

France is often seen by historians as a target used by Bismarck against which to direct German nationalism as a means of inducing the southern German states to unite with the North. Again, however, Bismarck employed several lines of diplomacy between 1866 and 1870. On the one hand, he hoped that German unification could be completed without force or undue haste. In May 1868, he observed: 'Our whole sympathy belongs to our South German brother to whom we are ready at any time to stretch out a hand, but we neither wish nor ought to force him to grasp it.'[10] Every effort should be made to link the southern states to the North German Confederation by common economic institutions like a Customs Parliament and a Customs Federal Council. On the other hand, Bismarck knew that Bavaria and Württemberg had leanings towards France; consequently, he used several blunders, made by Napoleon III, to alienate the South Germans from their western neighbour. For example, he publicized Napoleon's demands for the Saarland, as well as for Bavarian and Hessian territory in the Rhine area, concessions which Bismarck had once been prepared to consider in exchange for French neutrality in the Austro-Prussian War of 1866. Similarly, he used the Luxemburg crisis of 1867 to discredit France, although not, at this stage, to provoke a war. It seems that, by 1869, Bismarck had come to regard war with France as a distinct possibility, but not one which ought to be forced. Hence he told Werthern: 'I think it probable that German unity will be forwarded through violent events. It is quite another matter, however, to bring about such a violent catastrophe and to bear responsibility for the choice of time for it . . . Such arbitrary interventions in the development of history . . . have always had as their consequence only the striking down of unripe fruit.'[11] Only a year after this pronouncement, however, Bismarck's deliberate distortion of the message contained in the Ems Telegram goaded Napoleon's government into declaring war on Prussia. It seems that Bismarck had, by this time, come to the conclusion that war was unavoidable. The French government's demand for the withdrawal of Prince Leopold's candidature to the Spanish throne was so aggressively worded that compliance would have brought diplomatic humiliation to the Hohenzollern family as a whole. Besides, Bismarck realized, Prussia had by now outstripped France militarily and the southern German states were ripe for gathering. Bismarck was evidently confident that he could win a 'prize worthy of the sacrifices which every war demands'.[12]

There can be no doubt that Bismarck's success against Austria and France was due partly to the international situation in Europe during the 1860s. None of the powers could seriously consider opposing him or trying to restrain him because they were at loggerheads with each other. Each government had its own problems and priorities; to give one example, Britain was on bad terms with the French and, in any case, possessed during the 1860s a small army and a depleted navy. More than at any other time in the nineteenth century there was a power vacuum in Europe, and Bismarck was able to pursue his own designs unimpeded by the gravitational pull of international diplomacy. There no longer existed even a formal or moral restraint on aggressive statesmanship, as the Concert of Europe, which had maintained a rough balance of power between 1815 and 1854, had ceased to exist, and was not revived until the 1870s.

11

The Reforms of Alexander II

There can be no doubt about the importance of the period 1855–81 in modern Russian history. The 'Tsar Liberator' presided over an 'era of great reforms' which finally dragged Russia into the nineteenth century and provided the background to further changes under Nicholas II (1894–1917). Indeed, the scope of Alexander II's achievement has been compared by some historians with that of Peter the Great or Lenin.

At the same time, his measures were not intended primarily to innovate, but rather to inject new life into a flagging system. Hence there must be at least some reservations about their real effectiveness. This chapter will, on the one hand, point out the extent of change while, on the other, show the continuity between Alexander's ideas and methods and those of his predecessor, Nicholas I. It will also show the limited impact of some of the reforming edicts. The final section will deal with another, but related, duality: is it possible to divide the reign chronologically into two distinct periods, one dominated by reforming zeal, the other stagnating under dreary reaction?

*

Alexander was not by nature, or upbringing, a radical. He had a combination of progressive and traditional views, the result partly of the mixed education which he received from a liberal tutor, Zhukovsky, and a stern father. Although tolerant and always well-intentioned, he imbibed at an early age the autocrat's inherent

The Reforms of Alexander II

pessimism about humanity, once admitting to having 'a very low opinion of the human race in general and in particular'. Inevitably, therefore, he had a limited view of the potential for progressive change. According to D. Field, 'it is hard to find in Alexander the reformer's breadth of vision and harder still to find the strength of will'. Furthermore, 'his autocratic will did not manifest itself in bold strokes, but in passive tenacity'.[1]

When dealing with nineteenth-century Russia, it is worth bearing in mind that the term 'reform' can be given two meanings. First, it can be understood as action against the whole system of autocracy and a modification of the basis of Russia's political institutions; this was certainly the hope of the liberal constitutionalists on the accession of a new and less repressive Tsar in 1855. But clearly Alexander had no intention, at any stage in his reign, of breaking with past political practice. Nicholas I is usually seen as the embodiment of tsarist despotism, yet it was Alexander II who insisted that 'all legislation takes its authority from the unified autocracy'.[2] There was also continuity in their attitudes to parliamentary government and in their desire to uphold the social hierarchy; Nicholas, for example, had affirmed that 'the landowner is the most reliable bulwark of the sovereign',[3] while Alexander similarly regarded the nobility as 'the mainstay of the throne'.[4] The non-Russian fringes of the Empire were also unlikely to experience any radical concessions. To give Poland autonomy and a liberal constitution would only incite demands for similar privileges elsewhere and, in any case, Alexander saw no need to change Nicholas I's policy. When he visited Warsaw in 1856 he told the disappointed Poles: 'I will not change anything; what was done by my father was done well.'[5] He added, in what could be taken as an expression of intent for the whole of Russia: 'My reign will be a continuation of his.'

A second approach to 'reform', however, puts a much more favourable construction on Alexander's achievements. Autocracy would not be undermined, but it would be made to work more efficiently by modernizing and rationalizing the range of social and administrative institutions over which it presided. It was obvious that, by 1855, Russia was in desperate need of overhaul. Alexander had come to the throne at a time when Russia was in grave internal disarray; Nicholas had admitted that 'I am handing you command of the country in a very poor state'.[6] Defeat in the Crimean War showed the structural weakness of the army, the inefficiency of the financial administration and, above all, the dangerously archaic features of serfdom. Alexander was therefore impelled to take action, although what he had in mind was not a break with the past but controlled surgery to save the whole hierarchical body. There is, perhaps, too great a tendency to see Alexander as a tragic, potentially heroic figure struggling to break away from the grip of the tyrannical influence of Nicholas I. Although clearly the more progressive of the two, Alexander had no desire to revolutionize his inheritance. In fact, at times he even made use of the groundwork provided by various projects of reform initiated, but not completed, by Nicholas I.

The first and most important of Alexander's measures, and the one which earned him his unofficial title 'Tsar Liberator', was the emancipation of the serfs, carried against a protesting nobility by the 1861 Edict. From one viewpoint this can be seen as a monumental achievement. (M. S. Anderson states that 'the grant of individual freedom and a minimum of civil rights to twenty million people previously in legal bondage was the greatest single liberating measure in the whole modern history of Europe'.[7]) Peasants could now regulate their own private lives, own property, bring actions through courts and engage in trade. The 1861 Edict accomplished for Russia what had been done in France in 1789, in Prussia in 1807 and in Austria in the 1780s and again in 1849. Its lateral impact was also considerable, for the end of seigneurial jurisdiction necessitated reforms in the entire system of justice, local government and military service. The emancipation of the serfs was therefore the force behind a series of reforms which followed between 1864 and 1881.

From another viewpoint, however, the Edict of Emancipation can be seen as a major reform carried out in a traditional, even cautious, way. Alexander's own intention was to introduce a controlled measure in order to forestall the possibility of more sweeping changes extracted by violence. Hence he told the nobility in 1856: 'It is better to abolish serfdom from above than to wait until the serfs begin to liberate themselves from below'.[8] Moreover, the whole project of emancipation had deep roots within the previous reign. Nicholas I had also disliked serfdom, considering it 'the indubitable evil of Russian life'. He had established a secret committee, consisting of leading reformers like Speransky and Kiselev, to examine the feasibility of gradual liberation. When this committee reported, Nicholas went ahead with the freeing of the state

The Reforms of Alexander II

peasantry (about one half of the total) and, in 1835, added a Fifth Section to the State Chancellery to implement future changes. He placed this under the authority of Kiselev and allocated to it about 1.2 million roubles, the largest sum received by any department except war. From this time onwards, however, obstacles to complete emancipation became increasingly serious so that, in 1843, Nicholas felt obliged to reassure the nobility that no further changes were being contemplated. Alexander derived considerable experience from his service on the committee system and also made extensive use of the surveys which had been carried out on Nicholas's orders. In a sense, therefore, the 1861 Edict was the culmination of a long but intermittent campaign.

The aftermath also illustrates the cautious nature of emancipation. The details of the terms were drafted by the bureaucracy and the main aims were, as always, to uphold the social and economic status of the nobility and to prevent the emergence of a mobile and individualistic peasantry. Hence emancipation was hedged with restrictions and qualifications like redemption payments, which many of the ex-serfs found crippling and far in excess of the value of the small plots which they worked. In addition, the government vested responsibility for peasant affairs in a traditional commune system which, in most areas, organized the payment of taxes and allocated land on the complex principle of repartitional tenure rather than on the more straightforward hereditary basis. The overall result was a peasantry which was still bound, if not by the constraints of serfdom, at least by a system which would not allow the development of simple free enterprise in the rural areas.

What of the changes which followed in the wake of emancipation? The legal system needed a complete overhaul now that the central government could no longer delegate judicial responsibility to the nobility as part of their feudal power. The reforms of 1864 were far-reaching: they introduced key concepts of western jurisprudence like equality before the law, trial by jury and the separation of criminal and civil cases. They also reduced the appalling level of bribery which had affected the courts in the previous reign and did much to modify some of the more savage forms of corporal punishment. Again, however, there were signs of continuity as well as change. Nicholas I, although hardly renowned for his knowledge of judicial procedure, had shown some concern about the extent of corruption and therefore appointed a committee under Bludov, which struggled in vain to reorganize the courts. Alexander's reform may have transcended the narrower vision of earlier administrators and jurists like Bludov and Speransky but it cannot be seen as an entirely new departure. When it came to implementing the change the forces of tradition once again became apparent. The older ecclesiastical and township courts continued to deal with a variety of cases, while the military courts were given considerable powers to deal with cases involving threats to 'public safety'. The 1864 Statute also ensured that the government departments retained the means of initiating proceedings outside the normal court system.

Changes in the structure of local government were also a priority. The emancipation of the serfs broke the hold of the aristocracy on administration and policing and necessitated the emergence of new institutions. The formation of the *zemstvos* in 1864 has been seen as the first step in the evolution of representative institutions in nineteenth-century Russia. This was followed by the Statute of 1870, notable for the establishment of the *dumas*, the urban counterpart of the *zemstvos*. Chapter 18 explains the significance of the latter institution in later constitutional developments, and it is clear that Alexander's reign was an important formative period. Nevertheless, it should also be said that the future uses of the *dumas* and *zemstvos* were not anticipated by Alexander, who tried, as far as possible, to circumscribe their powers and keep them under the supervision of the central government departments. He left them in control of uncontroversial functions, such as the provision of primary education and the improvement of medical facilities, which they discharged with unprecedented zeal and efficiency.

There were two areas in which reforms were less inhibited by tradition, mainly because there was no point at which these reforms could become a threat to autocracy. The first concerned the army. As Minister of War between 1861 and 1881, Milyutin applied the lessons of the Crimean War and also of the Edict of Emancipation; the former showed the need for a chief of general staff and an effective system of regional commands, while the latter forced a complete review of the haphazard and appallingly harsh method of recruitment. Milyutin's reforms paid off more quickly and obviously than any other, with Russia's spectacular victory over the Turks in 1877. Meanwhile, Reutern had come to grips with some of the financial problems which had afflicted Nicholas I and had dragged Russia down during the Crimean War. He ended the wasteful

The Reforms of Alexander II

administration of revenue by separate government departments, introducing, instead, the principle of overall control by the treasury. He also reduced incompetence and corruption by more systematic auditing and a regular budget. The economy as a whole was given a much-needed boost by the import of capital from Western Europe. The main beneficiary was railway construction, and the overall mileage was increased from 660 at the beginning of the reign to 14,000 by the end. But some financial deficiencies, inherited from Nicholas I, were not remedied until much later in the century. Perhaps the most important was the continuing problem of the currency, which had collapsed during the Crimean War and did not recover fully until Witte put Russia on the gold standard in 1896.

*

There has always been a school of thought which has divided the reign of Alexander II into two distinct phases, the first dominated by reform, the second by reaction. The transition from one to the other, it is argued, occurred during the 1860s, with the actual turning point located at 1866, the year in which the ex-student, Karakozov, tried to assassinate the Tsar. It can certainly be shown that attitudes stiffened in response to the Polish Revolt and also to the growing unrest throughout Russia during the early 1860s and the 1870s. Alexander II and his ministers were affected psychologically by the emergence of radicalism, whether in the form of the *raznochintsi*, led by journalists like Chernyshevski, or the violent revolutionary societies of the 1870s, like *Narodnaia Volia* (People's Will). Hence, from the mid-1860s some progressive ministers were being replaced by arch-conservatives. Golovnin, for example, lost the Ministry of Education to Count Dmitri Tolstoy, who cancelled many of the earlier reforms, made sweeping changes in the curriculum of secondary schools, interfered directly with the appointment of university staff, and restored censorship on books, newspapers and pamphlets. Some ministers, who had once been liberal, changed with the times and moved conspicuously to the Right; thus Katkov, who had supported the emancipation of the serfs and the legal and local government reforms, became an important spokesman for reaction. Underpinning the whole edifice was Shuvalov who, from the time he became head of the Imperial Chancellery's notorious Third Section in 1866, did whatever he could to secure the appointment to the bureaucracy of anti-progressives. D. A. Milyutin complained in 1873 that there was a 'devastating and disgusting contrast with the atmosphere in which I entered the government thirteen years ago'.[9]

On the other hand, such changes in attitudes and personnel did not necessarily mean that the whole base of the regime shifted from enlightened reform to unyielding reaction. There are too many threads running through the reign as a whole to allow for such an unqualified break. There is evidence, for example, of the enormous influence of conservative bureaucrats in boiling down the proposals for emancipation before 1861, resulting in widespread discontent with the actual conditions of freedom. There was also a lack of effective co-ordination between the various sections of the unreformed central government, especially between the Departments, Chancellery and Council of State; this tended, from the beginning of the reign, to impede the full implementation of the edicts. The counterpart to reaction in the so-called era of reforms was reform in the phase of reaction. Obvious examples were the Municipal Statute of 1870 and Alexander's decision in 1881 to accept Melikov's plan for a limited consultative assembly of elected representatives of public opinion. The latter, in fact, was cancelled only because of Alexander II's assassination and the imposition of a far more reactionary regime by Alexander III.

A. J. Rieber has emphasized another type of continuity between the beginning and end of the reign. Alexander II's main concerns, the argument runs, were always military and fiscal; these provided the original impetus behind emancipation and continued to dominate all aspects of domestic policy throughout the period. Serfdom, Alexander realized, had 'spawned an outmoded army' and 'crippled the treasury'.[2] Emancipation was therefore a prelude to a more efficient army and a more modern fiscal system, the achievement of which were always given priority throughout the 1860s and 1870s. This argument, while drawing attention away from the value of some of the legal and social changes, does provide the period with a degree of stability and consistency. In any case, like his two immediate predecessors, Alexander II realized that effective autocracy must depend ultimately on sound financial management and military strength. This was a traditional Romanov approach and had as much to do with Alexander's reforms as any enlightened theories.

12

The Collapse of the Second French Empire

On 8 May 1870, the Empereror Napoleon III sought the approval of the French people for recently instituted liberal changes within the Second Empire. The result of the plebiscite was a massive vote of confidence: by 7,358,000 votes to 1,571,000. This was reminiscent of the plebiscite of 1852 which had produced a vote of 7,824,000 to 253,000 in favour of the proclamation of the Empire and the end of the Second Republic.

Only four months later, in one of the most dramatic and unexpected political changes of the entire period, the régime collapsed. France turned away from Bonapartism and drifted into the Third Republic.

The two factors primarily responsible for this reversal were the shock military defeat by Prussia, and the subsequent intervention of the city of Paris to oust a system with which, regardless of the loyalties of the rest of France, it had never really identified. The second development could not have occurred without the first; the first led to the second by exposing weaknesses in the Empire which only its most ardent opponents had previously suspected.

*

French military defeat came in a war which need never have been fought, and which was the climax of a sequence of diplomatic blunders over the issue of the Spanish Candidature.

When Prince Leopold of Hohenzollern Sigmaringen (a distant relative of the King of Prussia) announced his candidature to the

Aspects of European History 1789–1980

Spanish throne there were misgivings in many European courts. The spectre of a close dynastic connection between Spain and Prussia haunted Britain and Austria-Hungary as well as France. But French diplomacy failed to mobilize this concern and revealed instead the most glaring inconsistency. Indeed, two policies competed for ascendancy in Paris. Gramont and the Empress Eugénie advocated tough measures and immediate pressure, while Ollivier and the Emperor preferred conciliation and caution. What actually happened was a disastrous combination of both courses. The initial application of pressure was followed by conciliation, the benefits of which were destroyed by revived aggression.

This is apparent in the complex sequence of events of July 1870. When the candidature first became public knowledge the French government's immediate reaction was to despatch Count Benedetti to demand of the King of Prussia a guarantee of Leopold's withdrawal. In fact, a more appropriate course would have been to prevail upon the Spanish government to withdraw the offer of the throne, thus omitting Prussia altogether from the negotiations. Only when the King of Prussia had been thoroughly antagonized did Napoleon III force upon his ministers a more moderate approach. In a classic example of the use of roundabout and discreet diplomatic channels, the French Rothschilds were asked to establish secret contacts with Gladstone via the London Rothschilds. The British Prime Minister, in turn, communicated with Leopold II of the Belgians, brother-in-law of Leopold of Hohenzollern Sigmaringen. Meanwhile, Queen Victoria had also been approached to exert some of her influence. The result was highly satisfactory: a quiet withdrawal of Leopold's candidature, with the assent of Prussia. This considerable achievement was, however, destroyed and the crisis was reactivated when Benedetti was instructed to gain from Prussia an assurance that the claim would never be revived. The extent of Napoleon's personal involvement in this has never been precisely established, but it seems that he was pressurized by the French 'hawks'. Certainly the consensus of the *corps legislatif*, the Senate and the government ministers was that Prussia must be seen openly to have capitulated. Prussia's refusal to give this guarantee brought about a state of war-fever in France which was cleverly manipulated by Chancellor Bismarck in the way discussed in Chapter 10.

The advocates of war were noisy and numerous. In the *corps legislatif* Guyot Montpayroux thundered: 'Prussia has forgotten the

The Collapse of the Second French Empire

France of Jena and we must remind her!'[1] For the capitulation of the moderates to this type of reaction two reasons can be given. First, the Emperor was afflicted by a painful bladder condition which sapped his strength and lowered his resistance. Second, both the Emperor and Ollivier claimed to be sensitive to public opinion. Ollivier had stated in 1863 that war was legitimate only 'when it is desired by the whole nation';[2] in July 1870, the nation seemed to be insisting on one. The result was a war without a real cause and at the wrong time. Before the French declaration of war on 19 July, Thiers issued a note of dissent: 'Do you want all Europe to say that although the substance of the quarrel was settled, you have decided to pour out torrents of blood over a mere matter of form?'[1]

Presumably, France was sufficiently prepared to ensure a rapid victory? The majority of the *corps legislatif* seemed to think so, and the Minister of War, Laboeuf, promised that the army was at a peak of efficiency. The Emperor, however, was somewhat less confident. Speaking to the Senate, he warned: 'Gentlemen, we are entering upon a long and arduous war.'[3] There were good reasons for his reservations.

It is true that France did not lack experience of warfare during the Second Empire. She had, after all, been involved in the Crimean War (1854–6) and the War for Italian Unification (1859), and had sent overseas expeditions to China, Indochina and Mexico. Indeed, according to Marx, France was guided less by *liberté, égalité, fraternité* than by 'Cavalry, Infantry, Artillery'. In one sense, however, all this experience was inappropriate, since it was based upon far-off ventures rather than on the defence of the homeland. Napoleon I's victories had followed a period of intense national effort during the 1790s, whereas the vulnerability of France in the 1860s to war on her own frontiers was apparent in several ways.

First, there were serious deficiencies in the French system of conscription. The nation which had introduced the *levée en masse* in the 1790s had since lost the initiative to Prussia. Recruitment to the French army was always long-term and based upon a system of ballot. The result was a force devoid of any real contact with the people at large. Indeed, General Trochu openly stated that 'the ideal constitution is that which creates an army whose instincts, beliefs and habits make up a corporation distinct from the rest of the population'.[4] Prussia, by contrast, had long since adopted a system of short-term service and, by applying this universally rather than selectively, had built up a massive reserve power. Napoleon III was certainly aware of the discrepancy in the mobilizing capacity of the two countries and endeavoured, at the Compiegne Conference of November 1866, to gain support for short-term conscription. There was, however, strong resistance in the *corps legislatif*, and it gradually became clear that Napoleon's efforts to liberalize the Empire by strengthening its legislature had only increased the latter's capacity to obstruct military reforms; the middle class, in particular, wanted *La Gloire* but their parliamentary representatives would not consider genuine conscription. The eventual compromise of 1868, and the introduction of the part-time *garde mobile*, could not prevent the French armies from being completely outnumbered in 1870.

Equally serious was the cumbersome method of moving troops to the Front on mobilization. Prussia had adapted her railway network far more effectively to military demands, which meant that the advance of the Prussian armies encountered fewer delays. This was particularly unfortunate as French success would depend on a rapid invasion of the southern German states, to detach them from any alliance with Prussia. During the Franco-Prussian War, von Moltke and Bismarck were astonished at the delay and confusion of the French concentrations (even though French mobilization in 1870 was quicker than it had been in 1854 or 1859). Units from all parts of France reached the Front in disarray, imperfectly merged into their higher formations. The Prussians, who had expected to fight a war of defence, were able to seize the initiative and inflict severe defeats on the French in the Battles of Wissembourg, Fröschwiller and Forbach (August 1870).

The leadership of the French armies was also suspect. There was no shortage of famous names – Bazaine, Canrobert, Macmahon, Trochu. But these commanders formed an élite which resisted change and placed its trust in traditional methods. Napoleon III realized the need for greater co-ordination at the centre but, unlike Wilhelm I, his Prussian counterpart, he failed to form a war cabinet. Matters were made worse by unfortunate policy decisions. On the outbreak of war, for example, the assumption of overall command by Napoleon III destroyed any chance of independent action by the three Rhine armies. Even after the Emperor had been elbowed out of the way by Bazaine, defective decisions were made. The armies were hamstrung by the failure of the Paris government to allow any

The Collapse of the Second French Empire

large-scale adoption of defensive strategy. In August Macmahon's army was prevented from retreating from an insecure position at the Argonne; instead, it was ordered to join Bazaine, with the result that both were defeated at Beaumont. The ultimate catastrophe occurred when Paris urged Napoleon III to remain at the Front and not, as he intended, conduct an orderly withdrawal. Instead of regrouping for the possibility of a defensive victory, the remaining French forces were bottled up and forced to surrender on 2 September. There was to be no Valmy; only Sedan.

The outcome of the war might have been less catastrophic had France been assisted by one or more allies. The complete lack of diplomatic support in 1870 can be attributed to the widespread suspicion aroused by the Emperor's foreign policy. It is ironical that in the opening years of his reign he had been highly successful in gaining the recognition – even support – of other powers. He had always maintained high hopes of serving French territorial interests while, at the same time, harnessing the latent power of nationalism in the belief, expounded by Napoleon I, that: 'The first ruler who appeals to the peoples of Europe will be able to accomplish anything he wishes.'[5] His ultimate ambition was clearly to reverse the 1815 Vienna Settlement and to re-establish the hegemony of France in Europe.

Unfortunately, the type of revisionism pursued by Napoleon III eventually antagonized every state in Europe, effectively isolating France by 1870. Russia made an agreement with France in 1858, but remained suspicious of Napoleon's support for incipient nationalism. When the Emperor expressed sympathy with the Polish Revolt in 1863, Alexander II broke off diplomatic contacts with France and considered closer co-operation with Prussia instead. A more promising area of permanent friendship was Italy; after all, Napoleon III had committed French troops and resources to the cause of Italian Unification in 1859. The apparent absence of Italian gratitude, one of the great disappointments of Napoleon's reign, was attributable to the suspicion of Cavour and his successors that France had never intended to allow the establishment in the Italian peninsula of anything more than a series of satellite states. Certainly the Italian government never forgot the premature withdrawal of France from the war by the Armistice of Villafranca, while Garibaldi regarded the French garrison supporting Papal power in Rome as a direct betrayal of Italian nationalism, particularly since

Aspects of European History 1789–1980

French troops fired upon two Italian expeditions in the 1860s. Even the moderate Victor Emmanuel turned against France after Napoleon's annexation of Nice and Savoy in 1860 and, like Russia, cultivated closer relations with Prussia. The result was a military alliance between Italy and Prussia, drawn up in 1866.

What of the British attitude to Napoleon III's diplomacy? At first London's reaction was favourable; Palmerston had been so eager to recognize the new régime that he had landed himself in trouble with the Prime Minister and the Queen, although this had been on the question of procedure rather than principle. Within three years, France and Britain were formal allies in the Crimean War and the British government seemed quite content to allow Napoleon III to preside over the Paris Peace Conference of 1856. But five years more brought open British hostility, particularly to Napoleon's scarcely concealed dynastic designs in Italy and hopes of territorial acquisitions in Germany. Palmerston wrote to Russell in 1861: 'The whole drift of our policy is to prevent France from realizing her vast schemes of expansion in a great number of quarters.'[6] The lowest point in Anglo-French relations was reached in 1870. When Bismarck disclosed to the British government French schemes to partition Belgium, Gladstone declared that he was 'shocked and horrified'. British public opinion had been reinfected with its customary francophobia, and even literary circles joined in the castigation of Napoleon. Carlyle, for example, contrasted 'noble, patient, deep, pious and solid Germany' with 'vapouring, vainglorious, gesticulating, quarrelsome, restless and over-sensitive France'.

Of all the European states, Austria had the most cause for resentment against Napoleon III. After all, France had assisted the Italians in ejecting Austrian rule from Lombardy in 1859. Secondly, Napoleon had attempted to negotiate an agreement with Russia in 1858 which would have given autonomy to part of the Austrian Empire. Thirdly, the Austrian royal family had lost one of its members, Maximilian, in Napoleon's catastrophic Mexican venture (1863). Yet Austria also had the best reason for supporting France in 1870. Her own recent defeat by Prussia in the Seven Weeks' War (1866) had resulted in her exclusion from Germany and she would clearly welcome an opportunity to revive her previous connection with the southern German states. French diplomats were therefore active in Vienna in 1870, but they failed to produce any specific commitment. For one thing, Austria was militarily exhausted; for another, she had recently experienced serious constitutional and racial problems which even the 1867 *Ausgleich* had not entirely solved. Napoleon had to be satisfied with a vague undertaking that Austria would make common cause with France once the latter had actually invaded southern Germany. After being acquainted with the French disasters of August 1870, the Emperor Franz Joseph opted for 'friendly neutrality'. He no longer had any choice.

French isolation was symptomatic of the collapse of the basic structure of Napoleon's foreign policy. He had sought and, for a while achieved, dominance by fostering nationalism and reviving the Vienna settlement. But he had assumed that this nationalism would be the product of revolutions against authoritarian régimes and that it would seek ideological inspiration from the French Revolution. In fact, the nationalism which emerged in Germany in the 1860s was carefully pruned by Bismarck of any revolutionary connotations and rendered wholly conservative. France, therefore, was to be the victim of Bismarck's *Realpolitik*, not the benevolent guide and mentor envisaged by Napoleon III. Bismarck systematically exploited Napoleon's rash claims to the left bank of the Rhine, Luxembourg and Belgium, thereby casting France in the role of a predator. This destroyed the self-assurance which Napoleon had once possessed so that, according to von der Goltz, 'the Emperor seemed to have lost his compass'.[7] Thus, to return to the starting point of this section, the outbreak of war in 1870 was, for France, futile and unnecessary. It benefited only Prussia; by using it as a means of uniting Germany Bismarck was applying the dictum of Frederick the Great that 'diplomacy without war is like music without instruments'.

*

Military defeat did not by itself cause the collapse of the Second Empire. When Napoleon III went into captivity after the Battle of Sedan France could have been governed by a temporary regency of the type which had operated during the periods of insanity experienced by George III of England, or Frederick William IV of Prussia. Such an expedient, however, was made impossible by the intervention of Paris in the sequence of events, with the result that a

republic was proclaimed on 4 September. It is difficult to over-
estimate the hold which Paris had, at certain times, over the rest of
the country. Napoleon III believed that for half a century, 'France
has gone on only because of the administrative, judicial and
financial organization of the Consulate and [First] Empire'.[8] These,
of course, had been centred on Paris before 1815, and even the
Bourbon and Orléanist monarchies had not reversed the most complete form of centralization existing in any European state. Paris
had overthrown Charles X in 1830 and Louis Philippe in 1848. Could
Napoleon III escape the same fate?

He had certainly used the confused situation in Paris to climb to
power, first as President in 1848, then as President for ten years in
1851, and finally as Emperor in 1852. But, from the start, he had
tried to break the influence of Paris on the nation's destiny by
projecting himself as a national leader, appealing to all classes and
all areas. He hoped to break the vicious circle which Paris seemed to
keep in motion: according to Prévost-Paradol: 'France is republican
when she is under the Monarchy, and she becomes royalist again
when her Constitution is republican.'[7] The extent of his initial
support reflected the widespread disillusionment with the failures of
the Second Republic. The peasantry were reassured by his
guarantee of law and order; the bourgeoisie by his promise of
security for the unimpeded operation of market forces; and a large
part of the proletariat by his promise of social reform which was
motivated by his 'love of the suffering classes'.[9] Napoleon III stressed
the importance of balance between all sections of the population. At
the basic level France should not be 'incessantly troubled either by
demagogic ideas or by monarchist hallucinations'.[10] The underlying
ideology was radical but controlled: 'The Napoleonic idea springs
from the Revolution . . . it stands for the reconciliation of order,
liberty, the rights of the people and the principles of authority,
obeying neither the uncertain lead of a party nor the passions of the
crowd.'[11] Hence, the 1852 Constitution made the Head of State
'responsible to the nation', but gave him 'free and unfettered
authority'. The overwhelming majority of Frenchmen seemed to
approve.

But for how long? Election figures for the *corps legislatif* show a
significant change in voting habits as the reign progressed. The
proportion of government supporters to opposition deputies was as
follows:

The Collapse of the Second French Empire

4:1 in the 1852 election
4:1 in the 1857 election
5:2 in the 1863 election
4:3 in the 1869 election

Significantly, the opposition was concentrated in the twenty-two largest towns and cities. Paris elected no Bonapartist deputies after 1857; in fact, the last two elections gave, in Paris, crushing majorities to the republicans, against the national trend. The capital, which was the nerve centre of the imperial administration, therefore contained the most hostile part of the population. This was due partly to the rapid alienation of the urban proletariat by the régime's economic policies, and the deterioration of working conditions and wages in contrast to the growing prosperity of the bourgeoisie. The republicans attacked the Empire for creating a plutocracy; Duchêne, referring to the most powerful 200 families of the banking and merchant classes, complained that 'Antiquity does not contain any examples of an oligarchy so concentrated'.[12] Inflation affected the proletariat more than the middle classes. It has been estimated, for example, that the average wage in Paris rose by 30 per cent during the period of the Empire, while the cost of living increased by 45 per cent and rents by 100 per cent. It is hardly surprising, therefore, that Parisians should return to the anti-monarchist and pro-republican views which they had displayed before the appearance of Napoleon III. The process was accelerated by the propaganda which poured from papers like *La Lanterne* after the relaxation of the press laws in 1868.

Ironically, the opposition intensified as the régime became increasingly moderate. Napoleon III was unique among dictators in liberalizing his institutions and weakening the basis of his own authority. He had probably always intended to implement progressive policies once the opportunity arose; indeed, he considered that the main danger to his position lay in *resisting* change. 'March at the head of the ideas of your century and these ideas will follow and support you. March behind them and they will drag you after them. March against them and they will overthrow you.'[13] This view was also held by Ollivier, who was responsible for implementing the so-called Liberal Empire in 1870. He had argued as far back as 1861 that 'without liberty democracy is but despotism. Without democracy liberty is but privilege'.[14] Yet the concessions, designed to increase the influence of the *corps legislatif* and the Senate, failed to satisfy the republican opposition. In fact, Gambetta regarded the more moderate régime of 1870 merely as 'a bridge between the Republic of 1848 and the Republic of the future'. He added ominously: 'It is a bridge which we intend to cross.'[15]

If anything, Napoleon's reforms actually weakened the Second Empire. The *corps legislatif* and the Senate obstructed much of the Emperor's programme for domestic reform between 1868 and 1870, and resisted his proposals to bring the French army up to full strength. Furthermore, the growth of parliamentarianism undermined the hold of Bonapartism on France. Although Napoleon genuinely believed in democracy, he had always regarded himself as being above and outside the conflicts between the parliamentary groups. He therefore made no attempt to form a cohesive Bonapartist *party* which would pursue a consistent set of policies and become conversant with the intricacies of parliamentary strategy. Hence the Bonapartists were by far the most heterogeneous group within the *corps legislatif*, united only by their loyalty to Napoleon himself. Once the Emperor had been removed, most of them defected to the royalist camp where, at least, monarchist principles managed to survive without being personified.

It is hardly surprising, therefore, that the republicans were able to seize the initiative in 1870. Although they were in a minority in France as a whole, they dominated Paris and could rely upon a tight organization which thrived on opposition. In normal times Napoleon III could fend off attacks on his régime; he could prove that he had the confidence of the population as a whole by means of plebiscites which effectively masked the regional variations of support shown in general election figures. But the Franco-Prussian War brought about the collapse of normal government, and the Bonapartists were insufficiently organized to prevent the republicans from gaining control.

13

Bismarck and the German Political Parties 1871–90

The Constitution of the Second Reich (1871) gave Germany universal suffrage and an elected *Reichstag*, or lower chamber. Since the new state was a conglomeration of several different interests – industrial and agrarian, Protestant and Catholic – it was to be expected that such a major advance would favour the growth of political parties. From the beginning of his Chancellorship, however, Bismarck made every effort to prevent the evolution of parliamentary sovereignty on the British model, with account-ability of the executive to the legislature. Above all, he disliked the prospect of party politics, and had no intention of attaching himself permanently to any single faction. On the contrary, he avoided any long-term commitments so that he could preserve maximum freedom to manoeuvre between the various party leaders. He once described his objective as 'an understanding with the majority of the deputies that will not at the same time prejudice the future authority and governmental powers of the Crown or endanger the proficiency of the army'.[1]

This chapter will analyse Bismarck's relations with the four major groupings within the *Reichstag*: conservatives, liberals, centrists and socialists. In each case it will summarize the respective attitudes of the party leaders and the Chancellor, and will assess the degree of, and reasons for, the latter's success or failure in achieving his objectives.

*

Being a *Junker* himself, Bismarck had a close attachment to the Prussian Conservatives during the 1860s; with their assistance he purged the Prussian ministry of liberalism and increased the size of the German army in preparation for German unification. There would, therefore, appear to have been a natural basis for close and permanent co-operation.

But the German Chancellor and the Conservatives had, after 1871, what can best be described as a love-hate relationship. Only the Free Conservatives, an offshoot from the main party, guaranteed him permanent support. The Conservatives themselves initially feared for the future of Prussia now that German unification had been achieved. Bismarck had always maintained that unification meant that Germany would be absorbed into Prussia: 'Prussians we are, and Prussians we shall remain.' The Conservatives, on the other hand, considered that Prussia was being poured into Germany, suffering dilution in the process. They were particularly concerned about two of Bismarck's policies in the 1870s. The first was his flirtation with the National Liberals to complete the unification of Germany's legal institutions and currency; this, it was felt, would undermine Prussian predominance by removing the possibility of Prussian separatism. The second was Bismarck's struggle with the Centre Party. The *Kulturkampf* was roundly attacked by the Conservatives, since the state's anti-clerical measures could also recoil on Protestant interests, which conservatives of all types claimed to uphold. Meanwhile, a Conservative publication, *Kreuz-Zeitung*, was criticizing Bismarck as an opportunist upstart, a view held by many right-wing Prussians who felt that Bismarck had abandoned their interests altogether.

By 1878, however, there were signs of reconciliation. Bismarck turned his back on the liberals, agreeing with the Kaiser that 'the time has come to rule on more conservative lines'.[2] He now pursued a combination of economic, social and political objectives which largely succeeded in reassuring the Right. His economic policy was shaped by protective tariffs introduced in 1879. This move was particularly popular with the *Junkers* of East Prussia, who faced heavy competition from large American and Russian grain imports. Indeed, it would be no exaggeration to say that the *Junkers* were saved by protection. The swing away from free trade also benefited the industrialists and hence pleased the Free Conservatives. Aristocrats of both kinds – industrial and agrarian – were confirmed

Bismarck and the German Political Parties

in their control over German society and came together in a formidable alliance between 'steel and rye'. Meanwhile, Bismarck's efforts to eliminate the threat of socialism had earned him much sympathy from the Conservatives and confirmed that he and they still had common ideological objectives. This co-operation was strengthened by political changes made by Bismarck during the 1880s. For example, he recast several government institutions to re-establish the influence of Prussia and, assisted by the Prussian Minister of the Interior, von Puttkamer, he ejected the remaining liberals from the civil service. The vacancies created were naturally filled by right-wingers.

How complete was this reconciliation? The Conservatives and Free Conservatives remained dependable supporters of the Chancellor's policies during the crucial period 1879–89 and, in particular, provided the basis of the electoral alliance known as the *Kartell*. Without them, it is difficult to see how Bismarck could have held his own in the *Reichstag*. On the other hand, the Conservatives never possessed the same degree of influence in the *Reichstag* as in the Prussian Diet; consequently, Bismarck still had to negotiate with parties, like the National Liberals, with which he had less sympathy. Nor were *all* the Conservatives won over. The more traditional elements continued to distrust Bismarck, and they sided with the Kaiser against him in 1890, while Conservatives of all descriptions found it easier to get along with Bismarck's successors.

＊

Bismarck used, or abused, the German liberals more completely than any other part of the political spectrum.

He had disliked liberalism ever since his own conversion to conservatism after the failure of the Frankfurt Parliament (1848–9). In 1862 he had clashed with Prussian liberals over military expenditure and had made his position clear in his famous 'blood and iron' speech: 'Germany does not look to Prussia for her liberalism but for her strength.' He had subsequently eradicated the liberals from the state executive, and had conducted a fierce anti-liberal propaganda campaign. Elements of this conflict continued after the creation of the Reich in 1871. Both the National Liberals and the Progressives emphasized the importance of the legislature, and leaders like Bennigsen and Lasker pressed hard to make the

Chancellor's cabinet accountable to the *Reichstag*. Another cardinal point in the liberal programme was the control by the legislature of all funds supplied to the executive; this explains the opposition of the majority of the liberal deputies to the Tariff Bill of 1879, which was intended, among other things, to make the government more self-sufficient. The Progressives were also opposed to protection because they upheld *laissez-faire* as another article of faith. Finally, all liberals felt uneasy about Bismarck's heavy-handed measures to deal with the socialist threat. Most National Liberals and all Progressives resisted the first two drafts of the Chancellor's anti-socialist bill (1876 and 1878) on the grounds that they were a crude and discriminatory attack on basic social and constitutional freedoms and rights.

Despite this apparently unbridgeable gap, the period 1871–8 saw a strange co-operation between Bismarck and the larger of the two parties, the National Liberals. The main reason was that the National Liberals' greatest single aim was to complete German unification; since they had already compromised some of their principles by accepting the consequences of a 'blood and iron' policy, they had little to lose by using constitutional means to add the finishing touches to the new *Reich*. Hence they helped the head of the Chancellor's office, von Delbrück, put Germany on the gold standard, introduce a common currency and a code for commerce and industry, and establish the *Reichsbank*. The National Liberals, on their own initiative but with Bismarck's approval, introduced the legislation necessary to give the *Reich* a common civil and criminal law code. They were also prepared to support the central government in any struggle against what appeared to be regional or separatist interests. Hence they co-operated to provide the legislation necessary for the *Kulturkampf* although, it is true, there was a minority of dissident liberals led by Lasker and Bamberger. On the whole, Bismarck gained a great deal from this backing, although it is clear that he never had any intention of becoming permanently committed to liberalism; he valued his freedom of executive action too highly to make himself more accountable to the *Reichstag*.

The liberals, by contrast, suffered severely from their association with Bismarck. 1878 and 1879 proved to be the beginning of a long decline. A large section of the National Liberal Party compromised its belief in constitutional guarantees of individual liberty by supporting Bismarck's third anti-socialist bill in 1878, while 1879

Bismarck and the German Political Parties

saw a deep internal rift over the issue of tariff reform. The Centre Party leader, Windthorst, declared contemptuously that the liberal era had gone bankrupt. This was partly true. The National Liberals had over-zealously supported the establishment, with the result that much of their previous radicalism had disappeared. The 1880s brought further division to the liberal ranks. On the one hand, the National Liberals held on to their upper-middle-class support. Their intellectuals, like Treitschke, transformed the universities into pillars of orthodoxy, while their wealthy voters accepted without demur the closer connections with the Conservatives. The overall result was the growth of a curious and distinctively German phenomenon – right-wing liberalism. On the other hand, the Progressives, and the more radical elements of the National Liberals, reacted sharply against this trend and united, in 1884, to form the *Freisinnige* Party, led efficiently by Richter and dependent for its support on small merchants, minor officials and the more outspoken intellectuals. For a while this put up a better electoral performance than did the National Liberals, winning sixty-seven seats in the 1884 elections to the latter's fifty-one. It also had the patronage of the Crown Prince, the future Frederick III. But its decline from 1887 was rapid, and radicalism took a poor second place to 'conservatized' liberalism.

Bismarck had a great deal to do with this trend. Between 1887 and 1889 he appeared to have an uncanny ability to control the course of events. He had already reduced the National Liberals to manageable numbers and had integrated them electorally with the Conservatives by means of the *Kartell*, which won a large pro-government majority in the 1887 *Reichstag*. He was deeply concerned about the success of the *Freisinnige* Party and feared for his own office once the progressive Crown Prince came to power. His political manoeuvres, however, put paid to both threats. He provoked, in 1887, a conflict with the *Reichstag* over another army bill; this was really an excuse to have the *Reichstag* dissolved and new deputies elected. Because of the complex electoral manipulations of the *Kartell*. the *Freisinnige* lost over half their seats and Bismarck was able to confront the liberal heir to the throne with a predominantly right-wing *Reichstag*. His triumph was completed in 1888 with the death of Frederick III after only four months on the throne. The radical threat had now been eliminated. But Bismarck's success can be seen only in personal terms. The damage inflicted on

115

Germany by the splintering of a large and stable liberal party was incalculable.

*

In his relations with the Catholic Centre Party, Bismarck provoked an unnecessary conflict and eventually had to reverse his policy.

The Centre Party, formed in 1870, was highly critical of the Second Reich and firmly opposed the *Kleindeutsch* (see Chapter 10) pattern of unification because this favoured Protestant Prussia at the expense of the Catholic areas. In the former German Confederation, 52 per cent of the total population had been Catholic, and 48 per cent Protestant. In the Second Reich, as a result of the exclusion of Austria, the corresponding ratio was 37 per cent to 63 per cent. The Centre Party, therefore, found itself simultaneously pan-German, in the sense that it favoured close links with Austria, and particularist, as it defended the rights of individual Catholic states, like Bavaria, against the encroachments of Protestant Prussia. Since it could hardly expect to get Austria included in a new *Grossdeutsch* constitution, it settled for a programme of federalism and decentralization – anything which would dilute Prussian power. The Party also tried to inject a Christian ethic into politics. Its leaders opposed Bismarck's *Realpolitik*, with which the National Liberals had compromised, and also rejected the harsh economic extremes of *laissez-faire*, demanding, instead, protective social and industrial legislation along lines suggested by Father Kolping and Bishop Ketteler. Finally, they were determined to protect the Catholic Church and to act as its political agent.

Bismarck reacted swiftly to what he saw as a Catholic threat. He felt that the Centre Party revived two historic dangers: Ultramontanism and Frondism. The former was the more dangerous since it coincided with the Bull of Papal Infallibility, by which Pius IX hoped to reactivate the spiritual and temporal influence of Rome. This could, Bismarck reasoned, make Catholicism an international power for the first time since the seventeenth century. Needless to say, France and Austria would be involved in this, and this was a potential danger to Germany since the Centre Party could well seek their co-operation in spreading Catholic influence internally. The Frondeur element was also alarming. The Centre Party, Bismarck maintained, would, in resisting the Prussian monarchy, promote disruptive separatism and endeavour to cause the collapse of the

Bismarck and the German Political Parties

Reich. Bismarck's answer was the *Kulturkampf,* intended as a series of surgical measures to weaken the capacity of both the Catholic Church of Germany, and the Centre Party to be receptive to foreign and internal disruptive political influences. Falk's May Laws (1873–4) weakened Church control over education by insisting on government inspection of schools, brought the appointment and training of priests within the competence of the state, and increased the degree of secularization for example, by legalizing civil marriage. Bismarck was careful to emphasize that he was not attacking religion as such. He said in the Upper House of the Prussian Diet, in March 1873: 'The question before us is, in my opinion, distorted, and the light in which we see it is a false one, if we regard it as a religious ecclesiastical question. It is essentially a political question . . . it is a matter of the conflict which is as old as the human race, between monarchy and priesthood.'[3] This line of reasoning was reinforced in 1874 by the historian von Sybel: 'We can see that if ever a state has rebelled against clerical pretensions from sheer necessity, from the duty of self preservation, it is our state.'[4]

The *Kulturkampf* turned into one of the major failures of Bismarck's career. By 1878 he was searching for a way of withdrawing honourably from the conflict and, in 1887, he ended the last vestiges of the struggle. What were the main reasons for this reversal?

The first was the amazing resilience shown by the Centre Party, largely because of the extent and depth of its support. Bismarck fought what he considered to be a national struggle against an enemy which drew its strength from two types of backing. On the one hand, its appeal was supranational; it claimed the allegiance of Catholics everywhere, whether they were nobles, small traders, artisans, peasants or workers. On the other hand, it would also use infranational forces like Polish separatism and the anti-German sentiment of Alsace-Lorraine. The Party was also given an effective strategy by Windthorst, who has been described as the most brilliant parliamentarian in German history. Thus it achieved more consistent results than any other party between 1871 and 1890. In the 1884, 1887 and 1890 elections it won ninety-nine, ninety-eight and 106 seats respectively; this pattern continued beyond Bismarck's resignation, the Centre winning ninety-six, 102, 100 and 105 seats in the elections of 1893, 1898, 1903 and 1907.

The second reason was that Bismarck had planned the

Kulturkampf without his usual thoroughness and attention to detail. He even clashed with Falk over the basic method. The latter preferred to use legislative measures, while Bismarck hoped that the task could be carried out with administrative instruments; this would enable the government to keep to a minimum the contacts with Prussian and German parliaments. But the manoeuvre was badly judged, since it brought much sympathy within the *Reichstag* for a party which appeared to be struggling against heavy-handed and unconstitutional interference from the executive. The scope of the *Kulturkampf* was also inadequately defined. Despite Bismarck's original intentions, the campaign against the Centre did take on the appearance of an attack on the Church, particularly when the May Laws regulated the employment of the clergy and decreed the expulsion of Jesuits. Inevitably, the Catholic Church attracted widespread support, which did much to heal the earlier rifts caused by the controversy over Papal Infallibility. For once, Bismarck had been unable to perpetuate and exploit the divisions within the enemy camp; instead, he had unintentionally effected a reconciliation, as Catholics now hastened to support the Papal encyclical of 1875, which declared the measures of the *Kulturkampf* invalid.

Finally, the Centre Party was fortunate in that Bismarck lost enthusiasm for the struggle. By 1878 he had come to realize that he had overestimated the 'Catholic threat'. The Centre Party, after all, could hardly be called radical, particularly when compared with the SPD. It also seemed much less likely that the Centre would act in association with France which, in any case, was now well on its way to becoming an anti-clerical régime. Furthermore, the Centre Party had two potential assets which could be integrated into Bismarck's policies elsewhere. Its friendship for Austria could be used to good effect in gaining support for Bismarck's proposed rapprochement with the Habsburgs (see Chapter 15). And the support of the Centre Party deputies would, in conjunction with that of the Conservatives, overcome the opposition to protective tariffs from the National Liberals, Progressives and SPD. Hence Bismarck managed to salvage something from the wreck of the *Kulturkampf*. The Centre Party voted for the tariff law, in exchange for government concessions to the Church, and also supported Bismarck's policy of state socialism in the 1880s. Nevertheless, the Centre leaders remained wary of Bismarck's attention, and refused to be drawn into the *Kartell* of 1887. Bismarck, in turn, retained a respect for the Centre which he

Bismarck and the German Political Parties

had never shown the liberals, and his last political act was to attempt in 1890 to persuade Windthorst to form a new pro-government combination in the *Reichstag* which would counter-balance the disillusioned National Liberals and Conservatives. But the Centre wisely refused to convert limited support over specific legislative measures into total subservience to a discredited Chancellor.

*

Bismarck's most consistent opponent throughout his administration was the SPD (*Sozialdemokratische Partei Deutschlands*). This was the only party which he sought to eradicate and with which he never considered the possibility of compromise.

The SPD was an amalgamation between Lassalle's General German Workers' Union and the League of Workers' Clubs led by Liebknecht and Bebel. The Gotha Programme of 1875 showed a combination of Lassallean and Marxist principles, all hostile to the new *Reich*. The existing form of universal suffrage was considered a mere sham, and there was bitter criticism of the aristocratic and bourgeois hold on the economy, since this caused deep social divisions and permanent misery for the proletariat. The solutions proposed by the Gotha Programme were radical, including a 'free state and socialist society', the 'elimination of all social and political inequality', factory restrictions on female and child labour, and 'state supervision of factory, workshop and domestic industry'. The overall strategy of the SPD was, at this stage, twofold: to promote immediate social and political reforms and, in the long term, to bring about a socialist state.

To Bismarck such objectives threatened the entire structure of the new *Reich*. The SPD would subvert the 1871 Constitution, which was based on carefully considered checks and balances, and would also destroy the competitive power of German industry by imposing labour regulations. Above all, it would threaten the national base by fostering an international socialist conspiracy; Bismarck never forgot the moral support given by German socialists to the Paris Commune, nor their opposition to Germany's annexation of Alsace-Lorraine in 1871. Thus the campaign against the Social Democrats assumed the proportions of a crusade. In his determination to crush them Bismarck tried everything, changing his strategy several times in the process. In defence of his domestic *Realpolitik* measures,

119

he once observed: 'In dealing with Social Democracy the state must act in self-defence, and in self-defence one cannot be finicky about the choice of means.'[5] His most consistent policy was repression, embodied in the anti-socialist law of October 1878. This authorized the use of emergency powers for up to a year at a time, prohibited socialist assemblies and fund collections, and censored or banned publications of all kinds. As a result, forty-five out of forty-seven papers were removed from circulation, trade unions were virtually eliminated, and many socialist leaders were arrested. Yet Bismarck also considered it necessary to pursue an additional expedient. He made a bid for the support of the proletariat by a policy of state socialism, in which the government sponsored legislation covering sickness insurance (1883), accident insurance (1884), and old age and disability insurance (1889). Then, in 1889, he returned to the task of repression and sought to renew the anti-socialist law. The result was the crisis of 1890 which forced his resignation.

Bismarck's campaign against the SPD not only failed in its attempt to eliminate socialism but actually contributed to its eventual emergence as the strongest single element in the *Reichstag* by 1913. Bismarck failed to take into consideration the growth of the proletariat, a direct result of Germany's rapid industrialization. Steel production, for example, doubled during the 1880s, a decade which also saw the transformation of the ship building, electrical and chemical industries. Two basic reasons have been given for this industrial take-off: the protection afforded by the 1879 tariff, and the development of new methods of production like the Gilchrist-Thomas method of steel smelting. The effect on the composition of the German population was considerable. In 1830 the ratio of urban to rural inhabitants was about 1:4; this had shifted to 2:3 by 1860, and then accelerated from 3:2 in 1882 to 4:1 by 1895. The change was reflected in the increase in the popular vote for the SPD: 493,000 in 1877, 550,000 in 1884 and 1,427,000 in 1890.

Another factor in the survival of the SPD was the use of evasive tactics to reduce the impact of the anti-socialist law. Secret conferences were held abroad as, for example, in Schoss Wyden in 1880, Copenhagen in 1883 and St. Gall in 1887. Bowling, gymnastic and cycling clubs served as a front for local organizations which maintained close contacts with the party caucus in the *Reichstag*, avoiding government surveillance by elaborate deception. Ideas and propaganda were disseminated through the *Sozialdemokrat*, a newspaper founded in Zurich in 1879, and edited by Vollmar and Bernstein.

Thus, although they frightened some individual socialists, Bismarck's measures evoked a disciplined and purposeful resistance from the Party as a whole. As he came to realize this, he tempered repression with state socialism. Unfortunately for Bismarck, the government received little credit for its initiative and the proletariat refused to be won over. Any advances made were accredited by the workers to the pressures which had been exerted by the SPD and not to any generosity on the Chancellor's part. Besides, Bismarck ignored the real problem of poor working conditions. He was not in favour of restricting the power of the great industrialists by factory legislation, and the workers knew that they could expect no relief from the government in this quarter. It is hardly surprising, therefore, that state socialism was seen merely as a sop to free enterprise, just as parliamentarism was a 'fig leaf covering the nakedness of absolutism'.[6]

*

The balance sheet by 1889 was in Bismarck's favour. He had the committed support of the Conservatives and Free Conservatives; he had split the liberals and kept the larger section docile; and, although he had not succeeded in undermining the Centre, he encountered little obstruction from this source in the 1880s. Only the SPD remained totally hostile, but the loaded electoral system delayed the socialist take-off until after 1900.

Yet 1890 was the year of Bismark's greatest frustration and eventual failure. The problem was that a new and assertive Kaiser had made inroads into the authority which Bismarck had grown accustomed to wielding. Ironically, the most effective means by which the Chancellor could resist this encroachment was by claiming the support of the *Reichstag*, the very institution which he had for so long tried to weaken. But the crisis over the anti-socialist legislation showed the extent to which Bismarck had lost his political skills. He failed to maintain the *Kartell* which had so convincingly won the 1887 election, and antagonized the National Liberals and Free Conservatives as well as the Kaiser by refusing to compromise on the 'expulsion' clause of the anti-socialist bill. He even considered a *coup* against the *Reichstag*, to be followed by a new constitution which would be based on the consent of the German princes. He then abandoned this scheme in favour of another *Kartell* based on the Centre Party. Such schemes, however, served only to increase his isolation and intensify the demand for his resignation.

In the long term, Bismarck's chancellorship weakened the whole party system. Of all the major parties of the Second Reich, only the Centre and the SPD survived unchanged into the Weimar Republic; the others either disappeared or were re-established as new parties. One of the leaders of the Democratic Party, heir to the *Freisinnige* Party, observed in 1917: 'Bismarck left behind him as his political heritage a nation without any political education, far below the level which, in this respect, it had reached twenty years earlier.'[6]

14

The Survival of the Third French Republic 1870–1914

The Second Empire was replaced by the Third Republic in September 1870. As explained in Chapter 12, this was the achievement of Paris, largely in the face of the pro-imperial loyalties of the rest of France. But the permanence of this victory was by no means guaranteed, and it appeared that the provinces might well swing the pendulum back to authoritarian rule. The National Assembly which convened at Versailles in February 1871 contained an anti-republican majority and, under the temporary leadership of Thiers, took drastic measures to suppress the socialist and radical Commune of Paris. April's notorious 'Bloody Week' saw the massacre of over 20,000 people in the streets of the capital, a virtual re-enactment of the conservative and counter-revolutionary measures of Cavaignac during the 'June Days' of 1849. Cavaignac, in effect, destroyed the Second Republic. It would have come as no surprise had Thiers done the same to the Third.

Yet the Third Republic provided the longest period of continuous constitutional development in modern French history. It survived three periods of danger. The first was the attempt, during the early 1870s, to re-establish a monarchy. The second was the threat, made by Macmahon in the 1870s and Boulanger in the 1880s, to increase the powers of the executive at the expense of those of the legislature. The third was the deep cleavage in French politics and society caused by the Dreyfus Affair, and by the revolutionary dissent of both the extreme Right and the extreme Left at the turn of the century.

Aspects of European History 1789–1980

*

The Republic seemed, before 1875, to stand little chance of survival. Its supporters were compromised by the taint of the Commune and were, in any case, grouped into two antagonistic groups: moderates and radicals. The monarchists had, in 1871, an overall majority in the Assembly, with 400 seats out of 630. Although there were three claimants to the throne, schemes were advanced in 1871 and 1873 whereby the Comte de Chambord would be restored, to be succeeded by the comte de Paris; this formula appeared to reconcile the two main monarchist parties, the Legitimists and Orléanists. Throughout the first part of the 1870s there was no permanent commitment to a republic. The Assembly provided through the septennate of 1873 a temporary solution; it prolonged republican institutions only for a further seven years until a suitable alternative could be hammered out.

What saved the Republic at its inception was a combination of growing contention between the Legitimists, Orléanists and Bonapartists, and the electoral recovery of the anti-monarchists.

The political dispute between the three monarchist wings seemed to encompass many of the issues which had already divided them between 1815 and 1870. At first sight there was no real problem. The Legitimist Manifesto promised universal suffrage and parliamentary monarchy, and seemed content, in Cobban's words, to give up the substance of power in order to retain the shadow. The Orléanists, already committed to constitutional monarchy, found the new attitude of the Legitimists quite acceptable. But the monarchist challenge to the Republic was soon to divide along the seam of the tricoleur controversy (1871–3), despite a desperate mission to attempt to persuade the Legitimist comte de Chambord to give up his demands for the return of the white flag of the Bourbons. The comte, however, was adamant; if he were to be the next king of France he would not 'permit the standard of Henri IV, of Francis I and of Joan of Arc' to be snatched from his hands. The Orléanists were equally staunch in their refusal to abandon the tricoleur, the emblem which France had given herself. Behind this apparently trivial conflict lay deep and divisive constitutional issues, showing that Legitimism, Orléanism and Bonapartism were not easily reconcilable. The Legitimists were clearly resuming the stance of Charles X against the 1789 Revolution, determined to reduce its

The Third Republic to 1914

political and social influence. The Orléanists, by contrast, stood for the fusion of the Revolution with limited monarchy. The Bonapartists intended to restore the imperialist tradition of the Revolution in the form of a plebiscitary dictatorship. Thus, there appeared to be an intractable problem. The Legitimists and Orléanists agreed on the restoration of the kingdom rather than the empire, but the Legitimists held out against the Orléanists and Bonapartists on the issue of the tricolour. Since only a combination of Orléanists and Legitimists could ensure a monarchist restoration, the comte de Chambord, in effect, had the last word. Thiers was to be proved right in his belief that this would 'definitely establish the Republic'.

Religious controversy also played an important role in weakening the monarchist campaign against the Republic. It is true that all three wings supported the Church, and that the *noblesse* and upper bourgeoisie, monarchists to a man, were nearly all devout Catholics. But there were substantial differences of emphasis. The Legitimists wished to revive the temporal authority of the Papacy, even if this meant military intervention against the Italian government. They also laid heavy emphasis on the cult of the *Sacré Coeur*, regarding the construction of the Basilica at Montmartre as an act of national penance for decades of secularism. These attitudes found joint expression in the prayer proposed in 1871 by the French bishops: '*Sauvez Rome et la France au nom du Sacré Coeur.*'[1] The Orléanists and Bonapartists considered this Ultramontanism of the Legitimists entirely unacceptable, but could not find an alternative formula upon which they could agree. Many of the Orléanists were Gallicans, some even Jansenists, while the Bonapartists stood for a powerful Church which would act as a 'social cement' but which would avoid the eighteenth-century conflict between Ultramontane and Gallican interests.

The success of the monarchist offensive depended on speed. The longer the three wings took to agree, the greater the chance of survival they gave to the Republic. Leading members of the Assembly, once monarchists themselves, came to realize that the Republic was a viable alternative to the interminable disputes among the royalist factions. Thiers, who as an Orléanist had served under Louis Philippe and, as a Bonapartist under Napoleon III, now declared himself in favour of the Republic in 1872. His reason represented the feeling of a growing proportion of the Assembly: 'There is only one throne; three men cannot sit on it at the same time.'

Meanwhile, the republicans were gradually undermining the monarchist parliamentary majority: through a series of by-election victories between 1871 and 1873, and through the defection of a *bloc* of Orléanists to the republican camp after Chambord's final refusal to accept the tricolour. The Republic also benefited from the slow and cautious changes made by the 1875 Wallon Amendment and the 1875 Constitutional Laws. The institutions established included a seven-year presidency and an Upper Chamber, or Senate, both of which could conceivably be adapted to a monarchy some time in the future. This had a double advantage: on the one hand, it removed the urgency from the monarchist campaign against the Republic; the comte de Paris, for example, said: 'If we cannot make a monarchy we must make something as like to it as possible.' On the other, it gave the Republic a further opportunity for consolidation and retrenchment, even if the semi-monarchical appearance of the Constitution caused one newspaper editor to remark: 'We are entering the Republic backwards.'[2]

*

There is a saying that 'In France nothing lasts as long as what is only temporary'. The Constitutional Laws of 1875 were intended to be a stopgap: in fact, they remained in existence until 1940. Yet the Republic had to continue its struggle for survival for another fifteen years. This time it was confronted by the efforts of two individuals, Macmahon and Boulanger, to weaken the legislature, the main source of republican strength, and create a powerful Executive which would become the preserve of the Right.

President Macmahon's ultimate ambition was to restore the monarchy. In the meantime, he intended to use his own powers to the limits prescribed by the Constitution and to prevent the Republic from becoming more radical. As part of his onslaught against the republicans, he secured the resignation of Simon, the moderate prime minister, and installed the Orléanist duc de Broglie as his successor. When the Chamber of Deputies made it clear that it had no confidence in Broglie, Macmahon resorted to a legal, but typically Bonapartist manoeuvre. In May 1877 he obtained the Senate's assent to the dissolution of the Chamber in the hope that fresh elections would return a more docile majority. In preparation for these, Broglie's government weeded out the non-monarchists in the provincial prefectures and municipal councils. Notwithstanding such precautions, the outcome of the elections was a disaster for Macmahon. His manipulation of the Constitution failed to prevent a substantial victory for the Republicans over the Right by 326 seats to 207. Why?

In the first place, Macmahon was the wrong man for the attempt. Lacking personal charisma, he was unable to project any real appeal or confidence in his measures. His widespread publicity campaign fell flat; the distribution of posters and portraits elicited from the public comments like: 'He has an intelligent eye – the horse I mean.' He was clearly incapable of mounting any direct challenge to the constitution itself and yet, without this, any *coup* could only be, in the words of the Bishop of Poitiers, 'a sword stroke in water'. Indeed, Macmahon and Broglie were actually prisoners of the Constitution. They applied all the sanctions allowed by law against their opponents and used their authority to change the personnel of local government. But such methods served only to provoke more intense republican resistance and to forge unity where little had previously existed.

This reconciliation between the various factions of Republicans proved to be the main reason for the salvation of the Republic. The anti-monarchists adopted the slogan 'No enemies on the Left' to indicate that their factional feuds had ended. Partly responsible for this was the agreement between the different republican leaders. Gambetta, previously a radical, now purged his programme of all revolutionary connotations in an effort to gain the support of the bourgeoisie and the peasantry. His slogan 'We shall be prudent' merged with the promise of the more traditional Grévy that France would be guaranteed a 'safe republic'. Greater unity made possible a more effective attack on the government and its dangerous policies. The Republicans were able to play upon the fear of the growing influence of clericalism, of the possible consequences of any attempt to force the Italian government to restore to the Pope his temporal lands, and the threat posed to the legislature by Macmahon's abuse of the presidential prerogative of dissolution. The attacks were effectively conveyed in newspapers like *La République Française* and in the broadsheets distributed among the peasantry. Above all, Gambetta conducted a masterly campaign of aggressive speeches against the President. Attempts to silence him by prosecution only enhanced his reputation and increased his popularity.

Aspects of European History 1789–1980

Macmahon's failure was significant not only because it provided a further respite for the Republic, but also because it altered the nature of the next threat. Macmahon was replaced by Grévy, who decided to be 'submissive to the great law of parliamentary government'. From 1877 onwards the presidency was too weak to harbour any real opposition to the legislature. Consequently, any anti-republican move would have to come from outside the constitutional framework altogether. This inevitably meant that the next challenge from the Right would be more radical, even revolutionary. General Boulanger came close to destroying the Republic in 1889. After a series of remarkable election victories, he stood poised to seize power in a *coup d'état* which he intended to endorse with a referendum. His programme was anti-parliamentary and aimed at abolishing one of the Chambers, extending presidential powers, and replacing elections by plebiscites. It was the old Bonapartist formula of an authoritarian executive freed from legislative restraints, and deriving its support directly from the masses. Boulanger was a much more dangerous threat than Macmahon because he appealed to the radicals of the Left as well as those of the Right. He was, at first, supported by the Blanquists and Socialists who had become, during the 1880s, disillusioned by the high rate of unemployment and more critical of the parliamentary oligarchy into which they considered the Republic had descended. The Right were attracted by his appeal to national pride. Déroulède's League of Patriots, established in 1884, interpreted Boulangism as a means of achieving *revanche* against Germany for the loss of Alsace-Lorraine in 1871. The Bonapartists found Boulanger readily acceptable, the comte de Paris soon advised the Orléanists to give their support, and the overall campaign was financed by the Legitimist duchesse d'Uzès. The Church, traditionally anti-republican, gave its official sanction to Boulangism and set the seal on the new coalition.

Again, however, the Republic survived. The collapse of the movement was unexpected and dramatic. Boulanger, cowed by a government threat of impeachment, fled France in 1889. The elections of the same year gave the Republicans 366 seats to the Right's 216. In retrospect, the weaknesses of Boulangism are obvious. Its support was so diverse that a specific programme was never really possible. How could the radical Left and the conservative Right ever hope to agree on social and economic policies? How could the different concepts of democracy be reconciled? It seems that Boulanger was a powerful catalyst of discontent rather than the creator of a new ideology; indeed, Meyer called him, in 1889, *un talisman promis à tous les malheureux'*. The movement also had little support beyond Paris and the other major towns. The peasant masses remained indifferent to his appeal, or actively supported the Republic which had guaranteed their property. In this respect, therefore, Boulangism lacked the rural base which had been so vital for Bonapartism. Despite his charisma and electoral appeal, Boulanger lacked the capacity for strong and decisive leadership necessary for the personification of executive authority. Indeed, he was a mass of contradictions. An adventurer and opportunist, he declined three perfect opportunities to seize power. And, although immensely popular in Paris, he remained completely dependent on advisers like Laguerre, Naquet and Thiebaud to create an image for him.

The Republic showed characteristic resilience during the latter phase of the crisis. It mobilized the centre of the political spectrum and eventually managed to regain the support of the radical left. Boulanger's appeal to nationalism and clericalism pushed the Socialists back into the Republican camp and the old slogan 'No enemies on the Left' was revived. The attitude of the Possibilists was typical: 'We workers are ready to forget the sixteen years during which the bourgeoisie has betrayed the hopes of the people, we are ready to defend and conserve by all means the weak germ of our republican institutions against military threats.'[2] The Left also established the *Société des Droits de l'Homme et du Citoyen*, committed to forging an alliance between 'all those who remain faithful to the Republic' and waging a 'merciless struggle against any kind of reaction or dictatorship'.[3] With this range of support, the government was able to take the offensive. In a brilliantly conceived legal campaign it threatened Boulanger with impeachment, exposed his natural timidity, and precipitated his withdrawal. Having eliminated the leadership, it then took proceedings against Déroulède's League of Patriots and other groups which had threatened a *coup d'état*. The Third Republic therefore escaped the eventual fate of the First and Second, largely because Boulanger proved an inadequate successor to the Bonapartes. Never again was it to be severely tested by the cult of personality. By 1890 France seemed to have evolved out of her monarchist and authoritarian phases.

*

Aspects of European History 1789–1980

Deep divisions, however, remained in the social and political fabric. These were exacerbated between 1890 and 1914 by the Dreyfus Affair and, once this had been resolved, by attacks on the régime from *Action Française* and Syndicalism.

The Affair produced the last major threat to the Republic from the Right before 1914. The army considered that its reputation would be seriously endangered by the rehabilitation of Captain Alfred Dreyfus (who had been wrongly convicted of espionage) and therefore proceeded to cover up the greatest judicial crime of the century. In the process, it expressed quite openly its anti-Republican bias. This, in fact, had become more pronounced than ever before. While the major institutions had gradually been republicanized during the 1880s, the army had remained the preserve of the aristocracy, who now dominated the officer corps and the promotion boards. The army was given extensive support by Church leaders, particularly the Bishop of Toulouse, and by religious orders like the Assumptionists. Many Catholics suspected the Republic of spreading atheism, and Fr Didon saw the army as a possible instrument, 'a holy force whose mission is to make right prevail'. Anti-semitism and nationalism also reappeared, and Déroulède emphasized the link between the treason of Dreyfus the Jew, and the corruption of the Republican government itself. Yet the bitter denunciation of Dreyfus and his supporters was no substitute for a positive and concerted programme on the Right; once again, those who attacked the Republic were unable to offer any real alternative. Once again the Right was brought together by only a negative common denominator – resentment. This time, it even lacked a leader. There was no successor to Macmahon or Boulanger who, despite their shortcomings, had been a focal point for the loyalty of the activists of the different Rightist groups.

If the Dreyfus Affair produced a weaker attack on the Republic from the Right, it promoted a more vigorous response from the Left. This took some time to mobilize because of the initial implication of the Méline and Dupuy ministries (1898–9) in the injustice to Dreyfus, and also because the extreme Left at first regarded the whole Affair as a sordid bourgeois conflict. The turning-point, however, came in 1899, with the appointment of Waldeck-Rousseau as Prime Minister. Rousseau and his successor, Combes (1902–5), took a much tougher line and launched a massive offensive on the army and Church, ensuring, by a series of reforms, that these could never again involve themselves actively in political issues. The ministries were able to deal so confidently with the Right because they had sufficient backing from the different Republican groups to ensure an overall majority in the Chamber of Deputies. The threat from the Right, especially Déroulède's attempts to overthrow the Republic in 1899, had reactivated the old slogan 'No enemies on the Left'. The Radicals co-operated with the Socialists who, under the prompting of Jaurès, halted their campaign against the 'bourgeois Republic'. The Cabinet of Waldeck-Rousseau, in fact, contained the first Socialist to serve in any European government, together with Republicans of all other shades. Combes, in turn, co-operated closely with the *Délégation des Gauches*, a steering committee designed to preserve the unity of the Left. Meanwhile, political activity had been accompanied by extensive anti-Rightist and pro-Dreyfusard propaganda in papers like Clemenceau's *L'Aurore* and Guyot's *Le Siècle*. Organizations like the *Ligue des Droits de l'Homme* were also successful in mobilizing mass support from the lower-middle class and the urban proletariat.

The Republic achieved maturity as a result of the Dreyfus Affair and was evidently accepted by the vast majority of the electorate as the only régime possible for France. Between 1900 and 1914, however, activists continued their harassment of existing institutions. Maurras' newly established pressure group, *Action Française*, combined the most extreme elements of right-wing ideology and launched attacks on democracy, Protestantism, Jews, Freemasons and foreigners. It also pressed for a return to the monarchy and the structured society of the *ancien régime*. Yet Maurras could never expect, at this stage, to issue a major challenge to the Republic. His newspaper never achieved a circulation above 50,000 and the majority of the army and Church leaders considered him too radical. The extreme Left, meanwhile, had withdrawn their support for the Republican government in 1905, voting at the congress of the *Confédération Générale du Travail* to resort to direct action to make the régime more directly socialist. The result was a rash of strikes between 1907 and 1911 and a rapid increase in the influence of Sorel's Syndicalism. These, however, posed less of a threat than has often been maintained. The CGT had less than 400,000 resolute Syndicalists, compared with an estimated 10.6 million workers who were not militant. The government took forceful measures against the strikers. Clemenceau called out the troops in 1909, while Briand pressed railway strikers into the army as reservists in 1910. These measures were popular with the majority of the electorate, who cast a much larger vote for the moderate Republican parties in the 1910 general election.

*

How stable was the Third Republic by 1914? It appears, at first sight, that France had experienced a constant stream of political difficulties. Between 1871 and 1914, for example, there were no fewer than fifty ministries, twenty-six of which served between 1889 and 1914, and eleven between 1909 and 1914. The main factor preventing any real continuity was the absence of specific parties; deputies tended to group themselves more loosely into 'alliances' or 'federations', considering themselves free to move from one to another as circumstances dictated. The concept of party discipline, which divided the legislature between representatives of government and opposition, was alien to France. Consequently, new ministries had to be forged whenever there was a major disagreement on policy.

Three things, however, kept the Republic together throughout its times of crisis. The first was what has been called the stability of ministers rather than ministries.[4] Although governments changed frequently, the personnel who served in them reappeared regularly. Delcassé, for example, was Minister of Foreign Affairs six times between 1898 and 1905. Of the 561 ministers appointed between 1870 and 1940, no fewer than 120 served in five or more governments. Thus France was spared the prospect, which existed in other countries, that a new government might be completely inexperienced, or bring about a major change of course. Second, the French administration remained virtually unchanged throughout the prewar era. The major institutions, including the *conseil d'état* and the Inspectorate of Finance, continued to carry out the normal business of government, no matter what was happening at ministerial level; according to Guérard, 'so long as the bureaucrat is at his desk, France survives!'[4] Third, the majority of the population and, after 1875, over half of the parliamentary deputies, were supporters of the Republic. In quiet times their ideas of what form this Republic should take differed widely, resulting in major rifts between Radicals, Radical-Socialists, Socialists and Syndicalists. But whenever there was a major threat from the Right on the institutions of the Republic, these elements combined temporarily to meet it, apparently confirming the belief of Thiers that 'The Republic is the government which divides us least'.

15
German Foreign Policy
1871–1914

The emergence of Germany as a single state substantially altered the balance of power in Europe. Bismarck's victories had already indicated Germany's military superiority over Austria and France, while the rest of the century saw a rapid acceleration of the German economy, the result of a population explosion and an industrial revolution. It is hardly surprising, therefore, that German statesmen tended, after 1871, to dominate the European scene and that other continental leaders found the threads of their own diplomacy passing through Berlin.

*

By 1871 Bismarck considered that his task of uniting Germany had been accomplished and that consolidation and retrenchment should now replace conflict and *Realpolitik*. The Second Reich, he insisted, was a sated power; further additions of territory were therefore unnecessary and undesirable. Indeed, what had already been achieved 'could only be jeopardized by pressing for further expansion of German power'.[1] Instead, Germany should be 'appeased and peaceful',[2] for 'when we have arrived in a good harbour, we should be content and cultivate what we have won'.[3] His primary concern now was to anticipate and neutralize any forces which might disrupt the internal harmony of the new state or upset the international balance of power.

He therefore kept a close watch on the situation in both Eastern and Western Europe. He was well aware that his *Realpolitik* and

German Foreign Policy 1871–1914

deliberate aggression, used during the 1860s to unite Germany, had undermined the understanding which had previously existed between Russia, Prussia and Austria. There was now a danger either of Austro-Russian collaboration against Germany, or of an Austro-Russian war some time in the future into which Germany might be dragged. Somehow, therefore, he had to prevent relations between the Austrian and Russian governments from becoming too close or too strained. The situation in Western Europe was more immediately threatening. Throughout the 1870s and 1880s Bismarck was haunted by the prospect of an attempt by France to avenge her defeat of 1871. This had, after all, been a profound psychological shock, given a sharp edge of resentment by the cession, in the Treaty of Frankfurt, of Alsace-Lorraine. By herself, France constituted little military danger to Germany. But what if she could acquire an ally – Russia, perhaps? Bismarck's intention was that all continental disputes should be patched up without recourse to war, for an unsuccessful protagonist might otherwise seek any support available; France's price for *her* support would undoubtedly be an alliance against Germany. To guarantee Germany's security, therefore, France would have to be kept out of the mainstream of European diplomacy. As late as 1887 Bismarck still considered that 'France is the European state most eager for war, and European peace is assured with France's isolation'.[4] At the same time, Germany needed to be integrated into an effective defensive system, so that she was in accord with the majority of the European powers. Hence, he observed, 'when there are five [powers], try to be *à trois*'.[5]

In responding to these challenges, Bismarck tried to keep his options open as long as possible and he reserved the right to change course if necessary. He believed that 'in politics there are no such things as complete certainty and definitive results . . . Everything goes continually uphill, downhill.'[6] The result was a period of great complexity in German diplomacy.

At first Bismarck used ideological factors to restore the *rapprochement* between Germany, Austria and Russia, and to build a solid front against France. One of the agencies of destruction which he feared, and exploited, was revolution. In 1872, therefore, he formed the *Dreikaiserbund*, which committed the three governments to co-operate in their measures against socialism and other radical influences. The *Dreikaiserband* was also a means of fostering monarchical unity against republican France. Bismarck's attitude

135

Aspects of European History 1789–1980

towards France was typically double-edged. He certainly feared that the republicans would continue to demand revenge against Germany; but, on the other hand, he was reluctant to see France with any other form of government, for this would make her more respectable in the eyes of Austrian and Russian statesmen. In 1873 Bismarck actually reprimanded Arnim, the German ambassador in Paris, for supporting a monarchist bid to gain control in France. Why, he demanded angrily, should Germany seek to undermine a régime whose ideological base had, so far, ensured its own isolation?

Until 1875 Bismarck's measures appeared to be fully vindicated. Austria and Russia remained on good terms with each other, but through the agency of Germany, while no major power showed the least inclination to ally with France. In the second half of the decade, however, a situation developed which tested Bismarck's diplomatic acumen more completely. The Ottoman Empire, in decline for nearly two centuries, underwent a series of internal revolts and a new period of administrative chaos. Bismarck had to contend with two sets of diplomatic ramifications; these concerned Austria and Russia in the Balkans, and France and Italy in the Mediterranean.

Between 1875 and 1877 the Sultan was faced, in the Balkans, with insurrections by Bosnia, Herzegovina, Bulgaria, Serbia and Montenegro. Turkish reprisals reactivated Russia's traditional claim to protect the Balkan Christians which, in turn, aroused Austrian fears of Russian expansion into South-Eastern Europe, an area of special interest to Vienna after the loss of Austria's Italian provinces. Relations between Russia and Austria deteriorated rapidly after Russia declared war on and defeated Turkey. Bismarck now had a problem – and an opportunity. On the one hand, the Balkan imbroglio could easily cause a war between Russia and Austria which would upset the balance of power in Europe and endanger Germany. On the other, the Balkans could be used as an irritant to prevent other powers, including Russia and Austria, from coming together. By working on lesser antagonisms he could, therefore, prevent the build-up of a major confrontation. In an attempt to solve the problem, and seize the opportunity, Bismarck offered his services as an 'honest broker' at the Congress of Berlin (1878), playing a vital role in drawing up the eventual territorial compromise. The outcome, however, was far from satisfactory. The enmity between Austria and Russia was still potentially dangerous, while Alexander II bitterly attacked Bismarck's apparent support

German Foreign Policy 1871–1914

for Austria at the Congress and complained about the parsimonious territorial compensation received by Russia and the trisection of her client state, Bulgaria. Bismarck found that he had to take another initiative – this time the defensive Dual Alliance between Germany and Austria, directed specifically at Russia. There is some evidence that this was a precipitate and short-term measure, designed to break the impending threat of war by offering security to one of the protagonists while, at the same time, actively restraining it from aggression. It is sometimes said that the Dual Alliance represented Bismarck's final choice between Russia and Austria. This is not so. He still intended to keep his options open and hoped to revive the close connection with Russia in order to prevent the growth of a counter-alliance based on France. Bismarck did make a choice in 1879, but it was between Russia and Britain. He turned down the opportunity of a direct agreement with Britain because he knew that this would do more than anything else to alienate Russia permanently.

Meanwhile, the North African territories, over which Turkey had maintained the most tenuous of holds, were now coming under the attentions of the great powers. This time things worked more directly in Bismarck's favour. Britain became heavily involved in Egypt, and France in Tunisia – a situation welcomed by Bismarck because it would distract the Republic's attention from affairs in Europe. In fact, Bismarck used these involvements to promote a series of colonial collisions between France and Britain: he openly admitted to projecting the rivalries between the major powers into a safer continent, while working hard to keep them alive. There was also an immediate return from the Tunisia episode. The Italian government had, for some time, regarded Tunisia as being within its sphere of influence, a fact well known to Bismarck when he had given his blessing to the French annexation. When Italy approached Bismarck for help in 1882, Bismarck was able, by the Triple Alliance, to overcome two of the remaining weaknesses within his system. First, by ending the longstanding enmity between Italy and Austria he removed the threat from the latter's southern flank. Second, although Germany did not gain much from Italy's military support, at least France was deprived of a potential ally who would have given her an immense psychological boost.

During the 1880s Bismarck's policies became more and more tortuous as he had to deal with the complications caused by the Dual

Alliance; he was particularly concerned about the possibility of an alliance between France and Russia and tried everything to prevent it. At first, in 1881, he revived his original expedient of the *Dreikaiserbund*, in the form of the Three Emperors' Alliance. This, however, laid less stress on ideological unity, and more on specific territorial compromise between Austria and Russia in the hope that Russia would not seek accommodation with France through a sense of insecurity and isolation. By the mid-1880s, however, this arrangement (renewed in 1884) was on the verge of collapse because of the revival of the Bulgarian crisis. The threat of war between Austria and Russia was more serious than ever. The Austrian government objected forcefully to Russia's intervention in Bulgaria's internal affairs and her involvement in the abduction of Bulgaria's monarch, Alexander of Battenberg. In 1887 Bismarck resorted to a series of controversial measures designed to neutralize the conflict and to provide Germany with a means of avoiding direct involvement should an Austro-Russian war actually break out. By the Reinsurance Treaty he promised Russia full diplomatic support over Bulgaria. He obtained, in return, a guarantee of Russian neutrality in the event of a French attack on Germany, subject to a similar undertaking by Germany not to assist an Austrian attack on Russia. Bismarck was careful, however, to hedge his bets. His support for Russian claims in Bulgaria would not, he knew, result in a sudden increase in Russian influence in South-Eastern Europe, for Austria, Italy and Britain, who had negotiated the Mediterranean Agreement in the same year, would exert diplomatic pressure to prevent Russia from acquiring the vital Straits area. What he was doing, therefore, was reassuring Russia about Germany's friendship, while relying on others to frustrate Russia's plans in the Balkans. He was also careful to do nothing which would involve the desertion of Austria and the neutrality clause of the Reinsurance Treaty did not, technically, contravene the terms of the Dual Alliance.* He was, however, fully aware that his allies would not appreciate the subtlety of his diplomacy and, in order to avoid their inevitable suspicions about his motives, he kept the Reinsurance Treaty under the wraps of strict secrecy.

How successful was Bismarck's foreign policy? Certain advan-

---

* The Dual Alliance had provided for German support for Austria in the event of an attack on Austria by Russia; the Reinsurance Treaty only guaranteed German neutrality if Russia were attacked by Austria.

tages *could* be claimed for the complex system he developed. France remained completely isolated during the entire period of his chancellorship. He projected himself as the arbiter of Europe and took the credit for drawing the sting from the Balkan crises. He formed, in the Dual and Triple Alliances, a solid *bloc* of German-influenced territory in Central Europe. Yet he managed to prevent the growth of an armed camp based on France by keeping open contacts with Russia; the latter considered the Reinsurance Treaty so useful that she was to request its renewal in 1890.

There must, however, be serious reservations about his diplomacy. Complexity cannot, in itself, be considered a virtue, particularly since Bismarck had taken no measures to train a successor to maintain his system of checks and balances. He had been inflexible and dictatorial to his foreign office and diplomatic staff ('My ambassadors must fall into line like soldiers'[7]) and had systematically uprooted any signs of initiative or independent thought. The strongest personality was Baron von Holstein who, as it happened, strongly opposed Bismarck's Russian policy and, after the old Chancellor's resignation in 1890, instigated a major change of course. Bismarck could only fume at the 'mistakes' of his successors. Overlooking his own part in destroying the continuity of German foreign policy, he spoke of the 'criminal negligence' of Holstein and Caprivi and built up a powerful myth about his own supreme gifts as a statesman. This, in turn, was seized upon, elaborated and perpetuated by contemporary German historians.

It could be argued that the whole system was facing imminent collapse *before* Bismarck's resignation. He spent the last three years of his chancellorship trying desperately to juggle with apparently conflicting policies. His approach to Russia was especially faulty. He certainly exaggerated the importance of the Reinsurance Treaty. Russia was committed to neutrality only if France attacked Germany; she reserved the right, however, to join France if Germany were the aggressor. Hence the Reinsurance Treaty in no way precluded the possibility of a Franco-Russian alliance, a point which Bismarck ignored when he attacked the German cabinet for not renewing the treaty in 1890. Since accommodation between Russia and France was still a technical possibility, Bismarck should have devoted his energies to removing all possible motives. This he signally failed to do. In fact, his refusal to allow German investment in Russian state bonds contributed much to the Tsar's decision to take up French loans at the end of the 1880s. Meanwhile, the fall of Ferry's government in France in 1885 had ended the temporary improvement in Franco-German relations, while the emergence of Boulangism gave a new lease of life to Revanchism. France had, therefore, every reason to look beyond a mere economic agreement with Russia, while the latter had lost, in the welter of investment from Paris, its aversion to the prospect of a republican ally. Bismarck's peripheral arrangements were also looking increasingly unhealthy. Italy was an uncertain ally and, in any case, showed her extreme economic vulnerability during the Franco-Italian tariff war in 1888. The Mediterranean Agreement of 1887 could not be interpreted as a permanent arrangement, and Bismarck's offer in 1889 of a military alliance with Britain met a cold reception from the prime minister, Lord Salisbury. In 1879 Bismarck had foregone an Anglo-German Treaty in order to keep his options open with Russia. Now, in 1889, Russia was moving swiftly towards France, and Britain had long since retracted her offer. At no other time in his chancellorship had Bismarck's policy of being *à trois* appeared so threatened.

Bismarck's 'system' was also seen by a substantial section of the German population as anachronistic. Its dependence on restraint in diplomacy left dissatisfied the ever-increasing number of nationalists, while many of the army leaders had adopted the view that the threat of Germany's encirclement should be countered by military, not diplomatic, action. Above all, powerful economic pressure groups demanded a more active overseas policy to procure outlets for raw materials and markets for manufactured goods. Thus, by 1890, Germany was no longer a sated power. The statesman who had introduced this concept had, unfortunately, neglected to educate the German public into accepting it permanently.

*

The 'change of course' in German foreign policy after Bismarck's resignation should not, therefore, be seen as the cold-blooded abandonment of a thriving system. It was rather a change of tempo, or an acceleration of those forces which made German policy more aggressive and less cautious. With the removal of the master tactician of restraint, three main developments took place. The tenuous connection with Russia was abandoned, resulting in the formation, in 1894, of the Franco-Russian Alliance. Then, from the mid-1890s, Germany broke the European bounds to which Bismarck had constrained her and became involved in the more ambitious *Weltpolitik*. At the same time, a massive programme of naval construction was started, with the declared intention of challenging Britain's supremacy at sea. Why did these changes occur?

The first reason was that Germany's new leadership had bold designs but lacked the political wisdom to control them. Kaiser William II (1888–1918) was less disciplined and more impetuous than either of his predecessors, William I (1871–88) and Frederick III (1888). Modelling himself on Frederick the Great (1740–86), he showed a definite preference for military matters, giving greater attention to army and navy commanders than to his civilian ministers or to the *Reichstag*. After all, he believed that 'the soldiers and the army, and not the decisions of parliaments, forged the German Reich'.[8] Consequently, the ideas of Tirpitz, Schlieffen and Moltke were accepted without reservation, even though their emphasis on military strategy blunted the weapon upon which Bismarck had relied – diplomacy. The chancellors of the period 1890–1914 could not aspire to Bismarck's influence and were, in any case, a diverse mixture. Caprivi (1890–4) and Chlodwig-Hohenlohe (1894–1900) were inexperienced in foreign affairs, and lost the initiative to advisers like Holstein, as well as to the Kaiser's military circle. Bülow (1900–09) was more forceful but, as a product of the new generation, actively fostered both *Weltpolitik* and the naval programme. The last, Bethmann Hollweg (1909–17) had to struggle, in a period of growing international tension, with his own ignorance, and the pressure of the army commanders to decide Germany's course of action.

Recent historians have emphasized a second reason for the 'change of course'. They argue that serious internal pressures in German society and politics necessitated some form of distraction if the Second Reich were to survive; in this respect, the dilemmas and solutions of William II were similar to those of Napoleon III and Nicholas II. The inherent contradictions within Bismarck's Germany had become more and more obvious by 1890. The autocratic traditions of the Prussian-based monarchy and ruling élite appeared incompatible with the more recent concession of parliamentary democracy. The ruling class lived in fear of revolution from below, or at the least, control by socialists and progressives over the *Reichstag*. The working class, which had been considerably enlarged by Germany's massive industrial growth, resented the almost feudal class structure and suspected that the régime would, given the chance, conduct a *coup* to trim the powers of the legislature and reduce the size of the electorate. In the rest of the political and social spectrum, the middle classes shared the régime's fears of socialism, but were fully committed to upholding parliamentary democracy. The Kaiser and his ministers had become uncomfortably aware of the extent of the political stalemate by 1896. They therefore prepared to release internal pressures and turn them outwards, converting class and party dissension into patriotism and pride in empire. Hence, Foreign Minister Bülow said, in 1897: 'I am putting the main emphasis on foreign policy. Only a successful foreign policy can help to reconcile, pacify, rally, unite.'[9] Government policy was to encourage the aristocracy and the Conservative Party to seek political fulfilment in imperialism and to forget their hopes for an onslaught on the *Reichstag*. The middle classes would, in turn, become less obsessive about parliamentary issues and would respond quickly to the economic advantages offered by imperial expansion. The *Reichstag* could even become the means of disseminating interest in colonial issues and correspondingly fewer debates would be held on domestic problems. Above all, the government hoped to win more widespread popular support for the monarchy and achieve what had previously been considered impossible: the 'mobilization of the masses'. Bülow insisted: 'We must unswervingly wrestle for the souls of our workers.'[10] In this policy 'which mobilizes the best patriotic forces' and 'appeals to the highest national emotions', the government merely had to exploit and encourage the demand for expansion put forward by public pressure groups and by the Colonial, Pan-German and Navy Leagues. Remove Bismarck's constraints, concluded the Kaiser, Tirpitz and Bülow, and Germany could be given a more vigorous role, as a world rather than as a continental power, while domestic harmony could be achieved without repression.

There were, however, to be unforeseen results, for the 'change of course' brought reality to all Bismarck's fears of European anarchy and hostile coalitions.

Throughout the 1890s the main target of Germany's new policy was Britain. Holstein, for example, believed that colonial pressure would force the British government to make concessions and thereby acknowledge the legitimacy of Germany's new world role. A provocative line was therefore pursued; Germany refused to compromise over the Samoan Islands in 1894, challenged Britain's Congolese Treaty in the same year, supported Kruger in the Transvaal crisis of 1896, and seized Kiaochow in 1897. Tirpitz believed that pressure should also be applied to Britain's sea power, for then she would 'concede to Your Majesty such a measure of maritime influence which will make it possible for Your Majesty to conduct a great overseas policy'.[10] A key element of his design was to increase Germany's battleship strength, thereby forcing Britain to protect home waters at the expense of her far-flung imperial commitments. In the process of implementing this 'risk policy', Germany lost an opportunity to come to an agreement with Britain offered, in 1899, by Joseph Chamberlain. Under the influence of Tirpitz, the Kaiser's government was far advanced on a course of direct confrontation and not very well-calculated brinkmanship. In a sense, observes G. A. Craig, Germany's efforts to behave like a world power were clumsy, rude and excessive.[9]

Shortly after the turn of the century the 'new course' took its toll. The strategy of forcing British attention back to Europe certainly worked, but in a way which had not been expected by Germany. The British government thought the German threat sufficiently serious to abandon its continental isolation and to form, in 1904, the Entente with France. Further German miscalculation followed. The Kaiser and Bülow tried, by exploiting the Moroccan situation of 1905, to prove that this co-operation was only a temporary phenomenon. Far from splitting the Entente, however, German action at Algeçiras only served to tighten and perpetuate it. There was worse to come. Holstein had shown absolute confidence in the total incompatibility of Britain and Russia: 'Whale and bear could never come together.'[11] Yet, in 1907, the two powers settled their colonial disputes by the Anglo-Russian Convention, while the connection of both countries with France was reaffirmed by the Triple Entente. Even at this stage German diplomacy was basically aggressive. The Agadir Incident and the Second Moroccan Crisis (1911) provoked an official warning to Germany in Lloyd George's Mansion House Speech, and created an atmosphere in which Anglo-French and Anglo-Russian fleet manoeuvres were considered necessary.

Inevitably, this turn of events caused in Germany a fundamental sense of unease and necessitated a re-examination of her overall strategy. Far from improving Germany's position relative to the other powers, the pursuit of *Weltpolitik* and naval expansion had actually provoked Britain's return to continental diplomacy and tightened the alliance between France and Russia. Apprehension about Germany's geographical vulnerability revived, sharpened by the knowledge that *Weltpolitik* had actually drawn resources away from the maintenance of her continental hegemony. Bethmann Hollweg summarized the problem: 'Because of the navy we have neglected the army, and our "naval policy" has created enemies all around us.'[9] The only solution possible was another change of course and the return to a continental strategy which would enable Germany to break out of her encirclement. Unfortunately, this could no longer be achieved by diplomacy, for international relations were far less fluid than they had been in Bismarck's era. This absence of any political solutions enabled the military leadership to exert unprecedented influence on the government in two ways. First, the inflexibility of the Schlieffen Plan (1905), which allowed for a general assault on Russia only after the defeat of France, made it impossible to deal separately with Germany's two hostile neighbours. The sort of situation had arisen which Bismarck had always avoided: diplomatic options were limited by the demands of military schedules. Second, military commanders like Moltke and Ludendorff were, by 1912, putting pressure on the government to use war as a means of breaking out of a stranglehold which the current rearmament of Russia could only intensify in the future. Thus the civilian leadership was caught in a dilemma and resorted to the policies explained in Chapter 16.

16

The Outbreak of the First World War*

The debate on responsibility for the outbreak of the First World War has generated more heated controversy than any other within the survey of this book. The Allied Commission on War Guilt affirmed, in 1919, that 'The War was premeditated by the Central Powers' and that it was 'the result of acts deliberately committed in order to make it unavoidable'.[1] During the 1920s and 1930s the German government promoted a revisionist campaign in an effort to rescind the War Guilt clause of the Treaty of Versailles, by stressing collective responsibility for the outbreak of war in 1914. In this it was assisted by eminent historians like H. Rothfels[2] but, it has been suggested, it allowed only certain documents to be used, concealing any evidence which was likely to impede what had become an active political campaign.[3] Meanwhile, the whole concept of German war guilt had come under scrutiny elsewhere from both politicians and historians. Lloyd George, for example, expressed reservations about the post-war treatment of Germany, while H. E. Barnes,[4] S. B. Fay,[5] and G. P. Gooch[6] all enhanced the academic side of the revisionist case.

---

* The main steps in the outbreak of the First World War were as follows. On 28 June 1914, Franz Ferdinand was assassinated at Sarajevo. The eventual response of Austria-Hungary was an ultimatum to Serbia on 23 July. When Serbia rejected one of the terms of this ultimatum, Austria-Hungary declared war on 28 July. Russia mobilized in support of Serbia on 30 July. Germany declared war on Russia on 1 August and on France on 3 August. As part of her operations against France, Germany's forces entered Belgium; this was followed, on 4 August, by the British declaration of war on Germany. The ring was completed when, on 6 August, Austria-Hungary declared war on Russia. Italy, although allied to Germany and Austria-Hungary, remained neutral in 1914.

Europe in the First World War

The Outbreak of the First World War

During the 1950s the cycle of interpretation moved again towards the position of German war guilt, with the works of A. J. P. Taylor[7] and B. E. Schmitt.[8] A further and powerful push in this direction was given by F. Fischer[9] who maintained that Germany deliberately engineered the war in pursuit of expansionist aims which were really a prelude to the designs of Hitler. Fischer's position has, during the late 1960s and the 1970s, been variously challenged and defended. Critics include G. Ritter[10] and, more recently, L. C. F. Turner,[11] while elements of the Fischer thesis have been accepted by I. Geiss,[12] J. Röhl[13] and V. R. Berghahn.[14]

The interpretation presented here has three main ingredients: an assumption of basic German liability, a criticism of the negative policies of the Allies, and a broader survey of the whole system of alliances and war schedules.

*

The most aggressive powers are often the most insecure. Germany was, by 1915, confronted by several dangers. The first, described in Chapter 14, was the threat of containment at best and, at worst, of a war on two Fronts. To make matters worse, the Entente powers, and particularly France and Russia, had been greatly encouraged by the recent diplomatic embarrassment of Germany and Austria-Hungary in the Balkan Wars (1912–13) and were in the process of expanding their military capacity. The French government increased the period of conscription by one year in 1913, while the Russian army was undergoing a major programme of expansion, designed for completion by 1917. The German leadership – civilian and military – felt increasingly trapped between two powers which had considerable military potential and an apparent capacity to recover from internal crises. Russia was particularly worrying. According to Bethmann Hollweg in 1914, 'It grows and grows and hangs over us ever more heavily like a nightmare',[15] a view which was given greater edge by Jagow: 'In a few years, according to expert opinion, Russia will be ready to strike. Then she will crush us with the numbers of her soldiers.'[16] Even the economic front held few bright prospects. Bülow's trade agreement with Russia was about to lapse and, despite her clear industrial lead, Germany had fewer financial resources than France in the struggle to dominate Turkey. In an international situation which had clearly, since 1911, been

Aspects of European History 1789–1980

swinging in favour of the peripheral powers, Germany could not even feel certain of her allies. Italy was unreliable, while Austria was undergoing a serious internal crisis which was exacerbated by the growth of external Slavic pressures and which was rendering her 'weaker and more immobile'.[17] Bismarck's Dual Alliance, so long the lynchpin of German security in Central Europe, was therefore threatened with paralysis. Should the situation in the Balkans deteriorate further Austria might even fall apart, leaving Germany isolated amidst hostile neighbours, the eventuality feared above all others by Bismarck.

Was there a solution? Certainly there was no shortage of pressure groups whose shrill advocacy of forceful action reflected a confidence in the permanence of Germany's European hegemony. But the army clearly thought that such action would have to come sooner than later, for Germany's military advantage would be eliminated during the period 1912–17. On balance, the General Staff favoured a preventive war, although, it must be said, with declining enthusiasm. At a meeting between the Kaiser and his generals, held on 8 December 1912, von Moltke, the Chief of General Staff, said that war was inevitable and, he added, 'the sooner the better'.[18] Some time later, in May 1914, he acknowledged that the French were fast catching up and that 'delay meant a lessening of our chances'.[16] A preventive war could, however, still be won through the implementation of the Schlieffen Plan.

Faced with this unenviable dilemma, Bethmann Hollweg decided on what has been called a 'diagonal' policy; he sought neither to prevent a war by a diplomatic solution, nor to provoke one as openly as the army wished. In encouraging the Austrian government after Sarajevo to take military action against Serbia he was, in effect, taking a calculated risk. If Russia failed to react, Serbia would be destroyed, the Balkan threat would be eliminated, and the Entente would be weakened by a major humiliation. On the other hand, should Austrian action incur Russian retaliation, the war for which the generals were pressing would break out and Germany would smash the Entente by means of the Schlieffen Plan. Bethmann Hollweg, therefore, placed Europe on the brink in the full knowledge of what might happen, fortified by the belief that 'If war must break out, better now than in one or two years' time, when the Entente will be stronger'.[19] His whole attitude was a capitulation to the military leadership, confirming the breakdown of ultimate civilian control.

The Outbreak of the First World War

Indeed, he negated one of Bismarck's most important principles. 'We must both take care', the latter had argued in 1887, 'that the privilege of giving political advice to our monarchs does not in fact slip out of our hands and pass over to the General Staffs.'[20] The collapse of diplomatic options was so complete that Bethmann Hollweg could not pull back from war even though, at the last minute, he had second thoughts about his actions. By the beginning of August, therefore, everything had been subordinated to the most effective means of achieving a military solution. Kurt Breysig later conceded, in March 1919 that, although 'our army was the best in the world [it] perpetrated the world's worst politics'.[21]

What part did Austria-Hungary play in this crisis? The assassination at Sarajevo produced two main reactions. On the one hand, there were those, like the Foreign Minister Berchtold, and the Chief of Staff Conrad, who wanted to settle once and for all the supposed threat from Serbia. They feared that the Balkan Wars of 1912–13 had greatly increased Serbia's power, tempted her into dependence on Russia, and tipped the balance in South-Eastern Europe away from the Central Powers. They also felt that Serbia had the capacity to destabilize Austria-Hungary by inciting rebellion in southern provinces like Bosnia, Herzegovina and Slavonia. The implications of this were enormous: if the Empire's southern Slavs became restless, the northern Slavs, especially the Czechs, Poles, Slovaks and Ruthenes, might also be tempted into rebellion. The Sarajevo incident, therefore, offered an excuse to draw Serbia's sting. On the other hand, the Hungarian Prime Minister, Tisza, was more inclined to caution and negotiation, an attitude shared by some members of the governments in both Vienna and Budapest. For a time, it seemed possible that indecision might allow the assassination to slip into the past without reply. But then the resolve of the 'hawks' was stiffened by Germany's promise of unconditional support. The pendulum swung firmly in favour of those who demanded action, with the result that a harsh ultimatum was despatched to Serbia on 23 July. It is now considered unlikely that Austria-Hungary's leaders hoped that the ultimatum would make Serbia climb down, thereby giving Vienna a major diplomatic victory. Instead, it was intended to provoke Serbia's rejection, and therefore provide a pretext for an Austrian invasion. Berchtold was determined to destroy the Serbian threat not by diplomacy but by direct military action. Whatever the case, the tone of the

ultimatum antagonized most of Europe, including Austria's ally,
Italy. In fact, the Italian Foreign Minister, San Giuliano, notified
Italy's ambassadors in Berlin and Vienna that 'Austria has plainly
shown that she means to provoke a war', and that Italy was therefore
'under no obligation to go to the help of Austria' should the latter
'find herself at war with Russia'.[22]

*

Germany may, in collusion with Austria-Hungary, have precipitated the war, but the Allied powers did little to avoid it. Russia and
France appeared almost willing to accept the challenge, while
British policy, although commendable for its lack of hysteria and
pressure, was too equivocal to have any restraining influence.

Nicholas II, in an unusually aggressive mood, once said: 'The
Austrians should be forgiven nothing. They must be made to pay for
everything.'[23] This typified the intense Austrophobia into which
Russia had drifted since the Bosnian Crisis of 1908. This was due
partly to increased Russian involvement in the Balkans, itself a
reaction to defeat in the Russo-Japanese War of 1905 which had cut
off all prospects of further Russian expansion in the Far East. The
Tsar now increasingly identified Russian diplomacy with pan-
Slavism and with the aspirations of the Balkan peoples in holding
their own against the Ottoman and Austro-Hungarian empires.
There was also a profound fear that Russia was caught in the grip of,
in the words of *Novoe Vremya*, a 'tightening Teutonic ring'. The
Tsarist government found this spectre of Austro-German aggression
particularly useful as a means of diverting attention from serious
internal problems and of creating in the *Duma* a solid *bloc* of
government support from the Octobrists and Constitutional
Democrats. Little attempt was made, therefore, to moderate the
dangerous levels of chauvinism; even Sazonov and Kokovstsev had to
abandon, after 1911, Stolypin's pacific diplomacy. By 1914 there was
profound pessimism about the prospect of future peace. According to
a memorandum by Sazonov, a conference held by the Tsar on 8 (21)
February produced a consensus that a general European war was
likely, in view of the imminent collapse of Turkey and the impending Austro-Serb conflict. It was in Russia's interest to
postpone the collision until 1917 when her rearmament would be

The Outbreak of the First World War

complete, but Serbia should still be supported regardless of the consequences. The public, in the meantime, was assured that 'no clamour will frighten Russia; Russia is prepared for war'.[23] Mobilization plans had also been prepared, giving the same confidence to the Russian General Staff as the Schlieffen Plan gave to the Germans; in January 1914, for example, the Commander-in-Chief, Jhilinski, assured a dubious Kokovstsev that Russia was ready for a 'duel' with her enemies. The constant pressure from the General Staff served, in the long run, to blind the civilian leadership to Russia's military weaknesses. This, in turn, undermined the government's resolve not to react hastily to Austro-German provocation, so that in July 1914, Russia was the first of the major powers to undergo general mobilization.

French policies also had a strong hint of resignation to an impending struggle. Poincaré observed in 1912 that, although 'France does not want war,' nevertheless she 'does not fear it'.[24] In a powerful wave of anti-German feeling, the French military leadership under Joffre produced, in 1913, a new offensive plan designed to combat what had been deduced of German intentions. But the French government remained deeply concerned about the prospect of having to bear the brunt of a German attack. Consequently the main purpose of French diplomacy since 1911 had been to commit Russia to invading Germany with all possible speed in the event of war. This explains the virtual 'blank cheque' given to Russia by Paris during the 1912 Balkan Crisis as well as the pressure for Russian mobilization applied, in July 1914, by Laguiche and Paléologue. It would be interesting to speculate on two questions. Would France have been so anxious for Russia to play such an active role in Eastern Europe had she not been so concerned about her own security in the West? And would Russia have committed herself so irrevocably in July 1914, had she not been confident of French support, and comforted by the belief that the destination of most of the German divisions would be Paris?

The role of Britain in the July crisis erred on the side of omission rather than commission. The Foreign Secretary, Sir Edward Grey, is often blamed for not having made clear early enough, and with sufficient force, Britain's readiness to support France in the event of a German attack. There is, however, an alternative viewpoint: that Grey's intention was to defuse the situation by avoiding any aggressive statements of intent. In any case, Germany's course had already been plotted, regardless of whether or not Britain decided to intervene.[25] In a sense, the question of Britain's responsibility for the war is less significant than the change in the character of the struggle caused by her eventual entry. Events up to 1 August culminated in a European war, the result of a rash response from France and Russia to the desperate gamble of Germany and Austria. On 4 August, however, the European war became, with Britain's entry, a world war to be fought at sea and in the colonies as well as in Flanders and Poland. The British government was faced with a major dilemma. As an imperial power, it was not in Britain's interests to become involved in a continental struggle. Yet a German victory over France would destroy the continental balance of power which had enabled Britain to pursue imperial and maritime commitments. By 4 August, the Liberal cabinet had come to consider that intervention was inevitable although the justification, used to prevent a cabinet split, was the defence of Belgium against German aggression.

*

To move now to more general considerations, the climate in which Europe showed an almost suicidal willingness to rush into war was made up of three constituents. For years the Powers had harboured resentments and grievances, becoming accustomed to pushing claims in order to avoid diplomatic humiliation. This meant that the pursuit of policies of brinkmanship and the growth of a willingness to accept the risk of war. Such policies were carried out within the framework of an alliance system which had a complex pattern of military obligations, but without an international forum for diplomatic pressure. A modern equivalent would be a world in which NATO and the Warsaw Pact existed, but the United Nations Organization did not.

It used to be held that the system of alliances was, in itself, sufficient explanation for the outbreak of war; that the very existence of two armed camps made conflict inevitable sooner or later. But this approach has, for two reasons, an over-simple appreciation of the individual alliances. In the first place, the primary purpose of the alliances was defensive; the 1879 Dual Alliance had committed Germany to supporting Austria only if the latter were attacked by Russia, while the Franco-Russian Alliance

The Outbreak of the First World War

of 1894 also made mutual assistance contingent upon enemy aggression. Such terms could not, in themselves, have led to war; on the contrary, they were more likely to induce one ally to restrain the other from provoking an attack. Second, the way in which war actually broke out bore little relation to treaty obligations. Had the terms of the alliances been carried out to the letter, Germany would not have given Austria a 'blank cheque' after the Sarajevo assassination. Russia had no contractual obligation to assist Serbia and, in any case, her quarrel was with Austria, not Germany. What started as an attempt to mobilize against Austria ended as general mobilization, directed against Germany as well. Had she adhered strictly to the terms of the Alliance of 1894, France would have declared war on Germany as soon as the latter had declared war on Russia. In practice, however, it was Germany who took the initiative against France. Britain had a moral, although not a legal, obligation to assist the Entente powers, but actually entered the struggle after the German invasion of Belgium, a state with which she had no agreement at all. The alliance system also altered under the impact of the war itself. Italy and Romania pulled away from the Central Powers, later joining the Allies instead, and their place was taken by Turkey, who had had no formal diplomatic ties with Germany before 1914. It seems, therefore, that the alliances were actually less binding than their highly specific terms suggested.

There were, however, two ways in which the alliances *did* affect international relations and contribute to the growth of tension in Europe in the decade before 1914. First, they provided the links across which crises could spread from peripheral areas like North Africa and the Balkans to the major Powers themselves. Normally the dangers were seen and the connections cut; hence the Moroccan crises of 1906 and 1911 were allowed to fizzle out. But, as the sequence of events after Sarajevo showed only too clearly, the means existed whereby a local conflict could be transformed into a continental war. Second, the alliances had a direct bearing on the arms race and the development of military schedules. The Schlieffen Plan, for example, was designed to counter the Franco-Russian offensive which the German High Command assumed to be an integral part of the secret treaty of 1894. Russia would have preferred to concentrate on her major enemy, Austria-Hungary, but the Austro-German Alliance of 1879 forced her to devise a second plan, intended for use against Germany as well. As it happened, these schedules proved so inflexible that general war became inevitable once Russia mobilized on 31 July. The Tsar, faced with the choice of partial mobilization against Austria and total mobilization against Austria and Germany, started with the former but then switched to the latter. The German response was directed by the dead hand of Schlieffen. The military was committed to conquering France before tackling Russia. Thus the Tsar and the Kaiser had found themselves in a terrible dilemma. Russia's quarrel had been with Austria, but partial mobilization would have left Russia exposed to an attack by Germany. Germany's immediate need had been to put pressure on Russia, but this could not be done without first picking a quarrel with France. The military planners had concentrated so carefully on devising a technique to overwhelm the opposing alliance that they had left no room for half-measures. Each camp, obsessed with the fear of containment by the other, had allowed their General Staffs to plan only for total military victory, and not for the application of pressure backed by the threat of limited force. Clausewitz had once argued that military objectives must always be subordinate to diplomacy and that, only as a last resort, should war become 'a continuation of diplomacy by other means'. Unfortunately, the politicians of 1914 lost the initiative to the generals, who were unaccustomed to thinking in diplomatic terms.

There is a school of thought which stresses the parallels with the present nuclear confrontation. Since 1945, armed *blocs* have, as a result of their intense mutual antagonism, developed complex techniques for the deployment of offensive and defensive weapons. Sooner or later, the argument runs, these techniques will break through the political and diplomatic restraints. Political leaders will find themselves entrapped in a situation where the launching of war appears the only way out. Advocates of nuclear weapons, however, put another case. Today the very character of the weapons acts as a deterrent. War would be so fundamentally unacceptable that the balance of terror acts as a powerful restraint. This, it is held, is the basic difference with the situation in 1914. Then, war broke out largely because the prospective struggle was seen in the light of what had gone before – rapid campaigns and limited destruction. There was no new weapon, and the hints as to future developments, provided by the barbed wire in the American Civil War and the trenches in the Russo-Japanese War, had gone unheeded. The concept of the swift, clean kill was still the most powerful of all the

The Outbreak of the First World War

influences on military thinking. Ludendorff, for example, argued in 1910: 'Everything depends on our winning the first battles.'[26] It seems that Europe was looking back to the 1860s and Bismarck's spectacular victories, having, in the meantime, discarded the safeguards which he had attemped to build in the 1870s and 1880s.

17

The Collapse of Austria-Hungary and the Problems of the Successor States

Of the European powers the Ottoman Empire and Austria-Hungary were most directly vulnerable to the threat of internal disintegration. By 1914 the former had been forced to concede independence to its Balkan subjects. Austria-Hungary, however, still held together. More than ever, its existence was imperilled by powerful centrifugal tendencies, but these were, for the time being, restrained by centripetal influences. The future of the Habsburg Empire was literally in the balance.

The most obvious of the centrifugal forces was the Empire's racial tensions. Chapter 6 examined the problem presented to the German Austrians by Hungarian separatism. This had eventually been resolved by the *Ausgleich* (1867), which had granted Hungary autonomy within a federal state which was run by parallel institutions. But, between them, the Germans and the Magyars accounted for only twenty-two million of the Empire's fifty million inhabitants, and a new threat had emerged from the 23.5 million Slavs, who had been excluded from the privileges conferred by the *Ausgleich*. The Austrian half of the Empire, in particular, suffered from the conflict of sectional interests which affected, for example, the dealings between the Bohemian Diets and the Vienna government. Even the grant of universal suffrage in 1907 had not satisfied Slav opinion, for the electoral system was loaded in favour of the German voters. On the other hand, the Germans were still in a minority in the Austrian parliament and any legislative programme could be impeded by determined opposition from the Slavs. The

Austria-Hungary and the Successor States

situation was not helped by the Emperor Franz Joseph, who followed the traditional Habsburg dynastic policy of avoiding identification with any individual nationality, and promoting a balance of national antagonisms.

He also reckoned on his dominions being held together by centripetal forces, both internal and external. The strongest internal influence was the accord with Hungary. But there were also many instances of co-operation between the Germans and the Slav aristocracies of Croatia and Polish Galicia who valued their social status more highly than their racial affinities with the Czechs and Serbs. Another bond between the different regions of the Empire was the economic benefit conferred by one of the largest free trade areas in Europe. Hungarian grain, for example, had unrestricted access to Bohemian and Austrian markets, while Bohemian industrial products found outlets in Hungary. The greatest *external* check to disintegration was the existence, on the Empire's eastern frontier, of the Russian autocracy. This had fallen far behind in constitutional development and would, in its extreme pan-Slav fervour, attempt to dominate any newly emergent state. The peoples of Eastern and Central Europe also feared the prospect of interference by Imperial Germany should Austria-Hungary ever break up. Without exception, therefore, the subject races sought reform within the framework of the existing state. The Nationality Programme, drawn up in Brno in 1899, proposed a new *Ausgleich* which would give the Slavs the same status as that already conceded to the Magyars, while one of the leaders of the Austrian Social Democrats, Bauer, pressed in 1911 for a 'federation of autonomous nations'. When Austria-Hungary went to war in 1914 the main hope of the subject peoples was a rapid victory which would induce a grateful Emperor to preside over the necessary constitutional arrangements. Few people thought in terms of using the war to promote revolution or secession.

By 1918, however, the situation had changed dramatically. Military defeat caused the breakdown of government and consequently destroyed the centripetal influences. This released the centrifugal forces from their restraints and caused the Empire to disintegrate into its national components.

Austria-Hungary experienced a prolonged military crisis from 1915 onwards; the Russians occupied Galicia, and the Italians, who entered the war by the Treaty of London in the same year, threatened the southern frontier. Attempts to negotiate a separate armistice with the Allies failed miserably, and the Empire became totally dependent on Germany for its military survival. Meanwhile, the normal process of government had seized up, with the well-intentioned but inexperienced Emperor Charles being unable to maintain the constitutional ties with Hungary. Within the Austrian half of the monarchy the Slavs were alienated by the introduction of military zones and martial law. Even the economic arguments for imperial unity were fast disappearing. The entire Danubian basin was dislocated as a result of a series of bad harvests and the Allied blockades. Increasingly, therefore, each part of the Empire was forced into self-sufficiency. To make matters worse, the March Revolution of 1917 disposed of the bogy of Tsarist oppression and relieved Austria's Slavs of one of their greatest fears. Russia's new Provisional Government actually gave an incentive to separatism within the Habsburg Empire by openly acknowledging the 'right of the nations to decide their own destinies'. The Bolshevik Revolution (October 1917) seemed to confirm this policy and, in any case, turned Russia in upon herself. The other external restraint on disintegration, Germany, was finally defeated in November 1918. It is no coincidence that the imminence of this defeat accelerated the break-up of Austria-Hungary.

During the course of the war the different nationalities gradually came round to the view that their ends would best be served by complete secession from Habsburg rule. Hence Masaryk and Beneš, Czech leaders in exile, canvassed support in France for the creation of an independent Czechoslovakia, while the Serbs and Croats on the Yugoslav Committee signed the Pact of Corfu with Serbia and made preparations for the establishment of a southern Slav state. International conferences, like the Congress of Oppressed Nationalities held in Rome in April 1918, propagated the arguments for national self-determination and brought Slavs throughout the Empire into contact with their fellows in other countries. These external contacts helped to broaden political perspectives and to undermine any remaining particularist attachments to the Habsburg Empire.

What role did the Western Allies play in all this? The charge was later levelled against them that they deliberately promoted the collapse of Austria-Hungary as a means of guaranteeing victory against Germany in the West. The truth is rather more complex, revealing considerable interplay between the Allies and the

Austria-Hungary and the Successor States

nationalities of the Empire. At first the Allied war leaders favoured keeping Austria-Hungary intact as a bulwark against Germany and as a precaution against the 'Balkanization' of Central Europe. But, during the course of 1918, they were gradually convinced by the Slav émigrés and the congresses that the collapse of the Empire was inevitable. A key factor in this change was the failure to negotiate a separate armistice with the Empire; when the Spa Agreement of May 1918 tied the Habsburgs more closely than ever to the Hohenzollerns, the Allied leaders lost patience and became more explicitly in favour of creating separate states in the Danube region. In October 1918, President Wilson refused to accept the Emperor's offer of an armistice on the basis of limited provincial autonomy, insisting, instead, on self-determination, even if new states had to be brought into existence. This policy undoubtedly accelerated the collapse of the Empire as, indeed, it was intended to. By the time of Charles' abdication (11 November), Austria-Hungary no longer existed.

*

The Versailles Settlement formally acknowledged the existence of Czechoslovakia as a new state and, by the Treaties of St. Germain and Trianon, confirmed the cession of Galicia to Poland, Transylvania to Romania, Croatia and Bosnia-Herzegovina to Serbia, and the South Tyrol and Trentino to Italy. Austria and Hungary were now merely the German and Magyar rumps of the old Empire. Masaryk, like most of his contemporaries, applauded the new order which had 'shorn nationalism of its negative character by setting oppressed peoples on their feet'.[1] It soon became apparent, however, that the new states were engaged in a desperate struggle for survival, and some observers looked nostalgically back to the days of the multi-national Empire. One of these was the historian E. Eyck, who regarded the 'dismemberment of the Austro-Hungarian state' as a 'basic error'.[2] More recently, A. J. P. Taylor has pointed to the transitory nature of the Empire, but also to the difficulty of managing without it: 'The dynastic Empire sustained central Europe as a plaster cast sustains a broken limb; though it had to be destroyed before movement was possible, its removal did not make movement successful or even easy.'[3]

The Slav peoples of Central Europe were treated generously by the Versailles Settlement. The Allies made every effort to implement, in

159

(a) The structure and composition of Austria–Hungary 1867–1918 (* = Slavs)

Austria, comprising:
  Germans
  * Czechs
  * Poles
  * Ruthenes
  * Slovenes
  * Serbs and Croats
  Italians
  Romanians
  Magyars

Hungary, comprising:
  Magyars
  Romanians
  Germans
  * Slovaks
  * Croats
  * Serbs
  * Ruthenes
  Others

Bosnia–Herzegovina (annexed by the Empire 1908), comprising:
  * Serbs
  * Croats

(b) The break-up of Austria–Hungary

~ Boundaries shown are those for 1919–38

The extent of Austria–Hungary before break-up

Austria-Hungary and the successor states

their favour, Wilson's principle of national self-determination and, at the same time, to give them frontiers which could be defended and an economic base which had both industrial and agricultural potential. Poland, Czechoslovakia and Yugoslavia all emerged as larger and more populous states than either Austria or Hungary, whose boundaries were pulled back further than even the gloomiest pessimists had feared. Two problems emerged as a result of this disparate treatment. First, the formation of viable states was accomplished only by the inclusion of sizeable minorities. Of the twenty-seven million inhabitants in Poland, only eighteen million were Poles, while Czechoslovakia's 14.5 million people included 3.1 million Sudeten Germans who had been placed under Czech rule because their border area was an integral part of Bohemia's industrial economy. There was, among the advocates of national self-determination, a certain resignation to the inevitability of such anomalies; King Albert of the Belgians, for example, defended the decisions of the statesmen of Versailles thus: 'What would you have? They did what they could.'[4] The second problem was the uneasy relationship between the different types of Slavs who had been brought together as co-nationals. Slovaks accused Czechs of monopolizing government positions, a charge which was also levelled in Yugoslavia by the Croats against the Serbs. Some historians consider that the nationalist tensions which existed within the Danube area were worse after the dissolution of the Empire than they had ever been before. And yet the different peoples, with the possible exceptions of the Austrian Germans and the Croatian aristocracy, had no desire to see the restoration of the fallen dynasty.

Inevitably, the new states of Central Europe received disproportionate amounts of the resources, industries and agricultural land of Austria-Hungary. Czechoslovakia inherited only twenty-seven per cent of the Empire's population but nearly eighty per cent of its heavy industry, sufficient to enable her to compete successfully with many Western industrial states. Hungary was less fortunate; although she received between eighty per cent and ninety per cent of specialized engineering and wood processing plants, these had access to eighty-nine per cent less iron ore and eighty-five per cent less timber. There was also serious disruption in what had, since 1775, been a free trade area of some fifty million inhabitants. The connection between Hungarian agriculture and Austrian and

Aspects of European History 1789–1980

Bohemian industry has already been noted; the interrelationship could also be more specialized. In the textile industry, for example, most of the spinning was concentrated in Austria, and the weaving in Bohemia. From 1919, however, each of the newly independent nations had to build up those areas of their economies which had not previously been developed in order to create a more balanced agricultural and industrial base. Hence Hungary built up her heavy industry, Austria her weaving and Czechoslovakia her spinning. The result was frantic competition and the emergence of protective tariff barriers. By 1927 Austria's import duties averaged 18.6 per cent, Hungary's 30.7 per cent, Poland's 43.4 per cent and Romania's 99.2 per cent. Attempts *were* made to recreate a Danubian free trade area and to promote co-operation as well as competition, but these invariably foundered. In their struggle for economic survival, the new states of Central and Eastern Europe, with the exception of Czechoslovakia, came to accept the general principles of self-sufficiency and autarky. Whatever success they managed to achieve was, however, wrecked by the Great Depression. The resulting dependence on Germany and its sinister implications are dealt with in Chapter 22.

A great deal of thought had gone into the preparation of the constitutions of the successor states in 1918 and 1919. The view of the Allied leaders, especially President Wilson, was that future peace and stability in Europe would best be preserved by the spread of democracy. Consequently, all the most advanced features of Western democratic thought were enshrined in the new régimes, including universal suffrage, proportional representation, provision for referenda on key issues, and elected presidencies. One of the great disappointments in the inter-war period was that these constitutions failed to work properly in any country in Eastern and Central Europe, with the single exception of Czechoslovakia. Various reasons have been advanced for this. Much of the area had previously experienced only the autocracy of Tsarist Russia or the milder but very limited constitutional monarchy of the Habsburgs. It was, therefore, unduly optimistic to expect that a country like Poland, with no recent experience of self-government, could operate the type of constitution which baffled even the experienced politicians of the Third French Republic. Secondly, the new states, being heterogeneous in their racial composition, were bound to be sectional in their attitude to politics; hence the rivalry between

Austria-Hungary and the Successor States

political parties would often amount to open hatred. And thirdly, the pressure of economic problems, before and after 1929, hastened the emergence of authoritarian régimes. Hungary was the first to swing to the right as the Horthy and Bethlen régimes of the 1920s sought to eliminate the type of radicalism which had, in 1919, been implanted by Bela Kun. Pilsudski virtually scrapped parliamentary democracy in Poland in 1930, while Austria, torn apart by the conflict between Social Democrats and Christian Socialists, eventually succumbed to the corporate policies of Dollfuss and Schuschnigg. The most dramatic trend, however, was the growing reliance of the successor states on the Fascist dictatorships, especially Germany.

This confirmed the worst fears of those Allied leaders who had once argued for the preservation of Austria-Hungary. If, they had insisted, Balkanization occurred, it would be only a matter of time before some expansionist power brought the whole area under its influence. After 1920, two clearly defined *blocs* began to emerge among the successor states. One, which consisted of Austria and Hungary, sought to revise the Versailles Settlement and were the first to gravitate towards Germany during the 1930s, a trend completed by the *Anschluss* and Hungary's membership of Hitler's Anti-Comintern Pact. The second *bloc* comprised Poland, Czechoslovakia, Yugoslavia and Romania. These states formed close diplomatic links with each other and relied upon the guarantee of French protection against any external aggression. During the 1930s, however, French influence in Central and Eastern Europe collapsed dramatically and, as a result, this 'Little Entente' disintegrated. Romania and Poland made their own arrangements with Germany. Only Czechoslovakia held out against German influence, but she was set upon in 1938 by Germany, Hungary and Poland, all intent upon claiming their fellow nationals in the Sudetenland, southern Slovakia and Teschen. Poland, in turn, fell victim to the Nazi war machine in September 1939, and Yugoslavia followed in 1941.

18

The Last Years of Tsarist Russia

This analysis of the final two decades of Imperial Russia will be based on two propositions. The first is that Russia experienced a series of economic and social reforms, which were, particularly between 1905 and 1914, more substantial than is often realized. The second, however, is that the forces of tradition and reaction were a serious impediment to sustained progress. The resulting dichotomy imposed a severe strain on Russian institutions, leaving them exposed to the greatest externally induced crisis in Russian history, the First World War.

*

At first sight, the political and constitutional progress made after 1905 seemed very promising, particularly when contrasted with the negative and inflexible autocracy of Alexander III (1881–94). The October Manifesto (1905) was the first acknowledgement by any Tsar that an elected bicameral legislature had a role to play in Russia's constitutional future. The new state *Duma*, in fact, could be interpreted as a logical, if overdue, development of the concessions made by Alexander II in 1864 and 1870 granting permission for the establishment of provincial *zemstvos* and urban councils. Legislative powers, initially restricted to local government, had now reached the centre. This process did not, however, lead to the decline of local initiative. On the contrary, the early twentieth century saw an increase in reforms carried out by the *zemstvos*, affecting education, health, agriculture and communications, together with

The Last Years of Tsarist Russia

more systematic inter-provincial co-operation in the form of All Russian Congresses. An essential balance, therefore, seemed to have been reached. Local activism, so important in a country the size of Russia, in no way impeded the flow of broader legislative proposals from the *Duma*. Indeed, *Duma* deputies drew from the *zemstvos* experience of constitutional procedure while, at the same time, they broadened and redefined their reforming objectives as national party programmes. The Constitutional Democrats, for example, could be seen as a typical example of Western liberalism, evolving from a series of local interest groups into a cohesive and moderate force for progressive constitutional change. An encouraging sign for Russia's future political stability was that the Constitutional Democrats were usually in broad agreement with the Octobrists, or moderate conservatives. This made possible a broad consensus against attempts to interrupt the evolutionary process made by the extreme Right (especially the Union of Russian People), and by the extreme Left (including the Social Democrats).

Constitutional development was, however, impeded by official conservatism. The latter was given a powerful philosophical base by Pobedonostsev, Procurator-General of the Holy Synod between 1880 and 1905, mentor to Alexander III, and tutor to Nicholas II. His premise that humanity was infinitely corruptible and needed stability in the form of a permanently structured society led him to reject parliamentarism as 'the greatest falsehood of our time',[1] and to stress 'The whole secret of Russian order and prosperity is in the top, in the person of the supreme authority'.[2] His views, like those of Metternich, expressed the established order's growing fear of radical forces, and defined the nature of its response to them. It was unfortunate that the two traditional pillars of Tsarist power, autocracy and bureaucracy, should have been so well equipped with theoretical justification at the very time that the new 'constitutional experiment' was under way.

Nicholas II made it clear that the Constitution which he had been forced to concede as a result of the events of 1905 would not affect his basic powers. In a speech to the *Duma* in 1906 he announced: 'Let it be known to all that I . . . shall maintain the principle of autocracy just as firmly and unflinchingly as did my unforgettable dead father.'[3] This intention was soon embodied in Article 47 of the Fundamental Laws which made 'positive laws, statutes and regulations' directly dependent on 'the Autocratic power'. Everything possible was done to circumscribe the rights of the *Duma*. Although the interpellation of the Tsar's ministers by the *Duma* was a theoretical possibility, their removal was not; this immediately established that the legislature had no real control of the personnel of the executive. Although the budget could be debated, the *Duma* had no means of preventing its enactment, nor even of checking the calculations made by the State Comptroller; this removed the legislature's competence over financial matters. Although the *Duma*, together with the Upper Chamber (the State Council) could pass reforms, the Tsar retained the all-important power of veto; this was extended by Article 87 of the Fundamental Laws into a right to rule by decree when the legislature had been prorogued or dissolved. Thus, concessions granted with one hand had been snatched away by the other, leaving a parliament which was frustrated and embittered by the knowledge that it was a mere shadow of the Western institutions it hoped to emulate. Conflict between the executive and legislature disposed of the First *Duma* in 1906 and the Second in the following year. The alteration of the electoral law in 1907 produced a less belligerent parliament which lasted its full term until 1912, but the Fourth *Duma* (1912–17) revived the claims of the legislature against those of autocracy. One of the tragedies of the whole period was that the liberal intelligentsia were arbitrarily excluded from the reality of power, with the result that it became less and less inclined to co-operate with the Tsar's cabinet and bureaucracy.

The bureaucracy had, after the reforms of Speransky (1809–11), been a progressive force. By the twentieth century, however, many of its features were clearly anachronistic. It failed to co-operate with any representative institutions, and central government officials constantly tried to reduce the authority of the *Duma*, the *zemstvos*, and the numerous voluntary organizations which sprang up after 1900. Hence the volume of reforms produced by the *zemstvos*, although impressive, was far below their real potential. Gradovsky commented: 'In the hands of governmental offices and officials remained power without competence; in the hands of the *zemstvo* institutions was concentrated competence without power'.[4] There was also a serious absence of co-ordination between the various departments of the bureaucracy. The principle of collective ministerial responsibility still did not exist, and the Tsar continued to deal with each department individually. According to Jacob Walkin, the bureaucracy had, by 1914, 'become largely sterile and

The Last Years of Tsarist Russia

obstructive',[5] with urgently needed reforms being delayed or cancelled. The unfortunate complement to a weakened legislature was, therefore, an inefficient executive.

More obvious progress occurred in the Russian economy between 1890 and 1914, the result of a series of ministerial reforms.

Industrial growth is often regarded as the major success of Nicholas II's reign. The initial boost was given by Witte's policies in the 1890s, with their emphasis on government subsidies, derived largely from foreign investment, to heavy industry. The results were spectacular. During the 1890s Russia progressed from fifth to second place among the world powers in terms of railway mileage, while her coal and steel production doubled. By placing Russia on the gold standard in 1896, Witte ensured direct monetary contact with the rest of the world, and took maximum advantage of the prevalent low interest rates. After a depression lasting from 1900 to 1905, Russia experienced, between 1906 and 1913, a second boom, with an annual growth rate of 6 per cent and a corresponding increase in foreign trade. This period saw greater economic flexibility and a lessening of government involvement as conditions for private enterprise became more favourable. These included a greater demand among the peasantry for consumer goods, and a wider availability of domestic capital which reduced the necessity of government action to secure investment from abroad. Many industrialists and economists, inside and outside the country, believed that Russia was well on the way to catching up with the West.

But was she? In many ways, the industrial sector remained sluggish, and it is possible that government involvement, which had given it the initial shove, would eventually have acted as a brake as well. Russian industry found itself in a paradoxical position. On the one hand, there was a smaller entrepreneurial class than elsewhere, which could be supplemented only by government-sponsored activity. On the other hand, this activity was criticized, long before 1914, by the very industrialists it was intended to benefit. There were numerous complaints about inadequate statistical research and unnecessary bureaucratic regulations, while the Congress of the Representatives of Industry and Trade, established in 1906, applied pressure for more direct consultation by the Department of Finance. Above all, there was an underlying suspicion of the motives for industrialization. Nicholas II made no secret of his view that the whole process was intended to renovate and underpin political

167

Aspects of European History 1789–1980

autocracy. This anti-constitutional motive was separated by a huge gap from the more progressive political ideas which had accompanied industrialization in the West. Conscious of this, many Russian industrialists joined the agitation in the *Duma* for political reform, hoping thereby to exert more direct influence on government policies.

The real test of Russian economic progress was developments in agriculture. Between 1906 and 1910 Stolypin sponsored a series of measures to dispose of the anomalies which remained from Alexander II's emancipation of the serfs. Changes from 1906 enabled peasants to substitute hereditary for repartitional land tenure and to escape the enervating control of the commune. Other laws made available credit throught the Peasant Land Bank, promoted the colonization of Siberia, and abolished redemption payments. By 1913 considerable progress had been made in an economic sector which had induced deep despondency in Witte only fourteen years earlier. Over two million peasants had successfully transferred to hereditary tenure, and there was evidence of more widespread use of new farming implements and fertilizers, the inevitable result being higher yields of crops. At no stage, however, did Russian agriculture even approach the efficiency of that of the West. Moreover, Stolypin's reforms had been highly selective, intended to create a stratum of wealthy peasants which would promote political stability and provide a consumer outlet for industry. Hence, in his own words, his policy was only to 'take account of the sound and the strong'.[5] The poor and the weak, however, still made up the majority of the population, and the totally inadequate distribution of land ensured that the Russian peasantry would never emulate the conservative stability of its French counterpart.

Some historians see in the last years of Tsarist Russia an attempt by the government to spread the social base of its support through a variety of welfare reforms. The 1906 law on associations, for example, conferred basic trade union rights, and a scheme of health insurance was introduced in 1912. Annual expenditure on education quadrupled between 1900 and 1913 and the government showed greater willingness to consider the possibility of factory legislation. When compared with developments in the West, however, these reforms were inadequate and, in any case, hedged with restrictions. There is evidence that the degree of support for autocracy actually

The Last Years of Tsarist Russia

diminished in the first decade of the twentieth century. The proletariat was permanently alienated by the reception given on 22 January 1905 to Gapon's petition, and the inadequacy of government reforms after 1906 made the factory workers an ideal target for Bolshevik propaganda. The professional, commercial and industrial sectors of the middle class all resented the interference of the bureaucracy in the workings of the legislature over political and economic issues, and were made more articulate by the utterings of the intelligentsia. Finally, the nobility, for centuries the pillar of absolutism, was undergoing a crisis of its own. Some members had, out of conviction, joined the more progressive of the *zemstvos* or the liberal parties in the *Duma*, while the reactionary core were exasperated by growing economic problems. Indeed, it would be no exaggeration to say that the aristocracy no longer constituted a homogeneous class, a serious development for a régime which was becoming increasingly isolated from the rest of the people.

*

Judged by its own standards, Imperial Russia had produced some impressive achievements in the twenty years before 1914 and had experienced what was by her standards a rapid rate of evolution. But the obstacles in the way of further progress have led some historians, the 'pessimists', to conclude that revolution was inevitable, with or without the assistance of a catalyst like war. An alternative view, held by the 'optimists', is that Tsarism could have struggled on, at least into the foreseeable future. Even when it lacked the will to transform society and tried to insulate itself from radical pressures by repression, autocracy had considerable resilience and a definite capacity to survive. Revolutionary forces were, by themselves, insufficient to destroy absolutism, as was shown by the triumph of reaction in Central Europe in 1849, and, later, by the triumph of Stalin. An autocracy which was prepared to introduce basic reforms seemed to improve its prospects of overcoming radicalism. Liberals, for example, could be reconciled by the prospect of accelerated evolution; Shidlovsky, a leading representative in the *Duma*, observed before 1914: 'Give us ten more years and we are safe'.[6] To the extreme Left, reforms sponsored by the government were a serious threat. Lenin feared that Stolypin's measures could, if given time to work, insulate most of the peasantry from revolutionary activists. It seems, therefore, that Tsarism did have a chance, provided that it was spared external pressure, and that it could undergo a long period of retrenchment.

The outbreak of the First World War, however, made all the difference. Military collapse had a disastrous effect on the country's political institutions, accentuating the problems already referred to and provoking irreconcilable conflict between the executive and legislature. At the same time, the impact on the economy was so widespread that discontent reached the point of spontaneous eruption. As in Austria-Hungary, therefore, war acted as a catalyst for revolution. It did not actually cause the destruction of the existing régime, but it intensified the internal conflicts to such a degree that the basic capacity for survival was undermined.

*

Russia entered the war unprepared. The army was inadequately supplied, while leaders like the Grand Duke Nicholas, Yanush-kevich and Danilov, lacked the experience and expertise of great generals of the past or future, like Kutuzov and Zhukov. The training of the higher officer corps had been seriously defective and there was a grave lack of co-ordination between the Ministry of War and the Front. The inadequacy of the army was fully clear by mid-1915, by which time it had been compounded by a disastrous decision to imitate the scorched earth strategy of withdrawal used against Napoleon in 1812. Since this affected an enormous area, it had a devastating social and economic impact. It was criticized even by the Minister of Agriculture, Krivoshein, who warned: 'Of all the grave consequences of the war this is the most unexpected, the most threatening, the most irreparable.'[7] It also failed to prevent the slow but inexorable disintegration of the Russian army which, after all, was a microcosm of Russian society as a whole.

The collapse of the Russian offensive in 1915 convinced Nicholas II that his greatest duty was to lead the army in person. This had a disastrous impact on the administration, creating a vacuum at the centre which was filled by more irrational and arbitrary mani-festations of autocracy in the form of Rasputin and the Empress Alexandra. Although the extent of his influence was exaggerated at the time, Rasputin incurred the bitter opposition of the *Duma*, which formed a Progressive *Bloc* from the Constitutional Democrats and Octobrists to agitate for more direct legislative influence over the process of government. One of the greatest mistakes of the régime, in fact, was to ignore the efforts of voluntary associations, *Duma* committees and *zemstvo* councils to co-ordinate vital elements of the war effort like fuel, food and transport. Instead, the government assumed openly dictatorial powers, bypassing the *Duma* and issuing nearly 400 special decrees under Article 87 of the Fundamental Laws in two years. When the *Duma* was eventually prorogued until February 1917, its President, Rodzianko, warned that 'only a government that enjoys the confidence of the country could induce it to accept further privations'. Even more important than the conflict with representative institutions, however, was the alienation of the bureaucracy. The virtual abdication of the Tsar by 1915 from administrative responsibilities caused extensive disruption which produced, between 1915 and 1917, no fewer than four premiers: Goremykin, Sturmer, Trepov and Golitsin. This 'ministerial leapfrog' affected the entire bureaucracy causing, by 1917, total paralysis in the face of internal and external threats alike. According to Sazonov, 'the Government was hanging in the air and had no support either from above or below'.

The economic situation also became more and more desperate, rapidly undermining any progress made before 1914. Government policy, never renowned for creating a balance between withdrawal and involvement, now became more inconsistent than ever. At a time when the British and German governments were imposing extensive state control, the Russian administration adopted only half-measures relying, in effect, on a dual system of both state monopolies and private enterprise. These could not coexist, but when the government eventually suppressed the latter, the bureaucracy, depleted by political crisis, failed to adjust to the change. Meanwhile, the lack of systematic planning before the war resulted in serious shortages and contributed to hyper-inflation. Particularly serious was the inadequate supply of raw materials and foodstuffs; this was largely a problem of distribution and reflected badly on the decision, taken before 1914 by the Minister of Transportation, Rukhlov, to slash government expenditure on the railways. These shortages, together with a government decision to print paper money in vast quantities, stimulated price increases without allowing for corresponding adjustments in wages. The deteriorating standard of living inevitably fuelled popular discontent and was the most immediate factor in the February (March) Revolution of 1917.

The events of 23–8 February (8–13 March) were by no means

unprecedented in Russian history. The riots, strikes and demonstrations were almost entirely spontaneous and were regarded by the Empress as yet another of the country's 'hooligan movements'. The war, however, made a decisive difference. It swelled the numbers of those who were prepared to take to the streets, thus making impossible the task of enforcing law and order. In 1905 the Tsar had owed the survival of his régime to the backing of the army. By 1917, however, this had virtually disintegrated; in this respect the impact of the First World War was far greater than that of the Russo-Japanese War, which had left the army intact as an anti-revolutionary force. Finally, the government had become so discredited that the *Duma* was prepared to assume the leadership of the Revolution and put pressure on the Tsar to abdicate. Very little effort was made to resolve the problem of the succession to the throne, an indication that moderate as well as radical opinion now opposed monarchy as well as autocracy.

19

The Bolshevik Seizure and Retention of Power 1917–24

It is often assumed that the Bolshevik Revolution was completed in October 1917. Significant though this date is as one of the great turning points of modern history, the Revolution has to be seen in a broader context.

This chapter will therefore look at the whole period between 1917 and 1924, concentrating on the Bolshevik seizure of power in October 1917, the apparent vulnerability of the new régime in 1918, and its survival between 1918 and 1924.

*

There is inevitably a profound conflict of opinion over the deeper undercurrent of Russian history in 1917. This is best expressed by two of the leading protagonists in the struggle for power – Trotsky and Kerensky. At one extreme Bolshevik success is seen as part of the dialectical process, and as the completion of a movement towards a higher form of State. Trotsky, for example, argued that it represented 'the transfer of power from one class to another'.[1] The other main view is that the October Revolution was a freak occurrence, a perversion of Russia's historical trends. A well-organized minority group took advantage of administrative and social chaos to force Russian history into one of several alternative channels, and not even the widest one at that. Kerensky believed that the Bolsheviks succeeded 'only by way of conspiracy, only by way of a treacherous and armed struggle'.[2] These two views have since been echoed by

Soviet and Western historians who have been separated by the gap between the ideologies which influence their approach.

Despite the controversy about underlying trends, it is possible to find areas of agreement over the objective and immediate reasons for Bolshevik success. The analysis in this chapter will be based on the vulnerability and weaknesses of the Provisional Government, which ruled Russia from March to October, and the efficiency of the Bolsheviks who supplanted it.

The Provisional Government was precipitated into power by the spontaneous revolution in February (March) which, in turn, was the result of Russia's military collapse in the First World War. It had to pick up the pieces and create some sort of order from the chaos which it had inherited and which was not of its own making. A moderate régime, representing the centre and liberal left, it seemed to offer the prospect of reconciliation between Western and Slavic concepts of democracy. But events were against it from the start. As N. Berdyaev maintains, 'moderate people of liberal and humanist principles can never flourish in the elemental sweep of a revolution brought about by war'.[3] The situation in 1917 favoured the group with the firmest resolution, the greatest discipline and the most effective powers of coercion, attributes of the Bolsheviks rather than of liberals and moderate socialists. The collapse of a moderate régime was not, therefore, entirely surprising, especially in view of its extensive flaws.

Its main weakness was its dual base, the result of the emergence of two very different institutions. The Provisional Government itself originated from one of the committees of the *Duma*, and was formally constituted on 1 (14) March. Consisting mainly of liberals, like Lvov, Miliukov and Guchkov, it stood for the development of a Western type of parliamentary democracy. Meanwhile, on 27 February (12 March), the Petrograd Soviet had been set up to represent the working masses. It was dominated by the Left, particularly the Socialist Revolutionaries and Social Democrats who, in turn, had long been divided into Bolsheviks and Mensheviks. It was inevitable that there should be mutual suspicion between the two institutions. The Soviet, it is true, passed an early resolution to co-operate with the Provisional Government's laws 'in so far as they correspond to the interests of the proletariat and the broad democratic masses of the people'. The survival of the régime, however, depended on more than this. What was needed was nothing less than

The Bolshevik Seizure

the gradual convergence of the Provisional Government and Soviet so that any permanent constitution could embody both the parliamentary and mass traditions of Russian democracy.

What in fact happened was more complex. At first co-operation did seem possible as the Provisional Government drew some of its ministers from the Soviet. Kerensky, a Socialist Revolutionary, joined the Provisional Government from the start, while several others were invited into the broad coalition governments of May and July. From July onwards the Provisional Government was dominated by various shades of socialists rather than by its original liberal membership. But this did not guarantee harmony between the Provisional Government and the Soviet. On the contrary, they pulled apart over their conflicting policies on the continuation of the war and the redistribution of land. Kerensky increasingly identified himself with the Provisional Government rather than with the Soviet, which proceeded after April, to move further to the Left. Unfortunately, the Provisional Government appeared less and less homogeneous as Kerensky broke with the liberals as well. The latter actually pulled out of the government in protest against Kerensky's handling of the Kornilov revolt in August. By September, therefore, Kerensky had been left virtually isolated, in charge of a mere rump of a government which was separated by a wide gulf from the Soviet. To make matters worse, Kerensky became more and more aware of the tenuous nature of his claim to power. The Provisional Government was still, in the words of one historian, a 'pre-legitimate régime', as it had not yet been confirmed by parliamentary election. And yet, as Kerensky realized, to call for elections at this stage could only put the Left into power, perhaps irrevocably. He had thus become the guardian of moderation, but without the means of defending it.

Why, it could be asked, did the Socialist Revolutionaries and the Mensheviks in the Soviet not take the initiative and set up, as an alternative to Kerensky's régime, what would after all have been a majority government? The answer is that they stood for different types of socialism which could not readily be reconciled; besides which, neither had the necessary discipline or organization. Hence, the way was open for the Bolsheviks, originally a minority party, to move quickly into action and, by October, to win control of the Soviet. The difference in attitude between the Bolsheviks and the other parties of the Left had been shown in an incident at a meeting of the first All Russian Congress of Soviets in June. One of the Menshevik leaders, Tsereteli, argued that there was no real alternative to the Provisional Government. He concluded: 'At the present moment there is no political party which would say, "Give the power into our hands, go away, we will take your place." There is no such party in Russia.' Lenin was heard to say from his seat, 'There is.'[4]

Indeed, Lenin had for many years prepared for just such a situation and the Bolsheviks were in a unique position to take advantage of the weakness of the régime. Lenin had consistently emphasized the need for a tight party with a core 'of persons engaged in revolution as a profession'.[5] The Bolshevik Party was given a double objective in 1917. The first was to use its organization on behalf of the masses. Trotsky maintained that without this 'the energy of the masses would dissipate like steam not enclosed in a piston box'.[1] The Party would therefore accomplish what the masses by themselves could not: 'Just as a blacksmith cannot seize the red hot iron in his naked hand, so the proletariat cannot directly seize power.'[6] The second role was to take over the Soviet, using it as a front to legitimize the Party's revolutionary activities. From August onwards a process of political osmosis took place; the Provisional Government grew steadily weaker as support drained away from it, while the Soviet came more and more under the control of the Bolsheviks. When the latter actually achieved a numerical majority on 31 August (13 September), Lenin was able to claim that all future Bolshevik actions were to be conducted in the name of the Soviet. He said, for example, on 7 November: 'If we seize power today, we seize it not against the Soviets but for them.'[7]

Effective organization would have been to no avail without a clear overall strategy. The basic principle of the Bolsheviks was to have a fixed long-term objective, but a flexible short-term approach to it. The long-term aim was described in Lenin's *April Theses* as 'the transition from the first stage of the revolution, which gave power to the bourgeoisie . . . to the second stage, which should give power into the hands of the proletariat and the poorest strata of the peasantry'.[4] The short-term approach, however, would avoid any rigid or doctrinaire commitments. Three things, in particular, were emphasized. The first was the need for the right degree of force at the right time. Lenin spoke of a judicious alternation between withdrawal and attack, depending on the strengths and weaknesses of the opponent;

The Bolshevik Seizure

the effect, he said later, was 'an overwhelming preponderance of force at the decisive moment in the decisive points'. Secondly, the Bolsheviks should, for the moment, compromise with other parties and, if necessary, adopt elements of their programme. Thus they were prepared to help Kerensky overcome the threat of Kornilov, and they also won substantial support in the Soviet from the Mensheviks and Socialist Revolutionaries. Thirdly, the Bolsheviks made maximum use of any prevailing destructive forces in order to undermine the régime. For example, they promoted or supported regional nationalism in the local Soviets and the army, especially in the Ukraine. They realized that these tactics would break the power of the Provisional Government over all but the core of Russia.

What was the importance of Lenin's personal role in all this? There is general agreement among historians that the October Revolution could not have occurred without him.[8] They all point to his personal charisma and powers of oratory and, even more important, to his influence as the overall leader and strategist. His return from exile in April 1917 ended months of uncertainty and internal divisions within the Party and provided an authoritarian base which promoted a degree of discipline and unity which the other parties lacked. In a sense, Lenin's monolithic power base looked back to the days of the Tsar, providing the only realistic prospect of restoring order after the collapse of Tsarist rule. Above all, Lenin was entirely responsible for the timing of the October Revolution. He had realized that total commitment to the rising in July would have been disastrous, and he therefore urged restraint on that occasion. By October (November), however, he calculated that circumstances had changed sufficiently to warrant immediate action. On 6 November, therefore, he said: 'We must not wait! We may lose everything.'[7] In this respect, Lenin was similar to Napoleon, whose military victories depended on split-second timing. Both leaders illustrate the importance of individuals in promoting or accelerating historical trends.

*

Seizure of power in October (November) 1917 was by no means the end of the matter. The history of revolutions is littered with successful invasions from outside, or with internal Thermidorian reactions. Lenin was fully aware of this. 'It is easy for Russia in the specific, historically very unique situation of 1917 to *start* a Socialist revolution but . . . it will be more difficult for Russia than for the European countries to *continue* and consummate it.'[9] This was said in 1920, after the worst dangers had been overcome. How much bleaker must the situation have seemed in 1918?

There were two particularly serious threats to the new Bolshevik régime. The first was the possible impact of war. The Great War had been the most important catalyst in the destruction of Tsarist rule and also of the Provisional Government. There was now a danger that it would destroy the Bolsheviks as well, especially if, as was likely, it were complemented by civil war and counter-revolution. The second threat was internal. Russia could easily decompose into its national units and a political vacuum would rapidly result. By 1918, in fact, the Bolsheviks controlled an area the size only of fifteenth-century Muscovy, and even here the Socialist Revolutionaries were more popular than the Bolsheviks in electoral terms.

All the ingredients existed for the type of takeover which the Bolsheviks themselves had recently conducted. The Bolsheviks had, therefore, to switch from their previous destructive role to an unfamiliar constructive and defensive strategy. The latter was to prove far more difficult than the former.

*

The most serious danger in 1918 and 1919 was external. Aware of the new régime's vulnerability, Lenin decided to settle one struggle, the Great War, in order to concentrate on the anticipated counter-revolution and civil war. Hence, in the Treaty of Brest Litovsk (1918) he accepted the humiliating terms imposed by the victorious Germans, conceding that 'a disgraceful peace is proper, because it is in the interest of the proletarian revolution and the regeneration of Russia'.[10] The result was that the Bolsheviks were able to concentrate on the offensive launched by the Whites and the Allied powers. After initial difficulties in 1918, the Bolsheviks were, by 1919, close to victory over the White generals; the Allies considered the situation hopeless and therefore withdrew their troops and supplies. Why did this transformation take place?

The first reason was the geographical advantages possessed by the Bolsheviks. At first, they were confined to the rump of European Russia and surrounded on all sides by the enemy. Their location was, however, a source of strength; they were clearly defending the heart of the homeland, while the Whites had to campaign through more

The Bolshevik Seizure

unreliable peripheral areas. The Bolsheviks also controlled the main cities and industries and, above all, Russia's railway network, which radiated outwards from Moscow. The Whites, by contrast, had severe difficulties with transport, especially on the Trans-Siberian railway, which was usually clogged up by complex political and military disputes. The Bolsheviks made full use of their internal lines of communication, switching their defensive units rapidly as one front after another came under attack.

The second factor in the Bolshevik victory was their political homogeneity, a clear contrast to the serious disunity of their opponents. The Bolsheviks had a clear and systematic ideology and used their monopoly over all forms of communication to put across their skilfully prepared propaganda. Their opponents, by contrast, had no overall programme, let alone a single ideology. In fact, they represented the entire range of the political spectrum, ranging from left-wing parties like the Mensheviks and Socialist Revolutionaries, through liberal elements like the Cadets and Octobrists, to right-wing conservatives. Agreement on an alternative régime was out of the question, since the various possibilities were mutually exclusive. How, for example, could the advocates of a socialist republic hope to find common ground with those who wanted the return of Tsarist autocracy? The areas under actual White control were also subject to political problems and divisions – Siberia, for example, had no fewer than nineteen governments early in 1918. Even the Allies, whose interventionist forces were intended to assist the Whites, could not agree on the motives for their involvement, let alone their strategy. Japan and the United States, for instance, found themselves in bitter dispute over economic concessions in Siberia. Eventually the Western powers lost interest in the civil war and those statesmen who, like Churchill and Milner, wanted to continue the anti-Bolshevik crusade, were very much in a minority. By the end of 1920 the British government had heeded the threat of the trade union movement about the possible consequences of further involvement in Russia, while the French government had switched its strategy to containing Communism by preventing its spread to Poland and the rest of Eastern Europe.

Above all, there was an enormous difference between the military efficiency of the Bolsheviks and the shortcomings of the Whites. Trotsky's Red Army, created in 1918, made use of a large number of ex-Tsarist officers, but ensured their permanent loyalty by

179

subordinating them to political commissars who were, in effect, agents of the Party. At the same time, promotion was encouraged from the ranks; this eventually produced top-class generals like Voroshilov, Budyonny, Yakir and Timoshenko. Conscription, introduced in 1918, increased the size of the Red Army from 550,000 in September 1918 to three million in 1919 and 5.5 million in 1920. The Whites, meanwhile, were debilitated by the lack of overall command and of a basic strategy, so that their campaigns invariably fizzled out. Despite the formidable threat implied by Yudenich's advance on Petrograd, Kolchak's move towards the eastern frontier and Deniken's march on Moscow, all the White offences collapsed through poor timing. Even the supporting powers were indecisive; no specific military functions were given to the units landing at Murmansk and Archangel, and the numbers, in any case, were small because of the needs throughout 1918 of the Western Front in France. The Allies also failed to set up an overall War Council to co-ordinate their campaigns. Trotsky pointed out the enormous potential strength of the Allies and stated that when they 'manage to act unanimously and to undertake a campaign against us, we shall be lost'. But, he added, this would 'absolutely not occur'.[11]

In any civil war the attitudes of the civilian population are vitally important. Although they had only minority support in the 1918 elections to the Constituent Assembly, the Bolsheviks came to be seen by the inhabitants in the various war zones as less of a threat than the Whites to their livelihood. The peasantry, for example, feared that the Whites would return the powerful landlords and reimpose the former dues and obligations. Also, the White armies had to live off the land and some of their campaigns produced serious damage through pillage and looting. One of the Whites' major problems was that the peripheral areas under their control were strongly opposed to any programme for reunifying Russia. Self-determination was the key demand of the Ukranians, Poles, Baltic peoples, Caucasians and many others. Thus Deniken and Kolchak, committed to restoring the frontiers of Tsarist Russia, had to deal with highly unstable local politics; indeed Deniken had to divert some of his resources to deal with Ukranian separatists and bands of marauding peasants. Lenin and Trotsky followed a characteristically opportunist policy of supporting this separatism against the Whites and, once the Whites had been cleared out, of crushing it with the Red Army.

The Bolshevik Seizure

Meanwhile, the Bolsheviks had gained firm control over all the institutions of the state. The main development was a move away from a mixed democracy, with different types of representative institutions, towards a more homogeneous base consisting of Soviets and Party. The first casualty of this trend was the Constituent Assembly. At first, the Bolsheviks considered themselves committed to calling this, since Lenin had promised immediate elections. The result, however, was a sweeping majority for the Socialist Revolutionaries, who won 410 seats to the Bolsheviks' 175. Lenin now proceeded to attack the Constituent Assembly as a bourgeois institution, 'an expression of the old relation of political forces which existed when power was held by the compromisers and the Cadets'.[12] He was, therefore, determined to exclude the bourgeoisie from power and to move more directly towards the establishment of a proletarian state. The Constituent Assembly was dissolved and all future legislation was enacted by the Soviets. At the same time, the two new constitutions of 1918 and 1922 subordinated the new hierarchy of Soviets to the corresponding committees of the Party. A new form of democracy had therefore appeared; instead of the Party being forced to work within the constraints of the constitution, the constitution existed to transmit more effectively the policy of the Party. This was the recipe for permanent Bolshevik rule and accorded well with Lenin's concept of the dictatorship of the proletariat.

This process of Bolshevizing Russian democracy was accomplished by two techniques which, although different, were complementary: terror and concessions.

Terror had not originally been an integral part of the Bolshevik programme but, as Lenin was swift to point out, there had been numerous historical precedents, including the famous Jacobin Terror of the French Revolution. The Bolshevik leaders increasingly used violence to destroy all opposition and any remnants of either Western democracy or Tsarism. 'We want', said Lenin, 'to organize violence in the name of the interests of the workers.'[13] The question of the legality of such methods did not arise, for 'Dictatorship is power-based directly upon force, and unrestricted by any laws'.[14] Nor was morality an issue, for 'we say that our morality is wholly subordinated to the interests of the class war waged by the proletariat'.[13] It may well be necessary, Trotsky argued, to use extreme methods to achieve the desired results, for 'we shall not enter into the kingdom of socialism in white gloves on a polished

181

floor'.[15] Hence Bolshevik leaders were convinced of the need for institutions like the *Cheka** and for direct action against the Cadets in 1918 and the Socialist Revolutionaries in 1922. Since they had the complete monopoly of the use of Terror, the Bolsheviks made retaliation impossible; despite the widespread support which they undoubtedly commanded, the Socialist Revolutionaries had no vehicle for transmitting their opposition. The Bolsheviks also managed to avoid turning the Terror inwards. There was no repetition of the internecine conflict which had destroyed Hébert, Danton, Robespierre and other Jacobin leaders between 1793 and 1794.

To ensure that the Bolsheviks did not achieve a reputation for undiluted terror, Lenin also compromised whenever he considered that strategic withdrawal was necessary. Indeed, he seemed to follow the motion of two steps forward, one step backward. The period 1918–24 provides two major examples of this: his attitudes to federalism and the economy. Lenin had originally opposed on principle any form of national self-determination, except as a means of destroying the war effort of the Whites. But in 1918, and again in 1922, he acknowledged that federalism could prevent the threat of future disintegration, and he consented to the formation of the two largest federations in the world, the Russian Socialist Federated Soviet Republic and the Union of Soviet Socialist Republics. At the same time, the price of regional autonomy was close supervision at all levels by the appropriate organs of the Party. Lenin's retreat on economic principles was even more fundamental as in 1921 he transformed war communism into his New Economic Policy. His main reason was that coercion alone could 'ruin the whole course'. There was also an implicit admission that his economic strategy would take longer to achieve than he had originally anticipated because of the inherent conservatism of the peasantry. In the meantime, therefore, tactics should include a form of 'state capitalism', provided, of course, this in no way interfered with Lenin's political changes.

*

The years 1922–4 should have been a highpoint of the Bolshevik régime. The external threat had been overcome and Communism

---

* Extraordinary Commission for the Suppression of Counter Revolution, Speculation and Sabotage; the forerunner of the NKVD and the KGB.

The Bolshevik Seizure

had been established internally as a permanent and irrevocable system of government. Yet there were already signs of disenchantment. Victor Serge, a prominent Bolshevik, later complained that 'emergent totalitarianism had already gone half way to crushing us'.[16] Trotsky was by now attacking Stalin for aspiring to personal dictatorship. Lenin, clearly concerned about the possible trend of Bolshevism in the future, tried to demote Stalin and the *Cheka* chief, Dzerzhinsky. One of his main fears in the last year of his life was that the Bolsheviks had revived some of the underlying features of the detested Tsarist régime and had provided 'only a Soviet veneer'.

20

Two Views of the Terms of the Treaty of Versailles

The Treaty of Versailles, which dealt with Germany, was signed on 28 June 1919. In summary, it affirmed, by Article 231, the responsibility of 'Germany and her Allies' for the outbreak of the First World War and, accordingly, made provision for territorial adjustments, demilitarization and economic compensation to the victorious Allies for the losses which they had incurred. Germany was relieved of Alsace-Lorraine, Eupen and Malmedy, Northern Schleswig, Posen, West Prussia, parts of Southern Silesia, and all her overseas colonies. Limits were placed on her naval capacity, her army was restricted to 100,000 volunteers, and the Rhineland was demilitarized. A considerable quantity of rolling stock and merchant shipping was also removed, while France was given exclusive rights to the coal mines of the Saar region. Finally, provision was made for the payment of reparations by the German government, the amount eventually being fixed in 1921 at 136,000 million gold marks. Altogether, it has been estimated, Germany lost 13 per cent of her area, 12 per cent of her population, 16 per cent of her coal, 48 per cent of her iron, 15 per cent of her agricultural land and 10 per cent of her manufactures.

*

Was this a fair settlement? There is a longstanding tradition that it was not. This originated with the forebodings of contemporary diplomats and observers like Harold Nicolson[1] and Norman H. Davies, of the outspoken economist J. M. Keynes,[2] and of the

The Terms of the Treaty of Versailles

historian W. H. Dawson.[3] Although the sympathy for Germany was subsequently diluted by the rise of Hitler, there emerged a feeling that the Versailles Settlement could well have contributed to the destructive phenomenon of Nazism. It then became common to question, in retrospect, the wisdom of visiting the guilt of the Kaiser's Germany upon a moderate republic which had been engaged in a desperate struggle for survival against the forces of the extreme Right. German historiography, meanwhile, had maintained a constant attack on the Versailles *Diktat*, whether from the viewpoint of moderates like Brandenburg and Rothfels, or of the textbook writers for the *Nationalsozialistische Lehrerbund* (Nazi Teachers' Association). Although recent German historians like F. Fischer have, by reviving the whole question of German war guilt (see Chapter 16), brought about a re-examination of the Versailles Settlement, the majority of German writers still favour the traditional view; a typical example of the latter is Hannah Vogt, whose textbook[4] is of the type widely used throughout West Germany, and whose approach to the question is similar to that employed by many teachers in England.

By combining some of these sources it is possible to build up a composite criticism of the Treaty of Versailles. On the question of territorial changes there is some support for the implementation of national self-determination, but considerable criticism of the uneven use of the plebiscite. Why, for example, should this facility have been given to the Danes of Northern Schleswig and the Poles and Czechs of Southern Silesia, but not to the Germans of the Sudetenland or of Austria? Referring to the existence of large and disaffected German minorities in countries like Czechoslovakia and Poland, W. H. Dawson claimed that Germany's frontiers 'are literally bleeding. From them oozes out the life-blood, physical, spiritual and material of large populations'.[5] Poland, in particular, had been treated too generously at Germany's expense, a 'clear perversion' of the thirteenth of President Wilson's Fourteen Points.[5] As for the confiscation of Germany's colonies, many observers pointed to an element of hypocrisy. Wilson's avowed reason for removing regions like South-West Africa and Rwanda-Urundi from German administration was to protect the inhabitants from the proven harshness of German rule. Yet, some of the states which received them as mandates could hardly claim exemplary records: South Africa and Belgium, for example.

Aspects of European History 1789–1980

The most influential critic of the economic provisions of the Treaty was J. M. Keynes. He argued that the Settlement lacked wisdom in its aim to destroy Germany's very means of subsistence. The coal and iron provisions, for example, were 'inexpedient and disastrous'. Germany would be left with a capacity to produce only sixty million tons per annum, whereas in 1913 she had consumed 110 million tons. The situation was aggravated by the damage done to German commerce by the restrictions imposed on ship building and by the new system of protective tariffs against German exports. Above all, the indemnity being considered by the Allies in 1919 was well beyond Germany's means to pay. It was clear to Keynes, who resigned his position in the British delegation in protest, that the real dangers for the future lay not in boundary questions 'but rather in questions of food, coal and commerce'. He remained convinced that 'The Treaty, by overstepping the limits of the possible, has in practice settled nothing'. The subsequent economic crisis suffered by the Weimar Republic, including the collapse of the mark in 1923, seemed to provide immediate evidence to support his prediction.

Why did a treaty of such severity emerge in the first place? The reason most commonly given was that the ideals of President Wilson were heavily diluted by the revanchism of Clemenceau and the pragmatism of Lloyd George. In the words of Harold Nicolson: 'We arrived as fervent apprentices in the school of President Wilson: we left as renegades.'[6] According to H. Vogt, Clemenceau influenced the whole proceedings because 'he knew only one goal: security for France!'[7] The British delegation took a more moderate stance, but Lloyd George was, nevertheless, under heavy pressure from public opinion at home to make Germany pay for all the damage caused during the war. The bargaining position of Wilson was also weakened by disenchantment within the United States with the whole idea of involvement in European affairs. The overall result was inevitably the triumph of expediency over ideals leading, in Nicolson's view, to a 'deterioration of moral awareness'.[6]

There could be only one solution. Contemporary critics of the Settlement were unanimous in their demand for its alteration; according to Keynes, 'the revision of the treaty is the necessary and inevitable first step forward'.[8] There were certainly to be steps in this direction. In 1924, the Dawes Plan modified the method of paying reparations, while the Young Plan of 1930 extended the deadline, and the Lausanne Agreement of 1932 cancelled all out-

The Terms of the Treaty of Versailles

standing reparations. Meanwhile, all occupation forces were withdrawn from the Rhineland by 1930 and provision was made by the League of Nations for the full return of the Saar to Germany by 1935. But critics of the Treaty maintained that these concessions were too late to reconcile German public opinion to a settlement which it bitterly loathed. There was also a strong suspicion that the real beneficiaries of any pangs of conscience aroused in the victorious Allies by Keynes and Nicolson were not so much the statesman of the Weimar Republic as the Nazis who came to power in 1933.

*

Keynes, Nicolson and Taylor were enormously influential, but it was only to be expected that their views would be contradicted sooner or later. Not surprisingly, the image of a vengeful Clemenceau imposing a 'Carthaginian' settlement was first challenged by the French Prime Minister, Tardieu,[9] some of whose views were later elaborated by E. Mantoux.[10] An American, P. Birdsall[11] also went against the prevailing tendency to attack the Treaty, and they have been followed by many modern historians; examples can be selected from writers on France (like J. Néré[12]), Germany (W. Carr[13] and A. J. Nicholls[14]) and international relations (S. Marks[15] and G. Schulz[16]). The latest wave of interpretation has produced, in the work of M. Trachtenberg[17] and W. A. McDougall,[18] a more or less complete vindication of French policy, together with heavier criticism of Germany and, more controversially, of the United States and Britain.

Another picture of the Treaty of Versailles therefore emerges. By emphasizing three points it is possible to show that the treatment of Germany was not unduly harsh. First, her territorial losses in 1919 were tiny compared with the alterations which a German victory would have brought. According to F. Fischer, Germany's war aims included economic dominance over Belgium, Holland and France; hegemony over Courland, Livonia, Estonia, Lithuania and Poland in Eastern Europe, and over Bulgaria, Romania and Turkey in the Balkans; unification with Austria and the creation of a Greater Germany; and control over the entire Eastern Mediterranean and over a dismantled Russia. In sharp contrast the Allied plenipotentiaries, far from humiliating a defeated country, showed considerable restraint in removing only those ethnic minorities who

187

had clearly suffered from their inclusion in the German Reich. Second, some form of economic compensation was only to be expected, given the appalling scale of French losses; most of the Western Front had been within ten French *départements*, some of which had been totally ravaged by retreating German armies. German industries, by contrast, had largely escaped destruction since the Rhineland and Ruhr never came within the scope of Allied operations. There was, therefore, a straightforward argument for transferring some of the wealth of a complete industrial economy to assist the rebuilding of a shattered one. Third, it has not been proved conclusively that the Treaty of Versailles crippled Germany in the process of compensating France and Belgium. The chronic inflation between 1919 and 1923 was due at least as much to the German government's unrestrained issue of banknotes and to the heavy speculation by the Rhineland industrialists. There remains a strong suspicion that Germany could not meet the reparations bill because she had no intention of doing so. A general increase in taxation could have met all foreign debts and held the mark steady as well. No ministry, however, was prepared to risk the internal opposition which this would have brought; a short-term policy based on the reckless printing of paper money seemed a much easier option.

The role of France and Britain at the Paris Peace Conference has also been extensively re-assessed. (Néré, McDougall and Trachtenberg all refute the charge that France was the intransigent power and a source of constant irritation to the more moderate Britain.) It seems that France had every right to consider herself the aggrieved party between 1918 and 1923. The French originally sought to accomplish two objectives only: economic reconstruction and military security. These could be attained most effectively within the structure of an Atlantic community which would perpetuate the unity of the wartime alliance. Hence the Minister of Commerce, Clémentel, had in 1918 proposed an economic *bloc* which would operate a system of preferential tariffs and come to an agreement on currency matters. As for the future security of France, Tardieu, the French delegate, argued that a neutralized Rhineland would be the best guarantee against future German invasion. This should be related to a permanent pact between the Western powers. Once Western Europe had achieved a new strength and stability as a result of these agreements, Germany could be allowed to regain her economic and industrial status without the

The Terms of the Treaty of Versailles

danger of future aggression and war. Unfortunately, the French scheme collapsed. Clémentel's proposals were rejected by the United States, with the result that France had to depend for her economic recovery entirely on German reparations. Worse followed when, on 19 March 1920, the United States Senate refused to ratify the Treaty of Versailles. This meant that the treaty of mutual guarantee between France, the United States and Britain also crumbled. The United States withdrew from all military commitments in Europe, while Britain, whose membership of the alliance had been tied to American involvement, considered her own obligations to France ended by the Senate's decision. France was now virtually isolated and faced the prospect of containing, by herself, the inevitable revival of Germany. By 1923, moreover, it had become apparent that the German government was doing its utmost to evade fulfilling the terms of the Treaty of Versailles. Was it surprising, therefore, that Poincaré should have tried to restore the French initiative by ordering the occupation of the Ruhr?

Among the main critics of this action was the British government. But, it has been argued, the record of the British delegation at Paris was far from moderate or even consistent. The usual view that Lloyd George was a pragmatist, driven to occasional harshness only by pressure from British public opinion, will not do. If anything, the British position was more extreme than the French. Lloyd George, for example, appeared just as revanchist as Clemenceau; in 1918 he told the Imperial War Cabinet: 'The Terms of Peace must be tantamount to some penalty for the offence.'[17] In one of the sub-commissions, the British representative, Lord Cunliffe, claimed that Germany could afford to pay reparations of 120,000 million dollars, a figure which the French Minister of Industrial Reconstruction, Loucheur, rejected as too high. Although Lloyd George appeared, in his Fontainebleau Memorandum, to have been won over to moderation, the British government still put the reparations figure almost twice as high as did the French, and then complicated the proceedings by demanding the inclusion of war pensions and separations allowances as war damages. Largely because of British intransigence, the reparations figure had to be settled separately and was not announced until 1921. By this time the German government had taken comfort from the evident disintegration of the alliance between the victorious powers and had begun to probe for weaknesses in the Versailles Settlement. The country most seriously affected by this was France, who had taken a consistently reasonable line on the whole reparations issue.

No one could seriously argue that the Treaty of Versailles was a success. But, whereas the Treaty's critics maintained that the major need was fundamental revision, some of its defenders have put the case for more effective enforcement. The Settlement failed not because it was too severe, but because the alliance which formulated it fell apart with the withdrawal of the United States and Britain, and the isolation of France. Although the Treaty was propped up by Collective Security and the Locarno Pact (1925) it remained vulnerable to any German refusal to implement it. The modifications secured by the Dawes Pact (1924) were sufficient to win the temporary co-operation of moderate statesmen like Stresemann. But, in the long term, German public opinion continued to see the whole settlement as a *Diktat* and eventually supported its overthrow by the Nazi régime. Opponents of the Treaty argued that Nazism was one of its legacies; its defenders maintain that Hitler succeeded only because the Treaty was not enforced. Keynes, anticipating future problems, warned of the danger of visiting 'on the children of their enemies the misdoings of parents or of rulers'; Mantoux, looking back on an era of violence, concluded that what in fact happened 'was that the misdoings of a nation were visited on the children of its victims'.[10]

21

Mussolini

A. J. P. Taylor once described Mussolini as 'a vain blundering boaster without either ideas or aims', while the Fascism over which he presided had far less 'drive' than the Nazi movement.[1] This view will provide the basic terms of reference for the examination in this chapter of the career of Italy's dictator between 1922 and 1943. The first section will analyse his rise to power, focusing on his opportunism and the means by which he exploited the weaknesses of the establishment. The second will examine the methods by which he maintained his power, the extent to which he left the previous administrative structure standing, and the aura of the personality cult or 'Mussolinianism'. The third will deal with his decline – the result of personal defects, growing weaknesses within the system, and the damaging effects of the close connection with Nazi Germany.

*

The most striking thing about Mussolini's early years was his commitment to the extreme Left of the Socialist Party. He certainly had orthodox views on class struggle, stating in 1908 that 'the interests of the proletariat are opposed to those of the middle class. No agreement between them is possible. One or the other must disappear.'[2] He was also uncompromising in his condemnation of nationalism and imperialism, and he said of the Tripolitan venture: 'The national flag is a rag that should be placed in a dunghill'.

By 1922, however, Mussolini's beliefs had been transformed. He abandoned his attachment to the Left and announced in a speech:

'We declare war on socialism.'[3] He was also converted to the principles of the free market, claiming that capitalism constituted a centuries-old and irreplaceable set of values. Imperialism he now regarded as 'the eternal, immutable law of life',[4] while Catholicism, which he had once denounced, now became one of the sources of 'the imperial and Latin tradition of Rome'.[5]

The explanation of this *volte face* is that Mussolini's only really consistent belief was in the necessity of direct involvement. He claimed, in 1932, that 'My own doctrine . . . had always been a doctrine of action'.[2] Explaining his inconsistency over Italy's entry into the First World War, he argued: 'Only maniacs never change. New facts call for new positions'.[4] Above all else, therefore, he was an opportunist, and his real strength lay in his having no overall system and no ideological straightjacket.

This pragmatism enabled Mussolini to make full use of the chaotic conditions of post-war Italy. His rise to power was a combination of parliamentary manoeuvre and extra-parliamentary radical pressure. He played upon the weaknesses and divisions within the executive and legislature in such a way that the Fascists assumed far greater importance than the thirty-five seats which they had won in the 1921 general election would seem to warrant. He also instructed the local Fascist leaders, like Balbo, to create havoc, and early results of this activity were the capture of Ferrara by 63,000 Fascists and their successful move against the strike called by the socialists. The high point of Mussolini's emphasis on 'action', however, was the so-called 'March on Rome' in 1922, as a result of which Victor Emmanuel III was pressurized into summoning Mussolini to form the next government.

During the crucial period between 1919 and 1922 Mussolini had made the most of a critical economic situation and of the weak ministries of Orlando, Nitti, Giolitti, Bonomi and Facta. He launched a blistering attack on all the major parties in the Chamber. A headline in an issue of his newspaper, *Il Popolo*, warned: 'Gentlemen of the Government, make up your minds to grant the demands of the working masses.' Socialism he lampooned as 'a new tyranny that is merciless and also absurd'.[6] As for the liberal parties, they were basing all their policies on a 'scaffolding', behind which there was no 'structure'. He offered himself, therefore, as a unifier; hence 'Fascism draws its sword to cut the many Gordian Knots which enmesh and strangle Italian life.'[7] The opposition to his

Mussolini

emergence in the Italian parliament was weak and indecisive. Even after Mussolini had been made Prime Minister, Nitti and the moderates were opposed to any form of obstruction: 'The Fascist experiment must be carried out without interference: there must be no opposition from our side'.[8] Even the Left offered little direct opposition, except in the form of individual utterings. Matteotti, who made his own views so clear that he was murdered in 1924, rejected, nevertheless, a proposal from the Communist Party for a united front with the words: 'We are fighting Fascism for freedom: we cannot fight Fascism in the name of another dictatorship.'[8] It is hardly surprising, therefore, that contemporary observers spoke of the 'moral collapse' of parliament. Pietro Neni condemned the whole atmosphere of complacency in the Chamber in which party feuding prevented any form of united action against an organization which threatened the whole basis of the parliamentary system. Indeed, the mistaken impression arose that Mussolini could be used as a pawn in party politics and that he could be restrained from committing any excesses. Hence parliamentarians were 'under the delusion that they were cleverness itself. They fed the flame they should have quenched'.[9]

From which sections of the population did Fascism derive its support? At first it appealed to the displaced or marginal elements; like the Nazis, it was widely accepted among the unemployed. Then it attracted substantial numbers from the lower-middle class, disillusioned by their struggle for survival against the more powerful and better organized élite of the free market system. It also gained support from the demobilized soldiers and officers, students and peasants, who were won over by Fascist promises of grants to individual farmers rather than collectivization on Communist lines. Mussolini made an effort to extend the basis of his support among the urban proletariat by claiming that he agreed with the idea of workers' control of factories. At the same time, his promise to uphold capitalism and his opposition to strikes had the tacit approval of many large business corporations, while his aggressively stated brand of nationalism won favour among conservatives who were antagonized by Italy's parsimonious treatment by the settlement of St. Germain. Mussolini found it possible to appeal to such a wide cross-section of society by avoiding a definite commitment to a fixed ideology. When he finally defined Fascism in 1932, he stated that he had 'no specific doctrinal attitude in mind in these early years'.[10] His success at first was limited; in the 1921 general election, for example, he obtained only 6.5 per cent of the seats in the Chamber. Thereafter, his emphasis on 'action, action, action' paid handsomely, and the appeal of Fascism penetrated more deeply, assisted by a programme of intensive propaganda and the attractions of the cult of *Duce*.

*

How did Mussolini maintain himself in power? On being asked to form a government in 1922, he played the parliamentary game for only a few months before seeking to change the whole façade of the régime. Three constitutional laws ensured that he would not be obstructed by traditional party politics. The 1922 Electoral Law gave an automatic two-thirds majority in the Chamber of Deputies to the governing party, while the Chamber's legislative power was virtually destroyed when, in 1926, Mussolini was enabled to govern by decree. In 1928, a new electoral system was introduced whereby the Fascist Grand Council selected for a *bloc* vote the names of parliamentary candidates from lists drawn up by professional and industrial organizations. Meanwhile, opposition was carefully monitored by the secret police, OVRA. By 1929 Mussolini had shown clearly that 'Fascism is not able, does not know how, and, I add, ought not to become parliamentary'.[11] Furthermore, organized violence was 'more moral than compromise and bargaining'. Similarly, Mussolini implanted his own methods of control over the economy, through a series of 'battles' and public works programmes. Above all, he introduced the 'corporate state' under which syndicates of workers were established and brought within nationwide confederations.

One of the more surprising features of Mussolini's rule, however, is that he left a considerable part of the previous structure intact, especially the system of local prefects. In a circular issued on 5 January 1927, Mussolini ordered that Provincial Prefects must be obeyed completely by all citizens, even by prominent Fascists. The result was that the Prefects exercised far greater control over the Party than the Party possessed over the administration. Indeed, the Fascist Party contributed little to the formulation of policy and Mussolini ensured that it never became as cohesive as the Russian Communist Party or the German Nazi Party by playing off the members of the Grand Council against each other. He also insisted

Mussolini

on widespread membership of the Party, thus deliberately devaluing this privilege. Finally, he made the administrative machine more complex, increased the number of departmental personnel and, in A. Lyttelton's phrase, 'deliberately fostered untidiness and illogicality in the structure of government'.[12] Why?

The main reason was that Mussolini intended to rule by balancing the different elements which made up the state and the Party. His basic fear was that one or more of these elements might eventually challenge his authority, and the greatest immediate threat seemed to come from the Fascist Party itself. Hence he took the drastic but logical step of depoliticizing the régime. The result was a strange paradox: the strength of Fascism depended on the weakness of Fascist organizations or, to put it another way, a movement which was famed for its activism was encouraged by its leader to show inertia. Mussolini was deliberately creating a vacuum in the political and administrative structure where one would normally expect to find a ruling class or élite. The explanation for this was that Mussolini was actually opposed to the emergence of any group which was likely to compete with him for power or public support. The cult of the *Duce*, or Mussolinianism, was not an essential component of the Fascist programme, but rather an elaborate superstructure imposed on top of it. As far as Mussolini was concerned, however, it was the whole point of his rule; indeed, 'if Fascism does not follow me, no one can make me follow Fascism'.[5] Typical of Mussolini's self-projection was his claim to be the 'centre of convergence' for all the major 'forces' of Italy. He emphasized his role in reactivating Italy's glorious past by reintroducing the paraphernalia of ancient Rome, including the *fasces* (the bundle of rods, carried before the high magistrate, as an emblem of authority), the Roman salute, and the devices of the eagle and wolf. At the same time, he constantly emphasized the uniqueness of his personal appeal. He alone had the capacity to appeal directly to the people or to interpret their will. Indeed, he maintained that he possessed an intimate knowledge of crowd psychology, derived partly from the study of Gustav Le Bon's *Psychologie des foules*, and partly from active and extensive experience of mob oratory. Although he did give the impression of being a 'boaster', he was, to some, an impressive figure and the epitome of success. The Archbishop of Canterbury, for example, believed that he was 'the only gigantic figure in Europe', and Churchill called him 'genius in person'. It is hardly surprising that

Aspects of European History 1789–1980

Emile Henriot should have felt that 'the great man was in the process of becoming God'.[13]

*

This personality cult was also partly responsible for Mussolini's *decline*, for the 'great man' displayed several serious defects of character. He assumed, for example, that he could undertake successfully a vast range of administrative work. In 1929 he was personally responsible for eight key ministries: foreign affairs, the interior, war, navy, aviation, colonies, corporations and public works. By 1943, notwithstanding the pressures of war, he still retained five of these. He showed a lack of detailed administrative knowledge and made what was, for a supposed co-ordinator, an amazing confession: 'I never make a mistake in interpreting the feeling of the masses. I make mistakes in judging men'.[14] His mind was prone to over-simplification and over-confidence, showing little interest in anything which could not be solved by intuitive measures. Eventually, he became caught up in the very success of his own propaganda and convinced himself that he was indeed the focal point of Italy's energies.

Messianic confidence is not, in itself, an inevitable formula for catastrophe. Mussolini might have maintained himself in power indefinitely if no serious pressure had been exerted on his régime. During the 1930s, however, an increasingly active foreign policy put an intolerable strain upon the whole cult of the *Duce*.

During the 1920s Mussolini had seen himself as one of the arbiters of Europe and had played a prominent part in the policy of collective security embodied in the 1925 Locarno Pact. During the 1930s, by contrast, he was seen as one of Europe's aggressors. The root of this transformation was partly economic; the extensive American investments in Italy during the 1920s had restrained Mussolini's hand, but these were withdrawn in 1929 after the Wall Street Crash. During the subsequent depression Mussolini imposed more direct government control over the economy, gearing it for war and expansion. This made his diplomatic movement towards Nazi Germany a logical, if not inevitable, step. In one sense he gave Italy the type of glory which he had always promised: the conquest of Abyssinia and the acquisition of a new African Empire. On the other hand, the Rome–Berlin Axis brought ultimate disaster. Mussolini was hustled prematurely into a world war by his more powerful ally,

Mussolini

and suffered the humiliation of having to be given German support in Greece and North Africa. Military failure had a catastrophic impact on Mussolini's cult of personality; even before the war, the *Duce* had begun to suffer from comparisons made with the *Führer*. The final blow was the reaction of many of the Italian people against the import of Nazi doctrines, especially anti-semitism. By July 1943, Mussolini had been so discredited that he was removed from power by the Fascist Grand Council and the King. At this special session Count Grandi gave Mussolini a curt explanation of what had happened: 'You believe you have the devotion of the people . . . You lost it the day you tied Italy to Germany.'[15]

Why was Mussolini's fall so sudden and dramatic? Did military defeat have to result in so ignominious an end? The answer lies in the delicate balance between the different powers and institutions which Mussolini had been so careful to maintain. Under the strain of war this balance was destroyed, and Mussolini was left without any political protection. During the early 1930s he missed the opportunity of making the Fascist Party more homogeneous and eliminating corruption. He could have delegated this task to the reforming Secretary, Giuriati, but he chose instead to continue his policy of divide and rule. The result was the growth of cliques and factions, which proved to be useful until Mussolini found himself in difficulties in 1943. By this stage he could rely only on a small group led by Farinacci, while the majority of the Fascist Grand Council, under Grandi, turned against him, laying the blame for military defeat on the cult of personality. As Grandi stated in June 1943: 'It is dictatorship, not Fascism, which has lost the War.'[16] Mussolini's vulnerability was in total contrast to the loyalty which Hitler received from most of his subordinates. Hitler had, from the start, an approach which was very different from Mussolini's checks and balances. His aim had been to Nazify the state, not to depoliticize it. Hence all effective internal opposition, real or potential, had been eliminated long before the régime faced military defeat.

Mussolini's vulnerability was intensified by the existence of an alternative leadership in Italy. Unlike Hitler, Mussolini had never assumed the title as well as the effective powers of head of state. The monarchy, which had been left intact, became a rallying point for the Italian army in 1943, while the *coup* against Mussolini was backed and encouraged by Victor Emmanuel himself. It could also be argued that Mussolini had never really made his stamp on the

Italian army; the oath of allegiance, for example, was still to the state and not to the *Duce* in person. Nor had he managed to create an entirely loyal military élite like Hitler's *Waffen* SS. He had also been less careful than Hitler in anticipating trouble from his generals, and had not taken the trouble to shuffle their positions to prevent plotting or the build-up of opposition. Even his intelligence service was defective, for he was taken completely by surprise by the *coup* of July 1943. Despite his known contempt for Mussolini, Hitler was astounded by the *Duce's* fall and asked 'What is this sort of Fascism which melts like snow before the sun?'

22

The Great Depression

J. M. Keynes observed in 1931: 'We are today in the middle of the greatest economic catastrophe – the greatest catastrophe due almost entirely to economic causes – of the modern world.'[1] The Great Depression began in 1929, spreading outwards from the United States until it had affected almost all the countries in the world, whether industrial powers or underdeveloped primary producers. It brought severe dislocation in the form of falling prices, declining production, shrinking trade and rising unemployment. It also had a profound political and psychological impact, inducing in many states a swing away from constitutional democracy towards totalitarianism. The result was a major change in international relations during the 1930s and the envelopment of Europe by a resurgence of the militarism and nationalism which the Frst World War was supposed to have destroyed.

*

How and why did the Depression arise? Any analysis of such a complex phenomenon must be tentative, especially since economic historians still disagree on points of detail. Nevertheless, it is possible to provide a brief synthesis of generally accepted arguments.

The spread of a worldwide crisis presupposes the interdependence of the individual countries and the existence of channels through which influences can operate. Such a connection had developed

Aspects of European History 1789–1980

during the nineteenth century with the spread of international trade and the accompanying search for sources of raw materials, markets for manufactured goods and outlets for investment. This tendency had been interrupted, briefly, by the First World War, but was resumed during the 1920s, providing an ever increasing network across which problems could be transmitted as readily as prosperity. To some extent, these problems were predictable. During the nineteenth century internal (and hence international) economies had experienced cycles in which between seven and ten years of expansion would be followed by a temporary recession. There is some evidence that the major European countries were approaching the peak of a cycle in 1913, but that the war artificially postponed this until 1919–20, a slump following in 1920 and 1921. According to this trend, some sort of recession was likely by the end of the 1920s.

When it eventually came, however, it proved to be no mere 'routine' cyclic Depression. The basic reason was a severe imbalance of world economic development at the time, which meant that behind every appearance of success there lurked a potential crisis. This showed itself in several ways. Industrial production, for example, increased steadily in Europe during the 1920s. There was, however, over-emphasis on the staple industries, particularly coal, ship building and steel; this was largely at the expense of the newer industries which catered more directly for the consumer market. The United States, by contrast, developed the latter, especially the motor vehicle industry, and managed to achieve a growth rate which was considerably larger than Europe's. Hence the industrial progress made by European countries like Britain, France and Germany was actually accompanied by a proportionate decline in their share of the volume of world trade. Agriculture also experienced difficulties: greater efficiency and more widespread mechanization in Europe and North America increased production and lowered prices. This, in turn, had a serious impact on the producers of raw materials, who eventually had to reduce their import of manufactured articles from the industrial countries to compensate for falling revenues. In two sectors of the economy progress in the United States actually impeded the progress of other countries. In the secondary, or industrial sector, it flooded the world markets but remained unwilling to relax its tariff barriers against European goods, while in the primary sector of agriculture and raw materials it remained largely self-sufficient.

The Great Depression

Another contradiction between the capacity for recovery and liability to recession can be seen in the case of foreign investments. On the surface, widespread availability of capital was essential for sustained economic growth, and there was certainly no shortage of funds during the 1920s. American economic supremacy showed itself in the enormous loans to other countries amounting, between 1925 and 1929, to 2900 million dollars to Europe alone. This flow undoubtedly eased the problems of Germany, crippled by the demand for reparations which formed part of the Treaty of Versailles. The German government was able, with the assistance of American investment, to fulfil some of its obligations to Britain and France, and also to increase internal expenditure on industry and public works. In some ways, however, American investment had negative results, establishing what has been called a 'cycle of indebtedness'. There were two examples of this. The first was the pattern whereby American loans were incurred to help Germany pay reparations to Britain and France who, in turn, repaid interest on American wartime investment. The second was the dependence of many of the world's poorer countries on loans from the United States to repay previous loans; the only other form of reimbursement, through a balance of payments surplus, was precluded by American self-sufficiency. The willingness of American investors to export their capital during the second half of the 1920s meant that some countries, industrialized and underdeveloped, were dependent for up to 25 per cent of their assets on external suppliers. Unfortunately, the volume of trade in no way reflected the degree of investment received, which meant that repayment usually had to be in gold reserves. By 1929, the United States had accumulated most of the world's supply of gold and, as a result, distorted the operation of forms of exchange.

This brings us to a third contradiction. Several attempts were made to bring harmony to the international economy, but with little success. Britain, for example, returned sterling to the gold standard in 1925, encouraging other countries to follow her example by 1928. But this process, arguably, increased rather than reduced instability. Governments adjusted their currencies at different levels and at different times, or simply over-valued them and stimulated a further flow of gold to the United States. Long before 1929 there was growing apprehension about monetary, industrial or commercial anarchy. The Geneva Conference, which assembled in 1927 to

201

analyse the problem, found itself unable to suggest any solution, and governments were beginning to find increasingly attractive the prospect of protective legislation, including tariffs and quotas.

During the 1920s two things were, therefore, apparent. One was that the world's economies were closely linked, for good or ill, with that of the United States. The other was that they were all vulnerable. Consequently, an upheaval in the world's wealthiest country would set off a chain reaction. Or, to use a contemporary adaptation of an old metaphor: 'When America sneezes, the rest of the world catches cold.'

This happened in 1929. For a whole decade the rapid growth of American industry had been assisted by the ready availability of money, in part the result of deliberate policy by the Federal Reserve Bank. After 1925 speculation became increasingly common and when, in 1928, the Federal Reserve Bank tried to impose some sort of order by raising the interest rate, large sums invested overseas were immediately repatriated to the American market to swell domestic holdings. As long as the domestic boom continued, this degree of speculation would not actually damage the economy. But the peak of production was reached in July 1929, thus ending hopes that growth could be permanent and uninterrupted. The basic reason was that the supply of goods had finally outstripped consumer demand, necessitating a reduction in output, or an 'inventory recession'. The slump precipitated a crash as the Stock Market reflected a sudden loss of confidence by investors; 40,000 million dollars had been lost by the end of October. The Wall Street Crash, in part a reflection of the slump, also reacted with the slump to bring about 'the slide into depression. Gradually the crisis intensified as banks went under (as many as 1345 in 1930 alone) and the national income fell by 38 per cent between 1929 and 1932.

The impact of these developments on Europe was serious. Some of the industrial economies had already peaked (Germany in April, and Britain in June), while foreign investment was flowing out because of the higher interest rates in the United States from 1928. The Wall Street Crash accelerated this general trend. The sudden crisis of confidence virtually dried up the supply of loans to Europe and resulted in the further recall of investments to America to compensate for home losses. The uncertainty transmitted itself to the world's money markets, making those countries with extensive debts particularly vulnerable to any panic which might occur in the

The Great Depression

future. A major example of this was the 1931 financial crisis, which began with the collapse of the leading Austrian bank, *Credit Anstalt*, spread to the German banking system and then caused a severe strain in London; in the last case, foreign investors withdrew £200 million between July and August. It was obvious that any international monetary system which had ever existed had by now disintegrated. This was confirmed when, in 1931, Britain withdrew from the gold standard, to be followed by many other countries. Financial insecurity brought industrial atrophy which, in turn, led to an upswing in unemployment to 22 per cent of the total workforce in Britain and 44 per cent in Germany. The primary producers of South-Eastern Europe were ruined as the spreading depression eroded the previous price levels by up to 66 per cent and destroyed both external trade and internal consumer markets. Only two countries in Europe seemed, by 1932, to have held out against the depression: one was France, which had the highest level of gold reserves outside the United States, and was therefore able to ride the financial crisis of 1931. By 1934, however, this strength was undermined as France succumbed, belatedly, to the slump. The other exception was the Soviet Union, which was insulated from the international economy by Stalin's isolationist policies.

*

If ever there was a need for a concerted international effort to deal with an economic crisis it was in the early 1930s. It soon became clear, however, that little would be achieved in this direction. The 1932 Lausanne Conference merely confirmed what had for some time been considered inevitable: that payment of German reparations should end. The World Economic Conference, which assembled in London in 1933, achieved nothing at all. Increasingly, therefore, governments resorted to individual rather than collective policies, usually in isolation and often in conflict. Of these the most common was the import tariff, intended to protect domestic industries from foreign competition. Controls were applied vigorously all over Europe and even Britain finally revised eighty-six years of free trade by the Import Duties Act, 1932, and a series of bilateral agreements drawn up with the Dominions as a result of the Ottawa Conference. France adopted a similar, although more tightly organized, preference system with her own colonies. By 1933 the world was divided by a series of tariff walls through which access had to be negotiated by special arrangement.

Apart from the resort to protection, however, European states adopted different techniques, of which three are worth particular mention. The first was the use of deflationary policies. This was confined mainly to Germany until 1932 and France before 1934. In both cases wages were held down or reduced, and public expenditure slashed. In both cases the slump was intensified and prolonged, and the measures eventually had to be reversed. The second method was budgetary control, which applied particularly to Britain. It was less harsh than rigorous deflation, but was probably not all that effective. British economic recovery, which began in 1934, owed something to the availability of cheap money and a favourable atmosphere for private enterprise, in part an achievement of the National Government. But the real factor was the revival of domestic consumer demand which, in turn, promoted those areas of industry which had been relatively neglected during the 1920s. The result was a boom in house building and motor vehicle manufacturing, although this existed side by side with continued depression in the staple industries and the resultant levels of unemployment.

The third approach involved direct government intervention and presupposed the absence of any opposition. The main example was Nazi economic policy, which concentrated on the promotion of heavy industry and public works programmes. The result was the virtual elimination of unemployment as the level dropped from the peak of 44 per cent to 1 per cent in 1938. A new network of markets was established by a series of bilateral trade agreements with the countries of South-Eastern Europe. These guaranteed a flow of essential raw materials to Germany and, in turn, made states like Bulgaria and Romania totally dependent on Hitler. On the whole, German economic growth in the late 1930s was the most rapid in non-communist Europe. Two reservations, however, should be made. The economy was geared to militarism and was built at the cost of the most basic economic freedoms and at the expense of the consumer market; in this respect it moved in the opposite direction of the British economy. Second, the recovery which occurred after 1934 was not the work of the Nazis alone. The hyperinflation which had attacked the Weimar Republic in 1923 had forced many of the weaker industrial firms out of existence, and the remainder used the American investments which became available from 1924 to re-

The Great Depression

equip and modernize. Hitler therefore inherited an economic base in sound working order and could proceed to add his own super-structure.

*

A broadly accepted historical generalization is that economic crises have political repercussions. The Great Depression had a profound internal and international impact.

Europe consisted, in the 1920s, of a series of parliamentary democracies, many established immediately after the First World War. By the mid-1930s, however, these were confined to Britain, France, the Benelux countries, Scandinavia and Czechoslovakia. Even these countries experienced abnormal political trends; Britain, for example, switched from her normal pattern of single party administrations to a so-called National government, while the ministerial crises in France led, in 1936, to the establishment of Blum's Popular Front government. At the same time, pressure groups built up on the extreme Right to accentuate social insecurity; examples were Mosley's British Fascist Movement, the French Fascist Leagues and the Finnish *Lapua*. More disturbing, however, was the swing of most of Europe to dictatorship. There occurred, on a much wider scale, a repetition of what had brought Mussolini to power in Italy in 1922. Whole classes were destabilized by industrial and agricultural slumps or by financial crises. They gave their support to extremist parties who demonstrated their impatience with the cumbersome operation of parliamentary democracy. Thus the ruined agricultural interests backed right-wing régimes in the Balkans, while the defection of the middle-class voters from the moderate parties brought the Nazis to power in Germany. Italy, Europe's original Fascist régime, experienced what amounted to a second revolution, as Mussolini tightened his grip and imposed the National Council of Corporations. Even the Far East underwent constitutional changes. The initial response of the Japanese government to the Depression was to attempt a reduction of military estimates. But the Prime Minister, Hamaguchi Yuko, was shot in 1930 and the army became increasingly active in Japanese politics.

The failure to agree on common measures to deal with economic problems contributed, during the 1930s, to the heightening of political tension. Economic anarchy soon led to international anarchy, a process hastened by the three major powers who had

205

emerged from the Great Depression with their economies geared for imperial expansion and war. The Japanese invasion of Manchuria (1931) was the logical outcome of a search for new provinces on the mainland of Asia, but was given extra purpose by the need to control the outlets of the raw materials which were necessary for the new war machine. Italian Fascism, meanwhile, was being converted into an expansionist ideology which underlay the invasions of Abyssinia (1935) and Albania (1939). Partly responsible for this was the withdrawal of American investments after 1929, which had the dual effect of removing all restraints on Italian foreign policy and encouraging Mussolini to reformulate his whole economic strategy. By far the greatest blow to the international system, however, was dealt by Germany. Hitler's Four Year Plan was openly intended to prepare the Reich for war by 1940, and the increase in military expenditure contributed greatly to the growing confidence of Hitler's foreign policy by 1938 and 1939. At the same time, the main barrier to German expansion had been eliminated. The Depression ended French hegemony over Eastern Europe, replacing it with a special relationship between Nazi Germany and the new régimes of Bulgaria, Romania and Hungary. With reliable allies and a ready source of raw materials, Hitler could turn his attention to those states in Central and Eastern Europe which featured in his schemes for a Greater Germany and the achievement of *Lebensraum*. The results were the *Anschluss* (1938), the annexation of Czechoslovakia (1938–9) and the invasion of Poland (1939).

*

The world between the wars was the victim of a basic contradiction: countries were dependent on each other for the fulfilment of their economic needs and yet were not prepared to co-operate with each other, for fear that they might be making major concessions. But without co-operation the fulfilment of needs produced the two extremes of tightly controlled individual economies on the one hand, and a complete absence of international control, either economic or political, on the other. The result was so frightful that extensive efforts have been made, since 1945, to set up more carefully co-ordinated international institutions and to remove the fears which once led to the building of tariff walls.

23

Hitler's Rise to Power and the Nazi Revolution

Between the two world wars Germany regressed from the constitutional democracy of the Weimar Republic to the ruthless dictatorship of the Third Reich. This change, which occurred with Hitler's rise to power and the implementation of his own ideas, is generally described as 'revolutionary'.

National Socialism brought a profound upheaval to Germany. It directly attacked Western constitutional and libertarian traditions dating back to 1789 and beyond; indeed, Goebbels maintained that the Nazis had 'abolished' the French Revolution. The basic constituents of National Socialism were hardly novel. Pan-Germanism, imperialistic nationalism, the emphasis on race and *Volk* and, above all, anti-semitism, had all existed in the nineteenth century; they had, however, been held under constraint, and their more extreme exposition had been confined to the political fringe. Hitler moulded his own twisted version of these constituents into a cohesive body and, through his demagogic skill, injected it with demonic life.

But how was National Socialism to take control of Germany? Hitler was a resilient opportunist as well as an obsessive fanatic, and fundamentally altered his practical approach to revolution during the course of his career. At first he tried violence and conspiracy: his 1923 Munich *Putsch* was an attempt to overthrow the Weimar Republic as the essential prerequisite for constructing the National Socialist state. Failure at this stage forced him to rethink his method. He aimed, instead, at rising to power by means of the constitution and at introducing revolutionary changes from

207

above once his position was secure. (At the same time, he made no attempt to moderate the frantic tone of his speeches nor the intimidatory power of his mass rallies; his 'pseudo-legal' strategy was in no way intended to weaken what has been called a revolution in the techniques of communication.) His parliamentary success owed much to Germany's internal upheaval, accelerated, from 1929, by the Great Depression. The extension of his power and the systematic destruction of the Weimar Republic were accomplished between 1933 and 1934 by what was officially called the 'National Revolution'.

*

Hitler originally intended that any social and economic changes should be preceded by a military *coup*, the purpose of which was to destroy the existing régime. After all, Mussolini had forced the Italian Government to capitulate by the mere threat of a march on Rome. Hitler felt that he could do the same to the Berlin government. He was determined 'to know neither rest nor peace until the November Criminals had been overthrown'.[1] On 8 November 1923 he issued a communiqué: 'The Government of the November Criminals and the Reich President are declared removed. A new National Government will be nominated this very day here in Munich.'[1] With the revolutionary's concern about the judgement of posterity, he added: 'We can no longer turn back; our action is already inscribed on the pages of world history.'[1]

The whole undertaking was doomed to failure. It was inadequately prepared and confused in its execution. The Bavarian Commissioner-General, Kahr, was not unsympathetic to the Nazi cause, but felt impelled to put down the rising in case his own administration should collapse. Hitler, who had hoped for Kahr's support in acting against the Berlin government, therefore committed a serious error of judgement. He also over-estimated the degree of support for the Nazi Party in the rest of Germany in the early 1920s. In fact, the Nazis had no rating at a national level; they were regarded merely as a paramilitary pressure group, with no seats in the *Reichstag*. They were not even the main party of the Right, a role filled by the National Party. The radical vote was, at this stage, more likely to go to the extreme Left – to the Independent Socialists and the Communists.

Hitler's greatest mistake was to assume that the Republic was in

Hitler's Rise to Power and the Nazi Revolution

danger of collapsing as a direct result of the French occupation of the Ruhr and the inflation of the mark. The problem of 1923 was far more localized and less intense than the Great Depression in 1929 and, once the co-operation of the Allies had been secured, could be dealt with by the issue of the *Rentenmark* in 1923 and by the signing of the Dawes Plan in 1924. Prosperity and moderation were to be the keynote for the next six years, an unhappy time for extremists on both the Right and the Left.

*

The Munich *Putsch* is rightly represented as one of the more ridiculous and ignominious episodes of modern German history, but it was by no means insignificant. Hitler was not prepared to follow the example of another failed revolutionary, Kapp, and fade into obscurity. Ultimately, the *Putsch* was made to serve a triple purpose. First, it established the radical credentials of the Nazi Party, setting it permanently apart from the Establishment. As Hitler later observed: 'Let there be no mistake about it, had we not acted then I would never have been able to found a revolutionary movement. People would have justifiably told me: you talk like all the others and you act as little as they do.'[2] Second, Hitler's trial provided the Nazis with national publicity, enabling Hitler to rail openly against the Republic and to emphasize the constructive nature of his violence: 'If today I stand here as a revolutionary, it is as a revolutionary against the revolution.'[3] Third, the Nazi Party learned during the period of Hitler's imprisonment (1923–5) that it was essentially monolithic and that it would split into several sections unless it were returned to his leadership. On his release Hitler proceeded to eliminate the threat of his main rival, Gregor Strasser, to win over Northerners like Josef Goebbels and to assume complete control over Party strategy. He stated in 1934 that the *Putsch* had enabled him to wage the battle as he wished 'and not otherwise'.[1]

The failure of the *Putsch* also showed the need for a totally different path to power. Even while he was in Landsberg prison, Hitler developed a new strategy. Military revolt would now have to be replaced by participation in regular politics. 'Instead of working to achieve power by an armed *coup*, we shall have to hold our noses and enter the *Reichstag* against Catholic and Marxist deputies.'[4] This did not, however, involve any capitulation to the underlying principles of constitutional democracy. On the contrary, 'for us parliament is not an end in itself, but merely a means to an end.' Hence, 'the consitution prescribes the scene of the battle, but not its aim.' Hitler, in fact, eventually intended to scrap the constitutional process by which he expected to achieve power. As Goebbels put it in 1928: 'We are entering the *Reichstag* in order that we may arm ourselves with the weapons of democracy from its own arsenal. We shall become *Reichstag* deputies in order that the Weimar ideology should itself help us to destroy it . . . We are content to use all legal means to revolutionize the present state of affairs . . . Let no-one think that parliamentarianism is our Damascus. We come as enemies! Like the wolf falling upon a herd of sheep, that's how we come.'[5]

Hitler made no attempt to hide or explain away this double image of Nazism. Instead, he built up what was both a mainstream parliamentary party, with a superficial deference to constitutional principles, and a mass movement, with all the characteristics of a paramilitary pressure group.

On the one hand, Hitler created a more efficient party structure and adopted a more sophisticated attitude towards other parties and interests. Of particular importance was his temporary alliance, from 1928 onwards, with Hugenberg's National Party. Although he had no intention of obliterating the separate identity of the Nazi Party, Hitler was prepared to project a more evolutionary image until he had derived maximum benefit from Hugenberg's considerable resources. The Nazis gained extensive national coverage in Hugenberg's newspaper chain, to say nothing of valuable contacts with Germany's leading industrialists. Ultimately, Hitler's Nazis were to abandon the connection with the National Party, having drained its strength and replaced it as the major party of the Right. The process was accelerated by the injection of funds by major capitalists like the Ruhr coal magnate, Kirdorf, and steel producers Thyssen and Stinnes. They saw the Nazis as the major safeguard against Communism and were encouraged by the new Nazi 'constitutional' image which had already earned Hitler the nickname *Adolphe Légalité*. From 1930 onwards Hitler invested this money in the most extensive electioneering campaigns ever seen in Germany.

On the other hand, Hitler also extended the base of *mass* support for the Nazi movement, by means of a 'revolution in communication'.

Hitler's Rise to Power and the Nazi Revolution

His speeches, for example, reached an enormously wide section of the population; Albert Speer later asserted that 'Hitler was one of the first to be able to avail himself of the means of modern technology'. His speeches identified targets, like 'Jews', 'Bolsheviks' and 'November Criminals', which were oversimplified and caricatured in such a way as to stimulate emotional hatred rather than reasoned opposition. He also projected a sense of collective power, which he contrasted carefully to the insignificance of the individual (and hence of the liberal democratic tradition) and embellished with the imagery of natural forces, especially the survival of the fittest. This power was channelled, through mass meetings and rallies as well as by the violent methods of the S.A., into blind devotion to the leader. Hitler therefore 'personalized' politics and, in the process, appeared as both the prophet of doom and the national saviour.

What were the actual results of Hitler's revised strategy? Success was not instantaneous but, when it did come, it was spectacular. In the *Reichstag* elections of May 1928 the Nazis secured only 2.6 per cent of the popular vote,[6] which the Republic's system of proportional representation translated into twelve seats.[7] Then, from September 1930, the situation changed. The Nazis obtained 18.3 per cent of the vote and 107 seats, finding themselves, after the Social Democrats, the largest party in the *Reichstag*. Encouraged by the apparent success of his tactics, Hitler struck out for the highest office of state, the presidency. In two great election campaigns in 1931 Hitler was defeated by the incumbent, Hindenburg. The Nazis did, however, increase their popular support; in the first presidential election Hitler secured 11.5 million votes to Hindenburg's 18.6 million, while, in the second, Hitler narrowed the gap (13.4 million, to Hindenburg's 19.25 million). After failing to win the presidency, Hitler aimed at the chancellorship. He was assisted by a further boost in the Nazi performance in the *Reichstag* elections of 1932. In July the Nazis became the largest single party with 37.3 per cent of the vote and 230 seats. Goebbels, exasperated that electoral success had not yet produced a Nazi government, complained: 'We'll drop dead from winning elections.'[8] A slight loss of support in November 1932 still left the Nazis, with 33.1 per cent of the vote and 196 seats, easily the major force in the *Reichstag*. Despite his known dislike of the Nazis, President Hindenburg eventually summoned Hitler to the chancellorship in January 1933.

It is, of course, one of the major tragedies of the twentieth century that the Weimar Republic should have handed power to this mass movement posing as a parliamentary party. Two factors were largely responsible for this. The first was an economic catastrophe, the Great Depression, which destroyed the moderate parties and, by 1932, catapulted the Nazis into the position of the largest party in the *Reichstag*. The second was the constant drift of the Republic to the right and the eventual emergence, after 1930, of a series of authoritarian cabinets which had little compunction about doing a political deal with Hitler.

Hitler's tactics had made little headway in the period of comparative economic stability between 1925 and 1928. Something was evidently needed to crack open the whole political and social structure so that Hitler could remould the fragments. German society had, for some time, been vitiated by internal tensions which constantly threatened to break into open conflict; it was, therefore, vulnerable to any major crisis. The Great Depression, which hit Germany from 1929 onwards, released these tensions and cut away much of the previous support for the Weimar Republic. It was the catalyst for a massive change in the voting habits of a large part of the German electorate. The main casualties were the liberal parties – the People's Party (DVP) and the Democratic Party (DDP) – as well as the traditional Nationalists (DNVP). What happened was that the middle classes transferred their support from this area of the political spectrum to the extreme Right, a process caused by demoralization and panic.[9] Farmers, artisans, white-collar workers, shopkeepers and professional men all expressed their disillusionment with the Establishment. Their savings and pensions had been destroyed for the second time within a decade, and the Great Depression was especially hard to bear as it followed a period of economic improvement. They could have transferred their votes to the Social Democrats (SPD), but this would have involved a decline in social status since, at this time, the SPD was primarily a working-class party. Besides, the Nazi Party had concocted an attractive programme which promised much to the different sections of the middle class. In particular, it stressed the importance of the 'small man' as an economic unit, and promised to control some of the more unpredictable forces of capitalism as well as to destroy forever the threat of Communism. Thus the parties which had been involved in most of the Republic's coalition governments were abandoned as a normally stable part of the electorate sought relief in more radical

Hitler's Rise to Power and the Nazi Revolution

and sweeping programmes, even if their implementation involved the risk of eventual dictatorship.

This contraction of support for the Republic was spectacular but not entirely unprecedented. Ever since its foundation in 1918 the Republic had been opposed by various right-wing interests and political groups. The military, for example, were alienated by the so-called 'stab in the back'. Of the two wartime Commanders-in-Chief, Ludendorff defected to the Nazis, and Hindenburg imposed an authoritarian stamp on the presidency after his election in 1925; other army officers even toyed with the idea of a military *coup*. In some instances whole states rejected the new democratic ethos of the Republic and, like Kahr's Bavaria, remained virtual dictatorships. There were also many right-wing activists and writers: men like Moeller, van den Bruck and Junger, who looked back with nostalgia to the Second Reich and anticipated a Third in the near future. Even the liberals and socialists, who were responsible for drawing up the Republic's constitution, seemed to have reservations about Germany's capacity to sustain democracy indefinitely; they therefore allowed, in Article 48, for the discretionary use of extensive presidential powers in an emergency. According to Theodor Heuss, the first President of the German Federal Republic, 'Germany never conquered democracy for herself',[10] a point which became more and more obvious after 1929. The sudden economic crisis caused by the Great Depression destroyed the previous pattern of coalition cabinets and government by consensus, as the formulation of policy became more and more complicated. Increased reliance was therefore placed on Hindenburg, who was known to favour a paternalist approach to government, and who was impatient of the more complex manoeuvres of party politics. He and Brüning resorted to Article 48 of the Constitution, increasing the number of presidential decrees from five in 1930 to sixty in 1932. During the same period, the sittings of the *Reichstag* decreased from ninety-four to thirteen.[11]

This swing to the Right provided a congenial atmosphere for the suddenly strengthened Nazi Party and made Hitler's emergence as a possible national leader seem less outrageous than it would have been in the 1920s. And yet Hitler actually achieved power in an unexpected manner. He did not acquire it directly, as his attempt to dislodge Hindenburg from the presidency in 1931 had failed. Instead, he became Chancellor after a series of backdoor manoeuvres with and between right-wing Chancellors von Papen and Schleicher, with the connivance of Hindenburg himself. The traditional Right, particularly the Nationalists, tried at first to control the new Right, or Nazis. (Schleicher, for one, hoped to detach leading Nazis, like Gregor Strasser, by offers of posts in his 1932 cabinet.) When it became clear that the Nazi Party could not be divided in this manner, the traditional Right changed its tactics. Schleicher, knowing in January 1933, that his cabinet was about to fall, was in favour of letting Hitler form a government of his own. To try to keep the Nazis out of power much longer might well provoke another *Putsch*. In this event Schleicher, as army commander, would be in the unenviable position of having to put down the revolt in the name of the Republic he hated. Papen had already been prepared to concede Hitler the chancellorship; the Nazis could then be used by the Nationalists to do the dirty work of destroying the fabric of the Republic. Hindenburg was persuaded to appoint Hitler, although he hoped that experience of office would moderate some of Hitler's policies and bring a closer identity between the Nazis and the old Right.

Was there no way of preventing Hitler from being given power in this sordid way? Even allowing for the catastrophic impact of the Great Depression, electoral support for the Nazis could not be guaranteed to remain at 37.3 per cent. Indeed, it showed signs of declining and Hitler reacted with dismay to the 33.1 per cent received by the Nazis in November 1932. A concerted opposition, surely, would have been sufficient to keep Hitler out of power? Could it even have forced Hindenburg to moderate his use of emergency decrees as, according to the last sentence of Article 48, presidential decrees 'may be rescinded on the demand of the *Reichstag*'?[12] After the election of November 1932 the Nazis and National Party had, between them, 247 seats. The moderate parties (People's Party, Centre, Democrats and Social Democrats) controlled 237 seats, while the Communists possessed one hundred. Could a combined front, consisting of the moderates and far Left, therefore, have impeded the progress of the extreme Right? Two main factors prevented this from being a serious possibility. First, the Communists and moderate parties were not prepared to co-operate. The Communists competed directly with the SPD for the vote of the proletariat in the mistaken belief that they could attract the working-class vote in the same way that the Nazis had won the support of the middle class. Second, the use of decree laws *was* attacked by the *Reichstag*. But the chancellors (one of whom, in any case, had been the leader of the Centre Party) could always respond by seeking a dissolution. It does, therefore, seem that any real parliamentary constraints had been severely weakened by the beginning of 1933.

*

Hitler had become Chancellor with a semblance of legality, but had no intention of abiding by the Republic's Constitution. 'We are not', he had always emphasized, 'a parliamentary party.'[13] In fact, 'once we possess the constitutional rights we shall . . . pour the state into the mould which we consider the right one'. The 'National Revolution', therefore, started within weeks of his appointment, gained momentum in 1934 and 1935, and reached its climax after 1941.

Hitler's first priority was to make his authority unassailable by kicking down the ladder by which he had ascended. Ironically, the first stage of Hitler's revolution, the creation of a personal dictatorship, was accomplished by measures which were, technically at least, within the ambit of the Constitution.

The process began on 28 February 1933 with a decree from President Hindenburg which, under Article 48 of the Constitution, suspended normal civil liberties. The pretext was a Communist 'plot', which had included the destruction of the *Reichstag*. Then, in March, Hitler proceeded to shatter the Constitution itself, again by means allowed by the Constitution. The amendment of an entrenched, or constitutional clause, required a two-thirds majority. In the elections of 1933, the Nazis and National Party had won considerably fewer seats than required, although they had a slight overall majority. Hitler solved the problem by using the Decree of 28 February to expel the eighty-three Communist deputies and by negotiating for the support of the Centre Party. The result was a majority, by 441 votes to 94, for the Enabling Law, which empowered the Chancellor to issue legislation for four years without the consent of the *Reichstag*. This eradicated Article 68 of the Weimar Constitution: 'Reich laws shall be enacted by the *Reichstag*.' Other measures followed, including the Law against the New Formation of Parties (July 1933), which wiped out the entire opposition, thus obliterating the principle of legislative restraint on the executive. Although it had not been formally abrogated, the Constitution was now so undermined by the new regulations as to be totally useless. The way was now open for the extension of Nazi control over the whole range of Germany's institutions.

The next stage was hastened by pressure exerted from within the Party by the SA. Röhm and Strasser, in particular, wanted a second revolution in which the SA would take control of the army. Hitler, however, proceeded in his own way. Convinced that a 'brown revolution' would wreck his own position and invite a military counter *coup*, he did a deal with the *Wehrmacht* commanders. In return for eliminating the SA in the 'Night of the Long Knives' (30 June 1934) Hitler acquired the direct backing of the *Wehrmacht* for his régime, as well as an oath of loyalty to the person of the *Führer*. The purge of the SA also served to initiate Hitler's own 'second revolution'. It ended the myth of the 'legal changes' and clearly demonstrated that he would depend, in future, on a permanent state of emergency – all designed to uproot the remnants of constitutional democracy. The SS and Gestapo, effectively united in 1934, provided a secure base for the régime, while a new juridical sanction emerged as a result of drastic changes in the concept of justice and the role of the courts. The traditional notion of the law circumscribing the power of the government and the ruling parties was replaced by the principles of 'National Socialist philosophy, especially as expressed by the utterances of our Führer' (Hans Frank).[14] There was now no impediment to the use of coercion and terror and the total destruction of that part of the Weimar Constitution entitled the *Fundamental Rights and Duties of the Germans*. The most extreme departure was the systematic persecution of Jews and other minority groups. Article 109 of the Weimar Constitution had affirmed: 'All Germans are equal before the law.' Article 111 had stated: 'All Germans shall enjoy liberty of travel and residence throughout the Reich.' According to Article 135, 'All inhabitants of the Reich enjoy full religious freedom of conscience.'[12] These safeguards were shredded by the Nuremberg Laws (1935) and by the extensive use of the SS and Gestapo system of concentration camps.

The 'positive' aim of the Nazi system was the creation of a new social order. The emphasis was on expansionist nationalism, which was given extra force by its association with notions of Aryan purity and racial superiority. Attempts were made to subordinate

Hitler's Rise to Power and the Nazi Revolution

every sector of the media and education. Goebbels, who described his aim as 'total propaganda', presided over a new Ministry of Propaganda from March 1933, while draconian measures were taken to ensure ideological conformity by the press. Education was another obvious target; it was through the systematic indoctrination of Germany's youth that the qualities of fanatical loyalty and unquestioning obedience could be implanted into the next generation of citizens. Education was also given a paramilitary emphasis: boys enrolled in the Hitler Youth were rigidly disciplined and, according to the 1936 Law Concerning the Hitler Youth, were to be 'educated physically, mentally and morally in the spirit of National Socialism, to serve the nation and the racial community'.[15] Higher education was also drastically revised. Pure research was replaced by studies intended to uphold Nazi racial concepts – hence the emergence of 'German' or 'Aryan' physics and mathematics. The basic tone was set by the Minister of Culture, who announced to university professors assembled in Munich in 1933: 'From now on it will not be your job to determine whether something is true, but whether it is in the spirit of the National Socialist revolution.' Meanwhile, the Reich Cultural Chamber, created in September 1934, endeavoured to redirect the nation's aesthetic tastes and to eradicate 'degenerate' tendencies in art, literature and music. Underlying the whole process of indoctrination was the moulding of a race which would not question the fact of its superiority. Its aggressiveness and self-confidence were built up by mass rallies and spectacular events like the 1936 Olympics, so that, in the future, war would come to be accepted as a natural means of attaining the extra territory which it would inevitably need. Anticipating future conquest, of course, necessitated an economic policy subordinated to the demands of heavy industry and rearmament, and the Four Year Plan (1936–40) departed from normal practice in western countries by starving the consumer sector.

During the Second World War the Nazi Revolution entered its third and most fanatical phase. Any remaining constraints on expansion and persecution disappeared as Hitler conquered vast areas of *Lebensraum* in Eastern Europe. The annexation of Poland in 1939 and of large parts of European Russia in 1941 brought the Nazis into contact with millions of Jews and tens of millions of 'inferior' Slavs. This intensified the search by Nazi leaders for the ultimate fulfilment of Hitler's ideas, and the views first expressed in

Mein Kampf were sublimated in the extermination of much of European Jewry at Auschwitz-Birkenau, Sobibor, Treblinka and other camps. This genocide, organized so methodically by Heydrich, Himmler and Eichmann, went far beyond what is normally understood by the term 'revolution'; it has been seen as nothing less than the overturning of civilization itself. But then, as Hitler once boasted, 'We are ruthless . . . . Yes, we are barbarians! We want to be. That is an honourable epithet. We are the ones who will rejuvenate the world. The old world is done for.'[16]

＊

Although Germany experienced, between 1933 and 1945, a profound and even unprecedented upheaval, there is ample evidence of inefficiency and structural weakness in the Nazi Revolution.

One of Hitler's original objectives had been that 'all future institutions of this State must grow out of the [Nazi] movement itself'. This was broadly similar to the Bolshevik aim of replacing state institutions with its own. In practice, however, the Nazis never managed, nor even attempted, such a clean sweep. (K. D. Bracher and others have argued that much within the Third Reich was improvised; 'Almost everywhere the régime operated on two planes simultaneously: penetrating and compromising the old institutions yet at the same time building up new, separate rival machineries above them.'[17]) The traditional civil service, for example, was dominated by, but was still separate from, the new Nazi bureaucracy. As a result, their functions were often duplicated and always complicated. The Nazi political order was inherently untidy and unsystematic, dependent on the *Führer* himself for its continued functioning.

Indeed, the Nazi Revolution as a whole hinged entirely on the personal charisma of one man. This affected the movement in two ways. First, Hitler remained consistently more popular than his Party and there was a serious, if unacknowledged problem concerning the long-term future of the Nazi state. Who else could assume the task of sorting out the 'jurisdictional thicket of party agencies and state machinery'?[17] Second, Nazism was too firmly based on Hitler's personal obsessions to develop into a systematic ideology capable of future growth; in fact, any attempts to make the theory of the Party more scientific incurred Hitler's hostility. During the final phase of the Revolution, Hitler's policies became increas-

Hitler's Rise to Power and the Nazi Revolution

ingly irrational and, even under the shadow of imminent defeat, one of his main concerns was still the completion of the 'Final Solution'. In April 1945, while Russian artillery pounded Berlin, Hitler urged his successors 'Above all . . . to uphold the racial laws and resist mercilessly the poisoner of all nations, international Jewry'. Deprived of any other rationale and faced with imminent military collapse, the 'Thousand Year Reich' outlived its founder by just one week.

24

German Foreign Policy 1918–39

It is often assumed that 1933, the year in which Hitler came to power, represents a turning point in the development of German foreign policy, and that the objectives of the Third Reich were fundamentally different from those of the Weimar Republic. This chapter will deal with two basic issues arising from this. First, did the Nazis depart completely from the policies of statesmen like Cuno and Stresemann, or is there at least some evidence of continuity? Second, if Hitler's ambitions and projects can be considered essentially new, does it necessarily follow that the Second World War was their inevitable consequence?

*

The Nazi Revolution started, in the domestic sphere, within a year of Hitler's appointment as Chancellor. Changes in foreign policy, however, were at least five years behind, giving politicians in Britain and France cause to hope that National Socialism would eventually apply to Germany's internal problems the moderation apparent in its early diplomacy.

There were two basic reasons for the continuity of Germany's foreign policy during the early and mid-1930s. One was that the governments of the Weimar Republic had been under constant pressure from the more conservative elements of the social spectrum, particularly the National People's Party (DNVP), who had inherited the views and policies of the Conservatives and right-wing National Liberals of the Second Reich. At first, these traditionalists had been kept under control by the coalitions of the 1920s because the Democrats and Social Democrats had considerable electoral support. After 1929, however, the swing to the Right in the *Reichstag* elections put the conservatives into power. While von Schleicher and von Papen were Chancellors, the foreign ministry was filled with men like von Neurath and von Bülow, who constantly looked back to the Wilhelmine era of *Weltpolitik*. The Republic's ambassadors were drawn largely from the former aristocracy and had a similar commitment to seeing Germany re-emerge as a major power. Most of these officials were retained by Hitler during the first four years of the Third Reich, with the result that the continuity of personnel made any sudden and dramatic switch in policy unlikely. Indeed, for a while, Hitler was anxious to establish a reputation as a moderate in diplomacy, and he was actually less outspoken than the National Party leader, Hugenberg. He was also prepared to harmonize his views with those of the conservative leaders of industry, like Thyssen, or of the old-fashioned right-wing economists, like Schacht, even if this meant temporarily ignoring the purists of Nazi theory, like Rosenberg and Strasser. Hitler also found himself in agreement with the decision of the ex-republican leaders of the early 1930s when they accepted limited rearmament as a means of countering the worst effects of the Great Depression; he used this as a stepping stone towards achieving his own more distinctively militarist aims. Given the prevailing right-wing inclination of the Republic's policies and institutions after 1930, it is hardly surprising that Hitler needed to change so little in the early years. He could even keep the existing leaders of the *Reichswehr*, including von Blomberg and Beck, and he went so far as to purge his own radicals, like Röhm, who wanted to Nazify the army immediately.

The second reason for the continuity of German foreign policy during the transition from Republic to Reich was the existence of a common and longstanding programme to revise the Versailles Settlement. The Allies had removed from Germany 12 per cent of her population, 13 per cent of her territory and much of her industrial capacity, as well as imposing on her a total reparations debt of £6600 million. All Germans condemned the Settlement, whether they were moderate supporters of the Republic, traditional conservatives or radical Nazis. Hugo Preuss, a leader of the Democratic Party and architect of the Republic's constitution, referred to the

Aspects of European History 1789–1980

'criminal madness of the Versailles *Diktat*'.[1] Hence, during the 1920s, Republican statesmen and conservatives alike agreed that a revisionist policy was essential, even though they disagreed bitterly over the measures to be used. The overall aims of the moderate coalitions of the SPD, Centre Party, Democrats and People's Party, were itemized by Stresemann, Foreign Minister between 1923 and 1929. He insisted that the reparations question must be solved in 'a sense tolerable for Germany', that assistance should be given to 'those ten to twelve millions of our kindred who now live under a foreign yoke in foreign lands', and that Germany's eastern frontiers should be liable to 'readjustment'.[2] Von Stülpnagel, head of the *Reichswehr*'s operations section, put a similar case for 'the regaining of full sovereignty over the area retained by Germany' and 'firm acquisition of those areas at present separated from her'.[3] Meanwhile, the High Command was quite happy to evade the ban placed by the Treaty of Versailles on military manoeuvres by arranging for the training of German troops in Russia, a device made possible by the treaties formed with the Soviet Union by Rathenau in 1922, and by Stresemann in 1926.

Thus the elements of revisionism which featured in Hitler's foreign policy were by no means original. Although the moderates had been shocked by his withdrawal from the League of Nations in 1933, they had to admit that his methods did bring spectacular success. The conservative (as distinct from Nazi) Right were more enthusiastic about Hitler's diplomacy than they had ever been about Stresemann's, even though the High Command questioned his lack of military caution over the reoccupation of the Rhineland in 1936. Indeed, a glance at Hitler's diplomatic record before 1939 shows that he had accomplished all the targets of the republican revisionists. Germany had regained full sovereignty over all internal territories, including the Rhineland in 1936; the limitation on armaments had been ignored since 1935; and the Germans of Austria and the Sudetenland had been incorporated into the Reich by the *Anschluss* and the Munich Agreement of 1938. The popularity of his foreign policy was evidenced by the overwhelming majorities which he gained in his plebiscites; 99.08 per cent, for example, voted in favour of the *Anschluss*. Even allowing for a degree of electoral manipulation, it is certain that the German people accepted this early phase of Hitler's diplomacy with greater unanimity than they did his internal measures, perhaps because they were relieved by the

German Foreign Policy 1918–39

apparent harmony of its transition from one régime to another. British and French statesmen, too, regarded the first five years of diplomacy as the moderate face of Nazism and concluded that Hitler, although a radical, had reasonable and fixed objectives.

In retrospect, however, it is obvious that the continuity between the diplomacy of the Weimar Republic and the Third Reich was misleading. The crucial fact, which ultimately showed Nazi foreign policy to be as revolutionary as its domestic counterpart was that Hitler saw revisionism merely as a means of moving towards projects which were well beyond the ambitions of any of the republican statesmen. At the theoretical level, the differences between the aims of the moderates and the conservatives, on the one hand, and the Nazis, on the other, were obvious, although optimism and wishful thinking tended to minimize them. Conservatives, especially in the National Party, looked back to the era of the Second Reich, expecting a revival of *Weltpolitik* with its emphasis on colonies and naval power as well as continental military strength. But the boundaries of Germany herself would be those of 1914; after all, even Bismarck had opposed any drastic territorial changes for fear of weakening the Prussian base of the Reich. The moderates of the Republic faced a dilemma. They did not regret the passing of the Second Reich, and hoped that international co-operation would replace military rivalry. Stresemann, for example, saw Germany as a 'bridge' which would reconcile West and East and bring about the harmonious development of Europe. Consequently, he committed the Republic to a policy of collective security by the formation of the Locarno Pact (1925), and gave Germany a voice in international decisions by securing her membership of the League of Nations (1926). Unfortunately, the conditions of the Treaty of Versailles infused Stresemann's policy with more opportunist and less idealistic tendencies. He felt obliged to resort to covert measures to secure at least the beginning of German rearmament and to open the way for regaining lost territories. At no time, however, did he extend this policy of revisionism into one of expansion for its own sake. His main concern was to 'get the stranglehold off our neck' and not to create an enlarged Reich.

Hitler's aims encompassed nothing less than conquest on a continental scale and the destruction of Germany's neighbours. His views were stated explicitly in *Mein Kampf* and, more lucidly, in his *Secret Book*.[4] The latter contains a number of observations which

223

point to the radicalism of Hitler's basic thought. For example, he claimed that all previous governments had been restricted in their policy by the notion of the 'fixed frontier'. Even the Conservatives and neo-Bismarckians were wrong to hark back to the territorial arrangements of 1914, for 'the German borders of the year 1914 were borders which presented something incomplete'. As an alternative to the 'border policy' of the 'national bourgeois world', the Nazis would follow 'a territorial one', the whole purpose of which would be 'to secure the space necessary to the life of our people'. The limited policies of Bismarck had, perhaps, been necessary to establish and build up the 'power structure' for the future. But Bismarck's successors (the very statesmen who were now being lauded by the Conservatives) had denied Germany her natural process of expansion and had pursued an 'insane' policy of alliance with Austria-Hungary and maritime conflict with Britain. Now the mistakes of history could be rectified, *Lebensraum* could be achieved, and the 'inferior races' could be deprived of the territory to which their low productivity and potential gave them no natural right. Returning to the theme of struggle which had permeated *Mein Kampf*, Hitler affirmed: 'Every healthy, vigorous people sees nothing sinful in territorial acquisition, but something quite in keeping with its nature.' Besides, peace bred submissiveness and there was always the danger that 'whatever will not be a hammer in history, will be an anvil'.

Reduced to more explicit stages, Hitler's objectives were as follows: his first priority was to destroy the Versailles Settlement and revive Germany's military power. With this there was little dissent among his subjects. The next stage was to establish a Greater Reich by dismantling Germany's neighbours. This policy accorded with the views of some of the more extreme members of the National Party, but was generally viewed with reservations when it became apparent. The third step was to take lands in the East, as far as the Urals, for the future settlement of up to 100 million Germans. By this time, Germany's mastery of the Continent would be assured. It has sometimes been suggested that Hitler was considering a fourth aim: world dominance, to be contested, if necessary, against the opposition of Britain and the United States. Clearly, the last two projects would have been discounted by many conservatives as impossible, while Hitler's intentions in relation to the fourth have never been clearly established.

German Foreign Policy 1918–39

How did Hitler progress through these stages? Between 1933 and 1936 he emphasized the importance of firmness in achieving the destruction of the Versailles Settlement, but of moderation in the methods used. It would seem that his main concern was to prevent an Allied attack on Germany, and he warned his generals that 'the most dangerous time is that of the building of the armed forces'.[5] Hence he removed obstacles to German rearmament by withdrawing from the League of Nations Disarmament Commission in 1933, but also affirmed in public speeches that he had no intention of settling disputes with any other country by military means. To back up his self-projection as a man of peace, he formed the Nazi-Polish Non-Aggression Pact in 1934. This was received with undisguised relief by other European powers, but Hitler was merely playing for time and trying to undermine the French security system in Eastern Europe. Indeed, he observed in a moment of frankness, 'All our agreements with Poland have a purely temporary significance. I have no intention of maintaining a serious friendship with Poland.'[6] He showed particular skill in dividing potential opponents and in assessing the likely reaction of other statesmen to a *fait accompli* on his own part. For example, he managed to split the Stresa Front, formed in protest against Germany's announcement of military conscription, by offering a naval agreement which would apparently ensure permanent British superiority. He also affirmed that any departure from the Versailles Settlement should not be construed as a prelude to war, and that he certainly had no intention of annexing Austria. He made similar promises after his reoccupation of the Rhineland in 1936, a *coup* which succeeded because he correctly anticipated that neither the French nor British governments would be prepared to use force to resist.

Greatly encouraged by the success of his diplomacy in these early years, Hitler became increasingly aggressive in his methods and moved into the newer area of territorial expansion. In November 1937, he revealed to the leading personnel of the Foreign Ministry and to military chiefs like Blomberg, Fritsch and Raeder, the basic purpose of his policy, including the schemes for an enlarged Reich and *Lebensraum*. The meeting, recorded as the Hossbach Memorandum, revealed the reservations and even dismay of the non-Nazi elements. Beck, for example, described the programme as 'inconceivable', while Blomberg and Fritsch expressed concern about possible retaliation by Britain and France. Hitler responded by breaking all remaining links with the Weimar Republic. He dismissed those officials who had served it and who were now refusing to see that what had so far been accomplished in foreign policy was only a means to achieving a much greater end. Neurath was replaced as Foreign Minister by von Ribbentrop, while Blomberg and Fritsch were both removed by somewhat devious methods. Altogether, sixteen generals were retired and another fourty-four relocated. In one blow, Hitler had ended the partnership which had previously existed between the Nazis and the *Wehrmacht*; he now transformed the army into yet another institution which he dominated personally. Meanwhile, the economy, too, had been transformed. The pragmatic agreements with the industrialists and with the traditional economists were replaced, from 1936, by the deliberate preparation of a war machine to carry out Hitler's foreign policy. Schacht resigned his post in 1937 and, instead, Goering was given responsibility for the Four Year Plan which was intended to prepare Germany for war by 1940. Hitler's thinking here was revealed in the Hossbach Memorandum. He told his generals that Germany's expansion would have to be accomplished by 1943, or at the latest 1945, for, by this time, Germany's military advantage would have worn off as other countries would have begun to close the gap.

1938 and 1939 saw the completion of Hitler's enlarged Germany and the beginning of the quest for *Lebensraum*. Hitler moved quickly in 1938 because Britain and France hoped that the *Anschluss* and the demand for the Sudetenland were the final stages of a revisionist policy inherited from the Weimar Republic; in fact, they were merely a prelude for the expansion of Germany into Eastern Europe. This was eventually confirmed when, in 1939, Hitler incorporated the whole of Bohemia into the Reich, announced that Slovakia was to be a German protectorate, and launched a full-scale attack on Poland. In November 1939 he finally renounced the use of diplomacy and told his generals: 'All hope for compromise is childish.'[7]

*

The Nuremberg Judgement maintained that the Second World War was the outcome of Nazi policy and of Hitler's resolution 'not to depart from the course he had set for himself'.[8] There are two ways of looking at this whole question of responsibility. The first is that the conflict between 1939 and 1945 was unquestionably 'Hitler's War'. It is true that he had pursued a cautious foreign policy during the first few years after his appointment as Chancellor and that some of his objectives seemed directly in line with the revisionist approach of his predecessors. Yet there is no logical reason why these should not have been short-term measures designed to ease the way for the achievement of a more ambitious scheme – the conquest of Eastern Europe. *Mein Kampf*, the *Secret Book* and the Hossbach Memorandum all point to militarism and virtually unlimited expansion as being the only real objectives of Hitler's policies. Hitler was also obsessed with the notion that struggle and war were fundamental human activities and needs. 'War is the most natural, the most ordinary thing. War is a constant; war is everywhere. There is no beginning, there is no conclusion of peace. War is life. All struggle is war. War is the primal condition.' The logical conclusion, therefore, is that Hitler *wanted* war, partly to achieve his long-term objectives, partly to strengthen the Aryan race. As we have seen, the turn of the decade seemed to offer the best chance of successful aggression, as the rearmament of Germany's main rivals was still at an early stage. The majority of historians have been, and remain, convinced that war was the only possible outcome of Hitler's diplomacy. R. J. Sontag, for example, argued that Hitler's policy in 1939 was, 'like the annexation of Austria and the Sudeten districts of Czechoslovakia, merely preliminary to the task of winning "living space" '.[9] There have been critics of this line of reasoning, the most important being A. J. P. Taylor, who maintained that the war broke out through 'blunder' rather than design. Hitler's projects, as outlined in *Mein Kampf* and the Hossbach Memorandum, were 'in large part day-dreaming, unrelated to what followed in real life'. In his opinion, 'statesmen are too absorbed by events to follow a preconceived plan. They take one step and the next follows from it'.[10] This, however, remained very much a minority viewpoint, and the responsibility of Hitler for the conflict was reaffirmed by H. Trevor Roper, in a critique of Taylor's thesis. He demonstrated Hitler's commitment to long-term aims, all explicitly stated in *Mein Kampf*, and added: 'All the experience of the 1930s showed that Hitler still intended to carry them out.'[11] This line was also followed by a German biographer of Hitler, J. Fest, who reaffirmed the orthodoxy that 'who caused the war is a question that cannot be seriously raised'.[12]

Aspects of European History 1789–1980

These conclusions do not rule out a degree of responsibility, outside Germany, for the outbreak of war. In this case, however, responsibility is associated less with 'guilt' than with 'misinterpretation', 'inconsistency' and 'default'. It can be argued that Hitler's progress towards war was unintentionally accelerated by Western leaders, paradoxically, because of their very hatred of war. Daladier and Chamberlain, who found war morally repugnant, assumed that the rationale of all diplomacy pointed towards peace. Chamberlain, in particular, made the crucial mistake of assuming that even Hitler had specific objectives, and that if these were conceded to him, the causes of international tension would be removed. Hitler, of course, was greatly encouraged by the pressure exerted on the smaller states by the British and French governments and mistook forbearance in the interests of peace for weakness and diplomatic capitulation. This explains the increasingly aggressive stance which he adopted during the Sudeten crisis of 1938. By 1939 Chamberlain had at last got the true measure of Hitler and decided to extend military guarantees to Poland and Romania. This sudden switch appeared a desperate turn within a bankrupt policy and clearly lacked credibility with the Nazis. Hitler was by no means deterred in his designs against Poland and told his military commanders on 22 August that Britain and France would not, he was certain, react to a full-scale German invasion. B. Liddell Hart compared the pre-war crisis with someone stoking up a boiler until the steam pressure rose to boiling point – and then closing the safety-valve; while A. J. P. Taylor considered that British foreign policy fell between two stools: war could have been avoided by 'greater firmness' or 'greater conciliation'.

25

Soviet Foreign Policy 1918–41

This chapter will outline the development of Soviet foreign policy between the wars and provide explanations for the frequent alterations of course made by Lenin and Stalin. At its best, Soviet policy was skilful, confident and effective; at its worst, it was blundering, uncertain and ruinous. Throughout the period there was an internal – it might be said dialectical – conflict between ideological motives on the one hand and, on the other, a pragmatism which bordered on cynicism.

*

The Bolshevik Revolution brought an upheaval in international relations as well as in Russia's domestic situation. There were two reasons for this. The first was that the Bolshevik leaders displayed an intense ideological hostility to the Western powers, believing in the inevitability of their eventual collapse and also in the necessity of this as a precondition for the survival of the new Communist régime. Lenin argued in 1918: 'There can be no doubt that the prospects for final victory of our Revolution would be hopeless if it were to remain alone and if it were not for the revolutionary movement in other countries.'[1] The choice, therefore, was between causing revolution in capitalist states, or sitting back and allowing an eventual capitalist onslaught against Communism. According to Trotsky, 'Either the Russian Revolution will create a revolutionary movement in Europe, or the European powers will destroy the Russian Revolution.'[2]

Aspects of European History 1789–1980

The second reason was that the Bolshevik Revolution was followed by Russia's withdrawal from the First World War, a development which upset the military strategy of the Western Allies in their struggle against Germany. Lenin had consistently opposed Russia's involvement in what he regarded as a conflict between monopoly capitalists and, on coming to power, he opened the Tsarist archives, published all secret treaties and declared in favour of 'an immediate peace without annexations and without indemnities'.[3] By agreeing to the Treaty of Brest Litovsk with Germany in March 1918, Lenin showed that the Bolsheviks were prepared to suffer a temporary diplomatic humiliation in return for greater freedom to direct the revolutionary forces which would soon render all diplomacy superfluous.

Such calculations soon had to be replaced by a more urgent defensive strategy for survival. For Western reactions to the new Bolshevik régime and to Russia's separate peace with Germany were thoroughly hostile. Russia's capitulation at Brest Litovsk enabled the Germans to launch a new offensive on the Western Front on 21 March 1918, and the Allied Supreme War Council decided at Versailles that Russia should be brought back into the conflict even if this should require military intervention. Hence British expeditionary forces were despatched to Murmansk, Archangel and the Caspian Sea area, the French invaded the Black Sea region, and Eastern Siberia and Vladivostok were occupied by the Japanese and Americans. This intervention rapidly became caught up in support for counter-revolution as aid was given to the White armies of Kolchack, Yudenitch, Deniken and Wrangel. The Bolsheviks, however, managed to contain the threat, combining effective personal leadership with the emergence of the highly effective Red Army from the Revolutionary Military Committee. They had the advantage of complete control over Russia's railway network, which radiated outwards from Moscow, and they succeeded in eliminating most internal opposition to the war effort through the offices of the *Cheka*. But the Soviet régime was less successful in dealing with the Polish threat in 1920; although the Red Army threw back the initial Polish invasion, its own counter-attack was reversed by a second Polish offensive made possible by the reorganization carried out by Marshal Pilsudski and General Weygand. By the Treaty of Riga (1921) Russia suffered a second territorial amputation in three years.

Soviet Foreign Policy 1918–41

These events brought about an important change in Soviet foreign policy. The Bolshevik régime had survived a series of attacks from capitalist and counter-revolutionary forces without collapsing. At the same time, however, the Western powers themselves showed no signs of disintegration under the impact of revolutionary activity. The Spartacist rising in Berlin had been crushed in January 1919 and the Soviet Republic of Bavaria had been destroyed a few months later. Even the Bolshevik-inspired Hungarian revolution had collapsed and there seemed no immediate prospects of workers' risings in any other Eastern or Central European state. It made sense, therefore, to redirect the basic strategy of foreign policy and to think in terms of coexistence. In November 1921, Lenin acknowledged that his predictions of a swift world revolution had not been justified. Hence a period of internal consolidation had now to be the most urgent priority. Furthermore, the civil war had brought home the importance of adequate armaments and a balanced economy. The most direct way of achieving the industrial growth essential for both was through Western investment. According to Kamenev in 1921: 'We can, of course, restore our economy by the heroic effort of the working masses. But we cannot develop it fast enough to prevent the capitalist countries from overtaking us, unless we call in foreign capital.'[4]

Between 1921 and 1924, therefore, Soviet leaders resurrected the art of diplomacy and stunned the West with their mastery of the unexpected *fait accompli*. The target chosen for this activity was Germany, isolated and vulnerable as a result of defeat in the First World War and the harsh terms of the Treaty of Versailles. The Soviet Foreign Minister, Chicherin, conducted secret negotiations with his German counterpart, Rathenau. These reached their climax in Genoa in 1922. Ostensibly, Russia and Germany were themselves the objects of discussion among the other major powers, but the tables were turned when the Russo-German Treaty of Rapallo was announced. Great skill had been shown by the Soviet delegation in using as a lever the German fear that Russia might invoke Article 116 of the Treaty of Versailles unless such an agreement were reached. Although the Rapallo Agreement was not an alliance, it did provide for German investment and valuable military advice.

It should not be assumed, however, that this meant the end of

231

Trotsky's vision of worldwide revolution. On the contrary, the role of *Comintern* was still to foment Communist revolt where possible as, for example, in Germany in 1921 and 1923. Even the use of Western capital could be justified on ideological grounds. According to Kamenev: 'While strengthening Soviet Russia, developing her productive forces, foreign capital will fulfil the role Marx predicted for it when he said that capital was digging its own grave.'[4]

*

When Stalin emerged as Lenin's successor in 1924, Soviet foreign policy became even more complex. Although it is difficult to generalize about the whole spectrum of ideas and methods, certain underlying influences can be detected.

Before 1924 Stalin had had comparatively little contact with diplomacy and had always shown far more concern for the domestic base of socialism than for its external spread. Consequently, he had already come into conflict with Trotsky's belief in 'Worldwide Revolution', maintaining that Russia's only viable course was 'Socialism in One Country'. Stalin was an orthodox Marxist in that he believed in the ultimate, global victory of Communism. He argued, however, that the best way of achieving this was through military methods rather than through external insurrections; war, not revolution, would be the instrument of victory. Russia's role in this ought to be twofold. On the one hand, intensive preparations should be made to develop heavy industry so as to provide a solid military base for victory. On the other, Russia should avoid direct aggression, while being prepared to take advantage of the inevitable conflict between the capitalist powers. He told the Party Central Committee in 1925: 'If war begins . . . we shall have to come out, but we ought to be the last to come out. And we should come out in order to throw the decisive weight on the scales.'[5] How effectively did Stalin carry out these ideas?

*

At first Stalin was content to maintain the policy which had been outlined at Genoa by Chicherin in 1922, 'the parallel existence of the old social order and of the new order now being born'.[6] The Soviet régime obtained, during the course of 1924, recognition from Britain, Italy, France and Japan, and Stalin had high hopes of persuading foreign trade union movements to put pressure on their

Soviet Foreign Policy 1918–41

governments to lessen their ideological animosity towards Russia. He also intended to pursue a moderate course in China. Although Trotsky argued that the Chinese political situation was directly comparable to that in Russia in 1917, Stalin considered that a narrowly-based Communist revolution would be far less likely to succeed than a coalition of different radical forces; hence he urged Mao Tse Tung's Communist Party to join Chiang Kai Shek's organization, the Kuomintang. Before 1927, therefore, Stalin appeared to the capitalist world as a moderating influence and a welcome alternative to the subversive emphasis of Trotsky.

Then came the first of Stalin's changes of strategy. Deutscher maintains that the world had rejected the Bolsheviks as revolutionaries by the end of 1923, and then as conciliators by 1927. Certainly, events had not taken the course Stalin had expected. The major Western governments, with the possible exception of Germany, had grown increasingly hostile; the Soviet embassy in London had been raided and diplomatic relations were severed in 1927. Meanwhile, the Communists in China had broken with the Kuomintang and Stalin's policy of a broad-based coalition had therefore collapsed. There was also a domestic reason for Stalin's change of attitude. By 1927, he had gained complete control over the CPSU and was intent on expelling the rightist element consisting of Bukharin, Kamenev and Zinoviev, as well as the Trotskyists. He intended to abandon Kamenev's attempts to secure loans from the West and to reconstruct the Soviet economy on the radical lines put forward by Preobrazhensky. Agriculture would be collectivized and would subsidize the development of heavy industry in a series of Five Year Plans, the ultimate purpose being to convert the Soviet Union into a major military power. It no longer mattered, therefore, whether foreign powers were unsympathetic, provided that there was no direct military confrontation. In fact, Stalin found it necessary to project the capitalist states in the worst possible light in order to justify his economic upheavals to the Russian people.

How did Stalin explain his new position? In December 1927 he announced that capitalism had entered a phase of instability. This meant that 'the period of peaceful coexistence recedes into the past, giving place to a period of imperialist attacks'.[5] He saw the Great Depression, which struck the capitalist world in 1929, as the fulfilment of his prediction and argued that 'the world economic crisis will turn into a political crisis in a number of countries'.[7] The West, meanwhile, was showing its instability through increased aggression and militarism.

Assuming that his intention was to play a waiting game and, at the same time, to enforce industrialization and rearmament on a backward economy, Stalin's vilification of the West had an unquestionable logic. But he committed a major error in pursuing this logic to its extreme conclusion over Germany. The Great Depression had boosted the electoral performance of the Nazis and, between 1930 and 1933, Hitler made several bids for power, his target being the presidency or, failing that, the chancellorship. Stalin, however, saw little difference between the Nazis and the Social Democrats, the largest obstacle to Hitler and, until 1930, the major party in the *Reichstag*. He regarded them both as fascist; indeed, 'social democracy is objectively the moderate wing of fascism'.[8] He had the word of the German Communist leader, Thälmann, that 'the bourgeoisie would never let Hitler anywhere near power'[8] and, even should this be proved wrong, the real manipulator of the government would be, as always, great industrialists like Thyssen. If Germany moved from the rule of the 'Social fascists' (the SPD) to that of the 'National fascists' (the Nazis), she would be approaching the final internal upheaval which, the dialectic decreed, would destroy capitalism altogether. Consequently, German Communists were instructed not to assist the SPD and other moderate parties in keeping Hitler out of power. From his remote exile, Trotsky issued numerous warnings about the dangers of this policy. He accused the leadership of *Comintern* of 'leading the German proletariat towards an enormous catastrophe' and, in an alternative analysis of fascism, showed that it differed radically from social democracy. Indeed, 'should fascism come to power it will ride over your skulls and spines like a terrific tank . . . only a fighting unity with Social Democratic workers can bring victory. Make haste, you have very little time left!'[5] Trotsky's predictions were entirely accurate. To use another metaphor, Stalin helped create the very monster against which he had been warned.

How did Stalin adapt to the new situation? Although somewhat disconcerted by Hitler's success in 1933, he assumed that coexistence was possible and that Nazi Germany would pursue a Bismarckian policy of restraint towards Russia. After one year, however, Stalin abandoned this view. Hitler's elimination of all internal opposition showed that the Nazi régime was more

Soviet Foreign Policy 1918–41

dangerous than the 'social fascism' of the Weimar Republic. Furthermore, Soviet security seemed imperilled by the 1934 Nazi-Polish Non-Aggression Pact, which provided the basis for a possible anti-Russian alliance. Stalin, therefore, swiftly reverted to diplomacy.

His new policy comprised three elements. The first was a search for collective security in Eastern Europe; this would be made up of interlinked mutual guarantees and would, like the Locarno Pact of 1925, include Germany. When this scheme fell through, Stalin turned to the West for an agreement to outflank Germany. This resulted in the Franco-Soviet Pact and the Soviet-Czechoslovak Pact. These arrangements were accompanied by a third policy, the formation of popular fronts all over Europe to resist the growth of fascism and to prevent any repetition of the internal catastrophe which had befallen Germany. *Comintern* now instructed Communists in Spain, France and elsewhere to sink their differences with social democrats and even liberals. The situation in Spain, however, presented Stalin with a dilemma: the establishment of a Communist régime in order to prevent Franco gaining power would only alienate Western Europe and smash the Soviet Entente with France. He therefore instructed the Spanish Communists to avoid demands for the expropriation of property or state control over industry. He even played along for a while with the principles of the Non-Intervention Committee, until it became obvious that these were being openly flouted by Hitler and Mussolini in their military support to Franco.

By mid-1938, however, Stalin felt that the Western powers were unreliable allies. The Anglo-French response to German territorial expansion was governed by the policy of appeasement, and Stalin was shocked by the ease with which Hitler accomplished the *Anschluss* and absorbed the Sudetenland into the Reich. The Soviet Union alone offered military assistance to Czechoslovakia, but failed to gain French co-operation or permission from Poland or Romania for the transit of Soviet troops. It appeared, therefore, that Germany would be allowed to rearm and expand without hindrance from the Western Allies. To make matters worse, Russian and Japanese troops clashed several times in 1938 and 1939 on the borders of Manchuria and Mongolia. The European problem, therefore, required immediate settlement in case Stalin had to commit divisions to the Far East.

Aspects of European History 1789–1980

What were his options? He could maintain the Soviet relationship with Britain and France, but on revised terms; he could, for example, insist on more definite military commitments. Or he could seek rapprochement with Germany and draw up a territorial settlement which would eliminate any potential causes of conflict with Russia. During the first seven months of 1939 Stalin seemed willing to incline towards either alternative and managed to play off the rival powers with great skill. Foreign Minister Litvinov and General Shaposhnikov offered more clearly defined terms to the Western powers, but their response was too slow. Although Churchill urged the British government to draw up the alliance which Stalin seemed prepared to grant, Chamberlain hesitated, admitting to 'the most profound distrust of Russia'. Meanwhile, Stalin leaked details of these negotiations to Berlin and succeeded in drawing to Moscow a German delegation under von Ribbentrop. The result was the conclusion, on 23 August 1939, of the Nazi-Soviet Non-Aggression Pact, with its secret protocol agreeing to the division of Eastern Europe into Nazi and Soviet spheres of influence. This time Stalin provided no ideological justification; it was obvious to all that this was the most opportunist and pragmatic agreement of the century.

How necessary was the Pact for Russia? Soviet historians today make no mention of Stalin, but argue that 'subsequent events revealed that this step was the only correct one under the circumstances. By taking it, the USSR was able to continue peaceful construction for nearly two years and to strengthen its defences.'[9] There is, however, another view. A modern Western historian[10] maintains that it should not be assumed that, without the Pact, Germany would have attacked Russia in 1939. Hitler was too preoccupied with Poland, and with the declaration of war by France and Britain, to draw off divisions from the *Wehrmacht* for yet another campaign. More telling is the observation that even if Hitler *had* moved immediately, the Soviet Union would have been better off. By 1941 German military production had grown, proportionately, more rapidly than Russia's, enabling Hitler to launch, in Operation Barbarossa, the sort of offensive which would have been quite impossible in 1939. It would appear that Stalin had simultaneously over-estimated and under-estimated his rival in 1939. He had over-rated German military resources in comparison to Russia's, forgetting that his own Five Year Plans had boosted Soviet heavy industry. But he had underrated the effectiveness of the German

Soviet Foreign Policy 1918–41

Blitzkrieg strategy which shattered Poland and France. Stalin had, in fact, hoped that the final internecine struggle between the capitalist powers had at last arrived. By 1940 he was uncomfortably aware that Hitler had regained the initiative.

Even so, his policy was now to do nothing. For this inactivity during the course of 1940 and 1941 Stalin has been heavily criticized. Khrushchev, for example, said in 1956: 'The threatening danger which hung over our Fatherland in the first period of the war was largely due to the faulty methods of directing the nation and the Party by Stalin himself.'[11] Churchill had earlier described Stalin and his commissars at this stage as 'the most completely outwitted bunglers of the Second World War'.

The indictment rests on Stalin's strange behaviour in the face of the growing threat from Germany. He must have been aware that relations between Russia and Germany were deteriorating rapidly as a result of the Soviet seizure of the Baltic states. Yet he took no action to prepare Russia for the eventuality of war. In April 1941 he received information from Churchill, via British intelligence, that Hitler was moving Panzer divisions to southern Poland, and similar warnings from the United States and his own agents in Berlin. He refused, however, to accept that such manoeuvres were a prelude to a German attack, and he referred in *Tass* to the 'obvious absurdity of these rumours'.[12] He failed to place the Red Army on the alert, concentrating instead on maintaining good relations with Hitler by providing essential supplies of strategic raw materials, even though the Nazis had stopped paying for them. He even issued instructions that the Red Army should not resist any German border incursions in case these provoked a war which he felt that the Germans did not really want. The result of this was that when the *Wehrmacht* did invade, in June 1941, a spectacular Russian collapse occurred, and several million Soviet troops surrendered in the first six months.

This is a summary of the usual interpretation of what happened in 1941. It is, however, possible to adopt a more positive view of Stalin's policies; it could be argued that his appraisal of the situation was wrong not because it was irrational but rather because it was based too heavily on the type of logical reasoning to which he was always accustomed. Stalin doubted whether Hitler had any real motive to attack Russia unless he were actually provoked. It was, therefore, important to keep communications open and to keep stressing that 'The friendship of the peoples of Germany and the Soviet Union, cemented by blood, has every reason to be lasting and firm'.[5] Stalin was convinced that as long as the Soviet Union provided Germany with essential raw materials this coexistence could be maintained indefinitely. At the same time, Soviet policy would be firm and positive in other directions, for Stalin had no intention of adopting the appeasement strategy of Chamberlain. Hence Stalin would remind Hitler of Soviet power by annexing extra territory from Finland, the Baltic states and Romania, thereby strengthening the Russian frontier and cutting off access for a direct German invasion along the coast. Should the two countries appear to be drifting towards war, the symptoms would be recognizable and Stalin could make well-timed concessions to satisfy Hitler. What the Soviet Union had to avoid was alarmism and the possibility of being rushed into war by Churchill, who naturally wanted an ally against Hitler. Stalin did not disbelieve reports about troop movements; but his own interpretation was that they were intended by Hitler as a diplomatic move to put pressure on Russia, possibly as a counter to Russia's territorial annexations. To see in them the beginning of an attack would, in the words of his *Tass* article, be yielding to 'a clumsy propaganda manoeuvre of the forces arrayed against the Soviet Union and Germany'. Up to the very last day, indeed, Stalin was convinced that Hitler could not rationally contemplate widening the scope of the war.

1941, therefore, was dominated by two minds; one tuned to the intricate logic of the dialectic failed entirely to comprehend the other, which was visionary. Then, from the beginning of 1942 onwards, Stalin assumed that the final struggle with capitalism had arrived. It was not in the form which he had intended, but his industrial preparations in the form of the Five Year Plans ensured eventual victory over Nazism.

26

The League of Nations

The League of Nations was established, largely on the initiative of President Wilson, in 1919, the Covenant being drafted at the Paris Peace Conference and subsequently being incorporated into all the treaties which made up the Versailles Settlement. The main institutions were the Council, comprising the major powers and some lesser states elected in rotation; the Assembly, in which all member states were represented; and the Secretariat, which acted as the League's bureaucracy. Associated with the League, but not part of it constitutionally, were the Permanent Court of International Justice, and a series of specialist agencies, like the International Labour Organization. The League's membership totalled forty-one in 1919, rising to fifty by 1924 and sixty by 1934.

This chapter will examine the League of Nations under three main headings: its achievements, the main reasons for its eventual eclipse, and the foundations which it provided for its successor, the United Nations Organization.

*

The League of Nations was not the first attempt to establish institutions for international diplomacy and arbitration; between 1814 and 1914 there had been, under the generic description of 'Concert of Europe', eight Congresses attended by heads of government, and eighteen Conferences of Ambassadors. These had, however, been convened for specific purposes and were intended as an occasion for governments to elaborate their policy rather than as a forum for genuine international debate. They had, moreover, been somewhat exclusive and had represented only the handful of major powers. Other institutions had also been set up during the nineteenth century. These included about 400 non-political organizations and a range of bodies requiring close inter-governmental co-operation, like the International Telegraphic Union (1865) and the Universal Postal Union (1874). Against this background, the League of Nations performed two important functions. It provided a permanent framework for inter-governmental consultation which was more regular and systematic than the *ad hoc* conferences of the nineteenth century. It also extended the range of this framework to incorporate non-political as well as political bodies. The result was greater co-operation, made possible by the unprecedented use of the Secretariat, with all its resources for gathering and collating information and statistics. The system established in 1919 was far from perfect, but it did represent a considerable advance on the scattered institutions of the previous era.

Despite experiencing severe difficulties and eventual collapse, the League achieved several political successes by the mid-1930s. It provided a means whereby a small area could be removed from a defeated power, either temporarily or permanently, without being absorbed by one of the victors as would have been the case before 1914. The Saar, for example, was administered until 1935 by a Governing Commission, and Danzig by a High Commissariat. The League also carried out plebiscites in accordance with the principle of national self-determination embodied in the Treaties of Versailles and St. Germain; three examples were Upper Silesia, Schleswig and East Prussia. In order to give minorities a chance to air any grievances caused by boundary changes, a Minorities Subcommittee of the Council was established, although it possessed no actual jurisdiction within the affected areas. More successful was the action taken by the League, mainly during the 1920s, to settle disputes between some of the lesser states, particularly between Finland and Sweden over the Aaland Islands, Turkey and Iraq over the Mosul, Greece and Bulgaria, and Albania and Yugoslavia. The Commission on Mandates, meanwhile, ensured that those major powers which had received colonies from the defunct German Empire did not cover their administration under a veil of secrecy. Conscious of the League's right to criticize and investigate, if not to interfere directly, the imperial powers refined their colonial governments and took care to avoid the type of excesses which had often marred their record before 1914.

The most worthwhile and significant of the League's achievements were undoubtedly in the social field. The Health Organization conducted research into leprosy, gave advice on vaccines and standardized drugs in common use, while the Epidemics Commission dealt with the outbreaks of typhus and cholera which resulted from warfare in Eastern Europe. Refugees, casualties of the same problem, were the subject of the Nansen Report, which tried to ease their absorption into other countries. Various forms of exploitation were also investigated. The League was particularly concerned about the continuing traffic in women and children and the employment of young children in the Persian carpet trade. The International Labour Organization, meanwhile, tried to persuade governments to standardize conditions of labour and to regulate relations between employers and employees; many governments responded by passing the legislation recommended by the Organization's General Conference. Finally, the League sponsored a series of technical organizations which were concerned, above all, with rail transport, inland navigation and electrical power. In general, the League became so heavily committed to non-political activities that the Bruce Report of 1939 recommended extensive institutional changes to cope with the ever-increasing volume of work. This came out at a time when the political activities of the League had been all but suspended.

*

In retrospect, it is possible to see the enormous, perhaps unparalleled, difficulties of the inter-war period. Four empires had been destroyed, which had resulted in the most extensive territorial changes for centuries. Powerful ideologies developed on the extreme Left and the extreme Right, the latter assisted by economic catastrophe in the early 1930s. Any international organization was bound to find this environment overwhelmingly hostile, and, if it were to have the remotest chances of success in the political field, it needed the support and goodwill of the majority of the great powers and a structure through which to deal instantly with major disputes, by preventive action where possible, punitive where necessary.

This was not, however, the form taken by the League of Nations. It was not constructed to survive a period of crisis but rather to uphold what was optimistically regarded as an impending period of peace. There was widespread support for the belief of H. G. Wells that the Great War had been the 'war to end wars'; hence Europe had to get away from the traditional view, expressed early in the nineteenth century by Clausewitz, that 'war is the continuation of diplomacy by other means'. War, in fact, was now to be outlawed. By the Kellogg-Briand Pact of 1928, for example, the sixty-five signatories agreed to 'condemn recourse to war for the solution of international controversies and renounce it as an instrument of national policy in their relations with one another'.[1] Britain and the United States, in particular, approached the formation of the League from the assumption that institutions were needed for collective and voluntary agreement rather than for coercion. Hence the League was heavily influenced by Anglo-American notions of liberal democracy, both in the structure of the Council and Assembly and in the responsibilities allocated to them. The French delegates at the session for drafting the Covenant saw matters differently; they pressed for a more tightly knit body, with stronger coercive powers. Eventually, however, the Anglo-American view prevailed. The League would be the medium for peaceful arbitration, with pressure of any kind being used only as a final resort. Since the French amendment to set up a military force was rejected in 1919, the League had no agency with which to enforce its resolutions and therefore relied entirely on the co-operation of the major powers. Hence, in the words of P. Raffo, the League 'depended for its very existence and effectiveness on that unity of purpose and international goodwill which it was itself designed to promote'.[2]

The League Covenant illustrates these deficiencies clearly. Article 10 expressed the basic intention: 'The Members of the League undertake to respect and preserve as against external aggression the territorial integrity and existing political independence of all members of the League.'[3] Article 11 provided that the League should 'take any action that may be deemed wise and effectual to safeguard the peace of nations'. Unfortunately, there was no further ruling on what procedure should be taken in such an emergency. Article 10 stated that the Council should 'advise' on the means whereby members' obligations should be fulfilled, but the effect of this was virtually destroyed by a Canadian resolution in 1923 which gave to each individual government the right to interpret its obligations in its own way. Even more debilitating to

The League of Nations

any form of joint action was Article 5, which stated that 'decisions at any meeting of the Assembly or of the Council shall require the agreement of all the members of the League represented at the meeting'. This 'unanimity clause' severely undermined the League's attempts, under Article 11 to deal with the Japanese invasion of Manchuria (1931) and made it extremely difficult to enforce the sanctions allowed by Article 16. The Covenant assumed throughout that the great powers would always play by the rules even if the process of arbitration should fail; Article 12, for example, provided for a 'cooling off' period of three months before either side in an intractable dispute could resort to war. The events of the 1930s, however, demonstrated that Japan, Italy and Germany acknowledged no rules which could not actually be enforced, and Article 12 made little sense to Fascist régimes which based their foreign policy on surprise and the *fait accompli*.

Two attempts were made, during the 1920s and early 1930s, to make the League more effective as a peacekeeping organization. The first was to reduce the level of international tension through the process of disarmament provided for in Article 8 of the Covenant. The period 1926–34, however, brought total failure. The Commission for the Geneva Disarmament Conference spent five years producing an outline report which contained no details or statistics, while the Conference itself was irreparably damaged by Germany's withdrawal in 1933, and eventually adjourned indefinitely in 1934. The other attempt was more realistic. French pressure from within the League produced proposals for tightening up the procedures for concerted action in a crisis; the most promising were the Draft Treaty of Mutual Assistance and the Geneva Protocol. But these never got off the ground, largely because the British government, supported by the Dominions, attacked them as an unwarranted commitment. Instead, a system of 'collective security' came into existence, based on the 1925 Locarno Pact and guaranteeing the frontiers between France, Belgium and Germany from unilateral revision. The Locarno Pact was not directly connected with the League, although it provided for arbitration by the League in the event of disputes between the three protected states. The device was reasonably effective during the period 1925–9 when German foreign policy was directed by Stresemann, but it was rapidly dismantled by Hitler after 1933. Besides, Collective Security did not cover the more vulnerable and dangerous trouble spots of

Aspects of European History 1789–1980

Eastern Europe and therefore amounted to no more than a temporary reconciliation between Germany and the countries of Western Europe, giving, in the process, an illusion of safety.

Failure to give the Council any corporate peace-keeping powers confined the League to a role of arbitrating between the lesser states. Acts of aggression by major Powers often invoked a diplomatic response from outside the structure of the League. For example, the 1923 Corfu Crisis, engineered by Mussolini, was eventually resolved by the traditional expedient of a Conference of Ambassadors rather than by the League Council. Attempts by the Council to effect withdrawals from Manchuria by the Japanese, and from Abyssinia by the Italians, failed so dismally that, during the second half of the 1930s, the League was almost always bypassed. Britain and France resorted to a bilateral policy of appeasement towards both Italy and Germany, while the Non-Intervention Committee, set up to prevent the Spanish Civil War from overspilling into the rest of Europe, never came under the League's jurisdiction. (See Chapter 27.) The future of Czechoslovakia was decided, in 1938, by the heads of four governments, and President Beneš did not even bother to appeal to the League against their decision. Of all the states attacked in 1939 only Finland attempted to use the League machinery.

The institutional weaknesses of the League were exacerbated by the policies of the individual powers, to which we now turn. What stands out most clearly is the indecisiveness of the governments who formed and subsequently claimed to uphold the League – the United States, Britain and France – and the mortal wounds inflicted by Japan, Italy and Germany in pursuit of *Lebensraum*.

By far the most ardent advocate of the League of Nations was President Wilson and there can be no doubt of his intention to commit the United States to permanent membership. By 1919, however, the Senate had been captured by the Republicans and, under the forceful leadership of Henry Cabot Lodge, demanded substantial revision of the Covenant which had been submitted to it by the President. The Republicans were particularly concerned about the commitments which the United States would be expected to undertake in terms of Article 10, and stressed that the administration should retain the right to decide for itself in what issues it should become involved. President Wilson, however, rejected this view and undertook an unsuccessful nationwide campaign to seek support for his own interpretation. The outcome was the rejection of

244

The League of Nations

the Covenant in the Senate and the complete withdrawal of the United States from the League. The impact was enormous; many historians consider the American return to isolation undermined the League from the very beginning. S. Marks, for example, argues that 'In its larger role the League foundered on the twin rocks of the unanimity clause and the absence of America'.[4] Certainly, American isolation made it impossible to consider any specific action over Manchuria in 1931; Austen Chamberlain observed: 'We ought to know by this time that the USA will give us no undertaking to resist by force any action of Japan short of an attack on Hawaii or Honolulu.' Similarly, sanctions against Italy were pointless without American participation, and Roosevelt's refusal to become involved in the European crises of the late 1930s considerably enhanced the cause of fascism.

Britain and France were the only powers to retain their membership of the League throughout its course and, as such, came to be regarded as the organization's main pillars. Unfortunately, serious misunderstandings arose between them, undermining their efforts to keep it going. One of these concerned the very nature of the League. British governments regarded the League as a device for arbitration and as a forum for the expression of different ideas. The French, by contrast, wanted a tight system of security and a means of guaranteeing the 1919 peace settlements; they were therefore bitterly disappointed by Britain's rejection of the Geneva Protocol and refusal to assist the defence of the new frontiers in Eastern Europe. At times, relations between the two states reached rock bottom; Britain was completely out of sympathy with the French search for security in the Ruhr in 1923, while France refused to accept the naval ratio negotiated at the London Conference in 1930. Such disharmony benefited those powers whose main concern was not to place a definitive interpretation on the Covenant but to exploit its loopholes.

The first to do this was Japan. Although she had been one of the original signatories of the League Covenant in 1919, Japan had never been more than a half-hearted member of the League. She resented the heavy-handed refusal by the European members of the League to include within the Covenant an affirmation of racial equality. She was also dissatisfied with the policies of the Western powers, whether inside or outside the League; she was unhappy with the levels of ship building negotiated at the Washington Conference

(1921) and the London Conference (1930) and also with the restraints on her commercial expansion into mainland China. The Great Depression acted as a catalyst for change, transforming compliance, but dormant resentment, into defiance, and direct aggression. The economic crisis destroyed the remnants of democratic government and provided opportunities for political intervention by the army. This in turn led to a ruthless and opportunist foreign policy, beginning with military action in Manchuria. The League's reaction was too weak to prevent Japan from establishing the puppet state of Manchukuo, but just strong enough to invoke violent Japanese hostility. The new régime denounced the League as a western clique and ended Japan's membership in March 1933. Thereafter it acknowledged no external restraint on its actions and proceeded in 1937 to attack the rest of China, and in 1941 to dismantle the British, French and Dutch Empires in the Far East.

Italy was another power which had never really been committed to the League. As early as 1923 the British ambassador in Rome had remarked that Italy saw in the League's force antithetical to the vital necessities of her own future expansion'.[5] Mussolini certainly saw in the Covenant an obstacle to his plans for revising the parsimonious treatment of Italy by the Versailles Settlement. Yet, during the 1920s Mussolini followed a cautious policy; he usually projected an image of diplomatic reasonableness, showing an aggressive edge only occasionally, as in the Corfu Incident of 1923. As with Japan, however, the Great Depression brought a transformation. A second 'Fascist Revolution' occurred which, this time, encompassed foreign policy. By 1935 Mussolini was in full pursuit of imperial expansion, helped by the ambivalent attitudes of Britain and France over Abyssinia. On the one hand, he was encouraged by apparent Anglo-French capitulation in the Hoare-Laval Pact; on the other, he was infuriated by the attempt to impose economic sanctions, and withdrew Italy from the League in December 1937. Mussolini has often been seen as the leader who administered the death blow to the League, enabling Hitler to take advantage in the late 1930s of the resulting diplomatic free-for-all.

Germany's attitude to the League underwent a complete change. The statesmen of the parties within the coalition governments of the Weimar Republic favoured and worked for entry, which was eventually accomplished in 1926 by Stresemann. The main intentions were to revise the Treaty of Versailles and gain acceptance for the

The League of Nations

foreign policy objectives described in Chapter 24. By 1929 however, there was widespread dissatisfaction with the League, and growing support for the National Party's charge that the League had never been anything more than a 'syndicate of victors'[6] designed to enforce the Treaty of Versailles to the full. Military leaders like Groener, and diplomats like Bülow, openly stated that the League was irrelevant to Germany's needs; Bülow, for example, argued that if the League's purpose really was the preservation of the *status quo* and the prevention of future wars, then it was 'an objective in which we can have less interest than the other, especially the allied powers'.[7] Hitler, therefore, found a considerable groundswell of opinion against the League, as was demonstrated by the overwhelming majority in the plebiscite approving Germany's withdrawal in October 1933. His subsequent actions revealed open contempt for the League as either the guarantor of the Versailles Settlement or as an arbitrator in disputes. It took time, however, for other governments to realize that the objectives of his foreign policy were incompatible with any form of peaceful diplomacy.

The Soviet Union also underwent a change in its attitude to the League. Lenin had accused the League of upholding the forces of capitalism and colonialism, while Stalin had originally felt that any commitments would place the Soviet Union in an anomalous position: 'We do not want to be either the hammer for the weak nations or the anvil for the mighty ones.'[8] Stalin preferred, during the 1920s, to make his own arrangements, largely with Germany. But the spread of fascism during the 1930s convinced him that he would have to co-operate with the Western democracies. He therefore took the Soviet Union into the League in 1934, hoping that it would provide an alliance with Britain and France. As it turned out, however, the League and Russia gained little from their association with each other. Stalin became disillusioned by the Anglo-French policy of appeasement towards the fascist states, while the British and French governments were disgusted with Stalin's pact with Hitler in August 1939, and his subsequent attacks on Poland and Finland. In December 1939 the League carried out its last decisive act: the termination of Soviet membership.

*

The last session of the League of Nations was held in Geneva on 9 April 1946. One of the speakers, Lord Cecil, concluded with the

247

words: 'The League is dead: long live the United Nations!' This reformulation of the old French salute *Le roi est mort; vive le roi!* was intended to stress the connection between the two organizations; the United Nations had been born in 1945 while the League still existed officially, and the transfer of power was not carried out until August 1946.

Why was it necessary to form a new organization and to go through the rigmarole of transferring power? As we have seen, the League had proved inadequate to deal with the problems which had emerged in the 1930s and the Covenant was regarded as completely outdated. By 1945 the world's leaders were questioning the wisdom of tying an international organization to the specific peace settlement as the statesmen of 1919 had tied the Covenant to the Treaties of Versailles and St. Germain. What was now needed was an institution which would be able to *transcend* a peace settlement and adjust to future problems. At the same time, the great powers wanted to be certain of preserving their own interests without re-enacting the withdrawals of the 1930s. The veto was considered the best safeguard, but this was not provided for within the League Covenant. For this and other reasons, a mere revision of the League would have been inadequate, even if the enormous technical and legal difficulties could have been overcome.

But, although the United Nations would be a new and more complex institution, it would derive much from the League's background. Lord Cecil made this point in his speech of 9 April: 'But for the great experiment of the League, the United Nations could not have come into existence', a view with which a modern historian agrees: 'In most respects, indeed, the United Nations was the recognizable offspring of the League experience.'

This can be illustrated by comparing the institutions of the League and the United Nations. The drafters of the UN Charter kept the basic idea of a Council but decided to allocate its functions more precisely. The League Council was, in effect, replaced by three organs. The first was the Security Council, which was charged specifically with preventing or dealing with disturbances to world peace. The League's emphasis on unanimity was abandoned in favour of majority voting, with each of the five permanent members (the United States, the Soviet Union, Britain, France and China) being given the right of veto. The Security Council was empowered to raise an international peace-keeping force under the command of

The League of Nations

the Military Staff Committee; this remedied one of the greatest deficiencies of the League Covenant. Secondly, the Economic and Social Council was established to assume responsibility for non-political questions. Such an institution had already been recommended by the 1939 Bruce Committee as a means of removing one of the burdens of the League Council. The third new institution, the Trusteeship Council, was also designed to separate a specialized function from the primary task of peace keeping.

Other institutions within the United Nations Organization also had their ancestry within the League. The United Nations General Assembly was clearly the successor to the League Assembly, although experience suggested certain modifications. The General Assembly was given fewer peace-keeping powers but was compensated by a more meaningful role in other areas; it was, for example, given charge of the Trusteeship and Economic and Social Councils. The United Nations maintained with few modifications the League's methods of upholding international law. The League had operated through a Permanent Court of International Justice, although this had been officially outside the League structure. In practice, however, the PCIJ had been fully involved in the life of the League and the fiction of independence was therefore ended by the Charter, which made the new International Court of Justice a primary institution of the United Nations. Direct continuity was also apparent in the case of the Secretariats, although the United Nations version was to become more complex and to have greater responsibility because of the existence of the extra Councils. The UN Secretary General was generally considered more powerful than his League counterpart and, because of deep ideological differences between the major Powers, it became customary to choose candidates from the minor states, a contrast to the League's tendency to select British, French or Russian officials. This, however, can be seen as one of many results of the replacement of a European-based organization by one representing almost every nation on earth.

27
The Spanish Civil War

Historians have pointed to two main elements in Spain between 1936 and 1939. The first is a struggle between two broadly-based coalitions, with sharply contrasting ideologies, for the right to shape the country's future social and political institutions. The second is the impact of this struggle on the rest of the Continent. E. H. Carr, in fact, described the Spanish struggle as a 'European Civil War fought on Spanish territory'.[1] This chapter will suggest reasons for the victory of the Right in the domestic conflict and examine the implications for the European powers.

*

Both sides in the Spanish Civil War were heterogeneous and ranged, in each case, from the centre to radical extremes. Since they incorporated such diverse elements, they were described as Fronts. The National Front (or Nationalists) included conservatives, monarchists (especially Carlists), Falangists and other semi-Fascist groups, army commanders, and higher clergy. The Popular Front (or Republicans) comprised liberals, socialists, Communists, and anarchists. Like all broad coalitions, both of these were subject to internal fissures, but the National Front was better able to withstand them and showed the degree of unity necessary to win the war.

In the first place, the Right was susceptible to fewer ideological divisions than the Left. There was, for example, broad agreement between conservatives and Falangists on the necessity for an authoritarian régime. Any disagreements tended to be secondary:

The Spanish Civil War

on the precise nature of the authority and on the role of paramilitary organizations. Republican divisions, however, were more fundamental, perhaps because left-wing ideologies are usually more diverse and complex than those of the Right. A three-sided conflict developed between libertarian constitutionalists, authoritarian socialists or Communists, and libertarian anarchists. Any agreement between these was nearly always on a negative basis and was induced by common fear of a Nationalist victory. The National Front possessed greater ideological cohesion, the bond being strengthened by the commitment of the Catholic Church to Franco's victory. Pope Pius XI gave to the Nationalists a crusading zeal, arguing that the enemy had never been so clearly identifiable: 'The first, the greatest and now the general peril, is certainly communism in all its forms and degrees.'[2] The Popular Front, however, was divided between adherents of Marx and Bakunin, or were even, in the case of Azaña and his supporters, admirers of Cromwell. On the whole, the Right were able to implement opportunist policies, and changes of course could be accomplished by its leadership with minimal internal opposition.

The continuity of this leadership was the Right's greatest asset. Franco was not one of the century's great intellects; indeed, Puzzo states that 'His head was a cemetery of dead ideas'.[3] Nevertheless, he was the focal point which the Left lacked. Republican leaders like Azaña, Caballero and Negrin found it impossible to emulate the way in which he held disparate groups together. Franco was expert at rendering disputes superficial and preventing any deeper rift. He gave a meaningful role to all the Nationalist factions, while retaining ultimate power in his own hands. Hence the Carlists were satisfied by the 1938 Clerical Laws and the Falangists by the role assigned to them in propaganda. His first National Council incorporated a complete cross-section of the Right, including twenty Falangists and eight Carlists, and he managed to postpone indefinitely any decision to restore the monarchy, assuming himself Mussolinian powers under the title *Caudillo*. The factions of the Left, by contrast, regarded any attempt to impose a strong leadership as an obstacle to the pursuit of their individual programmes. Hence fighting broke out in Barcelona in 1937 between anarchists, socialists and Communists, while Caballero and Negrin were both ousted from below for attempting to put their own stamp on the Republican war effort.

Aspects of European History 1789–1980

The effectiveness of political organization and the fortunes of war were closely related. The degree of political organization influenced military performance but, equally, military success or failure strengthened or weakened political coalitions. The National Front possessed, in addition to a capacity for greater cohesion, the crucial advantage of extensive assistance from Germany and Italy. German aid was of the highest quality, including 16,000 military advisers, the latest aircraft, and the participation of the Kondor Legion. Italy provided even more assistance: nearly 50,000 troops, 763 aircraft and the use of ninety-one warships. On three occasions all this support was of vital importance to the National Front and held the rebellion together. The first was the transporting of Franco's troops from Morocco to Spain in German and Italian aircraft (1936), an essential preliminary to Franco's conquest of Andalusia. The second was the boost given to Nationalist morale by the sudden inflow of equipment in 1937. The third was the acceleration of Franco's offensive in Catalonia by a final massive consignment of arms and transports in 1939.

The Popular Front, it is true, received much assistance from the Soviet Union and from the thousands of volunteers, from a score of countries, who joined the International Brigades. But it also faced severe disadvantages. Stalin was unwilling to commit Russia too fully; Soviet supply lines were longer and more vulnerable than those of Italy, and Stalin was anxious not to over-commit himself in case he should leave Russia vulnerable to invasion by Germany. It was, however, in its relations with the Western powers that the Republic encountered its greatest obstacles. A series of French governments, headed by Blum and Daladier, carefully avoided involvement in the war for fear that this would destroy the stability achieved by the temporary consensus on the French Left. The British government, meanwhile, established the Non-Intervention Committee in 1936 in an attempt to prevent the provision of either side. Unfortunately, while Britain, the United States and France adhered to the Committee's regulations by not supplying the Republicans, Germany and Italy openly flouted them by assisting Franco. The result was that the transfusions given to the rebel forces were denied to a democratically elected government, a tragic anomaly in international conduct.

*

252

The Spanish Civil War

The Spanish Civil War reflected the ideological divisions within Europe, and excited intense passions among writers and artists, especially from Malraux, Borkenau, Lorca, Picasso, Cornford, Spender, Auden, Orwell and Hemingway. It also shaped the whole course of international relations between 1936 and 1939 by causing several basic diplomatic trends to converge.

The first of these trends was a growing *rapport* between Europe's two Fascist leaders. Italy had, during the 1920s, been firmly aligned with Britain and France. But a serious rift had opened over the Abyssinian crisis and the application of economic sanctions against Mussolini's régime destroyed the ten-year-old system of collective security. Italian involvement in the Spanish Civil War ensured that this alienation would be permanent and that there would be no reconciliation with the Western democracies. The war, indeed, added a further momentum to this diplomatic change and tipped Italy into the German camp. Hitler skilfully exploited Mussolini's resentment of France and Britain, knowing that the inevitable sense of isolation would result in a major diplomatic realignment. According to Hassell, the German ambassador in Rome: 'The role played by the Spanish conflict as regards Italy's relations with France and England would be similar to that of the Abyssinian conflict, bringing out clearly the actual opposing interests of the Powers. All the more clearly will Italy realize the advisability of confronting the Western Powers shoulder-to-shoulder with Germany.'[4] This expectation was entirely accurate. Ciano, the Italian Foreign Minister, expressed Mussolini's relief at the prospect of a new Italo-German *rapprochement*. 'Italy has broken out of her isolation; she is the centre of the most formidable political and military combination which has ever existed.' This 'combination' included the 'Rome-Berlin Axis', the Anti-Comintern Pact which Italy joined in 1937, and the Pact of Steel, a formal military alliance established in 1939.

Co-operation between Italy and Germany had far-reaching consequences, the most important of which was the removal of Italian constraint on Hitler's policy of expansion in Central Europe. Although he had clearly indicated in *Mein Kampf* that he intended to construct a Greater Germany, Hitler had been impeded by Mussolini's own interest in Austria. Military involvement in Spain, however, absorbed Mussolini's attention, allowing Hitler to carry out, without Italian opposition, the annexation of Austria in 1938.

Meanwhile, the Spanish Civil War also helped condition the Anglo-French response to Hitler's aggressive diplomacy. Eden, Chamberlain and Daladier all feared that the Spanish Civil War could easily overspill into a European war unless cautious policies were pursued. Eden preferred the principle of containment implicit in the Non-Intervention Committee, while Chamberlain opted for appeasement; both were appalled by the prospect of the damage and loss of life which a mechanized attack would inflict, as had already been demonstrated by the bombing of Guernica and Madrid. These reactions were carefully exploited by Hitler, who had, by the conclusion of the Munich Settlement in 1938, achieved most of his short-term objectives. Anglo-French policies, in turn, provoked a major change in Soviet policy; by 1939 Stalin had decided to abandon the Western powers and seek accommodation with Hitler. (See Chapter 25.) Thus Hitler made enormous gains through the agency of the Spanish Civil War. A new bond existed between Italy and Germany, collective security in the West had been wrecked on the policy of appeasement, and the Franco-Soviet Pact of 1936 was replaced, in August 1939, by the Nazi-Soviet Non-Aggression Pact.

The war also had an important effect on the development of weapons and military strategy. Again, Germany appeared to benefit most directly. Hitler used Spain as a testing ground for the products of his rearmament plan, exploiting especially the opportunity for training German pilots. The German experience derived from the war helped shape the *Blitzkrieg* tactics used against Poland in 1939 and France in 1940, which brought immediate and spectacular success. It is doubtful, however, if Italy received the same benefits. Her commitment was more total than Germany's and the advantages derived from experience were cancelled by the threat of military exhaustion. Mussolini was not unaware that, in 1939, Italy was in no fit state to embark upon another war, and he expressed reservations about Hitler's invasion of Poland. Russia, too, derived no benefit from her involvement in Spain. It could be argued that Russian strategists drew the wrong military conclusions; one of the reasons for the rapidity of the German advance into Russia in 1941 was that Soviet tanks were used, as in Spain, for infantry support, rather than as independent units. If, however, governments erred in their assessment of the war's lessons, many individuals did not. Before 1941 the most active resistance to German occupation came in France and Yugoslavia from partisans, who had served as

The Spanish Civil War

volunteers in the International Brigades.

Finally, the Spanish Civil War further demonstrated the ineffectiveness of the League of Nations as an international organization. The League had already failed to prevent the Japanese occupation of Manchuria, or to secure the withdrawal of Italian troops from Abyssinia. From 1936 onwards, however, the League was even deprived of direct access to major crises. The Non-Intervention Committee, it is true, was inspired by the League Covenant, which insisted that member states should not interfere with each other's internal affairs. But the Committee itself was outside the immediate range of the League's activity. It was a body which reflected the political aims of its founding states and not, as it should have been, an institution with a broader juridical base. Azaña argued, in 1937, that the Committee could in no way substitute for the League, 'for it is not an emanation of that body, it has not the powers of that body, if it is not in conformity ... with the principles which the Covenant sets forth'.[5] The League was, in effect, cut off from international decision making by *ad hoc* bodies claiming to carry out its principles. The point was later taken by the founders of the United Nations Organization, who took care to ensure that there was a more effective structure of contacts and referral between the different committees and the central institutions.

28

The Contradictions of the Third French Republic 1918–40

This period of French history is often bypassed by the student and general reader, as its fragmented details and enormous complexity make it difficult to generalize about trends and themes. One way out of the problem is to label the period 'France in decline' and then find reasons for French military collapse in 1940. There is much to be said for such an approach but, inevitably, a very one-sided picture will emerge of France between the wars. An alternative method, followed by this chapter, is to highlight the complexities as a series of unresolved contradictions affecting the constitution, the economy, diplomacy and military planning.

*

During the first phase of its existence (1870–1914) the Third Republic had had to struggle to overcome the threats of rightist forces to destroy it. The preoccupation with this had been so intense that the process of contest and reconciliation, essential for the progressive evolution of any political institutions, had been inadequately worked through. The legacy for the second phase (1918–40) was political deadlock. The basic problem, in outline, was a lack of true balance and harmony between the two main components of the Constitution: the legislature and the executive. The 1875 Constitutional Laws had made these of roughly equal status. During the 1870s and 1880s, however, the legislature, or National Assembly, had come into conflict with the executive, or President, and had emerged with greatly enhanced authority. Indeed, the presidency

The Contradictions of the Third French Republic

had been so severely weakened that an alternative form of executive power had to emerge, this time from within the legislature itself. The major executive functions were now assumed by the prime minister and his cabinet colleagues, all of whom were elected members of the National Assembly. At first sight this would seem an ideal compromise, based on the best traditions of parliamentary democracy. But what happened was that the conflict between the Assembly and the President was now replaced by internal strife within the Assembly, between groups which tried to form the country's governments. The result was chronic ministerial instability. Between 1918 and 1939 there were no fewer than thirty-six governments, formed by twenty separate prime ministers; the British record, during the same period, was nine ministries under five prime ministers. Several reasons can be advanced for what amounted to a twenty-two-year crisis.

The first was an example of how the evolution of the French political system had stopped prematurely. Léon Blum, the Socialist leader, pointed to the greatest single deficiency: 'If only there were political parties in France.'[1] To be effective, a legislature must have a well-developed party system, for otherwise, its powers are dissipated in the constant search for a governing majority. In other words, attention comes to be focused on short-term political manoeuvres rather than on long-term legislation.

France did possess the normal range of political ideologies, together with the sort of class divisions which should have promoted party politics. But the major problem was the absence of effective party *organization*. Largely responsible for this was the electoral system, the *scrutin d'arrondissement*, which emphasized the individual candidate rather than any wider loyalties he might have to a party caucus. The result was a somewhat unusual contradiction. France, the most centralized state in Europe, was represented and governed by deputies whose real strength came from narrowly-based provincial support. It is hardly surprising, therefore, that parties were relatively small, and that their leaders found it exceptionally difficult to establish any lasting unity. Blum, for example, had to contend with Pivert and Zyromski, both of whom had strong local support for their virtual secession from the Socialist Party (SFIO) during the late 1930s. The Radical Party, under Herriot and Daladier, was reformed during the 1920s and 1930s in an effort to keep pace with 'changing facts'.[2] Eventually,

257

however, internal divisions reappeared and reforms were pulled apart. The party had too many local interests and conflicting policies; in D. Johnson's phrase, it was 'an amalgam of contradictory ideas'.[3]

Thus the parties were too small and too weak to stand much chance of commanding the sort of parliamentary support that goes with stable government. But was this necessarily a bad thing? Would there not be an inducement to form coalitions and *blocs* which would represent a wider range of views both in the Assembly and among the electorate? Much of the political history of France between the wars concerns the effort to do precisely that. Coalitions of the centrist and right-wing parties included the *Bloc National* formed by Clemenceau in 1919, and the National Union set up by Poincaré in 1926. The Centre and Left combined, under Herriot, in the *Cartel des Gauches* from 1924 and, under Blum, in the Popular Front in 1936. Unfortunately, such attempts to find common ground always failed, for beneath the appearance of co-operation lay another contradiction. On the one hand, the struggle for power continued within the coalitions so that governments rose and fell with undiminished rapidity. On the other hand, this was not, as might be thought, caused by any refusal to compromise on policies, but rather the reverse. All parties had to limit their proposed legislation and abandon any contentious projects of reform. What happened, therefore, was that the parties became less distinctive in their philosophy, but no less competitive in their pursuit of cabinet posts. The paradox applied especially to the Radicals, who supplied ministers for most of the inter-war governments. In the words of a perceptive contemporary, they were reduced to the practice of 'moderation with extreme vehemence'.[1]

The weakness of the party system was made the more serious by the strength of the National Assembly. By the First World War the Assembly had come to dominate the political scene more completely than the 1875 Constitutional Laws had ever envisaged. In the first place, each of its two parts, the Chamber of Deputies and the Senate, had the right to impeach ministers. All governments between the wars faced extensive questioning, and most of them fell as a direct result of the *ordre du jour*, in effect a vote of no confidence. Secondly, the Assembly had developed a series of standing committees which, after the First World War, interfered increasingly in the process of government. The former, says D. Thomson, 'served excellently to sacrifice ministerial stability to parliamentary control over policy'.[4]

The Contradictions of the Third French Republic

Such powers had not, unfortunately, made the Assembly receptive to constitutional reform. The electoral system, for example, was in dire need of change. The introduction of proportional representation might well have tightened the party system by allowing national issues to predominate over local interests. But the Assembly allowed only a limited experiment, and ended even that.

Some constitutions possess a device for emergency government in the event of the normal process seizing up. The French presidency could have fulfilled such a role. Although it had declined dramatically since the days of Macmahon and Grévy, attempts were made by Poincaré from 1913 to give the presidency a meaningful function. The Assembly, however, was anxious to prevent any revival of presidential power, fearing a possible slide into authoritarian government. It therefore voted down all proposals for the election of the president by the public at large, and gave the office to politicians of little standing. Thus, in 1920, the Assembly denied the presidency to Clemenceau, who could have served with distinction as an elder statesman, and gave it to the little known Deschanel, who had to be removed a few months later because of insanity. The presidency had, in effect, become a wasted office and it was unable to take any initiative in reconciling party disputes. This was one more factor which led Reynaud, one-time prime minister, to observe in 1937 that 'the parliamentary régime had failed to function'.[5]

*

Political crises usually coexist with economic problems. In the case of France these were partly brought about by the war, and partly inherited from the period before 1914. The war had affected France more severely than any other Western combatant. She had suffered immense destruction in ten of her north-eastern *départements* and had lost 1.5 million men, including about 30 per cent of her male population between the ages of eighteen and twenty-eight; clearly the latter would have a serious long-term effect by causing a dramatic fall in the future birthrate. Of the inherited problems two were especially serious. France had a much smaller industrial base than her western competitors (in 1913, for example, she was producing only about one-seventh as much coal as Germany). Future expansion would therefore be much more difficult, and would have to be accompanied by extensive modernization. Secondly, the fiscal system was one of the most antiquated in Europe, having

Aspects of European History 1789–1980

changed hardly at all since the days of the Revolution. Many historians have pointed to the selfishness of the wealthy classes and to the ridiculously unfair system of extracting revenue which actually prevented the introduction of income tax until 1920. In 1918, therefore, France faced the double task of reconstruction and renovation. All attention, however, was directed to the former, in the confident expectation that the latter would inevitably follow. Enormous hope was pinned to the reparations which were to be taken from Germany. Not only would these pay for making good the war damage, they would also make possible the modernization of industry, and the adjustment of the whole economy to twentieth-century conditions. France, therefore, suffered a profound psychological shock once it became apparent that these reparations were smaller than had been expected, that they were to spread over a long period, and that they were extremely difficult to enforce.

The first lesson of the early 1920s, therefore, was that there was no straightforward formula for economic recovery or growth. In fact, France faced serious inflation, industrial stagnation and a permanent shortage of revenue which made her social services among the most primitive in Europe. Government attempts to deal with these problems were, for two reasons, cautious and unadventurous. First, no minister could afford to antagonize the bankers or the wealthy sections of the community by proposing extensive fiscal reform, for in the indignant outcry among many deputies and senators, it would undoubtedly be toppled. Second, France was, as yet, completely uninfluenced by recent and progressive economic theory; Keynes, for example, was to make no impact at all. Hence French economists considered it the government's function not to push the economy along, but only to create the environment for natural economic growth. During the late 1920s and early 1930s governments attached overriding importance to a strong currency in the belief that inflation was the worst enemy to economic stability. Thus there was an obsessive determination never to repeat the 1928 devaluation of the franc. By 1931, in fact, industry had picked up, and general economic revival seemed to be indicated by the accumulation of the largest gold reserves anywhere in the world, outside the United States. A strong currency backed by international confidence – this, according to official thought, was a guarantee against future crisis.

Then came a major contradiction. For a while, the strength of the

The Contradictions of the Third French Republic

franc and the huge gold reserves appeared to shield France from the impact of the Great Depression which had hit the rest of the industrialized world by 1931. But, in reality, great damage was to be done by the government's determination to underpin the value of the franc. In the first place, the arrival of the Depression was merely delayed, so that France suffered the worst effects just as other countries were beginning to recover. Secondly, the government made matters far worse by following a policy of savage deflation in order to save the franc from sinking in value, even though governments elsewhere had decided to leave the gold standard and let their national currencies find their own levels. The parties of the French Centre and Right were the victims of defective logic. Monetary policies, they argued, had protected France for three years against the Depression. Now they must be intensified to push France out of the Depression. What such views failed to realize was that France had been less immediately affected by the Depression not because of the strong franc, but because she had been less heavily industrialized and more self-sufficient than most of the other major economies. Far from being a shield against Depression, deflation exerted a powerful drag against recovery. This was emphasized by the Left, which had the chance to remedy matters when the Popular Front came to power in 1936. Unfortunately, the sudden switch to reflation, government spending and higher wages proved too sudden and only brought further chaos. It was not until 1938 that the French economy could really be considered to be on the mend, by which time Britain, the United States and, more ominously, Germany, had widened the gap of industrial production. Compared with these countries, France was now worse off than she had been in 1928.

*

French foreign policy had, since the 1870s and 1880s, been based on avoiding isolation and on forming against Germany alliances with states in Western and Eastern Europe. Unfortunately, such connections proved dangerously unstable between the wars. France's wartime allies in the West both wanted to avoid further European commitments once Germany had been defeated; hence the United States withdrew from the League of Nations into voluntary isolation, while Britain refused to ratify the Geneva Protocol and officially denounced the French invasion of the Ruhr (1923). During the 1930s the British government set the precedent for appeasement, a policy which France had no alternative but to follow. One by one the clauses in the Treaty of Versailles, intended to safeguard France and Belgium, were torn up by Hitler as it became evident that Baldwin and Chamberlain were not prepared to risk war to help France enforce them. Germany proceeded to rearm in 1935, occupied the Rhineland in 1936 and expanded territorially from 1938.

French connections with Eastern Europe proved no more profitable in the long run. The Bolshevik Revolution and Lenin's repudiation of all debts to France caused the French government to abandon the once invaluable Russian alliance. Instead, alliances were built up with the smaller Eastern European states, including Poland (1921 and 1925), Czechoslovakia (1925) and Yugoslavia (1927). But this was a poor substitute for the support of a single major power. Then, during the 1930s, successive French governments found themselves confronted by an impossible dilemma. At the very time that she was being forced on to the defensive by a revived Germany, France was also faced with the appalling prospect of having to contemplate assisting her client states in the East against Hitler. Far from distracting Germany, therefore, the French system looked like draining France. There was one possible solution – reconciliation with Russia. But even the 1935 Franco-Russian Alliance fell apart. Paradoxically, the connection with Russia weakened France still further. Stalin suspected that France expected the Soviet Union to fulfil the role of containing Germany in the East without any corresponding French effort from the West. He watched with alarm as Daladier, conscious of France's vulnerability to German attack, conspired with Chamberlain to abandon Czechoslovakia in 1938. Convinced that the French Alliance offered Russia nothing, he compounded French insecurity by seeking accommodation with Germany instead. By 1939 France had been through the motions of concluding alliances with every state of significance in Eastern Europe and yet had emerged diplomatically enfeebled and dependent once again on the support of Britain, the very power whose lukewarm attitude in the 1920s had pushed France into this hectic activity in the first place.

Then, at the time of greatest French weakness, there occurred a diplomatic revolution. Both Chamberlain and Daladier reversed their appeasement of Nazi Germany and, in 1939, extended a guarantee of protection to Poland. This policy, although honourable, was suicidal, for Germany was growing stronger by the month in the

The Contradictions of the Third French Republic

West and had no longer anything to fear from the French network of alliances in the East, which had long since collapsed. Above all, France was without the lynchpin of her previous war effort against Germany, the support of Russia. But for this backing in the First World War, France could not have won the Battle of the Marne; and the absence of Russian troops to draw off a large part of the German offensive in 1940 must count as the most important single reason for French defeat then.

There is another irony which highlights the muddle of French diplomacy in the 1930s. Although Germany was considered the major enemy and the most serious potential military threat, the French government gave more attention to Italy and the situation in the Mediterranean, for it was generally assumed that the Rhine would be an area of stalemate and defensive strategy. And yet the latter was the only point at which France could exert any pressure in defence of Poland. It seemed, therefore, that France had recovered an active role at the very time that she had lost the means of fulfilling it.

*

How well equipped was France to fight a war in 1939? It used to be thought that the French armies were overwhelmed by superior German forces. More recent estimates, however, have shown that this was not the case at all. Against the 103 German divisions on the Western Front, France mustered ninety-nine which, of course, were supported by British contingents as well. The Allies had a slight superiority in tanks (3000 against 2700) and a massive advantage in large warships (107 against thirteen). The French were able, in addition, to put up 11,200 artillery pieces against the 7710 German guns. The only real deficiency of the Allies was in airpower, where the *Luftwaffe* had a clear advantage.

On paper, therefore, the combatants were evenly matched. Yet France suffered the most rapid and humiliating defeat in her entire history. This was the more shattering because military preparations had been made by strategists who had for years been convinced that war was inevitable. In retrospect, however, we can see the under-lying flaws in strategic thought, a sad counterpart to the failure of French foreign policy.

The expectation of a German invasion was entirely in accord with precedent; after all, France had been attacked through Alsace-Lorraine in 1870, and via Belgium in 1914. It also seemed logical that a country with a population of forty million could not reasonably be expected to do more than fend off a power with sixty-five million people and a stronger industrial base. Common sense, therefore, called for effective defences. What emerged, however, was an inflexible system which proved entirely unable to counter Hitler's revolutionary *Blitzkrieg* tactics. The French General Staff put their entire confidence in the Maginot Line, constructed at great expense between the wars. This symbolized France's commitment to fighting a static war across an extended front – a repetition, in other words, of the 1914–18 struggle which had eventually worn down the superior German war machine. But history did not repeat itself. In 1940 the Germans bypassed the Line and punched a hole into the supposedly impenetrable (and therefore lightly defended) Ardennes, before racing to the Channel ports. The French forces were taken by surprise and were unable to manoeuvre with sufficient speed to plug the gaps. By committing themselves so completely to extended linear defences, the French strategists invited a bold and concentrated German blow on a vulnerable section. It is ironical that one of the most expensive and carefully planned defensive walls in history should also have been one of the most useless.

As we have seen, the French army was by no means short of modern equipment. In fact, French tanks were considered superior in armament and firepower to their German rivals, and a concerted effort had been made during the 1930s to keep them rolling off the assembly lines. And yet there was no attempt to integrate the new technology into revised military thinking. A Committee of Generals made the revealing statement in 1936 that 'it does not believe this technical progress sensibly modifies the essential rules hitherto established in the domain of tactics'.[6] Thus, while German commanders like Guderian were establishing independent and highly manoeuvrable tank units, the French view was still, in the words of Major Laporte, that 'the tank must above all be considered as one of the auxiliaries of the foot soldier'.[6] The result was that the heavier and better constructed French machines were, nevertheless, no match for the lighter and more effectively deployed *Panzer* divisions. Similar ignorance was shown over the destructive potential of the aircraft. While the *Luftwaffe* were experimenting, at the expense of Spanish civilians, with *Stuka* dive-bombers, and were devising a strategy to gain control of the air, the French Commander-in-Chief, General Gamelin, believed that 'There is no such thing as an aerial battle. There is only the battle on the ground'.[6] In view of what happened from 1940 onwards, this must rank as one of modern history's more remarkable statements. If any single factor can be said to have destroyed the morale of the French army in July 1940, it was surely the ease with which the *Luftwaffe* controlled the skies over France.

One of the main defects of the administration was its complexity; much the same can be said of the structure of command within the army. France had her fair share of military statesmen, Weygand and then Gamelin replacing First World War leaders like Joffre, Foch and Pétain. But they were often cut off from their immediate subordinates. Gamelin was desperately anxious to direct personally all aspects of military strategy but, because of his inefficient delegation of duties, ended up controlling very little. This is what de Gaulle had in mind when he referred to Gamelin's headquarters as 'his ivory tower at Vincennes'.

*

Some contemporaries thought that the collapse of France was due to the loss of her previous vitality and the transformation of strength into weakness. Hence Pétain blamed 'our moral laxness', while an English observer considered the Third Republic 'graft-ridden, incompetent, Communistic and corrupt'. The real problem, however, was that France lacked internal harmony because many of its strongest forces were turned inwards. Hence, in the words of Paul Guerin in 1939: 'The régime is paradoxical, conservative in purpose, revolutionary at heart, extremist and idealist in its programmes, opportunist and moderate in its actions.'[7]

29
The Soviet Economy 1917–80

On assuming power in October 1917, the Bolsheviks intended to redirect the Russian economy as quickly as possible according to Marxist principles. The 1918 Constitution of the RSFSR (Russian Socialist Federated Soviet Republic) advanced 'the fundamental aim of abolishing all exploitation of man by man, of eliminating completely the division of society into classes'.[1] Lenin hoped to promote harmony between the industrial and agricultural sectors and exploit all the most modern techniques: 'Communism is the Soviet power plus the electrification of the whole country.' He also intended to promote state ownership through all levels of industry and agriculture, referring, for example, to collectivization as the 'indispensable theoretical truth'.[2]

It soon became obvious, however, that the disturbed time between 1917 and 1929 made impossible any systematic application of Marxist theories. Instead, Lenin's economic policy was based on trial and error, with a changeable mixture of ideology and pragmatism.

At first the emphasis was on caution, as Lenin concentrated on establishing the Bolsheviks politically. Hence the new régime was relatively lenient towards private enterprise in both industry and agriculture. By the middle of 1918 only the banks, foreign trade, and strategic industries like armaments works, had been nationalized. The Decree of November 1917 had even restricted the right of workers on factory committees to representation only, and specifically prevented any contribution to decision making. The peasants

The Soviet Economy 1917–80

were allowed considerable concessions. Lenin had allowed them to seize the estates of the nobility in the hope of gaining their political support for the whole Bolshevik programme. Once the estates had changed hands there was no question of the peasantry agreeing to voluntary collectivization. They were fiercely determined to keep possession of their small individual holdings. Lenin realized that he would have to consolidate his own political power before he tried to change their minds.

By the middle of 1918 the Bolsheviks considered that conditions had changed sufficiently to warrant a new approach. Because of the threats of invasion and counter-revolution, Lenin now emphasized the need to tighten up internally and, at the same time, to try to put the Marxist programme into top gear. The result, between 1918 and 1921, was the policy of War Communism. This was basically an attempt to replace the free market by state control over all forms of production and distribution. The main measures included the introduction of state farms, the requisitioning of grain to supply the cities, the abolition of banks and credit, the nationalization of all industries, and the allocation of special production targets. This was the first attempt at a state-controlled economy, but it was carried out with inadequate planning and few directives. It resulted in confusion and resistance from the population, especially the peasantry. It also caused a decline in initiative and output; industry, for example, managed in 1921 to reach only 13 per cent of the production level of 1914. Worse still, the Bolsheviks were threatened with widespread disobedience; the 1921 Kronstadt Revolt was based on a demand for 'Soviets without Communists'. Complete failure was imminent. Not only had total state control been ineffectual, it had actually impeded the Bolshevik war effort and clearly had to be reversed. Lenin covered his failure by explaining that the policy had been forced on Russia 'by war and ruin' as 'a temporary measure'.[3]

His strategic withdrawal took the form of the New Economic Policy, announced in 1921. Lenin now emphasized the scale of the problem in moving Russia along the road to socialism, arguing that the time-span should be measured not by years but by decades. 'Our poverty and ruin are so great that we cannot *at one stroke* restore full-scale factory, state, socialist production.'[4] To think only in ideological terms was naïve. 'If certain communists were inclined to think it possible in three years to transform the whole economic foundation, to change the very roots of agriculture, they were

267

certainly dreamers.'[5] The basic strategy was now to restore to the economy a degree of capitalism and private enterprise, although no departure was to be allowed from the strict party control over political institutions. About 91 per cent of industrial enterprises were returned to private ownership or trusts, the currency was restored, and requisitioning was replaced by new regulations allowing the peasantry to dispose freely of their surplus produce on payment of a tax. Some concessions were made to socialist principles: every effort was to be made to persuade the peasantry to move away from their obsession with private ownership, and collective farms and co-operatives were to be promoted. The keynote, however, was to be patience.

The early results were disappointing, as the economy experienced further setbacks with a famine in 1921–2 and a financial crisis in 1923. By 1928, however, recovery was substantial. More food was available for the cities, and industrial production had increased steadily: 35.5 million tons of coal were mined in that year, compared with 29.1 million in 1913. But, like all strategic compromises, the New Economic Policy posed the problem of what course was to be followed in the long term.

*

In fact, from the earliest stages of the NEP, the Bolsheviks were divided over the best means of promoting economic growth. During the first half of the 1920s the so-called 'rightists', under Bukharin, argued that the NEP should be maintained for the foreseeable future. The key to future growth was improvements in agriculture; this meant that socialism should be introduced slowly and steadily – 'at the speed of the peasant nag'.[6] The peasantry should be given strong incentives to produce more. 'We have to tell the whole peasantry, and all its strata: "get rich, accumulate, develop your economy".'[7] The 'leftists', who included Trotsky and Preobrazhensky, disagreed with Bukharin's emphasis on agriculture, caution and personal incentives. Preobrazhensky argued that 'We won't be given much time to build',[8] the hostile capitalist states would see to that. To promote private enterprise among the peasantry was asking for trouble because this would inevitably lead to a new bourgeoisie in the form of wealthy peasants, of *kulaks*. These *kulaks* would become hostile to the whole ethos of the Communist régime, and could be expected to identify with 'world

The Soviet Economy 1917–80

capital'. The only strategy to follow, therefore, was to force the pace of industrialization. This would, within a short period, give Russia the means of defending herself against the West and, since all the resources of agriculture could be used by the state to assist the process, the *kulak* class would be eliminated. Far from wishing to prolong the NEP, therefore, the 'leftists' hoped to end it as quickly as possible and return to a more effectively planned form of war Communism.

The man who eventually dictated the course to be followed appeared, during the 1920s, to be inconsistent in his ideas. At first Stalin used Bukharin's ideas to attack the leftists, then, having safely disposed of Trotsky and Preobrazhensky, he turned on Bukharin. It is clear that Stalin's whole approach was based on *political* considerations and that what interested him most was the best means of consolidating his own power. Only gradually did he put together an economic strategy, and even this did not develop any concrete form until after the grain shortage of 1928.[9] From 1929, however, Stalin became more explicit about his economic aims. In the first place, the whole base of the Soviet economy had to be transformed in order to meet the threat of foreign invasion. Only the leadership could design the institutions to achieve this, which fitted in well with Stalin's search for personal power. The whole process would be subsidized by agriculture, which would be reorganized on a collective basis. Although he did not acknowledge it, Stalin had taken over Preobrazhensky's ideas. The main difference was that he intended to go to greater lengths in implementing them.

His instruments were a series of Five Year Plans, the targets for which were devised by Gosplan, with the personal intervention of Stalin himself. The first Five Year Plan (1928–33), which overlapped collectivization of agriculture, boosted heavy industry. The second (1933–8) extended heavy industry to previously undeveloped areas like the Caucasus and Siberia and also improved major canal and rail networks. The third Plan, launched in 1938, concentrated mainly on the development of strategic industries and armaments. All the Plans were accompanied by state coercion. Stalin revived the *Cheka*, in the form of the OGPU and then the NKVD, dispatched 'dekulakization squads' to overcome peasant resistance to collective farming, reduced trade unions to the status of 'Party transmission belts to the masses', and conducted the most extensive political purges in European history.

269

Aspects of European History 1789–1980

There has been some controversy over the impact of such changes. Stalin's measures were initially praised by Soviet historians and condemned by the West, but recently, as one writer points out, 'the roles are to some extent being reversed'.[10] It is certainly possible to advance both positive and negative arguments.

Stalin's positive achievement was concerned almost entirely with heavy industry. Between 1928 and 1941 steel and coal production increased fourfold and sixfold respectively and, by 1937, the Soviet Union had become the world's second largest manufacturer of heavy vehicles. Even a strong critic of Soviet economic measures, L. Pietromarchi, argues that the credit for setting up the Soviet industrial base must go to Stalin. Indeed, Stalin made three main contributions. First, he accelerated the whole process, breaking away from the much more cautious mentality of Bukharin and perhaps even of Lenin. Second, he extended the range of industrialization by equipping Siberia with plants and factories; these were to be the most important factor in the Russian fight for survival against the Nazis after 1941. Third, he found the resources to transform Russia's economic base without having to seek Western investment. In using agriculture to subsidize industry and squeezing every drop of money out of the ordinary consumer, Stalin devised a ruthless but effective method of accumulating capital.

On the other hand, Stalin's industrial measures are open to extensive criticism. There is evidence that he exaggerated Russia's industrial deficiency in 1929. The Tsars had developed a considerable industrial capacity, based on five main centres: Moscow (textiles), Petrograd (heavy industry), the Donetz region (coalfields), Baku (oil) and the Ukraine (iron and steel).[11] In a sense, the spadework had already been done, so that it is not altogether surprising that Stalin should have achieved such rapid results. He was also reluctant to acknowledge that most of his plans for widespread electrification and the development of Siberia were inherited from Lenin. At times Stalin became so obsessed with the statistics of production that some of the advances were cosmetic. Worst of all was the severe deprivation which accompanied industrial growth. Russia was unique in European economic history in experiencing an industrial revolution without corresponding improvements in the quality of life of the inhabitants. The serious shortage of consumer goods of all types was reflected in a popular riddle of the time: 'Why were Adam and Eve like Soviet citizens? Because they lived in

Paradise and had nothing to wear.'

The case against Stalin's agricultural measures is even more substantial. In the first place, he launched collective farming with inadequate information and statistics. He then sought to absolve himself from responsibility for the ensuing chaos by blaming local officials for being over-zealous. Secondly, collectivization policies inflicted appalling suffering on the peasantry, both through the activities of the dekulakization squads and the confiscation of grain supplies by the state. It is hardly surprising that the early 1930s should have seen massive resistance from the peasantry, who destroyed up to 50 per cent of the grain crop, 50 per cent of the total number of horses and 66 per cent of the sheep and goats. There was a greater threat of rebellion during the 1930s than there had ever been in the 1920s. Many peasants were even prepared to welcome the Germans in 1941, until they discovered that Hitler's plans for them were even nastier than Stalin's. Finally, Stalin could be charged with having set back agricultural production by twenty-five years, and with having set a dreadful precedent for the future.

The special problems following the Second World War make it difficult to integrate the last phase of Stalin's rule (1945–53) with the preceding period. Priority had to be given to reconstruction, with the emphasis again being placed on heavy industry. In the fourth and fifth Five Year Plans the consumer continued to suffer, partly because of post-war conditions, and partly because Stalin was determined not to weaken his resolve. Agriculture was reorganized into new collectives, but production remained as low as ever. By 1953 the total agricultural production was only 10 per cent more than it had been in 1914, while the number of livestock was 10 per cent down.

Referring to Russia's historically agricultural base, Stalin had once claimed that the country was 'walking on two unequal legs'.[9] By 1953 he had made the USSR the world's second industrial power, but the strengthening of this leg had been accomplished by crippling the other.

*

Considerable efforts were made after 1953 to redress the balance and to develop both sectors of the economy. At the same time, policies became more pragmatic and varied from one period to another. The main reason for this was the end of the long era of monolithic dictatorship. Stalin's successors (Malenkov until 1955, Khruschev until 1964, and the collective leadership of Brezhnev and Kosygin after 1964) possessed fewer powers and took care to avoid the extremes of Stalinist coercion.

The strongest area of the Soviet economy was still heavy industry. No real alteration of Stalin's emphasis was envisaged except, for a short period, by Malenkov, who hoped to promote the consumer industries. Khruschev, however, pulled the economy back on course after Malenkov had been off-loaded as a 'deviationist'. Production figures were as impressive as ever and, by the 1960s, the Soviet Union led the world in hydro-electric schemes and in heavy engineering, especially in turbines. It also had the capacity to sustain an enormous conventional war machine and to deploy nuclear weapons. By the 1970s it had achieved parity with the United States in the military and heavy industrial spheres.

An examination of the whole range of Soviet industry, however, reveals three problems. The first is the complexity and sometimes the inefficiency of its organization. Soviet leaders were always conscious of this and, from time to time, tried to alter the structure. Khrushchev, for example, scrapped the various ministries in 1957 and substituted 105 regional economic councils. But Brezhnev and Kosygin considered these inadequate and so devised another system. This, too, proved less than fully efficient as a vehicle for state planning. The second problem was that industrial growth still penalized the consumer. Malenkov tried to give a boost to light industry, but Khrushchev postponed any further improvements until the ill-fated Five Year Plan of 1956. Brezhnev and Kosygin did rather more; the Five Year Plan of 1971–5 gave priority to consumer industries. There remained, however, a large gap in consumer goods between the Soviet Union on the one hand and the West, or even the rest of Eastern Europe, on the other. The third snag was that industry generally became, during the 1960s and 1970s more and more dependent on advanced technology. In the 'high priority' areas like weapons and space research, Soviet technology was well-advanced, but during the 1970s the West opened up a lead in electronics and computers,[12] especially where these were related to the consumer market.

Agriculture, since the death of Stalin, experienced a major change of policy. It was no longer considered merely as a means to subsidize industrial growth and was given recognition in its own right.

The Soviet Economy 1917–80

Khrushchev gave it particular attention as, indeed, he had strong personal connections with agriculture. He increased investment and promoted the exploitation of virgin lands and the planting of alternative crops like maize. He also guaranteed higher prices and wages and encouraged a rapid increase in the output of meat and milk. The result, between 1953 and 1958, was a period of unprecedented agricultural growth, which raised hopes of overtaking the West. But this was to prove only a temporary phenomenon and problems re-emerged between 1959 and 1963. The exploitation of the virgin lands had been unbalanced, leading to widespread soil erosion; maize had been imposed, by central decision, on many areas for which it was quite inappropriate; and meat production had outstripped the availability of animal feed, necessitating the slaughter of thirty million out of seventy million pigs. To make matters worse, there was a harvest failure in 1963. Khrushchev's reputation had been so badly damaged by the slide that he was edged out of power in 1964. Brezhnev and Kosygin tried to force recovery by pouring in new investment, estimated as one-quarter of the total capital available in the eighth and ninth Five Year Plans (1966–75). The results were varied, with an apparent alternation between good years (1968, 1970 and 1973) and bad ones (especially 1972).

Western observers agreed that agriculture was consistently the weakest area of the Soviet economy and that comparisons with the United States were distinctly unfavourable. In the 1960s the United States had two-thirds of the Soviet cultivated area and one-fifth of the Soviet labour force, yet produced about three-fifths more.[13] It was also estimated that about five times as much investment had to be put into Soviet agriculture to achieve a return comparable to the United States.[14] The Soviet leadership saw the solution in technical developments and the improved organization of the collective farms. American opinion, however, questioned whether collectivization could work satisfactorily. State control had clearly produced results in industry but, it was argued, agriculture is a different matter. There is always a greater need for individual judgement in the field than on the assembly line. It is also more difficult to direct agriculture efficiently from the centre because local peculiarities make it impossible to standardize production on anything like the same scale as in industry. Naturally, such an interpretation was rejected by the Soviet leadership, not least because any extensive decentralization would mean a step backwards towards the NEP.

Aspects of European History 1789–1980

Solutions, therefore, would have to be sought within the existing ideological framework.

In other ways, the leadership proved more adaptable. One of the major changes after 1963 was in the Soviet attitude towards the West. Stalin had always maintained a policy of strict isolation, whereas Brezhnev and Kosygin specifically sought economic contacts with the West. A change in United States policy made it possible for the West to reciprocate. Originally, American Presidents saw any large-scale commercial contacts with the Eastern *bloc* as a means of helping the Soviet advance towards industrial and military parity with the United States. By the late 1960s, however, it was obvious that this parity would soon be achieved anyway and that economic contacts would make little difference.[15] The commercial agreements which followed Nixon's visit to Moscow in 1972 were of particular importance to two areas. First, the consumer could be protected against the results of bad harvests by huge imports of grain from North America – a sharp contrast with the indifference of Stalin's régime to the suffering caused by shortages. Second, the purchase of computers and electronic technology made up for some of the deficiencies in Soviet industry.[16] In 1980, however, such contacts were affected, although not ended, by the decline of political détente which was accelerated by the Soviet invasion of Afghanistan (see Chapter 31). The long-term implications of this remain to be seen.

30

The Defeat of Nazi Germany

By June 1940 Hitler had conquered a greater area of Europe than any other leader in history. Under direct Nazi rule lay Poland, Slovakia, Norway, Denmark, the Benelux countries and France. Bohemia and Austria had become provinces of the Reich; while Italy, Hungary and Romania were military allies. Hitler had also demonstrated the effectiveness of the revolutionary *Blitzkrieg* and had modified the old Schlieffen Plan to achieve the stunning victory which had eluded the German High Command in 1914.

Yet, in under five years, the Third Reich lay in ruins and German military paramountcy had been destroyed. The period from 1941 onwards is a classic example of the misuse of a nation's resources in the pursuit of unrealistic and inappropriate policies. This chapter will concentrate particularly on Hitler's strategic and military errors, and upon the huge industrial disparity between Germany on the one hand, and the two major Allied powers on the other.

*

Although his war designs succeeded brilliantly against Poland and France, Hitler badly mismanaged the conflict against Britain, the Soviet Union and the United States.

Britain he had never regarded as a total enemy; indeed, in his *Secret Book*, he had referred to Britain as 'Germany's natural friend'. Consequently, he was always prepared to seek reconciliation, even 'on the basis of partitioning the world'.[1] His early strategy was based on forcing Britain back into neutrality, and he made the grave blunder of not committing Germany's total military capacity in 1940 to the invasion of Britain. Britain's survival was the first step towards the ultimate decline of Hitler's Reich. Alone, she did not possess the military or industrial capacity to defeat Germany. She was the wrong type of power in that her real strength was maritime rather than continental. But, as during the Napoleonic Wars, this gave her the potential for prolonged resistance. Churchill's crucial role was to keep the war going in the West and to extend the conflict to the periphery, especially North Africa and the Atlantic. Hitler made some effort to come to terms with this strategy, including an unsuccessful attempt to engage Franco's Spain in an offensive against Gibraltar. But he reacted with little interest to Admiral Raeder's proposals for breaking British contacts with the Empire and for an all-out campaign against Malta, Suez and North Africa. He also rejected Raeder's advice that further projects in the East should be postponed to ensure the mobilization of all Germany's resources for the struggle in the West. The effect of Britain's role in the war gradually became more serious as German commitments in North Africa and, after 1942, in Italy, weakened the *Wehrmacht's* offensive in Russia. Britain also acted as a stepping-stone for the United States' bombing attacks on Germany as well as a base for the combined Allied invasion of Normandy in 1944.

The invasion of Russia (1941) was undoubtedly the major mistake of Hitler's career, the decision being taken against the advice of the General Staff who stressed that country's hostile geography and climate. It appears, however, that Hitler was immovably committed to his ultimate design which would simultaneously give the Aryan race its promised *Lebensraum* and eradicate the centre of European Jewry and international Bolshevism. His strategic justification was more rational but no less questionable. He argued, for example, that the invasion of Russia would isolate Britain and that 'if Russia is destroyed, Britain's last hope will be shattered'.[2] This, however, directly contravened his opinion of November 1939 that 'We can oppose Russia only when we are free in the West'.[3] His premature invasion undid all the gains of the Nazi-Soviet Non-Aggression Pact, and brought about the very problem which much of his diplomacy in the 1930s had sought to avoid, a war involving Germany against major powers on two fronts. His claim that he had to have direct access to the oil supplies of the Caspian Sea area was also unconvincing, for Stalin had shown no signs of interfering with

The Defeat of Nazi Germany

the flow of fuel and essential minerals. The effect of 'Operation Barbarossa' was to commit Germany to war with a power which was three times her size in population, eighty times as large in area, and of much greater industrial capacity. It is hardly surprising that the major military setbacks experienced by the *Wehrmacht* occurred in Russia. These, in turn, took the pressure off Britain and greatly assisted the latter's peripheral war effort in the Mediterranean and North Africa.

Hitler showed his greatest ignorance over the United States, on which he declared war in 1941. He was convinced that her ethnic and racial mixture made America a degenerate power and that, as a result, she was 'permanently on the brink of revolution'.[4] He also assumed that the US war effort would be confined to the Pacific in a struggle which the Japanese were bound to win. Here Hitler made another great mistake. In January 1942 Roosevelt pledged to Churchill that he would give priority to the defeat of Germany, his reasoning being that American concentration on Japan might result in a Nazi victory over Russia and Britain. The Western Allies also agreed to co-ordinate their strategy and High Commands in the Combined Chiefs-of-Staffs Committee; in effect, they fought the war as one power, and achieved a degree of unity which never existed between Hitler, Mussolini and Tojo. The entry of the United States reactivated the war in the West, and made possible a more direct southern strategy which included the invasion of Italy in 1943. Throughout 1943 and 1944 Germany also suffered numerous bombing raids which demonstrated, in Roosevelt's words, that Hitler's 'fortress Europe' was a fortress 'without a roof'. Meanwhile, Hitler was unable to attack the United States directly, which meant American industrial output was never disrupted by air-raids. The climax of the Anglo-American war effort came with the opening of the Western Front in France in 1944. Instead of remaining an anvil for the Russian hammer, the Western powers had now become a hammer in their own right.

Hitler's mistakes of strategy were monumental. This was characteristic of a mind which encompassed the extremes of bold generalization and obsession with finicky detail, but which was guided by intuition rather than reason. After his initial successes in 1939 and 1940, Hitler became over-confident, developing, in Jödl's words, an 'almost mystical conviction of his own infallibility as leader of the nation and of the war'.[5] Manstein criticized his lack of method in similar terms: 'Ultimately, to the concept of the art of war, he opposed that of crude force, and the full effectiveness of this force was supposed to be guaranteed by the strength of will behind it.'[6] His conduct of military operations showed the same shortcomings. Convinced that 'the fate of the Reich depends only on me',[7] he destroyed any independence left to his commanders by assuming complete control of the *Wehrmacht* in December 1941. Since he had no personal experience of military command, he possessed no real understanding of the problems confronting generals on the front, and only impeded their initiative by refusing to allow them to take emergency measures without his permission.

Several examples can be given of Hitler's weakness as a military leader. The first was his total mismanagement of the campaign against Britain in 1940 and 1941. Goering had promised the destruction of British air defences within four days and conditions which would be ideal for invasion within four weeks. The *Luftwaffe*, however, was diverted from destroying air bases to bombing cities and industrial targets, with the result that the RAF survived what could have been a sudden and crushing blow. Although out-numbered numerically, the RAF gradually gained the ascendancy, largely through the superior training of its pilots, the greater manoeuvrability of British fighters like the *Spitfire* and *Hurricane*, and the early use of radar as a warning system. Hitler was unable to use the *Luftwaffe* to its greatest effect, mainly because it had been designed to back up ground forces in a *Blitzkrieg* operation rather than to fight as an independent unit of command. He also failed to learn from his mistakes and to devote his attention to redesigning the *Luftwaffe* and eliminating the British scientific lead. Instead, he lost interest in the unfamiliar theatre of aerial warfare and returned to his tested ground tactics.

But the Russian campaign also revealed the negative qualities of Hitler's military command. He was utterly convinced that 'Operation Barbarossa' would be concluded before the end of 1941, for 'we have only to kick in the door and the whole rotten structure will come crashing down'.[8] Consequently, German troops were not even equipped with winter uniforms, despite the delay in launching the campaign caused by the necessity of dealing with the trouble in the Balkans in the summer of 1941. Hitler also changed his mind over the most important objectives to be attained. Originally he emphasized the importance of Leningrad, whereas Brauchitsch,

The Defeat of Nazi Germany

Halder, Book, Guderian and Hoth all urged a massive attack on Moscow. He then switched his attention to the Ukraine and, according to Halder, lost the opportunity of knocking Russia out of the war in 1941 by his inconsistency. The Soviet leadership made full use of the breathing space granted by the reprieve of Moscow, to gather strength and launch a counter attack. In the ensuing battle for Stalingrad, Hitler refused to allow von Paulus to conduct an orderly withdrawal, with the result that Zhukov was able to surround the Sixth Army and force it to surrender in January 1943.

Stalingrad was undoubtedly the turning point of the war. From 1943 onwards Hitler was increasingly on the defensive, a role which he found distasteful and difficult. Instead of an orderly contraction of all his front lines, he adopted what Schramm has called the 'wave-break doctrine', whereby positions had to be held even after the enemy had swept past and isolated them. He also placed undue confidence in inadequate defences like the 'Atlantic Wall', despite the misgivings frequently voiced by commanders on the spot, like von Rundstedt. By 1945 German units were spread all over Europe, which meant that the Reich was under-defended against invasion by Soviet, American and British troops. The reason for this strange policy is that Hitler never lost hope of victory, hoping to switch from defence to attack at the first favourable opportunity; thus his advance positions had to be maintained whatever the cost. He likened his situation to that of Frederick the Great in 1761, and awaited the deliverance which, he felt, would follow the inevitable break-up of the Alliance opposing him. He told his generals in 1944: 'All of the coalitions in history have disintegrated sooner or later. The only thing is to wait for the right moment.'9 In the meantime, he hoped to grind his enemies down by a war of attrition. These, however, were policies born of desperation and delusion. The Soviet Union and the Western Allies did not allow their differences to stand in the way of crushing the Third Reich, whilst attrition proved far more damaging to the defenders than to the invaders.

*

The Second World War was primarily a mechanized war. Although he controlled the finest war machine in Europe in 1939 and 1940, Hitler lost the advantage from 1941 onwards as Germany faced the two greatest industrial powers in history.

The Soviet Union had been caught by surprise by 'Operation

279

Barbarossa' in 1941, but her subsequent recovery owed much to Stalin's economic policies since 1929. The Five Year Plans had transformed Russia's economic base, and had established the plant for sustained industrial production. The transition to a wartime economy was accomplished with remarkable speed. The commissariats of armaments supervised the switch to the mass production of tanks and aircraft in factories which had been removed from European Russia and reassembled, beyond the range of the *Luftwaffe*, in the Urals, Kazakhstan, Western Siberia and Central Asia. The constant supply of war material to the Red Army from 1942 onwards meant that the *Wehrmacht* had to fight against increasing odds. Hence Tippelskirch admitted: 'After 1943 it was no longer possible to upset the enemy's absolute control in the air over the regions of military operations.'[10] The same applied to ground equipment; Soviet tanks had an unassailable numerical advantage at the Battle of Kursk, and Guderian came to the conclusion that the Russian KV and T–34 tanks were superior in performance to the German equivalents. Soviet field artillery was also more advanced, and included the BM–13 rockets (or *Katyusha*) which were employed with devastating results at Stalingrad and later at Berlin. Altogether, the Soviet Union acquired an unassailable lead in the armaments race, as the total production figures for 1942 indicate:

	USSR	Germany
Tanks	24,700	9,300
Aircraft	25,400	14,700
Artillery	127,000	12,000

Of the two totalitarian ideologies, Communism proved more adept than National Socialism at regulating all areas of the economy and subordinating them to the quest for military victory. At no stage did Nazi Germany even approach the level of Soviet military expenditure which amounted to 57 per cent of the 1942 budget.

The transformation of the American economy to wartime production followed an entirely different pattern. Indeed, Goering doubted whether it could be accomplished at all, adding: 'The Americans can't build planes, only ice boxes and razor blades.' By 1941, however, the assembly-line techniques which had produced a constant flow of consumer goods, had been regeared for the manufacture of weapons. This transition was accomplished not by Five

The Defeat of Nazi Germany

Year Plans, but by Roosevelt's Lend-Lease policy. The intention had been to subsidize American armaments industries in order to provide assistance to any country whose integrity was considered vital to that of the United States. Thus, by the time she had entered the war, America had already become the 'arsenal of democracy' and her armaments production soon exceeded that of all the Axis powers together. Between 1940 and 1945 American factories and plans manufactured 300,000 aircraft, 86,000 tanks and 71,000 naval ships. During the course of 1942 German aircraft production was only thirty-one per cent of that of the United States, a factor which gave the Allies air superiority over Germany from 1943 onwards.

The German economy, meanwhile, faced increasing difficulties. Although it had been converted to a war footing by the Four Year Plan of 1936, it relied essentially on plundering other countries rather than on making maximum use of domestic resources. It is true that the German people experienced none of the hardships of the Russians under Stalin's Five Year Plans, but the cost was that the German economy was never intensively exploited until it was too late. Speer, Hitler's Armaments Minister, maintained that the *Wehrmacht* could have been twice as well supplied in 1941, and he constantly criticized the reluctance of Nazi officialdom to employ German women in munitions factories as a means of releasing up to three million men for active service. Germany's dependence on foreign resources and labour was partly responsible for the rapidity of her defeat from 1943 onwards. Deprived by Zhukov's victories of her *Lebensraum* in the East, she could not hope to match the resources and armaments of the two industrial giants who were inexorably rolling back her frontiers.

31

The Cold War

'Cold War' is a term used to describe the confrontation of the two power *blocs* organized into defensive pacts, armed with nuclear weapons and guarding spheres of influence. This rivalry took shape during the Second World War, or more specifically, with the involvement of the Soviet Union and the United States. At first there was co-operation between Russia and the West against a common enemy. Churchill, for example, said in June 1941: 'The Russian danger is our danger.'[1] There was a possibility of permanent reconciliation and Roosevelt, in particular, favoured institutional experiments and the construction of the United Nations Organizations on the foundations of the wartime Alliance. Gradually, however, a darker side emerged, as Russia and the West attached different interpretations to agreements negotiated at wartime conferences like Yalta and Potsdam, or clashed over the treatment of the defeated powers and liberated states. Attitudes hardened, especially when the self-proclaimed moderate Roosevelt was succeeded by Truman, whose tougher policies resembled more closely those of Churchill.

If the Cold War emerged during the last phase of the struggle against Nazi Germany, it had roots which extended back to the second decade of the century. The confrontation of armed alliances was made more intense by the existence of profound and long-standing ideological differences. Trotsky had once personalized the gulf between Russia and the West by calling Lenin and Wilson 'the apocalyptic antipodes of our time'.[2]

The Cold War

It is customary to see the Cold War as the response of one side to the aggression of the other. This chapter will retain that approach, examining the attitudes of *both* sides. It will concentrate particularly on the long background of mutual distrust, the concern about strategic security, and the different ideas about freedom and democracy. The final section will consider briefly the main developments since the early 1960s.

*

Notwithstanding their temporary co-operation during the Second World War, there was deep mistrust between the two sides, based on historical precedent. The Western suspicion of the Soviet Union derived from two sources. The first was a traditional fear of Russian expansionism which the Bolsheviks were suspected of having inherited from the nineteenth century. Hence the French Minister of the Interior, Sarraut, complained in 1927 that 'the leaders of Muscovite Communism hope to bring forth a new imperialism out of some vast Slavic hegemony'.[3] Secondly, the West was profoundly disturbed by the Trotskyist policy of 'worldwide revolution' and the Leninist maxim that ideological differences made conflict inevitable. Despite the threat of Fascism, therefore, there was a marked reluctance to trust Soviet diplomacy during the 1930s. Besides, the Soviet leadership was notorious for its changes of course in foreign policy and seemed, at times, to be blinded by inflexible dogma. Stalin actually believed in the late 1920s and early 1930s that Germany's Social Democrats were, like the Nazis, a manifestation of Fascism. This was hardly likely to inspire confidence in those democracies which possessed moderate socialist political parties. Chamberlain summed up the prevalent view in 1939 when he confessed to 'the most profound distrust of Russia'.[4]

There was no less suspicion on the Soviet side. Western intervention against the new Bolshevik régime in the civil war had come as a savage blow and did much to shape the subsequent view of the West as aggressive and militarist. Western European states were also seen as unreliable diplomatic partners during the 1930s. Litvinov, the Soviet Foreign Minister, observed in 1938 that Britain and France preferred to coexist with Italian Fascism and German Nazism and to make 'endless concessions to them'.[5] He considered the Munich agreement the ultimate folly of appeasement, leaving Russia with no alternative but to make her own arrangements with

Germany. Even when the Soviet Union and Western capitalism sank their differences in 1941, Stalin remained convinced that Churchill and Roosevelt were deliberately using the Russian war effort for their own ends. From 1941 onwards, Stalin consistently urged Britain and the United States to open a second Front against Hitler by invading France. He regarded Churchill's 'soft underbelly' strategy against Italy as an easy option for the West and as a means of using up Russian lives. 'All is clear,' Stalin said in August 1942. 'They want us to bleed white in order to dictate to us their terms later on.'[6] When Roosevelt announced that the invasion of France could not take place until 1944, Stalin bitterly reproached his Allies: 'Your decision . . . leaves the Soviet Army, which is fighting not only for its own country, but also for its Allies, to do the job alone.'

Against this atmosphere of mutual recrimination, the Grand Alliance against Hitler can be seen as an artificial and short-term expedient. There was little possibility of a permanent compromise; even before the ashes of the Third Reich had cooled, the Alliance had disintegrated under the impact of strategic rivalries and ideological differences.

*

The major factor in the development of the Cold War was undoubtedly a preoccupation with military security. As a direct result of the war against Germany, both the United States and the Soviet Union projected themselves more forcefully onto the world political and military scene. The former abandoned the isolationism of the inter-war period, while Stalin revised his previous policy of waiting on the sidelines to pick up whatever was left after the 'death struggle' he anticipated between the capitalist countries. Hitler had unwittingly mobilized the two greatest industrial and military giants in history. It is hardly surprising that these superpowers should have turned on each other with a display of power politics on an unprecedented scale.

The confrontation was intensified by the analysis made by each side of the motives and methods of the other. The United States was influenced by detailed theoretical analysis of Soviet diplomacy by experts like G. F. Kennan. Soviet conduct, it was believed, was based on supreme confidence of ultimate victory. Hence 'the Kremlin is under no ideological compulsion to accomplish its purpose in a hurry';[7] it could apply pressure wherever possible, withdrawing

ARCTIC OCEAN

Reykjavik ICELAND

ATLANTIC OCEAN

NORTH
SEA

FINLAND

Helsinki

UNITED
KINGDOM

Oslo

Stockholm

Moscow

EIRE
Dublin

DENMARK

USSR

The Hague

Copenhagen

London

WEST

EAST
Berlin

Warsaw

Brussels

Bonn
GERMANY

POLAND

Paris LUX

Prague

Berne

CZECHOSLOVAKIA

FRANCE

SW.

Vienna
AUSTRIA

Budapest

HUNGARY

ROMANIA

ITALY

YUGOSLAVIA

Bucharest

BLACK
SEA

Belgrade

Lisbon
PORTUGAL

Madrid

Rome

Tirane

BULGARIA
Sofia

TURKEY

Ankara

SPAIN

GREECE

MEDITERRANEAN SEA

ALBANIA

Athens

	Members of the European Community
	Members of the European Free Trade Association (Norway, Sweden, Switzerland, Austria, Portugal, Iceland, Finland)
	Full members of the North Atlantic Treaty Organization
	Members of the Warsaw Pact
	Members of the Council for Mutual Economic Assistance (Comecon)

Military and economic alignments in Europe in 1973

when this became counter-productive. The only way of countering this was by adopting a deliberate policy of containment. This confirmed the views of both Churchill and Truman. Indeed, the latter observed in 1946: 'Unless Russia is faced with an iron fist and strong language, another war is in the making. Only one language do they understand – "how many divisions have you?"' '[1] The Soviet analysis of Western behaviour, meanwhile, was based on the view that 'capitalist' states were still dangerous and aggressive, the more so because they were trying to uphold a system which Stalin, and later Brezhnev, believed to be in a 'general crisis'. Hence, Stalin maintained, 'the perils of capitalist encirclement' had not disappeared 'with Hitlerite Germany'.[8] In turn, Western observers pointed to the inherent instability of an ideology and political system which could become so obsessed by outside 'threats' and internal disintegration. Some claimed that this feeling of insecurity dominated the Kremlin's whole outlook and made it dangerously unpredictable.

Four examples can be used to show the interplay of Western and Soviet fears: the original flashpoints of the Cold War – Poland and Germany, the wider strategic area which includes the Western hemisphere and the Soviet frontiers, and the Third World countries of Asia and Africa.

Poland was the first area of real contention between the Soviet Union and the Western Allies. There were, during the course of 1944 and 1945, disputes over the proposed boundaries and government of the reconstituted Polish state. These soon assumed wider strategic implications. Stalin was determined to create, down the entire length of Eastern Europe, a broad band of Soviet-dominated territory which would act as a buffer against any future invasion of Russia from the West. He considered that control over Poland was the most urgent priority, not least because Poland had been strongly anti-Soviet between the wars – in her own right between 1919 and 1934, and as a German satellite between 1934 and 1939. Molotov summed up in September 1939 the uncertainties generated by Russia's western neighbour: 'Poland has become a convenient ground for all sorts of fortuitous and unexpected eventualities that might create a threat to the USSR.'[9] The West, meanwhile, became increasingly hostile to Soviet ambitions over Poland. While they were prepared to acknowledge the Soviet claim to Polish territory east of the Curzon Line, Roosevelt and Churchill were profoundly unhappy about the possibility of permanent Soviet control over

The Cold War

Polish institutions. Churchill had always regarded Poland as an outpost of Western influence in Eastern Europe, and as a vital barrier against the spread of Communism. Although he and Truman eventually had to accept as a *fait accompli* Soviet control over Poland, they were fully alerted to the scope of Soviet intentions and were determined to make a stand elsewhere.

Germany, meanwhile, had become the greatest single source of conflict between East and West. Details of zoning bedevilled relations at Potsdam in 1945, while the subsequent Berlin crises of 1948 and 1961 had far-reaching significance. What did Germany actually mean to the two sides? Its importance to Western countries was that it acted as a buffer between themselves and the Soviet *bloc*. The first Berlin crisis patterned the whole Western response to the Soviet threat. It resulted, for one thing, in the creation of the German Federal Republic, designed to fill the power vacuum which had existed in Central Europe since 1945. For another, it led to the formation of the North Atlantic Treaty Organization which, by the early 1950s, consisted of the United States, France, Britain, Belgium, the Netherlands, Luxembourg, Denmark, Norway, Iceland, Italy, Portugal, Greece, Turkey and Canada. Its avowed purpose was entirely defensive; by Article 5 of the NATO Charter the signatory powers undertook 'that an armed attack against one or more of them in Europe or North America shall be considered an attack against them all'.[10] The decision to arm West Germany and admit her to NATO in1955 seemed to provide further security and appeared to be justified by the renewed Soviet pressure on Berlin between 1958 and 1961.

The Soviet view was conditioned by a profound distrust of Germany. Russia, after all, suffered devastating losses at the hands of the Nazis in the Second World War. These were itemized by Molotov in 1947 as 1710 towns and 70,000 villages, 31,850 industrial enterprises and 98,000 collective farms. Above all, between twenty and twenty-five million people were killed, the largest casualty figure sustained by any country in human history. The creation of the German Federal Republic was interpreted as the rebirth of fascist militarism, while her admission to NATO was considered the last straw. Bulganin saw the whole process as intended to provide the 'means for new aggression' to 'yesterday's aggressors'.[11] The immediate Soviet response was the formation of the Warsaw Pact, which comprised obligations for mutual defence

Aspects of European History 1789–1980

between the USSR, Poland, Hungary, Czechoslovakia, Romania, Bulgaria and Albania. Still concerned about the German problem in the late 1950s, Krushchev sponsored the Rapacki Plan to demilitarize West Berlin. Then, to prevent what he regarded as attempts by the West to bring about economic collapse in East Germany, he sealed the border and ordered the construction of the Berlin Wall (1961). The Soviet leadership subsequently regarded the survival of Ulbricht's régime and the emergence of East Germany as one of the major industrial powers of Europe as a direct result of this policy.

Apprehension also existed over a wider area. American presidents stressed the need to contain Communism behind its frontiers in Asia and, therefore, sponsored military alliances like CENTO and SEATO. They also took the precaution of establishing, at various stages, military bases in Turkey, Iran, Pakistan, Taiwan and Okinawa. Above all, the Monroe Doctrine (which, in 1823, declared that the United States would not countenance any European interference in the American continent) was revived and given new force in two ways. The first was institutional; the Organization of American States was designed as yet another military alliance and as a device for minimizing Soviet influence in Latin America. The second was the precautionary action taken by President Kennedy in 1962 to prevent the Soviet Union from maintaining nuclear weapons in Castro's Cuba. In a public broadcast he announced that Khrushchev had defied 'American hemispheric policy'.[12] In order to exert maximum pressure on Moscow he decided to quarantine Cuba, preparing, as a last resort, the possibility of a surgical air strike on the new missile bases. At the same time, Adlai Stevenson delivered a strong attack in the Security Council on the long sequence of aggressive Soviet actions which had culminated in the Cuba Crisis. Khrushchev, for his part, had complained for some time of the virtual encirclement of the Soviet Union by American air bases. He pointed out, in a letter to Kennedy at the height of the crisis, that Turkey, which contained American missiles, was actually closer to the Soviet Union than was Cuba to the United States. 'Do you consider, then, that you have the right to demand security for your own country and the removal of those weapons which you call offensive and do not acknowledge the same right for us?'[12] As far as Khrushchev was concerned, nuclear war was prevented only by the restraint of the Kremlin.

The Third World entered the calculations of the superpowers

The Cold War

during the late 1940s and early 1950s. United States policy was based, until the late 1960s, on the 'domino theory'. An extension of the argument of containment, this maintained that each state which fell to Communism would trigger the process in a neighbour. The result was American support for régimes in Latin America and South Korea, and also involvement in Vietnam, the longest and most expensive war in United States history. The official justification was always that military aid was defensive and that it was accompanied by other forms of co-operation, especially economic. Soviet leaders, by contrast, referred to the 'expansionist' tendencies of the United States. Brezhnev, for example, spoke of the 'aggressive war waged by US imperialism in Vietnam'. Soviet relations with Third World countries, it was stated, were not intended to be subversive but assistance to combat the return of colonialism could well be part of a wider aid programme. Each side clearly disbelieved the statements of the other, attributing to all types of aid a great deal of strategy and very little altruism.

*

These strategic rivalries were given a particularly sharp edge by ideological differences as profound as any in history. Adlai Stevenson spoke in the United Nations Security Council in 1962 of 'the conflict between the absolutist and pluralist conception of the destiny of mankind'.[12] Both sides claimed to uphold democracy; both justified their diplomacy in the name of freedom and in the interest of peoples. Soviet Communism stressed the need to eliminate economic and class 'exploitation' by means of irreversible political and social changes. To the West, this implied dictatorship and a denial of the fundamental right of a people to change the system through free elections. There has also been a basic difference in their respective views on political parties and constitutions. Marxism-Leninism operates in a one-party state, the purpose of the constitution being to transmit reforms and changes to the people in the most efficient way possible; in practice, if not in official theory, the constitution merely lubricates the Party. The Western democratic tradition, on the other hand, is that the Constitution circumscribes the powers of the various political parties which compete for power within it. This would be regarded by the Soviet Union as an extension to politics of the interplay of capitalist forces, the emphasis being on the rules of procedure rather than on social reform. In return, Western liberal and social democrats see in the removal of such rules by the Soviet régime a permanent danger of tyranny which will probably destroy any reforming impulses.

Western views on the future of democracy in Europe were carefully formulated in the Atlantic Charter, prepared by Churchill and Roosevelt in August 1941. 'They desire to see no territorial changes that do not accord with the freely expressed wishes of the peoples concerned.' Furthermore; 'They respect the right of all peoples to choose the form of government under which they will live.'[13] It seemed, at first, that this formula was acceptable to Stalin, who signed the Declaration on Liberated Europe, along with Churchill and Roosevelt, at Yalta in 1945. Under this the three powers promised to help the liberated peoples 'to create democratic institutions of their own choice'. Before long, however, Churchill was attacking Stalin for converting popular front governments into Soviet satellite régimes in Poland, Hungary, Romania and Bulgaria. In his 'Iron Curtain' speech, delivered in Fulton in March 1946, Churchill warned: 'police governments are prevailing in nearly every case' and that 'there is no true democracy'.[14] In the following year Truman told Congress: 'I believe it must be the policy of the United States to support free peoples who are resisting attempted subjugation by armed minorities or by outside pressures.'[1] Western leaders reacted with horror and disgust when Soviet troops invaded Hungary in 1956, and Czechoslovakia in 1968. In the latter case, President Johnson represented the feelings of the Western world when he accused the Soviet Union of having invaded a 'defenceless country to stamp out a resurgence of ordinary human freedom'.[15]

The Soviet perspective was inevitably different. It was argued that Russia never undertook to introduce a Western-style of democracy into Eastern Europe, and that her subsequent actions were designed not to subvert the freedom of smaller countries, but to preserve their socialism from corrupting or destructive influences. Replying to a resolution in the United Nations condemning the invasion of Hungary, Sobolev argued that Hungary had been threatened by 'counter-revolutionary elements', which had succeeded in 'deluding the workers by mendacious propaganda'.[16] A similar theme was used by Brezhnev in 1968 to justify the occupation of Czechoslovakia. He was forced, he said, to take an 'extraordinary step dictated by necessity'. Such necessity arises

The Cold War

when 'internal and external forces that are hostile to socialism try to turn the development of some country towards the restoration of a capitalist régime'.[17] The common assumption of all Soviet leaders, therefore, was that Western powers, especially the United States, were trying to destabilize Eastern *bloc* countries by exploiting any signs of socialist weakness. Furthermore, it was argued, the United States established a vast economic network, attempting to dominate Europe through the Marshall Plan. The unification of the Western zones of Germany was an example of the collusion of Western capitalism, since, according to Molotov, 'it facilitates the penetration of American and British monopolists into German industry and opens to them wide opportunities for subordinating the German economy to their influence.'[18] The American response to this accusation was that the zones were being united and economic assistance granted to prevent Germany from being permanently crippled and impoverished. Besides, it was often pointed out, the Western Allies did not strip their zones of all their industrial assets, unlike Stalin, who insisted on 10,000 million dollars from an already exhausted and impoverished people, thereby adding economic slavery to political subjugation.

*

Two distinct developments are discernible in the period since the early 1960s: the movement towards co-operation and détente and the revival of tension which had always been so characteristic of the Cold War.

One reason for the growing desire for coexistence during the 1960s was the grave perils of nuclear warfare and mass destruction, made dramatically clear by the 1962 Cuba Crisis. In a less tense atmosphere, several major agreements were drawn up, including the 'Hot Line Agreement' (1963), the Partial Test Ban Treaty (1963) and the Nuclear Non-Proliferation Treaty (1968). Another impetus was the *rapprochement* between the Soviet Union and the countries of Western Europe. This was initiated by de Gaulle's search for a special relationship between France and Russia in the early 1960s and was enhanced by Brandt's policy of '*Ostpolitik*' at the end of the decade. The result was the 1970 Treat between the German Federal Republic and the Soviet Union, to be followed by the Four Power Agreement on Berlin (1971), the Treaty with the German Democratic Republic (1972) and the Treaty with Czechoslovakia (1973).

Aspects of European History 1789–1980

The diplomacy of détente focused, in the 1970s, on two major issues. One was the relationship between the superpowers. Clearly the greatest need was for agreement on the control of nuclear weapons, and the Helsinki negotiations eventually produced the Strategic Arms Limitation Treaty (SALT I) signed at the 1972 Moscow Summit by Nixon and Brezhnev. Further talks, between Ford and Brezhnev, resulted in the Vladivostock Accords (1974) which, in turn, were intended to form the basis of SALT II. Meanwhile, the improvement in US-Soviet relations was reflected by agreements on commerce and the transfer of high technology (see Chapter 29).

The other major issue concerned Europe. Ever since the 1950s Soviet leaders had aimed at ratifying the status quo in Eastern and Central Europe by means of an all-European conference. In 1973 Helsinki was the scene of an assembly of representatives of all the European states except Albania, together with delegations from the United States and Canada. This 'Conference on Security and Co-operation in Europe' (CSCE) has been described as the closest Europe would ever come to producing an official end to the Second World War by broad-based multilateral agreement. The Final Act, or Helsinki Declaration (1975), contained a wide range of 'baskets', one of which was a set of guarantees of human rights.

Throughout the 1970s, however, détente clearly had its limitations. President Nixon pointed out that it was 'not the same as lasting peace' and that 'the world will hold perils for us as far ahead as we can see'.[19] Crises continued to occur, if at less frequent intervals, one example being the military alert called by Nixon at the height of the 1973 Arab-Israeli War. From 1974 onwards a series of factors conspired to undermine détente and, eventually, to wreck the SALT II agreements. One was the disillusionment of the Carter administration with the Soviet record on human rights; another was the fear aroused in Washington by the sudden increase of Soviet activity in the Third World, especially in Angola (1975–6) and Ethiopia (from 1976). The final blow was the Soviet invasion of Afghanistan in 1979 which confirmed that détente was seriously endangered and which raised the question had a new cold war begun?

32

Economic and Political
Integration in Western Europe
Since 1945

The idea of European unity is not new. As far back as the eighteenth century several people, including the Abbé de Saint-Pierre and Jeremy Bentham devised schemes for a European legislature. The term 'United States of Europe', coined in the nineteenth century, was frequently used in the early twentieth century by the Austrian statesman, Coudenhove-Kalergi, and the French politician, Briand. Any hope that Europe was evolving towards a federation was, however, destroyed by the emergence during the 1930s of the most extreme form of nationalism ever known which, in turn, brought militarism and dictatorship to over two-thirds of the Continent's states, as well as the most destructive conflict in history.

The Second World War generated profound disillusionment with Europe's unpleasant habit of producing a major conflict every generation. It is not surprising that the anti-Nazi resistance movements should have led the field in denouncing the destructive forces of nationalism, and in advocating political and economic integration. Their Manifesto, drawn up at Ventotene in 1940 by Ernesto Rossi and Altiero Spinelli, defined the main objective for the future as 'the definitive abolition of the division of Europe into national sovereign states'.[1] This was followed by the formation of the European Federalist Movement (1943) and by a series of conferences which gave practical expression to the belief of the French writer Camus that 'the European resistance will remake Europe'.[1] This 'grass roots' federalism, in turn, influenced post-war politicians and economists who were equally anxious to learn from the experience of

293

Nazi tyranny – men like Adenauer, de Gasperi, Spaak, Monnet and Schuman. The idealism and enthusiasm of the Resistance leaders therefore influenced the new governments, so that, for the first time ever, European integration became, in several states, official policy.

How far did this policy progress between 1945 and 1950? On the whole, practice fell far short of theory, with alliance or inter-governmental co-operation being emphasized at the expense of supranationalism and political unity. This can be seen in the development of the period's three major sets of institutions. The first was the Organization of European Economic Co-operation (OEEC) set up in 1948 to co-ordinate the distribution of American aid in the Marshall Plan. This might have developed into a customs union but any such scheme was strongly opposed by the British government. Secondly, fears for future security brought about the Brussels Treaty (1948) between Britain, France, the Netherlands, Belgium and Luxembourg. But when this was expanded into the North Atlantic Treaty Organization in 1949, and incorporated Canada and the United States, it lost its exclusively European base and adopted a more traditional framework of collective security. The third trend seemed, at first, to be more promising. Numerous conferences were held for the specific purpose of preparing for political unity and the most important of these, at the Hague, resolved 'to transfer certain sovereign rights to the nations in order to express them in common'.[2] The direct result was the Council of Europe, set up in 1949 and consisting of a consultative Assembly. This Council, however, had very few powers and was clearly a much diluted version of the original plan.

The basic reason for the limited success of these ventures was a clash between two different approaches to integration. Some governments favoured a federal model on the lines of the United States, while others preferred a confederal scheme which would resemble the looser structure of the United Nations.

Federalism was ardently supported by the Benelux countries, which had so frequently been caught up in the destructive cross-currents of Franco-German conflict. The French government, still trying to recover from the humiliation of 1940, saw a federation as the most effective way of containing Germany in the future, while the Germans sought a vehicle for reconstruction and reconciliation. Confederalism was the choice of the peripheral states of Western Europe, especially Britain and Scandinavia. Britain had a long

Economic and Political Integration in Europe

tradition of separation from Europe, except over considerations of the 'balance of power'. Hence, Churchill had remarked before the war, 'We are with Europe, but not part of it'.[3] In any case, Britain had maritime and imperial interests, together with a 'special relationship' with the United States. In a conversation with de Gaulle in 1944, Churchill had made Britain's priorities quite clear: 'Whenever we have to choose between Europe and the open sea, we shall always choose the open sea. Whenever I have to choose between you and Roosevelt, I shall always choose Roosevelt.'[4] Above all, Britain was the one country in Europe which was not disillusioned with the appeal to patriotism: Churchill's wartime oratory combined with the experience of victory to reaffirm Britain's complete faith in her own institutions.

Hence there was, by 1950, a clear division between those countries who wanted European unity and those who did not. The latter remained suspicious of all schemes for integration and attempted, where possible, to weaken them. The former, meanwhile, had still to work out between themselves a clear goal and a realistic means of attaining it.

*

The answer was provided by Jean Monnet, director of the French reconstruction programme and a longstanding advocate of European unity. In a memorandum to the French Foreign Minister, Schuman on 4 May 1950, he argued that all the means previously adopted had led to an *impasse* and that this could be broken only by initial concentration on *economic* integration. In time, this would develop an irreversible momentum towards political integration; the Schuman Declaration, issued on 9 May, reflected this view. He stated, as an article of faith, that 'The European federation is indispensable to the maintenance of peace'. On the other hand, 'Europe will not be made all at once, as a single whole: it will be built by concrete achievements which will first create *de facto* solidarity'.[5]

The practical expression of this aim was the European Coal and Steel Community (ECSC). Formed by the Treaty of Paris (1951), this consisted of France, West Germany, Italy, Belgium, the Netherlands and Luxembourg. In the High Authority it possessed Europe's first genuinely supranational institution and one which was intended to have 'legal personality'. In 1957 the leaders of the six members agreed, by the Treaty of Rome, to enlarge the scope of the ECSC by establishing the European Economic Community (EEC) and Euratom. The main institutions of the EEC comprised the Commission, which had powers to instigate and exercise joint economic programmes, the Council of Ministers, in which the key decisions were taken by representatives of each of the member governments; the Parliament, whose deputies were nominated by the national legislatures; and the Court of Justice. A transition period of twelve years was allowed by Article 8 for the establishment of a customs and economic union, which would involve the removal of all internal duties and the adoption of a common external tariff. Common policies would also be adopted for industry, agriculture, transport, capital and services. Ultimately, it was envisaged, progress could be made towards the transfer of political sovereignty to a supranational authority.

Both the ECSC and the EEC were formed without the membership of the Scandinavian countries or Britain. The former preferred their own arrangements, like the Nordic Council (1952). Britain, anxious to avoid any binding commitments, declined two invitations, issued in 1951 and 1956. The first decision was taken by a Labour government which had no desire to place the recently nationalized coal and steel industries under the control of an external body; a Labour Party NEC document argued that: 'No socialist party could ever accept a system by which important fields of national policy were surrendered to a European representative authority.'[6] The second decision was that of a Conservative government which feared the possible influence on Britain of a continental type of economic planning. Both parties, however, saw the advantage of a free trade area without strings attached. Britain therefore took the initiative in establishing, in 1959, the European Free Trade Association (EFTA), with Austria, Denmark, Norway, Sweden, Portugal and Switzerland. Non-Communist Europe had, in effect, divided into two economic zones; the 'inner Six' and the 'outer Seven'.

Meanwhile, another attempt had been made to establish a political and military system in Europe. In 1950 the French prime minister, Pleven, proposed the formation of a European Defence Community (EDC). His main motive was to allow Germany to rearm, but within a European context; German contingents would be fully integrated into a European defence force under a Minister of Defence, a Council of Ministers and an Assembly. This would have the triple advantage of using German power as a means of replacing

Economic and Political Integration in Europe

United States influence in Europe, preventing the re-emergence of aggressive German nationalism, and providing much needed resources to counter the growing threat from the Soviet *bloc*. The French regarded British support as essential for the success of the scheme, as only a combination of Britain and France could guarantee effective control over German rearmament. The British government, however, was unimpressed by the idea of the EDC, preferring the Atlantic connections offered by NATO. Ernest Bevin declared in the House of Commons that the proposal for a European Army was 'too limited in scope . . . European unity is no longer possible within Europe alone but only within the broader Atlantic community.'[7] Meanwhile, the French Parliament, long divided over the project, finally refected the EDC, which therefore collapsed in 1954. Eden's government tried subsequently to establish a more loosely structured alternative by enlarging the 1948 Brussels Treaty, through the inclusion of Italy and West Germany, into the Western European Union.

By 1960 it was clear that the only real chance of integration, either political or economic, lay with the EEC. It now remained to be seen whether the aims of the 1950s could be achieved during the 1960s.

*

In one respect the EEC was remarkably successful. De Gaulle described as an 'economic miracle'[8] the rapid enrichment of all six member states and the creation of the world's largest single trading *bloc*. Between 1958 and 1967 the exports of the EEC as a whole trebled, while the volume of world exports only doubled. The indices of the gross national product showed a similar improvement; taking the 1953 index as 100, the GNP of the EEC had increased to 188 by 1965, in comparison with 154 for EFTA and 149 for the United States. Progress was also made in implementing the economic targets of the Treaty of Rome. By July 1968 all internal barriers had been eliminated on industrial goods, iron, steel, coal and agricultural produce; a common agricultural policy and uniform tax system (based on VAT) had been introduced, a common external tariff was in operation, and the member states had adopted a concerted policy on tariff negotiations with countries outside the EEC.

By contrast, the movement towards political unity had slowed down. Economic success had certainly helped remove tension

297

Aspects of European History 1789–1980

between the nations of Western Europe but had not given a positive boost for federalism. It has been argued[9] that a federation can be established only if a political factor, external or internal, reacts with a background of economic integration. Hence the economic unity of the Thirteen Colonies was transformed into the tighter political structure of the United States as a direct result of the conflict with the British Crown, while the German *Zollverein* was converted into the Second Reich by the statecraft of Bismarck. No such political catalyst had yet appeared within the EEC. If anything, France and Germany pursued, during the 1960s, foreign policies which placed national considerations far above the ideal of political federalism.

On becoming prime minister and then president of the Fifth Republic de Gaulle made it his business to revive France's influence in Europe and to reassert a powerful French identity. Never a convinced federalist, he preferred to focus on '*une certaine idée de la France*' and openly declared as his principle: '*Les nations, ça existe.*'[10] Three distinctively Gaullist policies followed. First, in his determination to reduce French connections with the United States, he withdrew France from the military arm of NATO, committing her to becoming a nuclear power in her own right, and seeking détente with the Soviet *bloc*. Second, he sought a traditional bilateral agreement with Germany in contrast with the Fourth Republic's policy of Franco-German reconciliation within a European context. Third, and most important, he was determined to uphold to the limit French interests within the EEC itself. In 1965, a major crisis developed as de Gaulle insisted on a French veto on certain agricultural policies, even though these were acceptable to the other five members. It took nearly a year before the deadlock was overcome and the result was a severe setback to those federalists who wanted to accelerate the movement towards political unity. The Luxemburg Agreement (1966) provided a compromise which, in effect, acknowledged the right of one member to insist on 'unanimous agreement'. This enhanced the powers of the Council of Ministers, which represented the national governments, at the expense of the more genuinely supranational commission.

By the end of the 1960s and the beginning of the 1970s Germany had also begun to follow a distinctive foreign policy. The Christian Democrats, in power since 1948, had by 1969 been superseded by the SPD, who had always been less enthusiastic about the prospects of European unity. Indeed, the new Social Democratic Chancellor,

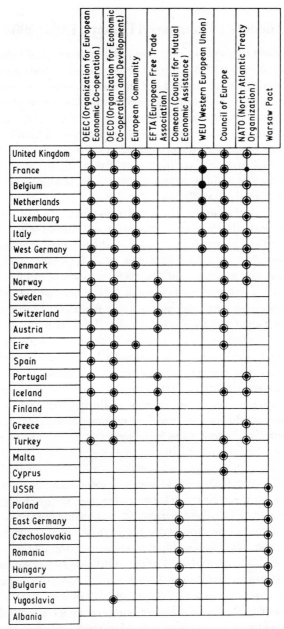

Fig. 1   European integration: membership of various organizations by
1973. Diagram after *The Bartholomew/Warne Atlas of Europe:
A profile of Western Europe* pp. 22–23 (Edinburgh and London,
1974)

Brandt, said in 1969: 'In the more purely political field I think we will have to depend upon intergovernmental operations [rather than upon] supranational methods.' This seemed to echo de Gaulle's policy, as did Brandt's search for a bilateral understanding with the Communist régimes in Eastern Europe; in August 1970, for example, the Russo-German Treaty was drawn up, followed shortly afterwards by an agreement with Poland. *Ostpolitik* was criticized by the CDU and CSU on the grounds that accommodation with Eastern Europe could be accomplished only at the expense of further integration in Western Europe.

There was *one* example of progress made during the 1960s. In July 1967 the executive bodies and Councils of Ministers of each of the ECSC, EEC and Euratom were combined into a single Commission and a single Council, within the more generally designated 'European Community'. Yet, by 1969, it was still clear that the spectacular economic progress made by the Six had not yet been accompanied by any real political change. Since the transition period of twelve years, allowed by the Treaty of Rome, had now elapsed, a decision would have to be made about the future of the Community. Yet this decision involved a dilemma. How, on the one hand, could the momentum of evolution be maintained so that premature stratification could be avoided? How, on the other, could further progress be made towards political integration without compromising the national interests considered so important by the Community's two most powerful members?

*

While the continental governments were experiencing these problems, successive British leaders were re-examining their whole attitude to the EEC. The Liberal Party had always been in favour of membership, but the first prime minister to be converted was the Conservative Macmillan. In a broadcast to the nation on 20 September 1962, he said 'all through our history . . . we have still been very much involved in Europe's affairs. We can't escape it. Sometimes we've tried to – but we can't. It's no good pretending.'[11] The Labour Party held out longer, partly because Gaitskell, leader until 1963, was a convinced anti-Marketeer. In 1966, however, Wilson committed his Labour government to seeking entry for Britain, and was determined that he would 'not take no for an answer'.

Economic and Political Integration in Europe

How did the negotiations fare? Five of the EEC members welcomed the British application, but entry was delayed for over ten years because of the vetos imposed in 1962 and 1968 by France. De Gaulle felt that Britain was profoundly 'insular' and 'maritime', and that 'the nature, the structure, the very situation that are England's differ profoundly from those of the continentals'.[12] He feared that Britain would use the EEC merely as a crutch for her own economic recovery; that she would upset the 'special relationship' recently worked out between France and Germany; and that she would act as a 'Trojan horse' within Europe for American political and financial influence. These views were not, however, universally held in France for, on de Gaulle's retirement in 1969, the new president, Pompidou, removed the veto. Negotiations were opened by the Heath government and the Treaty of Accession was signed in 1972, leading to membership in 1973. Subsequent renegotiations and the 1975 referendum, confirmed Britain's place within the Community.

These developments represented a profound reappraisal of Britain's role in the world which, in turn, came from a growing awareness of her economic and political vulnerability.

Britain's economic performance since 1945 had been far more sluggish than that of the EEC countries. For example, her exports grew between 1953 and 1963 by under 40 per cent, in contrast to the Community's average growth of over 140 per cent. Three reasons can be advanced for this: the first was the cost of victory. During the Second World War Britain accumulated enormous external debts and, at the same time, sold many overseas investments and cut back on services. These investments and services had, for over half a century, played a vital part in converting a balance of trade deficit into an overall balance of payments surplus. At first, the true extent of Britain's losses was disguised by American loans and by the post-war weakness of the defeated Axis powers – Germany, Italy and Japan. During the 1950s, however, Germany rapidly reconstructed her shattered industries and, in the process, replaced the type of obsolete plant which was still widely used in Britain. Gradually, the grim truth emerged that Germany's bomb damage was less difficult to repair than the contraction of Britain's investments. Indeed, it could be argued that the smaller degree of physical destruction in Britain actually discouraged systematic modernization in industry. Secondly, Britain continued to pursue an active political role as a major power which was quite out of step with her smaller economic base. One example of this was the determination of all post-war governments in Britain to defend the integrity of the sterling area; this was clearly a direct consequence of the commitment which Britain had, in the past, fulfilled as the focal point of a huge empire and as the world's largest trading nation. One historian, in fact, sees a direct conflict between Britain's post-war trading needs and the interests of the City of London.[13] Thirdly, British governments had adopted a more piecemeal approach to reconstruction than had Germany, France and the Benelux countries. Conservative policies fought shy of central control, but even the Labour Party's socialism lacked the consistency of the Continent's 'planned economies'.

By the 1960s British leaders considered that only association with Europe could bring about economic revival. Trade figures seemed to confirm that the future lay with the EEC. During this decade British trade with the Commonwealth increased by 29 per cent (from £1240 million to £1601 million), compared with a massive jump of 230 per cent (£463 million to £1530 million) with the Community. What was now needed was a greatly expanded market which would give British products the same advantage as their rivals. As Macmillan said, referring to Britain's existing limitations: 'How are we going to sell them if the base, the home market, is only a quarter of theirs?'

British decline had also been political. The Suez catastrophe of 1956 showed that Britain was no longer a world power, even though this lesson was not learned for several more years. It also loosened the 'special relationship' with the United States, as the latter had supported several resolutions in the United Nations Security Council condemning Anglo-French action. In the past, Britain might have withdrawn into 'splendid isolation', content to maintain close relations with the Empire. By the early 1960s, however, British colonies were receiving their independence and, in the words of US Secretary of State, Dean Acheson, Britain had 'lost an Empire and not yet found a role'.[14] The solution of the Conservatives was to look to Europe, while the Labour Party at first sought to foster and lead a democratic and multi-racial Commonwealth. Then two events in the mid-1960s, the Indo-Pakistan War and Rhodesia's unilateral declaration of independence, threatened the very existence of the Commonwealth and showed that Britain's leadership was extremely precarious. Membership of a European *bloc* became more and more attractive, especially since exclusion from that *bloc* could mean future isolation and insignificance.

Economic and Political Integration in Europe

Even the longstanding British reservations about the loss of national identity, through unwanted political integration, had been allayed. The policies of de Gaulle and Brandt showed that federalism was no longer the major target of Western European leaders. Heath had been able to say in 1961: 'That situation is fully safeguarded and we should not frighten ourselves by false apprehensions about these matters.' By 1970 the 'situation' was still the same. According to Sir Geoffrey Ripon: 'There is no question of the imposition of theoretical solutions from above; no threat of instant federation.'[15]

*

Britain's movement towards the EEC therefore coincided with the latter's considerations about its future. It also provided a solution. Political unification could again be postponed as a distant goal (especially in view of Britain's attitude), but the Community could be prevented from becoming static by a programme of enlargement. This, in turn, would necessitate the overhaul of the Community's economic policies and political institutions. Perhaps, the federalists now argued, gradualism and a broad base would provide the best prospects of political unity.

The Community's enlargement has been carried out by two processes: membership and association. New members have been Britain, Ireland and Denmark (admitted by the Treaty of Accession in 1972) and Greece, which entered the Community in 1981. Applications were also received in 1977 from Spain and Portugal, and are expected in the 1980s from Turkey, Cyprus and Malta. Two areas have been granted close association with the Community. The larger is the Third World: at first the connection was confined by the Yaoundé Convention of 1963 to ex-French and ex-Belgian colonies, but the scope was subsequently extended, in the Lomé Conventions of 1975 and 1979, to most of Africa, the Caribbean and the Pacific. Meanwhile, Mediterranean countries were also being given associate status, and a free trade area was established in Southern Europe for industrial, though not agricultural, products.

Economic reform has been designed to achieve 'positive integration', or common financial institutions, after the successful 'negative integration', or removal of tariffs, of the 1960s. One example was the formation of the European Monetary System in March, 1979. Efforts were also made to reform the process of budgetary contributions and disbursements, largely on the initiatives of Britain and Italy, against whom the Community budget had tended to discriminate. A major achievement has been the adoption of a more distinctively social policy after the 1972 Summit's resolution to give the Community a 'more human face'; this led to the European Development Fund (EDF) in 1975, from which both Italy and Britain have benefited. Further changes are likely in the 1980s as the British role in the Community remains uncertain, and the prospective members have less highly developed economies than the original Six.

Political reforms have kept the future in mind but have been far from spectacular. 1979 saw the realization of one of the long-term projects of the Treaty of Rome – direct elections to the European Parliament. The Community's executive, however, has not been substantially altered. It is true that several new institutions have developed, like the European Council and the Conference of Ministers Political Committee. But these have not yet merged with the existing Commission and the Council of Ministers. The present emphasis seems, as much as ever, to be on inter-governmental economic co-operation rather than on genuine supranationalism.

*

To summarize the argument of this chapter, European federalism was an age-old ideal, but became a real proposition only in the powerful reaction against nationalism after the Second World War. It originated as a grass-roots movement, and was then taken over as official policy by several governments. Early initiatives, however, were impeded by the lack of enthusiasm from Britain and other peripheral states. Decisions were therefore made by the Six to concentrate, during the 1950s, on economic integration in the form of the ECSC and the EEC, Britain choosing to remain outside both. The EEC produced spectacular economic success but no further political progress so that Britain, affected by economic and political decline, was able to revise her whole attitude to Europe by the early 1960s. Meanwhile, the EEC had reached the point of decision about future policy and went for enlargement and further internal changes in preference to more immediate political unity.

What are the prospects for political integration in the future? On the one hand they appear fairly good. The countries of non-Communist Europe show fewer political extremes now that neo-

Economic and Political Integration in Europe

fascism has left Spain, Portugal and Greece. There is also general acceptance that political unity can occur only within the context of the European Community. On the other hand, the very enlargement of the Community could increase the differences between its members to the extent that a United States of Europe would be considered neither possible nor necessary.

33

Nationalism

Among the numerous characteristics of nationalism three are worth particular mention. The first is an awareness, among members of the community, of a natural homogeneity in language, culture (especially literature and music) and social customs. The second is a mass acceptance of the authority of a central government, in the defence of specified frontiers against external enemies. The government sometimes seeks to convert this loyalty into veneration by promoting selected attitudes and transmitting certain values through education and the mass media. The third, the people's awareness of its own unique identity, can be used as a source of energy: either to extend a nation's frontiers at the expense of its neighbours or, conversely, to drive out intruders, whether foreign dynasties or imperial powers.

The nation state has roots which extend far back into the middle ages[1]; both France and England, for example, were incipient nations by the twelfth and thirteenth centuries. Then, during the early modern period, European monarchs gave these states complex bureaucracies so that they could transmit their will more effectively to their subjects. The nation state had, by the seventeenth and eighteenth centuries, become synonymous with centralized government and with the extension of this government's power to all the frontiers.

Nationalism, however, developed rather more slowly. Commitment and loy. · to the nation state certainly existed among the Spaniards, English and Dutch of the sixteenth century, and the

Nationalism

French of the seventeenth. Yet at this stage something was missing. Nationalism is fundamentally the expression of mass commitment above all other loyalties. During the period before the French Revolution, the inhabitants of most countries had other bonds which were still very powerful. One was the *local* connection which comprised a variety of feudal obligations and loyalties which were left over from the middle ages. Another was a profound attachment to *universal* values which, as in the case of religion, entirely transcended the individual state. Thus the commitments of the people were like two separate beams of light, one stopping well short of the national frontier and the other overshooting it. Before a nation state could be fully established the two beams would have to be made to converge *on* the frontier.

English nationalism was given a powerful boost by the puritan revolution, and later by the writings of Locke (1632–1704) and Burke (1727–97). The puritan spirit of English nationalism also spread, with the early settlers and pioneers, to North America. But the absolute monarchs of some of the continental countries were somewhat less likely to speed up the growth of nationalism as an ideology affecting their peoples. Their attention was divided between specific problems (like dynastic consolidation) and universal issues (like religious conflict). Besides, these rulers had no need, or desire, to mobilize mass support. The state, after all, was still considered the personal property of the ruler and the slogan '*l'état, c'est moi*' was hardly likely to promote nationalist fervour. Thus, before nationalism could make any further headway, there would have to be a redefinition of the relationship between the people and the state. This, in turn, would require a political and social upheaval.

*

Such an upheaval was caused between 1789 and 1815 by the French Revolution and the expansion of the Napoleonic empire. During this period nationalism took France by storm and was then transmitted to other parts of Europe, especially to the fragmented states of Italy and Germany.

Although the French Revolution started cautiously, it soon altered radically the individual's relationship with the state by uprooting a host of traditional local interests and sweeping away the remnants of feudalism. As France entered a more ideological phase

307

Aspects of European History 1789–1980

from 1793, she came more and more obviously under the influence of the ideas of Rousseau (1712–78). (E. H. Carr describes Rousseau as the 'founder of modern nationalism' in that he 'rejected the embodiment of the nation in the personal sovereign or the ruling class' and 'boldly identified "nation" and "people"'.[2]) Rousseau made two significant contributions to the growth of nationalism. First, he attacked the cosmopolitan outlook of the eighteenth-century Enlightenment and stressed, instead, the people's community base: *'chaque nation a son caractère propre et spécifique.'*[3] Second, he redefined the relations between ruler and ruled. In emphasizing the importance of the 'general will', he gave the individual a place within the community as a whole; in turn, the community had the right to expect his total allegiance. Thus *'La patrie est dans les relations de l'Etat a ses membres'.*[3] Jacobin leaders like Robespierre, Carnot and Danton used these ideas to develop a common national purpose. According to Danton, 'France must be an indivisible whole'. Mass conscription was introduced to mobilize citizen armies and, with this new weapon, French nationalism overspilled France's frontiers, becoming at the same time more and more messianic. Under Napoleon, nationalism lost some of its association with radical democracy but retained its connection with militarism.

France had a more profound impact on the rest of Europe than had any other power since the days of the Roman Empire. Napoleon, in particular, contributed in two ways to the growth of nationalism beyond the borders of France. First, he dismantled the old institutions and remnants of the feudal system and, in Italy and Germany, consolidated the scattered territories into larger states; he tried, in his own words, to 'simplify their monstrous complication'.[4] The second contribution was more negative, but no less important. His conquests and insensitive diplomacy aroused a series of national responses, ranging from Russia and Spain, to Italy and Germany. This resistance eventually caused the defeat of the French armies in the Peninsular War, the Russian Campaign and the War of Liberation.

During the early years of the nineteenth century Germany underwent a particularly profound upheaval, the catalysts for which were French ideological influence and conquest. German writers like Goethe (1749–1832) had been part of the mainstream of the eighteenth-century Enlightenment and had shared its cosmopolitan base. Gradually, however, German culture acquired a more regional

Nationalism

identity as, under the influence of Rousseau, the German Romantics rejected the universalism of the eighteenth century.

German Romanticism began with a linguistic emphasis, as writers like Arndt (1769–1860) stressed the importance of language in national identity: 'The Germans have not been bastardized. They have retained their original purity and have been able to develop slowly but surely according to the everlasting laws of time.'⁵ This was built by Herder (1744–1803) and Jahn (1778–1852) into a broader conception of the German race or *Volk*. Jahn confirmed the movement away from the cosmopolitan outlook of Goethe: 'We seek the same goal, but in Germanity instead of humanity.'⁵ Herder introduced the concept of collective creativity in the form of the *Volksgeist*: the cultural achievements of individual writers and painters were outlets for the genius of a whole people. Unfortunately, this people was not yet a nation and Fichte (1762–1814) concentrated his efforts on promoting a political revival and contributing to the defeat of Napoleon. Hegel (1770–1831) went further and emphasized that political regeneration could be accomplished only by greatly extending the power of the state. 'It must be that all the worth which the human being possesses . . . he possesses only through the state.' He added: 'The state is the Divine Idea as it exists on Earth.'⁶

Clearly these expressions added up to a profound change in the concept of the individual's relationship with the community and provided the theoretical ingredients for a powerful national consciousness. But Central Europe was still fragmented politically, a situation confirmed by the Congress of Vienna in 1815. The question which now arose was: how could the national sentiment acquire a political structure? As Jahn said, 'A state without a *Volk* is nothing, a soulless artifice'; but equally, 'a *Volk* without a state is nothing, a bodiless phantom'.⁵

*

One of the major characteristics of nationalism is that it is ideologically amorphous. It can change shape and adapt to virtually any other ideology, only to switch, if necessary, to something else which is totally different. The creation of nation states in Central Europe shows this quite clearly. During the first half of the nineteenth century German and Italian nationalism identified openly with liberal and social forces, usually in opposition to the existing establishment. After 1851, however, nationalism in this area increasingly underpinned the establishment and allied with authoritarian governments.

Italy had been deeply affected by the French Revolution, both ideologically and structurally. The Italian national movement was still influenced by France after the end of the Napoleonic Wars; the *Carbonari*, for example, was inspired by French ideas in its struggle against the Austrians. The most important of the Italian nationalist theorists, Mazzini, allied openly with liberal thought and rejected the more ruthless Italian tradition of power politics associated with Machiavelli. Indeed, he considered Machiavelli's era to have been one of 'corruption and degradation' which it was necessary to 'bury with the past'.[7] The 1848 Revolutions, however, showed that spontaneous nationalism, which aimed at establishing an Italian republic, stood little chance against the power of Austria. It therefore fell to the more conservative Cavour to direct the course of Italian unification with the aid of a somewhat unscrupulous approach to diplomacy. Mazzini, disgusted with this turn of events and with the apparent capitulation of his former disciple, Garibaldi, complained that Machiavelli had triumphed after all.

German nationalism also co-operated initially with liberalism as the middle-class search for political power and the desire for national unity coincided. Again, however, the 1848 Revolutions showed the need for a different approach to unification and, after 1851, the initiative passed to the authoritarian government of Prussia. There has always been some controversy as to whether this was mere capitulation, or whether it was a voluntary change of direction. Certainly the failure of the Frankfurt Parliament in 1849 closed the door on the liberal pattern of unification, but it could also be argued that the authoritarian approach was not entirely alien to German Romanticism, especially to the ideas of Hegel. Also, economic theorists like List (1789–1846) had constantly urged the need for economic and industrial progress. Prussia, as it turned out, provided the model for both state power and industrial might, and German liberalism resigned itself to what appeared the inevitable. Baumgarten, the liberal historian, epitomized the attitude to Bismarck in the 1860s. 'We thought that by our agitation we could transform Germany,' he said, conceding that the whole liberal approach had proved erroneous. But then, with Prussia redirecting

Nationalism

Germany's efforts, 'we experienced a miracle almost without parallel'.[8]

This 'miracle' was fully exploited, during the next fifty years, by a series of musicians, poets, philosophers and historians. Wagner, for example, intensified the mystical element of the German *Volk* in his operas, while Treitschke, Ranke, Droysen and Sybel all projected the Second Reich of Bismarck and the Kaiser as the logical, indeed, foreordained outcome of all previous German history. The fusion between the German Romantic spirit and Prussian militarism seemed complete. The way was open for a more assertive display of German power. German nationalism now showed unprecedented self-confidence; Treitschke, for example, boasted: 'From now on German policy can hardly commit any serious mistakes.'

*

We have seen that nationalism can change and adapt readily to different conditions. The period 1871–1914 also proved that it can exist at different levels. These eventually collapsed into each other, to bring about the First World War.

The main level consisted of the nation states which, after 1871, included Germany, France, Britain, Italy and Russia. Between these states rivalries became more and more intense, particularly those between Germany and France, and Germany and Russia. Before 1870 there had existed in France considerable admiration for German Romanticism, especially from Michelet and Quinet, while Victor Hugo had gone so far as to say: '*La France et l'Allemagne sont l'Europe. L'Allemagne le coeur, la France la tête.*'[9] This friendship, however, had never been returned by German writers, except, possibly, by Heine. Then came the shock of defeat in the Franco-Prussian War, which evoked from the French a bitterly anti-German response, which was to be further whipped up by the writings of Maurras (1868–1952) and Barrès (1862–1923). Indeed, Franco-German hostility was the key factor behind the emergence of the alliance systems of the last three decades of the century. Meanwhile, German nationalism had developed a feeling of deep contempt for the Slavs of Eastern Europe, while there evolved in Russia a powerful reaction against German influences; the expression of this took different forms, ranging from the novels of Dostoevsky to the official views of Pobedonostsev. A strong undercurrent of militarism pervaded Russia as well as Germany, intensified by Russian success in the Turkish War of 1877. Dostoevsky, for example, declared that: 'War rejuvenates men. It raises the spirit of the people and the recognition of their worth.' The corresponding German war fever was best expressed by Nietzsche (1844–1900): 'You should have eyes that always seek an enemy – *your* enemy ... Your enemy you shall seek, your war you shall wage'.[10]

Below the level of powerful and aggressive nations was the level of incipient nationalism. This existed mainly in Central and Eastern Europe in the multi-national empires of the Turks and Habsburgs. Because these two 'prisons' of nation states were of vital strategic importance to the other major powers, the Slavs remained locked up for the whole period in Central Europe, and until 1913 in the Balkans. Germany, for example, bolstered up Austria-Hungary, while Turkey was used by Britain as a bulwark against Russian expansion in the eastern Mediterranean. Power politics on this scale meant, in the long term, a dangerous accumulation of resentment among the Slav peoples. At the turn of the century this was not likely to concern the four governments which dominated Europe, and Joseph Chamberlain in any case believed that 'The day of the smaller nations has long since passed away'.

He also added 'The day of Empires has come.' Between 1870 and 1914 the nationalism of the great powers had overspilled normal frontiers. The resulting 'super' nationalism formed another level and consisted of two distinct varieties. The first was imperialism. Britain, France and Italy all competed for territories overseas, while Germany pursued a systematic policy of colonial acquisition and naval expansion which came under the general term *Weltpolitik*. The second form of expansionist nationalism was the type normally prefixed by the term 'pan'. The Russian variety, pan-Slavism, sought to liberate Bulgarians, southern Slavs, Czechs, Slovaks and Poles from Turkish and Austrian rule and, of course, to extend Tsarist influence to the heart of Europe. Pan-Germanism was based on two unquestioned assumptions: one was that Germany's frontiers should be extended to include all the German-speaking peoples of Europe; the other, that the German peoples were entitled to *Lebensraum* in the East at the expense of the Slavs. Herder had justified this concept far back in the nineteenth century with the statement that 'The Slavic peoples occupy a larger space on earth than they do in history'.[11]

Imperialism and pan-movements were both potentially lethal,

Nationalism

giving national rivalries a new edge. Although continental considerations had been the main determinants of the system of alliances
which developed after 1871, it was the spread of supernationalism
which promoted the armaments race, especially between Germany
and Britain, and Germany and Russia. By 1914 there was unprecedented tension throughout Europe, ideal conditions for the spread
of war. The *casus belli* occurred, in the area of incipient nationalism,
with the assassination of the Archduke Franz Ferdinand at
Sarajevo.

*

Nationalism has always had a tendency to schizophrenia. Between
1919 and 1945 it showed greater extremes than at any other time
before or since. On the one hand, there were high hopes of permanent
peace and harmony now that national self-determination had been
accepted as the guiding principle in redrawing Europe's frontiers.
On the other hand, military defeat and economic disaster provided
ideal conditions for the emergence of a new type of nationalism
which was revolutionary, militarist and destructive.

The victorious Allies drew up the peace settlement of 1919 on the
assumption that the Great War had been caused by the aggressive
nationalism of Germany and by the deprivation of the rights of
Germany's minority peoples, especially the Slavs. The answer,
therefore, was to follow the principle of national self-determination
and create a series of new nation states which would also possess a
balanced constitution – so that their nationalism could be demo-
cratized from the very start. Peace in the future could also be
guaranteed by the pursuit of internationalism in the form of the
League of Nations which, according to President Wilson's Fourteen
Points, would afford 'mutual guarantees of political independence
and territorial integrity to great and small powers alike'.[12]
Nationalism would be, at one and the same time, liberated and
controlled; the experience of 1914–18 would therefore come to be
seen as 'the war to end wars'.

At the other extreme, the inter-war period saw the emergence of
what has been called 'inflamed nationalism' in the form of Italian
Fascism, German National Socialism, and Eastern European adapt-
ations of the two. Fascism and Nazism had in common the rejection
of the traditional structure of authority and a contempt for class
barriers. They sought to redefine the relationship between the

313

individual and the state by stressing the people's corporate identity; according to Mussolini, 'In the Fascist state the individual is not suppressed, but rather multiplied'.[13] The main purpose of the renewed power of the state was to promote external expansion and victory at the expense of weaker neighbours. Hitler, for example, insisted that 'struggle is the father of all things' and that war was man's 'primal condition'.

There is a tendency to consider Nazism as a variety of fascism; but there are, in fact, some differences.[14] Italian Fascism was essentially the vehicle for Mussolini's opportunism and was always subordinated to the *Duce*'s cult of personality. Nazism had stronger and deeper ideological roots which combined the *Volk* of the early Romantics with the theory of racial dominance generated by Gobineau's *Essay on the Inequality of the Human Races*. The result was the transformation of the German *Volk* into the Aryan master-race, in the name of which Hitler oppressed the Slavs, endeavoured to exterminate the Jews, and eventually led Germany to destruction.

*

During the period of German occupation, European resistance leaders came to see the nation state as dangerous and obsolete.[15] Yet once again nationalism displayed a remarkable resilience and capacity for survival. Despite being discredited by the excesses of the 1930s and the Second World War, it became, after 1945, more widespread than ever before.

In the first place, it managed to sustain itself in Europe, although without the extremes of the period 1871–1945. There were those who hoped that Western Europe would abandon the nation state and seek political integration. But progress in this direction was very limited. Since governments invariably insisted on retaining full jurisdiction over domestic and foreign affairs, the nation state was perpetuated rather than undermined. Eastern European countries, too, lost none of their national consciousness. The spread of an international ideology like communism was counterbalanced by national responses to the heavy hand of the Soviet Union. Since 1945, another form of nationalism has gained ground in Europe, profiting from the removal of national tensions between the major powers. Several Western European states have experienced regional

Nationalism

nationalism. The Kilbrandon Commission (1969–73) acknowledged the importance of Scottish and Welsh nationalism within the United Kingdom, while the French government is having to come to terms with separatism in Brittany and Provence; the Italian government with claims from Sicily and Sardinia; and the post-Franco régime in Spain with the Basques and Catalans. Whether or not this regional nationalism can be adapted to the existing state and inter-state structures of Western Europe is likely to be a major issue for the rest of the century.

Nationalism began as a European phenomenon and was also an important factor in the spread of European imperialism. Yet, since 1945, it has also been used as a means of pushing back European rule in the Third World. Nationalism in Asia has developed as a series of Western influences implanted onto an historic and indigenous base; this applies particularly to India, Cambodia, Thailand, Vietnam, Burma, Iran and Indonesia, where modernization and the traditions of the strongest ethnic group merged to set in motion powerful liberation campaigns. At first sight, nationalism seemed less appropriate to African conditions, for imperial boundaries had incorporated many different tribes; Nigeria, for example, consisted of over 250 ethnic groups. Yet African leaders like Nkrumah and Nyerere aimed at creating a new allegiance which cut across tribal affiliations and which kept intact the boundaries drawn by the imperial powers. It is true that there were disastrous civil wars in the Congo and Nigeria, and that the numerous border conflicts have given Africa the world's largest refugee population. Yet the alternatives to the nation state, particularly small pre-imperial kingdoms or large political conglomerations, seemed far less likely to succeed. It has been pointed out that Africa contains the largest number of states of any continent on earth and that most of these are relatively stable. Besides, these African nations are no more unreal than those of the Belgians or the Yugoslavs, which have also been created 'from among the ruins of earlier empires'.[16]

*

Nationalism today affects a larger area of the world than at any other time in history and shows little sign of succumbing to other 'isms'. Even a universalist ideology like Marxism, which believes that 'the working man has no country', has settled into national

315

forms; indeed, A. D. Smith refers to 'a proliferation of Marxist nationalisms and highly nationalist Marxisms'.[17] Nationalism retains its dual character and still provides the means for either liberation or oppression. According to K. R. Minogue, therefore, 'There is room for both the Sleeping Beauty and the Frankenstein's monster view of nationalism'.[18]

34

Marxism and its Manifestations

The purpose of this chapter is to provide a brief survey and explanation of the different forms of Communism which have emanated from the ideas of Karl Marx. It will outline the basic elements of Marxist thought and show how individual reformulations of this thought reacted with changing material circumstances to produce a series of distinctively regional versions.

*

Despite the quantity and complexity of their writings, it is possible to identify three main constituents in the thought of Marx and Engels.[1]

The first was a determinist conception of society and of the relationship between economic circumstances and political power. The *foundation*, or base, of society was always the state of economic development reached by the ruling class. By the mid-nineteenth century this consisted of either bourgeois capitalism in the more advanced areas of Europe, or decaying feudalism elsewhere. The *superstructure* consisted of the political, juridical and religious institutions by which the ruling class maintained its grip. Alteration of these institutions could be achieved only be removing the economic base from which they sprang.

The second component was the theory of value and profit. The proletariat, Marx believed, was created and used by the bourgeoisie as wage labourers but were always paid far less than the real value of what they produced. The balance of the value therefore constituted profit, which was used as capital to exploit more wage labour. In this self-perpetuating process it was essential to find new outlets for investment and fresh supplies of labour. When home markets became saturated because of 'epidemics of over-production', capital spread to other parts of the world in the form of imperialism. At the same time, 'unbridled competitive struggle'[2] resulted in the elimination of smaller scale capitalism and the emergence of monopolies. Eventually, capitalism of all types would reach a crisis. This would coincide with the growing strength of the proletariat, which 'becomes concentrated in greater masses' and would seek to overcome its 'misery, oppression, slavery, degradation, exploitation'.[3]

The way in which this change was expected to occur was the third main element of Marxist thought. In their *Communist Manifesto* (1848), Marx and Engels argued: 'The history of all human society, past and present, has been the history of class struggles.'[4] This had not been fortuitous, but had followed a definite course in accordance with certain laws of history which, it has been claimed, Marx uncovered in much the same way as Darwin revealed the process of evolution. The basic pattern was dialectical, and derived from the intellectual methodology of Hegel: that each thesis developed, an antithesis and the resulting interaction produced a synthesis which, as a new thesis, generated a further antithesis and hence revived conflict. Marx developed this at two levels, 'of the external world and of human thought'.[3] Internally, the dialectic has been used ever since by Marxists, and by others, as a method of criticism, examination and analysis. Historically, it was made to show the way in which class conflict developed. Each economic system and class had created its own antithesis, which would inevitably interact with the thesis to form a new system. According to Engels, 'from its origin the bourgeoisie has been saddled with its antithesis: that capitalists cannot exist without wage workers'.[2] Thus, as the *Communist Manifesto* asserted, 'the bourgeoisie produces its own gravediggers. Its downfall and the victory of the proletariat are equally inevitable'.[4] In order to effect this change it might well be necessary to resort to violence, since 'Force is the midwife of every old society pregnant with a new one'.[5] The alternative to bourgeois rule would initially be the 'dictatorship of the proletariat', which would dismantle the capitalist superstructure and extend the powers of the state to cover credit, communication, education, land and the instruments of production. Eventually society and the economy

Marxism and its Manifestations

would become fully collective and co-operative in the spirit of communism. This would mean that the coercive elements of the state could disappear, followed by political institutions themselves. Engels believed that 'The interference of the state power in social relations becomes superfluous in one sphere after another, and then dies away of itself . . . The state is not "abolished", it withers away'.[3] What would be left is the Marxist ideal – the 'classless society'.

The actual method of bringing about the 'dictatorship of the proletariat' in the mid-nineteenth century was never clearly stated. Although, in the words of the *Communist Manifesto*, a 'spectre' did indeed 'haunt Europe', it was still mainly a theoretical one. Marx and Engels assumed that the dialectical process, by which capitalism would be destroyed, would operate more rapidly in those countries which had already reached an advanced stage of capitalism than in those which were predominantly feudal. After all, the most developed countries would possess the largest and most discontented proletariats, who would be able to seize the initiative as the economic system entered its period of crisis. On balance, Central and Western Europe seemed the most vulnerable areas; Marx affirmed in 1848: 'The Communists turn their attention chiefly to Germany.'

*

Between 1850 and 1914 the influence of Marx was widespread, but uneven. Two International Working Men's Associations were established, the first in London (1864) and the second in Paris (1869). French socialism, although inclined mainly towards traditional utopianism, developed an influential Marxist wing, while British labour movements combined a few Marxist sympathies with their predominant commitment to trade unionism. As Marx had predicted, however, the new ideology was strongest in Germany.

What had not been foreseen was that there would be a major dispute over the interpretation of Marxist principles. Although this occurred throughout Europe, the most important example was in Germany, which possessed the largest socialist party in the world. Formed by Bebel and Liebknecht, the SPD (*Sozialdemokratische Partei Deutschlands*) sharply criticized the political and social structure of the Second Reich, particularly during the chancellorship of Bismarck (1871–90). The Party's main Marxist theorist, Kautsky, was entirely orthodox, and revolution was an essential

319

feature of his policy. This, however, had to be understood in a social and not necessarily violent sense. Co-operation with parliamentary regimes would bring few gains but 'The elections are a means to count ourselves and the enemy and they grant thereby a clear view of the relative strength of the classes and parties, their advance and their retreat. They prevent premature outbreaks and they guard against defeats.'[6] On the other hand, democracy 'is not capable of preventing this revolution. Democracy is to the proletariat what light and air are to the organism; without them it cannot develop its powers'.[6] In contrast to this approach, the case for Revisionism was presented in the 1890s by Bernstein. Marxism should be rescued from its obsession with revolution and allowed to accommodate itself to parliamentary institutions. Once the SPD had attained a majority in the *Reichstag* it could deal with Germany's social iniquities by legislation. Indeed, legislation 'is best adapted to positive social-political work' because it acts as 'a systematic force'. Revolution, on the other hand, was unpredictable and destructive, since it was primarily 'an elemental force'.[7]

In addition to the orthodox and revisionist wings of German social democracy there also developed a more radical version of Marxism, led by Rosa Luxemburg and Karl Liebknecht. Before 1914 there was, therefore, a three-way split, and the ideological emphasis of the SPD still had to be settled.

Then came the First World War and with it a much more uniform policy. Far from everywhere destroying capitalism, as Lenin hoped, the war contributed to the breaking of the first wave of militant Marxism in Western and Central Europe. The real victor here was Revisionism. The socialist parties placed nationalism first in every country except Serbia and Russia, and supported their governments. In Germany, Bernstein was now joined by Kautsky (whom Lenin branded as 'renegade'); Kautsky believed that the dialectical process had not yet reached the stage where the overthrow of capitalism was imminent. Adherents to revolutionary Marxism now found themselves the exception rather than the rule and protested in their own way. During the war two offshoots from the SPD formed themselves into new parties. These were the Independent Socialists and the Spartacus League (soon to become the Communist Party, led by Liebknecht and Rosa Luxemburg). Ironically, these found themselves after the war in conflict with an established order which was dominated by the SPD. In January 1919 the government of the

Marxism and its Manifestations

Weimar Republic, of which the SPD provided both president and chancellor, suppressed a Communist rising in Berlin, in which both Luxemburg and Liebknecht were killed. A few months later it destroyed the Soviet Republic of Bavaria, which had been created by the Independent Socialists at the end of 1918.

The pattern was similar elsewhere in Europe. Many Marxists had emerged from the war as Revisionists, accepting the permanence of parliamentary institutions. A smaller number still favoured the revolutionary approach, but now looked to Russia, the new centre of Communism, for leadership and inspiration.

*

While it was becoming apparent that Western and Central Europe would not, after all, be the centre of radical Marxism, a revolutionary impetus was growing in Russia. This was in the form of a new movement, Marxism-Leninism, or Bolshevism. Lenin broke away in 1903 from the more moderate Mensheviks, having already attacked Legal Marxism and Revisionism. He moved in the opposite direction to Bernstein, adapting Marxism to revolutionary conditions rather than to parliamentary institutions. Substantial modifications were necessary, and he once observed: 'We do not regard Marx's theory as something completed and inviolable.'[8] As with other Marxist leaders, in fact, many of Lenin's changes to this theory arose from the force of reappraised circumstances.

Lenin's main theoretical contribution to Marxism was his belief that the first revolution could occur in a more backward country like Russia: that capitalism was most immediately vulnerable at the weakest link in its chain, rather than where it was most highly developed. The war, he maintained, revealed capitalism in decline everywhere, but the process of overthrowing old régimes would actually begin in Russia. Other, more developed countries would then benefit from Russia's revolutionary experience, in return for which Russia would be influenced by socialist developments in the West during the period of the 'dictatorship of the proletariat'.

In his preparation for revolution in Russia, Lenin combined deference to the dialectic with a strong element of pragmatism. He acknowledged that some parliamentary experience was desirable for the development of working-class consciousness and organization. It was even necessary to collaborate with the 'revolutionary bourgeoisie' to overthrow the Tsarist régime, since this would bring Russia nearer, dialectically, to the phase of proletarian revolution. At this point, however, Lenin disagreed profoundly with the Mensheviks. The latter, under Martov, argued for a substantial period of parliamentary rule which, in the long term, could be expected to evolve into a socialist system. Lenin, by contrast, considered that the dialectic must be accelerated, and he made this clear in his *April Theses* (1917). After the overthrow of the Tsar by the March Revolution, a Provisional Government was established, based to some extent on Western constitutional principles. Lenin now argued: 'The peculiarity of the current moment in Russia consists in the transition from the first stage of the revolution, which gave power to the bourgeoisie as a result of the insufficient consciousness and organization of the proletariat, to the second stage, which should give the power into the hands of the proletariat.'[9]

Forcing the pace like this obviously eliminated any possibility of a spontaneous revolution, and made a carefully formulated strategy essential. Lenin's solution was the development of a tightly organized Party Central Committee, which consisted of dedicated professional revolutionaries. After all, 'in its struggle for power the proletariat has no other weapon but organization'.[10] The Party adopted conspiratorial methods and the October Revolution, which overthrew the Provisional Government, was a vindication of Lenin's concentration of 'a great superiority of forces at the decisive point, at the decisive moment'. (See Chapter 19.)

The aftermath of the Revolution saw the establishment of Lenin's own version of the 'dictatorship of the proletariat' and the adoption of his interpretation of socialism as the first step towards the ultimate ideal of communism. Considerable coercion was used to accomplish this, although the roles were now reversed: the 'majority' now suppressed the 'minority'. But the possession of power also brought a divergence of views as to the future priorities of Marxism-Leninism. A profound ideological and tactical split developed between Trotsky and Stalin, resulting in the eventual expulsion and assassination of Trotsky.

Trotsky's main contribution was the theory of 'permanent revolution' (or 'uninterrupted revolution'), although this had already been partially incorporated into Marxism-Leninism during Lenin's lifetime. Revolution, Trotsky argued, would not end with the overthrow of bourgeois rule by the proletariat. It must continue, as

Marxism and its Manifestations

'permanent revolution', on both a national and worldwide scale. Nationally, it could end only 'in the complete liquidation of all class society'.[11] Internationally it could attain completion only in 'the final victory of the new society on our entire planet'.[11] Although this fitted in logically with the theory of the dialectic, in practice the worldwide emphasis seemed inappropriate in the 1920s because of a growing disillusionment with the prospect of Western revolutions. The Bolsheviks had been confronted by extensive Western intervention on the side of counter-revolution during the civil war (1918–20) and the spontaneous revolutions in Germany and Hungary in 1919 had been crushed. A sharp reaction therefore occurred; the priority was now to develop 'Socialism in One Country', to make Russia self-sufficient and invulnerable in a hostile ideological environment. This was the principal aim of Stalin, who used the power which he had accumulated by 1927 to restructure Marxist-Leninism in two ways.

First, he elevated the role of leadership to a new pinnacle by redefining, somewhat conveniently, the Marxist concepts of 'base' and 'superstructure'. 'The base gives rise to the superstructure, but this does not at all mean that it merely reflects the basis, that it is passive, neutral, is indifferent to the fate of its basis, to the fates of classes, to the character of the system. On the contrary ... it becomes the greatest active force, actively assists its basis to take shape and acquire strength, and makes every effort to help the new order to finish off and liquidate the old basis and the old classes.'[12] This directly justified the use of coercion and the development of repressive organs like OGPU and the NKVD, to say nothing of the interference of the leadership in all political decisions. The Party had now become, in effect, 'the instrument of the dictatorship of the proletariat'.[13] The logical conclusion was the systematic elimination of all opposition, since what was needed was 'absolute and complete unity of action on the part of all members of the Party'.[13] (This was actually in contrast to the earlier dialectical controversy which Lenin had encouraged within the Party.)

Second, Stalin greatly accelerated the construction of the Soviet state, concentrating on enlarging its workforce and industrial production. The main reason for this was his obsession with the threat of outside intervention, as he had no faith in the Trotskyist vision of assistance being rendered to Russia by worldwide revolution. To Stalin there was a stark choice. 'We are fifty or a hundred years behind the advanced countries. We must make good this distance in ten years. Either we do it, or they will crush us.'[14] His methods attained a new peak of ruthlessness. The superstructure redesigned the base in a series of Five Year Plans which forcibly collectivized agriculture and converted the Soviet Union into an industrial and military power. (See Chapter 29.)

In the last ten years of his rule, Stalin became the first agent for spreading communism, although not in the way envisaged by Marx, Lenin or Trotsky. Communism did not take over in Western Europe by a series of locally-planned revolutions inspired by the Russian example; instead, it spread over Eastern Europe in the wake of military conquest at the end of the Second World War. The satellite states which emerged were therefore very different from the more advanced societies Lenin had hoped would be a source of inspiration to Russia.

By 1953 Stalin had completely personalized the superstructure in the form of dictatorship. His successors, however, finding the hero cult and extremes of coercion equally unacceptable, proceeded to redress the balance. A destalinization campaign was initiated by Khrushchev, who affirmed in 1956: 'Stalin abandoned the Leninist method of convincing and educating for one of administrative violence, mass repression and terror.'[15] Hence it was necessary 'to eradicate the cult of the individual as alien to marxism-leninism'.[15] But Khrushchev's brand of revisionism did not entirely eradicate Stalinist influences. After Khrushchev was removed from power in 1964, the superstructure was once again strengthened, although Brezhnev stopped short of Stalin's excesses and made no attempt to restore the personality cult. Soviet leaders after 1953 did manage to remove some of the obsessions of Stalinism; they even found a way of using coercion without some of the horror which had once accompanied it. But the revised form of Soviet Communism became, in its turn, rigid and introverted. It was also no longer the only major influence on Communist movements elsewhere.

Stalin had always aimed to keep world Communism as a monolithic organization subservient to Moscow. By the late 1940s this concept was already being challenged by President Tito, who was determined to apply his own brand of Communism in Yugoslavia and who was subsequently expelled from Stalin's Cominform (Communist Information Bureau) for his pains. Worse was to follow as the Chinese Communist leadership emerged as a major rival to

Marxism and its Manifestations

Soviet hegemony in 1949. But it was Khrushchev's policy of destalinization which set the seal on the monolithic image of world Communism and promoted, quite unintentionally, what has been called 'polycentrism', or more pronounced regional variants. This occurred for two main reasons. First, the attack on personality cult undermined the focal point of unity and, because it also attacked one of the ingredients of Maoism, was bitterly resented by China. Peking therefore emerged as a centre to rival Moscow and, in an intensive propaganda war, denounced Khrushchev's line as 'revisionist'. Second, destalinization had a profoundly unsettling effect upon Eastern Europe. Already shaky Stalinist régimes were gravely embarrassed by Khrushchev's revelations of administrative terror and were faced with a series of disturbances which culminated in the Hungarian uprising of November 1956. Khrushchev's reactions to these disturbances shocked the rest of the world and seemed to show that the Soviet Union was more concerned with maintaining control over its satellite states than with preserving or reviving its moral claims for leadership of world Communism. It is ironical that, while the Soviet Union had finally emerged as a superpower with a régime less repressive than of its predecessors, it now inspired less commitment from other Communists than it had during the harsh era of Stalin.

*

An alternative form of revolutionary Marxism had, meanwhile, been developed in China by Mao Tse Tung, both before and after his overthrow of Chiang Kai-Shek's régime in 1949. Chinese Communism was partly a derivation of Russian Marxism-Leninism and partly an adaptation of Marxism to Chinese conditions.

Mao acknowledged his debt to Lenin and the 'salvoes of the October Revolution'[16] which brought Marxism to China. He also learned from the Bolsheviks the importance of organization and conspiracy, which undoubtedly influenced his view that 'A revolution is . . . an act of violence by which one class overthrows another'.[17] Moreover, 'The seizure of power by armed force . . . is the central task and highest form of revolution.'[18]

In some respects, however, Mao reinterpreted Marx and Lenin, adapting their ideas to Chinese thought and conditions. At a philosophical level, he imposed the dialectic on the traditional Chinese concept of *yin* and *yang*, opposites which exist harmoniously within every form or being. He substituted contradiction for harmony, but retained the notion of opposites. Thus 'A thing moves and develops because of such contradictions within itself'.[19] He emphasized, however, that there were two types of contradictions, which he labelled antagonistic and non-antagonistic. The latter contradictions, he maintained, would often have to reconcile themselves in order to deal with the former contradiction. Or, put in political terms, lesser differences should be resolved so that the major enemy could be disposed of.

This approach immediately opened the way for a flexible and pragmatic course of action in bringing about a revolution, and made Chinese Communism highly distinctive. There was to be less emphasis on the internal conflict between classes and more on a united front to overthrow feudalism and imperialism; the implementation of socialism could then follow. Hence he was able to recast some of the fundamental ideas of Marxism and Marxism–Leninism. To replace the regime toppled by revolution, he could conceive 'a joint revolutionary-democratic dictatorship of several revolutionary classes'.[20] He could thus adopt a more flexible and pragmatic approach to the situation in China. He emphasized: 'We are not utopians and cannot divorce ourselves from the actual conditions confronting us.'[21] Since the overwhelming majority of the Chinese were peasants, they had to become the revolutionary force and not remain, in Leninist and Stalinist terms, 'the reserve and ally of the working class'. This creation of a *rural* revolutionary vanguard was Mao's most important legacy, since it could be related to the concept of the 'people's war' and to guerrilla tactics designed for the countryside rather than the cities.

After 1949 trends in China puzzled the rest of the world and there was some controversy as to their real significance. One possible explanation is this. During the 1950s Mao encouraged widespread debate, thus putting into practice his views on contradiction. 'Let a hundred flowers blossom; and let a hundred schools of thought contend.'[22] By the end of the decade, however, Mao had become dissatisfied with the rate of industrial and agricultural growth in China and was concerned that debate was turning rapidly into criticism. Furthermore, he suspected that the Chinese Communist superstructure was becoming as rigid as its Soviet counterpart. He therefore unleashed the 'Great Proletarian Cultural Revolution' in an attempt to rediscover the Chinese revolutionary spirit, thereby 'preventing capitalist restoration and building socialism'. He also brought to a peak his own personality cult and eradicated all internal dissent and external Soviet influences. By 1969, however, the Cultural Revolution had burned itself out and Chinese Communism resumed a more pragmatic course during the 1970s. The most remarkable example of this was the accommodation between China and the West which followed Mao's death. In placing China's immediate strategic interests and intense hostility towards Russia above any ideological conflict with the West, Mao's successors seemed to be acting on the chairman's pre-Cultural Revolution dictum: 'In China and in the present circumstances.'[23]

*

In 1966 Lin Piao said: 'Taking the entire globe, if North America and Western Europe can be called the "cities of the world" then Asia, Africa and Latin America constitute "rural areas of the world".'[24] He added that, since 1945, the impetus of revolution has been 'held back' in the former areas but has accelerated in the latter. Events of the 1960s and 1970s seemed to support this analysis. The revolutionary initiative was captured by Third World Communism while, in Europe, the more moderate Eurocommunism adopted an evolutionary approach.

Third World Communism derived from Marxism, Marxism-Leninism and Maoism. Marx claimed that the bourgeoisie had created 'a world after its own image'. Lenin believed that this had led to the oppression of subject peoples by imperialism, 'the monopoly stage of capitalism'. Furthermore, 'wars waged by colonies and semi-colonies in the imperialist era are not only possible but inevitable'. Mao Tse Tung explained how the overthrow of imperialism could be accomplished, and also how a Communist régime could be established which was related to the needs of the more backward areas of the world; the former by guerrilla warfare, the latter by gearing Marxist-Leninist ideology to the peasantry rather than to the proletariat. He enumerated his tactics of guerrilla warfare in considerable detail, basing everything on the maxim: 'Fight, fail, fight again, fail again, fight again . . . till . . . victory; that is the logic of the people.'[25] Time and persistence were the vital factors, since imperialism was considered totally vulnerable to popular movements. Western powers were, in his view, no more than 'paper tigers'.

Lu Ting-yi (a member of the Chinese Communist Party Central

Committee) therefore had good reason for saying, in 1951, that 'the classic type of revolution in colonial and semi-colonial countries is the Chinese Revolution'.[26] But Third World revolutionaries were also swayed by conditions and circumstances within their own areas. Two particularly successful leaders, Ho Chi Minh of Vietnam and Castro of Cuba, were more pragmatic in their outlook even than Mao Tse Tung. Castro, on his own admission, became a Communist late in his career. Undoubtedly, this attention to circumstance has also affected the relations between Third World Communist régimes and the major Communist powers. Although they had a closer resemblance to China, both Cuba and Vietnam chose to maintain close links with the Soviet Union, largely for economic and strategic reasons. The same applied to Angola and Mozambique, the new Marxist states in Africa.

Marxism in Western Europe was characterized by its disillusionment, during the 1950s, 1960s and 1970s, with the Soviet Union. This was in complete contrast to the 1930s and 1940s, when the USSR, despite the excesses of Stalinism, had appealed to intellectuals of the 'far Left' as the 'fatherland of the international proletariat', and had managed to recruit many KGB agents like Philby and Burgess in Britain. One reason for this disillusionment was the emergence of the Soviet Union as one of the world's two military superpowers; Western Marxists began to feel that it was now concentrating entirely on national and strategic interests and had lost sight of its ideological role in the world. Another was the alarm felt at the subjection of Eastern Europe. The Soviet invasion of Hungary (1956) and Czechoslovakia (1968) came as a profound shock to Western Communist parties, who vied with each other in condemning Khrushchev and Brezhnev. Yet Western capitalism was still considered unacceptable, whether as free enterprise or in the form of the planned economies now favoured by Western Europe's socialist parties. What, then, was the answer?

Many of the Communist parties in European countries outside the Soviet *bloc* revised their strategies and re-examined their ideologies in a broadly similar way. They were referred to increasingly as 'Eurocommunists', although this label did not imply the loss of national identity by each party or the growth of any international body. Gradually, Communist leaders and spokesmen in Italy, Spain and France built up a new strategy. Radical change was still regarded as essential, in Napolitano's phrase, to end 'the anarchy of capitalist development'.[27] The process of change should, however, be accomplished by constitutional means and the Soviet system should be avoided. Indeed, Azcárate referred to this type of Communism as a 'parody of Marxism',[28] while Ellenstein declared: 'For us the Soviet system is neither an example nor a model.'[29] Eurocommunism therefore took the radical step of removing Leninism as a basic source of inspiration. Its approach to revolution was also anti-Leninist. Eurocommunists would not seek to disrupt a functioning constitution but, as Carrillo warned: 'In no way do we put aside the possibility of reaching power by revolutionary means, if the dominating classes close the democratic paths.'[29] In other words, revolution is seen as a defensive tactic to uphold democracy rather than as an offensive weapon with which to destroy it. It is hardly surprising that those groups in Western Europe who regarded themselves as truly revolutionary condemned the Euro-communist parties for being part of the establishment and for turning their back on internationalism.

*

The constant reformulation of Marxism led, by the 1970s, to its control of one-third of the world's population; at the same time, however, it revealed several general problems. One of the original hopes of Marx and Engels was that an ideology based entirely on materialism would be best able to guarantee a high standard of living and a permanent material wellbeing. In practice, the results of Communist rule were somewhat mixed. On the one hand, the overall productive capacity of most Communist states improved markedly (with some notable exceptions, like Cambodia in the 1970s). On the other hand the cost of this improvement was enormous; Soviet and Chinese collectivization produced many millions of human casualities and caused severe fluctuations in the standard of living. A major dilemma confronting every Marxist government was how to achieve a balance between a planned collective economy and a quality of life for its people which could compete with non-Communist Western societies. The latter, indeed, compounded the problem; far from falling into headlong decline, as Marx had predicted, they set a furious pace in economic and consumer growth, especially after the Second World War, with which even the Soviet Union had difficulty in competing. Hence most Marxist régimes were driven to modify some of their policies, and tended to oscillate between all-out pursuit of industrial and agricultural targets and periodic concessions to consumer demand. There was, of course, no ideological formula for this, each régime being influenced very much by its own problems and circumstances.

There remains a popular misconception that Communism is an *integrated* world movement. Events since 1945 have revealed a series of major splits. Yugoslavia broke away from the Soviet *bloc* in 1948; China and Russia entered a period of Cold War in the early 1960s; the Western Communists formally abandoned Leninism in the late 1960s; and finally, 1979 saw a major war between Vietnam, Cambodia and China. Constant reinterpretation may have enabled Marxism to adapt to many different environments, but it has also tended to obscure the original slogan 'Workers of the world unite!'

35

Imperialism

Between 1815 and 1880 there was a comparative lull in the imperial and maritime conflicts which complicated international relations in the eighteenth and late nineteenth centuries. Three of the five colonial powers had suffered heavy losses and could do no more than safeguard what was left. Spain, for example, had lost Central and South America to independence movements and had to content herself with Cuba, Rio de Oro and the Philippines. Portugal was confined, after being deprived of Brazil, to the African coastal enclaves of Guinea, Mozambique and Angola, while the Dutch were left with only the East Indies and Surinam, after ceding the Cape and Ceylon to Britain in 1815. The other two colonial powers continued to be active. France, deprived by 1815 of one empire, began the task of building another, conquering Algeria during the 1830s and 1840s, extending her influence to Senegal in the 1850s and acquiring direct control over Tahiti, the Marquesas and part of Indochina. Britain, who found her maritime strength enhanced by her gains in 1815, steadily spread her power over Australia and New Zealand, as well as appropriating Singapore (1819), part of Burma (1852), and Lagos (1861). Yet such expansion was relatively peaceful. British and French spheres of influence did not overlap as they had in the eighteenth century, and there was, in any case, an official understanding that the British Empire was replete. The Duke of Wellington, for example, said in 1829: 'I am anxious to avoid exciting the attention and jealousy of other powers by extending our possessions.'[1] In some quarters there was actually opposition to imperial commitments. Cobden, for example, put the fashionable Manchester School view that empire was irrelevant to trade, adding that it would be 'a happy day when England has not an acre of territory in continental Asia'.[1]

Then, during the last two decades of the nineteenth century and the immediate pre-war period, imperial rivalries were renewed, reaching a greater intensity than ever before. The Monroe Doctrine (1823) discouraged European states from turning their attention to the American continent, but Africa, the Far East and the Pacific all experienced partition. British acquisitions during the 1880s and 1890s included Egypt, Nigeria, East Africa, Uganda, Bechuanaland, the Rhodesias, Nyasaland, Sierra Leone, the Sudan, Swaziland, Burma, Malaya, New Guinea and Borneo. The French extended their dominion over the whole of Laos, Annam and Tong King in Indochina, and over the whole of the West African interior. Germany carved out the enclaves of South-West Africa, Togoland, the Cameroons and German East Africa, together with the Pacific possessions of Eastern New Guinea, the Bismarck Archipelago and the Caroline Islands. Italy annexed Eritrea, Somaliland and, in 1912, Libya. Finally, Russia extended her Asiatic frontier into the Liaotung Peninsula region of China. By 1914, therefore, most of the globe was under the rule of European countries or peopled by Europeans who had asserted their independence from the original metropolitan power. The only states which had managed to retain their autonomy were Japan (which had Europeanized itself), China (which had to put up with foreign enclaves and unfavourable trade agreements), Siam, Afghanistan, Ethiopia and Liberia.

This second wave of imperialism and, in particular, the 'scramble for Africa', has been the subject of considerable historical controversy, with emphasis accorded to economic, diplomatic, humanitarian and irrational factors. Such a variety of explanations is the inevitable result of the complexity of imperialism; the outward expansion of a country and, even more, of a continent, is caused by a variety of internal pressures, assisted by peripheral conditions as well. The next section of this chapter will, therefore, outline some of the main arguments that imperialism was the result of pressures within and between the European powers. The final section will deal with another approach: that European governments were not always keen on imperial ventures but were, on occasion, drawn reluctantly into colonization.

*

One of the first writers to analyse the pressure exerted by economic factors was the radical J. A. Hobson, whose *Imperialism* (1902) carried the argument that the European states had built up, through industrialization and financial development, a gross inequality of wealth. The concentration of wealth in the hands of the few created a crisis, for this 'surplus capital' could not 'find investments within the country' and had to seek outlets overseas. Thus Britain, Germany and France were forced 'to place larger and larger portions of their economic resources outside the area of their present political domain, and then stimulate a policy of political expansion so as to take in the new areas'.[2] The argument was subsequently elaborated by Lenin, although the latter rejected Hobson's belief that capitalism was redeemable provided that surplus wealth could be redirected to internal 'social investment' at home. Most historians have since pointed out that the Hobson-Lenin thesis does not fit the facts of imperial expansion. There was certainly a huge outflow of investment from Europe, but most of this went to areas which were not subsequently annexed, like Canada, the United States, Latin America and Russia. Hence the accumulation of surplus capital cannot be regarded as a general stimulus to imperial expansion. But this is not to say that economic factors had no influence at all. During the 1880s and 1890s successive British governments showed increased concern about the adoption of protective tariffs by Germany, the United States and other commercial competitors. The British prime minister, Lord Salisbury, for example, complained in 1895: 'Everywhere we see the advance of commerce checked by the enormous growth which the doctrines of protection are obtaining.'[1] Strong political pressure groups emerged, preparing official and public opinion for the transition from purely private enterprise to a more deliberate government policy towards imperialism. Joseph Chamberlain, in particular, sought to revive Britain's commercial supremacy by acquiring new sources of raw materials and outlets for finished goods. The German government, meanwhile, had been strongly influenced by the commercial interests of Bremen, Hamburg and Lübeck in the type of administration it had set up in South-West Africa and the Pacific Islands. Bismarck, on one

(a) The colonization of Asia by 1914

Colonization

occasion, referred to these protectorates as a 'business proposition', arguing that 'the flag follows trade'.[3] Furthermore, the new *Kolonialrat*, set up in 1890, was always attentive to the representations of the chambers of commerce of Hamburg, Bremen and Cologne.

Pressure groups of this type were not, however, the only force behind official imperialism in Britain and Germany, while in France, it has been argued, 'economic factors . . . were hardly ever responsible for the initiation of . . . colonial policy'.[4] W. L. Langer and A. J. P. Taylor accounted for the spread of imperialism in diplomatic rather than in economic terms,[5] an approach endorsed by D. K. Fieldhouse who believed that 'imperialism may be seen as the extension into the periphery of the political struggle of Europe'.[6] D. Thomson used a similar analogy: 'The naked power politics of the new colonialism were the projection, on to an overseas screen, of the inter-state frictions and rivalries of Europe.'[7]

Imperialism

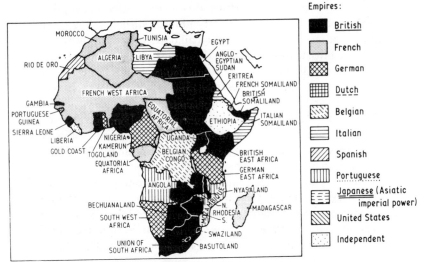

Empires:

- British
- French
- German
- Dutch
- Belgian
- Italian
- Spanish
- Portuguese
- Japanese (Asiatic imperial power)
- United States
- Independent

(b) The colonization of Africa by 1914

Colonization

It could be argued that Bismarck was mainly responsible for this. Concerned that France might try to build an alliance against the newly formed German Reich to avenge the humiliation of 1870, Bismarck sought to isolate the Third Republic and, if possible, to induce a certain degree of dependence on German goodwill. The most effective means of achieving these aims was by creating and exploiting rifts between France and her potential allies. Europe was too volatile for such a design, but collisions in Africa carried little danger of a major war. This reasoning was supported by the Chancellor's celebrated statement that 'my map of Africa lies in Europe'. He was assisted by a revival of French enthusiasm for empire as a means of recovering lost prestige. As Gambetta said, 'In Africa France will make the first faltering steps of the convalescent'.[8] Hence he secretly encouraged France to annex Tunisia in 1878. The result was that Italy, who had plans for the area herself, went through an intense wave of francophobia, eventually joining Germany and Austria-Hungary in the Triple Alliance of 1882. Bismarck also endeavoured to prevent any entente between France and Britain while, at the same time, encouraging the French government to forget the loss of Alsace-Lorraine by

335

seeking compensation in Africa. He told the French ambassador in 1885: 'Renounce the question of the Rhine; I will help you in securing all the satisfaction you require on all other points.'[9] As evidence of his good faith to France, Bismarck pursued a policy which was likely to challenge Britain's position in Africa and the Pacific. He laid claim, for example, to territory adjoining British spheres of influence, and proceeded to annex South-West Africa, Togoland, the Cameroons, Tanganyika and East New Guinea. There was also a domestic reason for seeking confrontation 'at a distance'. After 1884 Bismarck feared that the Kaiser's failing health would soon mean the accession of the Crown Prince Frederick. The latter, openly anglophile and liberal, would almost certainly dispense with Bismarck's services and construct a 'Gladstone cabinet'. On the other hand, his position would definitely be undermined if Britain were seen as a national threat. Herbert Bismarck later admitted, in 1890, that in order to weaken Frederick's power 'we had to launch a colonial policy, which is popular and can produce conflicts with England at any moment.'

How did Britain and France react to these machinations? Under the leadershop of Ferry, the Third Republic took full advantage of the favourable diplomatic situation by extending French influence well beyond the frontiers of Algeria and Senegal. By the time of the Berlin Conference (1885) it was clear that Britain had been out-manoeuvred and that her own interests might well be threatened unless more positive action were taken. During the 1890s, therefore, the 'scramble for Africa' accelerated, assuming a momentum of its own. The alternative to direct annexation was no longer independence but the certain intervention of a European rival. Hence French expansion eastwards towards the Nile, and German activities on the shore of Lake Victoria, threatened British interests in East Africa and Egypt, leaving her with little option but to annex Uganda. Similarly, the German presence in South-West Africa upset the delicate stability of the sub-continent and certainly hastened the colonization of Bechuanaland and the Rhodesias.

Less tangible than diplomatic factors were three other forces, which might be called curiosity, concern and national fulfilment. Curiosity prompted, and was, in turn, kept alive by, the work of explorers like Nachtigal, Barth, Flatters, Brazza, Speke, Burton, Livingstone and Stanley. The controversy over the source of the Nile was followed with passionate interest all over Britain and did much

Imperialism

to prepare public opinion to accept a new imperial initiative in 'Darkest Africa'. Similar enthusiasm prevailed in France over discoveries in West and Equatorial Africa. For a while, in President Macmahon's words, 'Geography [had] become the philosophy of the world'.[10] Concern assumed a variety of forms. Missionaries like Moffat and Redman sought to convert whole tribes to Christianity and to promote their material well-being by encouraging contacts with traders. Sometimes the missionary societies put pressure on governments to take a more active role in suppressing evils like the East African slave trade or threats to Christianity. Sometimes the government intervened anyway; the German annexation of Kiaochow in 1897 was a direct result of the killing of two Jesuits in China. Another manifestation of concern was the unquestioned assumption that the indigenous peoples must, for their own benefit, be put into contact with a superior European culture. It was also the duty of the white man to civilize the black. Lord Curzon affirmed in 1907: 'In the Empire we have found not merely the key to glory and wealth but the call to duty and the means of service to mankind.'[1] Other statesmen and theorists emphasized the importance of imperialism as a means of national fulfilment. This was particularly the case in Germany, where Kaiser Wilhelm II openly pursued a policy of *Weltpolitik*, and the historian Treitschke felt impelled to write: 'Every virile people has established colonial power . . . All great nations in the fullness of their strength have desired to set their mark upon barbarian lands.' He added: 'The colonizing impulse has become a vital question for every nation.'[6] The Italian Prime Minister, Crispi, went so far as to claim that colonies were 'a necessity of modern life'.[11]

*

It would be a mistake to consider the parts of the world which came under colonial rule as entirely inert. On the contrary, certain parts of Africa exercised considerable 'pull', particularly on British imperialism; this is an argument stressed by less Eurocentric historians. (According to R. Robinson and J. Gallagher, for example, Britain was drawn into Africa by 'the persistent crisis in Egypt',[12] and the threat posed to British interests by the Boer Republics in South Africa.)

The major concern of the British government was to protect British routes to India, the most valuable part of the Empire, through the Suez Canal and round the Cape of Good Hope. Unfortunately, local problems made the northern and southern tips of Africa very unstable. The Egyptian Khedive was threatened, in 1881, by a major revolt led by Arabi Pasha, who aimed at freeing Egypt from all European influence. The British occupation of 1882 was not the end of the matter, for the great Islamic revolt in the Sudan against Anglo-Egyptian rule necessitated military action by Kitchener, culminating in the Battle of Omdurman in 1898. British rule was dragged further up the Nile and into East Africa by the need to outflank the Islamic threat, and to counter the moves of France and Germany. Meanwhile, the Boer Republics of the Transvaal and the Orange Free State were threatening the long-term British scheme for a loose federation of South African states which would also incorporate the Cape and Natal. The alternative could well be a United States of South Africa, dominated by a republican Transvaal and bitterly hostile to any British influence. Again, therefore, the British Government was receptive to pressure to acquire territory as a means of outflanking or isolating the challenge, in this case promoting the colonization of Bechuanaland on the western border of the Transvaal, and the Rhodesias to the north. The overall result of the two separate processes of expansion was a stretch of British territory from the Cape to the Mediterranean broken only by the German colony of Tanganyika.

It is significant that British imperialism was most actively sponsored by men, like Rhodes, McKinnon and Goldie who operated from inside Africa. Rhodes, who had made fortunes from the diamond mines at Kimberley and the gold reef at Johannesburg, turned his attention to territorial expansion north of the Limpopo, his ultimate intention being to build a rail-route from Cape Town to Cairo. The British government, by granting a Royal Charter to Rhodes' British South Africa Company in 1889, directly sanctioned his activities in Matabeleland and Mashonaland as a relatively inexpensive means of outflanking the threat from the Boers. In extending the range of British influence beyond the Zambezi, Rhodes greatly exceeded the original expectations of the Colonial Office.

Similarly, McKinnon's British East Africa Company, which was given a Charter in 1888 to safeguard British interests against German and indigenous threats, eventually pulled the British Crown into the unexpectedly large areas of Kenya and Uganda.

Imperialism

Even West Africa, predominantly French, had the substantial British enclave of Nigeria, a direct result of the energy and ambition of another local empire builder, Goldie, operating through the Royal Niger Company.

The great powers were drawn into some areas, paradoxically, by resistance of indigenous cultures and leaders to growing European influence. In these circumstances outright conquest took the place of commercial agreements and treaties of protection. The one major indigenous success was the victory of the Ethiopian leader, Menelik, over the Italians at Adowa in 1896, but even this served only to strengthen Italy's commitment to Empire and, ultimately, to shape Mussolini's African policy in the 1930s. Elsewhere, Islamic states which tried through the *jihad* (holy war) to purge themselves of the infidel, succeeded only in laying themselves open to invasion. The British, for example, destroyed the Mahdist state in the Sudan, while the French intensified their efforts in West Africa because of the resistance of leaders like Samori, and peoples like the Ahmadu. Numerous Negro and Bantu states and confederacies were also laid low, examples being the Ashanti, Dahomey, Bunyoro and the Matabele. But, although the indigenous response proved counter-productive in the face of an assertive and aggressive continent, it did establish a precedent for the distant future. Fifty years later, Europe's comparative decline would render it less capable of dealing with colonial rebellions and nationalist independence movements.

36

Decolonization

The peak of Europe's dominance over other parts of the world was reached in the decade before 1914 and immediately after the First World War. Thereafter the process of imperial expansion was gradually transformed into one of withdrawal. This change, at first imperceptible and then gradual, became, during the 1950s and 1960s, an unscrambling of colonies which was even more rapid than the original 'scramble' itself.

This 'decolonization' can be explained in two ways. On the one hand, strong opposition developed within the colonies against the rule of the metropolitan power while, on the other, the power's resistance was lessened by a revised attitude to imperialism which eventually made pulling out seem inevitable. The time-scale of this change was compressed by war; the impact of the Second World War on Europe's Asiatic colonies was quite as devastating as had been the Napoleonic Wars on Spanish and Portuguese America at the beginning of the nineteenth century.

*

The reaction against the imperial powers was threefold: indigenous nationalism in Asia and Africa, worldwide anti-colonialism which was given a forum in international institutions like the United Nations, and, finally, the pressure for decolonization applied peripherally by the two superpowers – the United States and the Soviet Union.

The spread of imperial rule in the late nineteenth century had, in

Decolonization

some areas, encountered considerable resistance; this, in itself, was evidence of the deep roots of indigenous nationalism. Nevertheless, this defiance had been too weak in the face of European persistence, mainly because it had been expressed within the traditional context of the tribal war or of the Islamic *jihad*. During the twentieth century, however, anti-colonial movements became much more effective. For one thing, they assimilated European concepts of liberty, equality and self-determination, often combining these with a Marxist attitude to class struggle, and grafting the result to historic pride and cultural rediscovery. Hence political parties campaigned, in the best European tradition, for electoral reform and the control of colonial executives by more widely representative legislatures. At the same time, trade unions and other pressure groups sought to eliminate the economic and social manifestations of racialism. These new tactics were made possible by a social transformation; two colonial legacies which helped destroy colonialism were an educated indigenous élite conscious of its liberating role, and an ever-increasing mass following in the form of a more heavily concentrated urban proletariat.

The impact of the First World War on nationalism was widespread but uneven. It was, perhaps, most profound in the Arab areas of the Middle East. Egypt had a restive middle class, stirred by wartime inflation and ready to back Zaghlul's demands for extensive reforms and for self-government. Milner considered the situation so serious that autonomy was granted in 1922. Pressure also built up in the other Arab states, which had been liberated from Ottoman rule during the First World War only to be mandated to Britain and France. Imperial rule in the Asian sub-continent was also more precarious; the Amritsar Massacre of 1919 showed the depth of Indian opposition and discredited the imperial authorities, even while causing Gandhi to postpone his campaigns of civil disobedience. The British government eventually replied, in 1935, by introducing the Government of India Act which extended the powers of the provincial rulers. It was also generally accepted the sub-continent could, within the foreseeable future, be given dominion status along the lines of Canada and Australia.

Yet, with the major exception of Egypt, no European colonies were carried to full independence on the crest of the First World War. The draft, forced-labour and economic disruption had sharpened indigenous resentment but imperial rule remained, for the moment,

341

intact. The real collapse came with the Second World War. The Japanese conquered most of South-East Asia and Indonesia, and proceeded systematically to dismantle French and Dutch rule. European vulnerability was further demonstrated by the fall of British Malaya, Singapore and Hong Kong. The Japanese occupation of these areas stirred nationalism in two ways. The first was intentional; an intensive anti-European propaganda campaign was combined with the promotion of local officials to replace the newly interned French and Dutch administrators. The second, however, was an unintended by-product of ruthless subjugation: the emergence of patriotic leaders like Ho Chi Minh who were determined, through the use of guerrilla tactics, to eject all forms of foreign dominance, whether European or Asiatic. When, therefore, the French and Dutch attempted to return to South-East Asia in the baggage van of the American armies, they encountered stiff resistance from the Viet Minh and the Indonesian movement led by Sukarno and Mohammed Hatta. The result was the proclamation of the Indonesian Republic and, following the French defeat at Dien Bien Phu in 1954, complete French withdrawal from Vietnam. Meanwhile, in 1947, India had received the independence promised to her during the war; Attlee and Cripps, at least, were realistic enough to see that the clock could not be turned back to the era before the Japanese offensive.

The Second World War also affected the development of nationalism in Africa, although less directly and over a longer period. Extensive economic changes stimulated the growth of trade unionism, particularly in British West Africa. This, in turn, brought organization and militancy to the expression of both political and economic grievances. Nigeria, for example, experienced a general strike in 1945, and the Gold Coast one in 1950. Meanwhile, African nationalism was learning much from the example of liberation movements in South-East Asia and Indonesia. In this respect, as the *Listener* observed in 1954, there was now behind each colonial movement 'the heave of the great shoulder of Asia'.[1] Gradually, the leaders of Tropical Africa – Nkrumah, Azikiwe, Nyerere, Banda, Sekou Touré and Awolowo – manoeuvred themselves into the position which had been reached by Gandhi and Nehru in the previous decade. They hastened the departure of colonial powers who had lost the will to rule but who, nevertheless, considered their presence necessary for the time being. The breakthrough came with

Decolonization

the independence of Ghana in 1957, and a veritable host of French and British colonies followed in 1960 and 1961.

There is no doubt that the mobilizing of international opinion played a considerable part in pushing back colonial rule. The United Nations Organization persistently applied pressure on imperial powers and evolved a new understanding of human rights and freedoms. Its role, both political and ideological, became more militant in direct proportion to the number of new Nation States joining the Afro-Asian *bloc*. In 1960, the United Nations issued its *Declaration on the Granting of Independence to Colonial Countries and Peoples*. This was uncompromising in its message to the colonial powers: 'The subjection of peoples to alien subjugation, domination and exploitation constitutes a denial of fundamental human rights, is contrary to the Charter of the United Nations, and is an impediment to the promotion of world peace and co-operation.'[2] A UN Resolution in 1965 went even further; by this time, colonial rule had become 'a crime against humanity'.[3] Similar expressions of hostility to European control had already been expressed by Asian leaders at the Bandung Conference in 1955, and by the Organization of African Unity after 1963. A contrast indeed to Lord Curzon's celebrated statement in 1907 that Empire was 'the means of service to mankind'![4] Confronted by such profound hostility in the General Assembly and discovering a new meaning of the 'white man's burden', smaller colonial powers like Belgium followed Britain and France in dumping the possessions which had once given them a pretension to greatness. The single exception was Portugal who became the focal point of the wrath of the Afro-Asian *bloc* until domestic revolution forced her to decolonize in 1975.

Finally, powerful pressure was also applied by the two leading world powers, the United States and the Soviet Union. The former came into being as a result of the revolution of 1775 and incorporated into its constitution the world's first explicitly anti-colonial ideology. American influence has been exerted in two ways. First, official presidential policy has been to put pressure on European states to weaken and cut their imperial connections. In 1918, for example, President Wilson tried, unsuccessfully, to persuade his fellow victors to extend the principle of national self-determination to Africa and Asia as well as to Europe. In 1940, Roosevelt and Churchill differed over their interpretation of the Third Principle of the Atlantic Charter – the 'right of all peoples to choose the form of government under which they will live'. Roosevelt was looking far beyond the problem of Eastern Europe to the emancipation of British India and the sub-Saharan colonies. Since 1950, a second influence has been exerted by the United States, this time by the American Negro, and the main beneficiary has been West Africa. While the American Negro sought his racial and cultural roots, his African counterpart gained an insight into the organization and methods of civil rights campaigns. Meanwhile, ever since the 1920s, the Soviet Union had kept up a sustained and virulent attack on colonialism, equating it with political and economic exploitation on a massive scale, and offering an ideological pattern of liberation based on class struggle and revolution. There have been moments of co-operation between the superpowers over colonial issues, but these have not prevented them from competing with each other for influence over newly emergent nations and, in the process, accusing each other of 'neo-colonialism'.

*

Imperialism had been immensely popular in the late nineteenth century. Nevertheless, there had from the outset been forces attempting to pull it back. Marx predictably attacked the British initiative in India. 'The aristocracy wanted to conquer it, the moneyocracy to plunder it and the millocracy to undersell it.' Criticism also came from radicals within the Liberal Party, especially Labouchère, Morley and Scott. J. A. Hobson assembled, in 1902, the most complete, organized and logical denunciation of imperialism to date, while Lenin subsequently incorporated some of Hobson's arguments into his own tract *Imperialism: the Highest Stage of Capitalism*. Meanwhile, the British Labour movement had committed itself *en bloc* to Lansbury's 1896 resolution demanding the 'right of all nations to complete sovereignty'.[5] Similarly, the French Socialists and the German Social Democrats attacked government policy over Africa and the Far East. After the First World War opposition to imperialism became at once more specialized and more international. In 1929, for example, the League against Imperialism was established as a result of a conference held in Brussels. By 1939, most of the European Left had come to the conclusion that the continued possession of colonies would perpetuate two major evils. First, colonial administrations were, with varying degrees of justification, open to the charge of

racialism and economic exploitation. Second, the d
domestic resources into colonial investment was delay
reform at home and, with it, the emergence of the welfare

The conversion of the Right to decolonization came ve
later. During the Second World War Churchill affirmed: 'I
become the King's First Minister in order to preside o
liquidation of the British Empire.'[6] Yet, within ten years
Conservative Oliver Lyttelton was able to say: 'Certain broa
of policy are accepted by all sections of the House as being
party politics... First of all we aim at helping the colonial terri
to attain self-government.'[7] By the late 1950s a Conservative p
minister, Harold Macmillan, was referring to 'winds of cha
sweeping through Africa, while the colonial secretary, Iain Macle
spoke of 'a deliberate speeding up of the movement towards in
pendence' in the belief that 'any other policy would have led
terrible bloodshed in Africa'.[8] Two factors had made possible th
consensus across the whole political spectrum. Labour's election
victory in 1945 started a train of events within the Empire that even
the Churchillian wing of the Conservative Party could not reverse
after Labour's defeat in 1951. Besides, British withdrawal was made
to seem less catastrophic because of the framework of dominion
status into which the older colonies had already fitted; this had been
confirmed by the Statute of Westminster (1931) as a permanent and
regular constitutional device for delegating the powers of the British
Crown. Hence decolonization could be made acceptable to the
mother country on the grounds that the old Empire was, in effect,
being replaced by a new Commonwealth. The French government
was less fortunate in its experience. Although it tried to modify its
rigid pre-war policy of assimilation, it ran into trouble over its
scheme for a French Union; eventually its plans for decolonization
took on the appearance of a retreat from the South-East Asia
disaster of 1954. A significant change of heart followed Dien Bie
Phu as the new prime minister, Pierre Mendès-France, told
shocked nation that France would have to give up parts of Nor
Africa, a commitment honoured by de Gaulle after the formati
of the Fifth Republic.

Meanwhile, imperialism was being criticized by a new generat
of economists who challenged the whole concept of interlin
commercial and financial benefits which Joseph Chamberlain
once attributed to imperialism. After 1945, empires were

(a) The decolonization of Asia (with dates of independence)

Decolonization

increasingly as a strain on the expenditure of the mother country. After all, West Germany, free of all colonial obligations, was experiencing an economic boom long before it affected the rest of Western Europe. When the other states shed their empires their economies in many cases actually picked up. Fears that the Dutch loss of the East Indies would ruin the Dutch economy proved completely unfounded as firms which had previously operated in Indonesia now redirected their capital and their management skills to the home market, contributing greatly to the Netherlands boom of the mid-1950s.[9] The upheaval caused in Europe by the Second World War also had a tremendous impact on the whole area of policy and was bound to lead to a re-examination of basic priorities. The destruction of Nazi Germany and the Fascist régime in Italy had removed the edge from European nationalism; this meant that it was possible to plan schemes for Western economic integration and political co-operation and, at the same time, made Europe more

346

Decolonization

(b) The decolonization of Africa (with dates of independence)

Decolonization

introspective and less expansionist. This co-operation was also based on the need for organized defence against the other legacy of the war – an enormously strengthened Soviet war machine. Simultaneous commitments to the EEC, EFTA or NATO necessitated a complete re-examination of the whole meaning of overseas commitments. Naturally, there would have to be a permanent flow of raw materials, including oil, from the Third World to the industrial countries. But, whereas supplies had previously been guaranteed by political domination, it now seemed to make more sense to rely on the self-interest of liberated peoples. Was it not better to promote stable autonomy, rather than to try to maintain unstable dependence?

Post-war Europe, in brief, was in desperate need of reconstruction; but any real recovery would have to be based on an acceptance that she had shrunk in terms of power and influence.

Notes

CHAPTER 1

1 A. DE TOCQUEVILLE: *The Ancien Régime.*
2 J. C. DAVIES: 'Toward a Theory of Revolution', in J. C. DAVIES (ed.), *When Men Revolt and Why.*
3 J. LOUGH: *An Introduction to Eighteenth Century France*, Ch. III.
4 E. N. WILLIAMS: *The Ancien Régime in Europe*, Ch. 8.
5 P. GOUBERT: *The Ancien Régime*, Ch. I, Part 2.
6 K. KUMAR: *Revolution*, Introduction, Part 6.

CHAPTER 2

1 R. R. PALMER: *The World of the French Revolution*, Ch. 2.
2 J. M. ROBERTS: *The French Revolution*, Ch. 2.
3 P. H. BEIK (ed.): *The French Revolution: Selected Documents*, Document 24.
4 D. I. WRIGHT (ed.): *The French Revolution: Introductory Documents*, Document 17.
5 Ibid., Document 18.
6 Ibid., Ch. 5.
7 T. A. DI PADOVA: 'The Girondins and the Question of Revolutionary Government', in *French Historical Studies* (1975–6).
8 A. COBBAN: 'The Political Ideas of Robespierre during the Period of the Convention', in *English Historical Review* (1946).
9 J. J. ROUSSEAU: *The Social Contract*, Book I, Ch. VII.
10 D. I. WRIGHT: *Revolution and Terror in France 1789–1795*, Ch. 6.
11 See C. BRINTON: *A Decade of Revolution, 1789–1799* for a survey of the controversy.
12 G. LEFEBVRE: *Remarks on Robespierre*, trans. in B. HYSLOP: *French Historical Studies* (1958).
13 Quoted in D. I. WRIGHT: op. cit.

Notes

14 C. CHURCH: 'In Search of the Directory', in J. F. BOSHER (ed.): *French Government and Society, 1500–1850: Essays in memory of A. Cobban.*

15 M. LYONS: '9 Thermidor: Motives and effects', in *European Studies Review* (1975). Also, *France Under the Directory*, 1975.

16 L. HUNT, D. LANSKY and P. HANSON: 'The failure of the Liberal Republic', in *Journal of Modern History* (1979).

CHAPTER 3

1 R. B. HOLTMAN: *The Napoleonic Revolution*, Ch. X.
2 H. A. L. FISHER: *Bonapartism*, Ch. I.
3 F. MARKHAM: *Napoleon*, Ch. 17.
4 G. BRUUN: *Europe and the French Imperium, 1799–1814*, Ch. 4.
5 R. B. HOLTMAN: op. cit., Ch. VI.
6 Ibid., Ch. V.
7 A. SOBOUL: *The French Revolution 1787–1799*, trans. by A. FORREST and C. JONES: Conclusion.
8 R. B. HOLTMAN: op. cit., Ch. IV.
9 J. GODECHOT, B. HYSLOP and D. DOWD: *The Napoleonic Era in Europe*, Ch. 2.
10 *New Cambridge Modern History*, Vol. IX, Chapter XI: 'The Napoleonic Adventure'.
11 M. LATEY: *Tyranny. A Study in the Abuse of Power*, Ch. 7.

CHAPTER 4

1 F. MARKHAM: *Napoleon*, Ch. 9.
2 G. BRUUN: *Europe and the French Imperium*, 1799–1814, Ch. IX.
3 F. MARKHAM: op. cit., Ch. 14.
4 R. BEN JONES: *Napoleon; Man and Myth*, Part V.
5 J. M. THOMPSON: *Napoleon Bonaparte: His Rise and Fall*, Ch. XII.
6 Ibid., Ch. XI.
7 J. GODECHOT, B. HYSLOP and D. DOWD: *The Napoleonic Era in Europe*, Ch. 6.
8 J. H. ROSE: *The Life of Napoleon I*, Ch. XXX.
9 E. TARLÉ: *Napoleon's Invasion of Russia, 1812*, Ch. 1.
10 F. MARKHAM: op. cit., Ch. 7.
11 J. M. THOMPSON: op. cit., Ch. XIV.
12 E. TARLÉ: op. cit., Ch. 1.
13 J. M. THOMPSON: op. cit., Ch. IX.
14 G. LEFEBVRE: *Napoleon*, Ch. IX.
15 J. GODECHOT: op. cit., Ch. IX.
16 A. BRIGGS: *The Age of Improvement*, Ch. 3.
17 J. F. C. FULLER: *The Conduct of War 1789–1961*, Ch. III.
18 L. W. COWIE: *Hanoverian England 1714–1837*, Ch. XX.
19 J. H. ROSE: op. cit., Ch. XXIX.
20 *New Cambridge Modern History*, Vol. IX, Ch. III.
21 J. H. ROSE: op. cit., Ch. XXXII.
22 Ibid., Ch. XXII.

23 E. TARLÉ: op. cit., Ch. 6.
24 J. ROPP: *War in the Modern World*, Ch. 4.
25 J. H. ROSE: op. cit., Ch. XXI.
26 E. TARLÉ: op. cit., Ch. 2.

CHAPTER 5

1 W. A. PHILIPS: *The Confederation of Europe*, Ch. III.
2 J. DROZ: *Europe between Revolutions 1815–1848*, Ch. I.
3 M. S. ANDERSON: *The Ascendancy of Europe 1815–1914*, Ch. 1.
4 C. W. CRAWLEY: 'International Relations 1815–1830', in *New Cambridge Modern History*, Vol. IX.
5 W. A. PHILIPS: op. cit., Ch. V.
6 Ibid., Castlereagh's Memorandum.
7 E. L. WOODWARD: *The Age of Reform 1815–1870*; Book II, Ch. I.
8 W. A. PHILIPS: op. cit., Ch. VI.
9 A. MILNE: *Metternich*, Ch. III.
10 A. PALMER: *Metternich*, Ch. 10.
11 E. L. WOODWARD: op. cit., Book II, Ch. II.
12 G. VERNADSKY: *A History of Russia*, Ch. 9.

CHAPTER 6

1 H. F. SCHWARZ (ed.): *Problems in European Civilisation: Metternich, the 'Coachman of Europe'*, from extract by A. SOREL.
2 J. DROZ: *Europe between Revolutions 1815–1848*, Ch. I.
3 H. F. SCHWARZ: op. cit., from extract by H. KISSINGER.
4 E. L. WOODWARD: *Studies in European Conservatism*, Part I: Metternich.
5 A. MILNE: *Metternich*, Part I.
6 Ibid., Part IV.
7 A. PALMER: *Metternich*, Ch. 18.
8 C. A. MACARTNEY: *The Habsburg Empire 1790–1918*, Ch. 6.
9 A. PALMER: op. cit., Ch. 17.
10 Ibid., Ch. 15.
11 E. BURKE: *Reflections on the Revolution in France* (1790).

CHAPTER 7

1 P. N. STEARNS: *The Revolutions of 1848*, p. 50.
2 G. A. KERTESZ (ed.): *Documents in the Political History of the European Continent 1815–1939*, Document 44a.
3 D. WARD: *1848: The Fall of Metternich and the Year of Revolution*, Ch. IX.
4 M. KRANZBERG (ed.): *1848 – A Turning Point?*, extract by L. B. NAMIER.
5 E. EYCK (ed.): *The Revolutions of 1848–9*, Document II.6.A.
6 G. A. KERTESZ: op. cit., Document 88b.
7 Ibid., Document 84 (Mazzini's Instructions for Members of Young Italy, 1831).

Notes

8   E. J. HOBSBAWM: *The Age of Capital 1848–1875*, Ch. 1.
9   P. N. STEARNS: op. cit., p. 163.
10 F. FEJTÖ (ed.): *The Opening of an Era: 1848 – An Historical Symposium*, Conclusion.
11 P. N. STEARNS: op. cit., p. 91.
12 J. P. T. BURY: *France 1814–1940*, Ch. VI.
13 A. PALMER: *The Lands Between*, Ch. 3.
14 D. WARD: op. cit., Ch. XIII.
15 E. K. BRAMSTED: *Germany*, Ch. 6.

CHAPTER 8

1 See A. J. P. TAYLOR: *The Struggle for Mastery in Europe 1848–1918*, Ch. IV.
2 R. C. BINKLEY: *Realism and Nationalism 1851–1871*, Ch. 8.
3 J. A. S. GRENVILLE: *Europe Reshaped 1848–1878*, Ch. XI.

CHAPTER 9

1 D. MACK SMITH (ed.): *Great Lives Observed; Garibaldi*, Part 3.
2 A. J. GRANT and H. TEMPERLEY: *Europe in the Nineteenth and Twentieth Centuries*, Ch. XVI.
3 *New Cambridge Modern History*, Vol. X, Ch. XXI.
4 D. BEALES: *The Risorgimento and the Unification of Italy*, Document 8.
5 D. MACK SMITH (ed.): *Italy*, Ch. 4.
6 G. M. TREVELYAN: *Garibaldi and the Thousand*.
7 D. MACK SMITH (ed.): *The Making of Italy 1760–1870*, Part 18.
8 D. MACK SMITH (ed.): *Great Lives Observed; Garibaldi*, Part 14.
9 Ibid., Part 1.
10 D. MACK SMITH (ed.): *The Making of Italy 1760–1870*, Part 9.
11 Ibid., 'Cavour to Comtesse de Circourt', 29 December 1860.
12 D. MACK SMITH (ed.): *Victor Emmanuel, Cavour, and the Risorgimento*, Ch. 10.
13 J. RIDLEY: *Garibaldi*, Ch. 27.
14 D. MACK SMITH (ed.): *The Making of Italy 1760–1870*, Part 12.
15 J. RIDLEY: op. cit., Ch. 30.
16 D. MACK SMITH (ed.): *Great Lives Observed; Garibaldi*, Part 11.
17 A. J. P. TAYLOR: *The Struggle for Mastery in Europe 1848–1918*, Ch. VI.
18 D. MACK SMITH (ed.): *Great Lives Observed; Garibaldi*, Part 4.

CHAPTER 10

1 H. BÖHME (ed.): *The Foundations of the German Empire. Select Documents*, trans. by A. RAMM, Document 69.
2 J. M. KEYNES: *The Economic Consequences of the Peace* (1919), p. 75.
3 A term used by W. CONZE: *The Shaping of the German Nation. A Historical Analysis*, Ch. IV.
4 E. K. BRAMSTED: *Germany*, Ch. 5.
5 W. CARR: *Germany 1815–1945*, Ch. 3.
6 F. B. M. HOLLYDAY (ed.): *Bismarck*, Part 1.

7   W. CARR: op. cit., Ch. 4.
8   A. J. P. TAYLOR: *Bismarck: The Man and the Statesman*, Ch. IV.
9   O. PFLANZE: *'Bismarck's Realpolitik'*, in J. SHEEHAN (ed.): *Imperial Germany*.
10 H. BÖHME (ed.): op. cit., Document 147.
11 Ibid., Document 151.
12 A. J. P. TAYLOR: op. cit., Ch. IV.

CHAPTER 11

1   D. FIELD: *The End of Serfdom. Nobility and Bureaucracy in Russia 1855–1861*.
2   A. J. RIEBER: Alexander II: A Revisionist View', in *Journal of Modern History* (1971).
3   B. H. SUMNER: *Survey of Russian History*, Ch. III.
4   M. T. FLORINSKY: *Russia: A History and an Interpretation*, Vol. II, Ch. XXXIII.
5   W. E. MOSSE: *Alexander II and the Modernization of Russia*, Ch. 5.
6   G. VERNADSKY: *A History of Russia*, Ch. 10.
7   M. S. ANDERSON: *The Ascendancy of Europe 1815–1914*, Ch. 2.
8   H. SETON-WATSON: *The Decline of Imperial Russia 1855–1914*, Ch. II.
9   H. SETON-WATSON: *The Russian Empire 1801–1917*, Ch. XI.

CHAPTER 12

1   M. HOWARD: *The Franco-Prussian War*, Ch. II.
2   T. ZELDIN: *Emile Ollivier and the Liberal Empire of Napoleon III*, Ch. 12.
3   T. ARONSON: *The Fall of the Third Napoleon*, Ch. 4.
4   M. HOWARD: op. cit., Ch. I.
5   N. RICH: *The Age of Nationalism and Reform*, Ch. 2.
6   W. H. C. SMITH: *Napoleon III*, Ch. 12.
7   A. HORNE: *The Fall of Paris*, Ch. 2.
8   W. H. C. SMITH: op. cit., Ch. 13.
9   Ibid., Ch. 7.
10 J. A. S. GRENVILLE: *Europe Reshaped 1848–1878*, Ch. VI.
11 G. P. GOOCH: *The Second Empire*, Ch. I.
12 T. ZELDIN: *France 1848–1945*, Vol. I, Ch. 4.
13 T. ZELDIN: *Emile Ollivier*, Ch. 5.
14 Ibid., Ch. 6.
15 T. ARONSON: op. cit., Ch. 2.

CHAPTER 13

1   G. A. CRAIG: *Germany 1866–1945*, Ch. V.
2   E. EYCK: *Bismarck and the German Empire*, Ch. IV. 3.
3   W. M. SIMON: *Germany in the Age of Bismarck*, Document 38.
4   Ibid., Document 39.
5   T. S. HAMEROW (ed.): *Problems in European Civilisation. Otto von Bismarck: A Historical Assessment*, extract by J. ZIEKURSCH.

Notes

6 W. CARR: *A History of Germany 1815–1945*, Ch. 5. (The words are those of K. LIEBKNECHT.)

CHAPTER 14

1 A. COBBAN: *A History of Modern France*, Vol. 3, Ch. 1.
2 D. W. BROGAN: *The Development of Modern France 1870–1939*; Book II, Ch. II.
3 M. CURTIS: *Three Against the Third Republic*, Ch. II.
4 W. SHIRER: *Fall of the Third Republic*, Ch. 6.

CHAPTER 15

1 I. GEISS: *German Foreign Policy 1871–1914*; Ch. 1.
2 W. N. MEDLICOTT and D. K. COVENEY (eds): *Bismarck and Europe*, Introduction.
3 A. J. P. TAYLOR: *Bismarck: The Man and the Statesman*.
4 F. B. M. HOLLYDAY (ed.): *Bismarck*; Document: Secret Dispatch from Bismarck to Count von Hatzfeldt, 8 August 1887.
5 H. HOLBORN: *A History of Modern Germany 1840–1945*, Ch. 6.
6 O. PFLANZE: 'Bismarck's Realpolitik', in J. J. SHEEHAN (ed.): *Imperial Germany*.
7 E. EYCK: *Bismarck and the German Empire*, Ch. IV.
8 K. S. PINSON: *Modern Germany*, Ch. XII.
9 G. A. CRAIG: *Germany 1866–1945*, Ch. VII.
10 V. R. BERGHAHN: *Germany and the Approach of War in 1914*, Ch. 2.
11 H. HOLBORN: op. cit., Ch. 7.

CHAPTER 16

1 Report presented to the Preliminary Peace Conference 1919, in D. E. LEE (ed.): *The Outbreak of the First World War*.
2 See I. GEISS: 'The outbreak of the first world war and German war aims', in *Journal of Contemporary History* (1966) I.3.
3 See J. RÖHL (ed.): *1914: Delusion or Design?* (1973).
4 See H. E. BARNES: *The Genesis of the World War* (1926).
5 See S. B. FAY: *Origins of the World War* (1930).
6 See G. P. GOOCH: *Before the War, II. The Coming of the War (1938)*.
7 See A. J. P. TAYLOR: *The Struggle for Mastery in Europe* (1954).
8 See B. E. SCHMITT: *The Origins of the First World War*, Historical Association Pamphlet (1958).
9 See F. FISCHER: *Germany's Aims in the First World War* (1967).
10 For an appraisal of Ritter's views see K. EPSTEIN: 'Gerhard Ritter and the First World War', in *Journal of Contemporary History*, 1966; I.3.
11 See L. C. F. TURNER: *Origins of the First World War* (1970).
12 See I. GEISS: op. cit. Also *German Foreign Policy 1871–1914* (1976).
13 See J. RÖHL: op. cit. Also *From Bismarck to Hitler* (1970).
14 See V. R. BERGHAHN: *Germany and the Approach of War in 1914* (1973).
15 G. A. CRAIG: *Germany 1866–1945*, Ch. IX.

Aspects of European History 1789–1980

16   L. C. F. TURNER: op. cit., Ch. 4.
17   J. RÖHL: op. cit., quotation by RIEZLER.
18   V. R. BERGHAHN: op. cit., Ch. 19.
19   W. CARR: *A History of Germany 1815–1945*, Ch. 8.
20   G. A. CRAIG: op. cit., Ch. IV.
21   J. RÖHL: op. cit.
22   L. C. F. TURNER: op. cit., Ch. 6.
23   I. V. BESTUZHEV: 'Russian foreign policy February–June 1914', in *Journal of Contemporary History* (1966), I.3.
24   L. C. F. TURNER: op. cit., Ch. 2.
25   For a full examination of Grey's policy in 1914 see L. C. B. SEAMAN: *From Vienna to Versailles*, Ch. XIV.
26   V. R. BERGHAHN: op. cit., Ch. 6.

CHAPTER 17

1   I. J. LEDERER (ed.): *The Versailles Settlement*, extract by T. MASARYK.
2   E. EYCH: *A History of the Weimar Republic*, Vol. I, Ch. IV.
3   A. J. P. TAYLOR: *The Habsburg Monarchy*, Epilogue.
4   S. MARKS: *The Illusion of Peace*, Ch. 1.

CHAPTER 18

1   B. DMYTRYSHYN (ed.): *Imperial Russia. A Source Book 1700–1917*, Document 42.
2   A. E. ADAMS: 'Pobedonostsev and the Rule of Firmness', in the *Slavonic and East European Review*, XXXII.
3   T. RIHA: 'Constitutional Development in Russia', in T. G. STAVROU (ed.): *Russia under the Last Tsar*.
4   J. WALKIN: *The Rise of Democracy in Pre-Revolutionary Russia*, Ch. 7.
5   H. SETON-WATSON: *The Russian Empire 1801–1917*, Ch. XVII.
6   A. MENDEL: 'On Interpreting the Fate of Imperial Russia', in T. G. STAVROU: op. cit.
7   M. T. FLORINSKY: *The End of the Russian Empire*, Ch. 9.

CHAPTER 9

1   L. TROTSKY: *The History of the Russian Revolution*, trans. by M. EASTMAN, Vol. I.
2   A. KERENSKY: 'The Policy of the Provisional Government of 1917', in *The Slavonic and East European Review* (1932).
3   N. BERDYAEV: *The Origin of Russian Communism*.
4   Quoted in E. H. CARR: *The Bolshevik Revolution*, Vol. 1, Ch. 4.
5   V. I. LENIN: *What is to be Done?*
6   L. TROTSKY: op. cit., Vol. III.
7   A. E. ADAMS (ed.): *The Russian Revolution and Bolshevik Victory*, extract by M. FAINSOD.

Notes

8 See D. SCHUB: *Lenin* (1948). B. WOLFE: *Three who made a Revolution* (1948). L. FISCHER: *The Life of Lenin* (1964). A. ULAM: *The Bolsheviks* (1965).

9 S. N. SILVERMAN (ed.): *Lenin*, Ch. 3.

10 Ibid., Ch. 2.

11 J. SWETTENHAM: *Allied Intervention in Russia 1918–1919*, Ch. V.

12 S. N. SILVERMAN: op. cit., Ch. 2.

13 C. H. LEGGETT: 'Lenin, Terror, and the Political Police', in *Survey*, (1975).

14 V. I. LENIN: 'The Proletarian Revolution and the Renegade Kautsky', in S. SILVERMAN: op. cit.

15 E. H. CARR: op. cit., Ch. 7.

16 K. KUMAR: *Revolution*, 5.16.

CHAPTER 20

1 See H. NICOLSON: *Peacemaking 1919* (New York, 1939).

2 See J. M. KEYNES: 'Economic Consequences of the Peace (1919) and the Peace of Versailles', in *Everybody's Magazine* XLIII (September 1920).

3 See W. H. DAWSON: *Germany under the Treaty* (London, 1933).

4 See H. VOGT: *The Burden of Guilt: A Short History of Germany 1914–1945*, trans. by H STRAUSS (1964).

5 W. H. DAWSON: op. cit., Ch. XIII.

6 H. NICOLSON: op. cit.

7 H. VOGT: op. cit., Ch. II.

8 J. M. KEYNES: 'The Peace of Versailles', op. cit.

9 A. TARDIEU: *The Truth About the Treaty* (1921).

10 E. MANTOUX: *The Carthaginian Peace or the Economic Consequences of Mr Keynes*, written during the Second World War and published posthumously (trans. 1952).

11 P. BIRDSALL: *Versailles Twenty Years After* (1941).

12 J. NÉRÉ: *The Foreign Policy of France from 1914 to 1945*, trans. (1975).

13 W. CARR: *A History of Germany 1815–1945* (1969).

14 A. J. NICHOLLS: *Weimar and the Rise of Hitler* (1968).

15 S. MARKS: *The Illusion of Peace* (1976).

16 G. SCHULZ: *Revolutions and Peace Treaties 1917–1920* (1967).

17 M. TRACHTENBERG: 'Reparation at the Paris Peace Conference', (in *Journal of Modern History* (1979). Also: *Reparation in World Politics* (1980).

18 W. A. McDOUGALL: 'Political Economy vs National Sovereignty: French Structures for German Economic Integration after Versailles', (in *Journal of Modern History* (1979).

CHAPTER 21

1 A. J. P. TAYLOR: *The Origins of the Second World War*, Ch. 3.

2 M. GALLO: *Mussolini's Italy*, Ch. 1.

3 SIR I. KIRKPATRICK: *Mussolini, Study of a Demagogue*, Ch. 4.

4   M. GALLO: op. cit., Ch. 2.

5   Ibid., Ch. 5.

6   Ibid., Ch. 3.

7   SIR I. KIRKPATRICK: op. cit., Ch. 6.

8   M. GALLO: op. cit., Ch. 7.

7   SIR I. KIRKPATRICK: op. cit., Ch. 5.

10 E. WEBER: *Varieties of Fascism*, Document 1C.

11 M. GALLO: op. cit., Ch. 9.

12 A. LYTTELTON: 'Italian Fascism', in W. LAQUEUR (ed.): *Fascism: A Reader's Guide.*

13 M. GALLO: op. cit., Ch. 10.

14 P. MELOGRANI: 'The Cult of the Duce in Mussolini's Italy', in G. L. MOSSE (ed.): *International Fascism: New Thoughts and New Approaches.*

15 C. LEEDS: *Italy under Mussolini*, Ch. 5.

16 M. GALLO: op. cit., Ch. 15.

CHAPTER 22

1   P. PEARSON:. *The Origins and Nature of the Great Slump 1929–1932*, Ch. 1.

CHAPTER 23

1   A. BULLOCK: *Hitler, a Study in Tyranny*, Ch. 2.

2   J. C. FEST: *Hitler,* Book 2, Ch. 4.

3   A. J. NICHOLLS: *Weimar and the Rise of Hitler*, Ch. 10.

4   A. BULLOCK: op. cit., Ch. 3.

5   J. P. STERN: *Hitler: The Führer and the People*, Ch. 12.

6   Election figures in this chapter, given as a percentage of the popular vote, are taken from E. B. WHEATON: *Prelude to Calamity*, Table, Parties in the Reichstag 1919–1932.

7   Election figures in this chapter, given as seats in the *Reichstag*, are taken from S. DELMER: *Weimar Germany*: Table in Ch. 9.

8   J. C. FEST: op. cit., Book 4, Ch. 3.

9   See R. KNAUERHASE: *An Introduction to National Socialism, 1920–1939*, Ch. 2.

10 K. SONTHEIMER: 'The Weimar Republic and the Prospects of German Democracy', in E. J. FEUCHTWANGER (ed.): *Upheaval and Continuity.*

11 H. BOLDT: 'Article 48 of the Weimar Constitution, its historical and political implications', in A. NICHOLLS and E. MATTHIAS: *German Democracy and the Triumph of Hitler – Essays in Recent German History.*

12 L. L. SNYDER: *The Weimar Republic*, Document 18: The Weimar Constitution.

13 J. C. FEST: op. cit., Book 4, Ch. 2.

14 J. REMAK (ed.): *The Nazi Years: A Documentary History*, Ch. 4.

15 Ibid., 'Law Concerning the Hitler Youth'.

16 J. C. FEST: op. cit., Book 5, Ch. 1.

17 See K. D. BRACHER: *The German Dictatorship.*

Notes

1   J. C. G. ROHL: *From Bismarck to Hitler,*|Ch. V, Document 1.
2   Ibid., Ch. V, Document 7.
3   Ibid., Ch. V, Document 6.
4   Quotations from *Hitler's Secret Book (Hitlers zweites Buch)*, written in 1928 but not published until 1961, prepared for publication by G. L. WEINBERG and H. ROTHFELS.
5   H. HOLBORN: *A History of Modern Germany*, Vol. 3, 1840–1945, Ch. 12.
6   G. A. CRAIG: *Germany 1866–1945*, Ch. XIX.
7   J. FEST: *Hitler*, Book 6, Ch. 3.
8   J. L. SNELL (ed.): *The Outbreak of the Second World War*, extract from the Nuremberg Judgement.
9   R. J. SONTAG: 'The Last Months of Peace, 1939', in *Foreign Affairs*, Vol. XXXV (1957).
10 Quotations from A. J. P. TAYLOR: *The Origins of the Second World War*.
11 H. TREVOR-ROPER: 'A. J. P. Taylor, Hitler and the War', in *Encounter*, Vol. XVII (1961).
12 J. FEST: op. cit., 'Interpolation Three'.

CHAPTER 25

1   G. F. KENNAN: *Soviet Foreign Policy 1917–41*, Document 2.
2   A. FONTAINE: *A History of the Cold War from the October Revolution to the Korean War 1917–1950*, trans. by D. D. PAIGE, Ch. 1.
3   G. F. KENNAN: op. cit., Document 1.
4   X. J. EUDIN and H. H. FISHER: *Soviet Russia and the West 1920–1927*, speech by L. B. KAMENEV, 15 March 1921.
5   I. DEUTSCHER: *Stalin: a Political Biography*; Ch. 10.
6   J. DEGRAS (ed.): *Soviet Documents on Foreign Policy Vol. I*; pp. 298–301. Chicherin's opening speech at the Genoa Conference, 10 April 1922.
7   G. F. KENNAN: op. cit., Document 25.
8   W. LAQUEUR: *Russia and Germany: A Century of Conflict*, Ch. 11.
9   *A Short History of the Communist Party of the Soviet Union*, prepared by a panel of Soviet historians, p. 247.
10 See W. LAQUERE: op. cit., Ch. 12.
11 T. H. RIGBY (ed.): *Stalin, Great Lives Observed* series.
12 A. FONTAINE: op. cit., Ch. 7.

1   J. A. S. GRENVILLE (ed.): *The Major International Treaties 1914–1973*, p. 108.
2   P. RAFFO: 'The League of Nations', *Historical Association Pamphlet* (1974).
3   J. A. S. GRENVILLE (ed.): op. cit., pp. 60–1.
4   S. MARKS: *The Illusion of Peace*, Ch. 1.
5   R. HENIG (ed.): *The League of Nations*, II. 3A.
6   C. M. KIMMICH: *Germany and the League of Nations*, Ch. 1.

7   Ibid., Ch. 10.
8   I. DEUTSCHER: *Stalin: A Political Biography*, Ch. 11.

CHAPTER 27

1   E. H. CARR: *International Relations between the Two World Wars*, Ch. 13.
2   G. JACKSON (ed.): *Problems in European Civilisation: The Spanish Civil War*, extract by F. J. TAYLOR.
3   D. A. PUZZO: *The Spanish Civil War*, Ch. 2.
4   W. L. SHIRER: *The Rise and Fall of the Third Reich*, Ch. 9.
5   D. A. PUZZO: op. cit., Document 20 (Azaña's speech of 18 July 1937).

CHAPTER 28

1   A. ADAMTHWAITE: *France and the Coming of the Second World War*, Ch. 1.
2   M. SCHLESINGER: 'The Development of the Radical Party in the Third Republic: The New Radical Movement 1926–32', in *Journal of Modern History* (1974). The quotation is by MARCEL DÉAT, doctrinist within the Radical Party.
3   D. JOHNSON: 'Leon Blum and the Popular Front', in *History* (1970).
4   D. THOMSON: *Democracy in France since 1870*, Ch. III.
5   S. M. OSGOOD (ed.): *The Fall of France 1940*, extract by P. REYNAUD, trans. by editor.
6   W. SHIRER: *The Collapse of the Third Republic*, Ch. 12.
7   Trans. in D. THOMSON: op. cit., Ch. V.

CHAPTER 29

1   A. G. MAZOUR: *Soviet Economic Development: Operation Outstrip, 1921–1965*, Reading No. 8.
2   R. D. LAIRD and B. A. LAIRD: *Soviet Communism and the Agrarian Revolution*, Ch. 3.
3   A. G. MAZOUR: op. cit., Ch. 1.
4   A. ERLICH: *The Soviet Industrialisation Debate, 1924–1928*, Ch. I.
5   A. G. MAZOUR: op. cit., Ch. 2.
6   A. NOVE: *Stalinism and After*, Ch. I.
7   A. ERLICH: op. cit., Ch. I.
8   Ibid., Ch. II.
9   See M. LEWIN: 'The Immediate Background to Soviet Collectivization', in *Soviet Studies* (1965–6).
10   O. A. NARKIEWICZ: 'Stalin, War Communism and Collectivisation', in *Soviet Studies* (1966–7).
11   See L. PIETROMARCHI: *The Soviet World*, Ch. VII.
12   See R. AMMAN: 'Soviet Technological Performance', in *Survey* (1977–8).
13   W. KLATT: 'Fifty Years of Soviet Agriculture', in *Survey* (1967).
14   K. BUSH: 'Soviet Growth: Past, Present and Projected', in *Survey* (1977–8).

Notes

15 See J. BRADA and A. E. KING: 'The Soviet American Trade Agreements: Prospects for the Soviet Economy', in *Russian Review* (1973).
16 See A. WOLYNSKI: 'Western Economic Aid to the U.S.S.R.' in *Conflict Studies* No. 72, (June 1976); and V. SOBESLAVSKY: 'East-West détente and technology transfer', in *The World Today* (October 1980).

CHAPTER 30

1 K. HILDEBRAND: *The Foreign Policy of the Third Reich*, Ch. 5.
2 G. A. CRAIG: *Germany 1866–1945*, Ch. XX.
3 W. L. SHIRER: *The Rise and Fall of the Third Reich*, Ch. 19.
4 T. L. JARMAN: *The Rise and Fall of Nazi Germany*, Ch. XV.
5 P. E. SCHRAMM: *Hitler: The Man and the Military Leader*, Appendix II (Memorandum by General Jodl, 1946).
6 J. P. STERN: *Hitler: The Führer and the People*, Ch. 22.
7 W. L. SHIRER: op. cit., Ch. 19.
8 A. BULLOCK: *Hitler: A Study in Tyranny*, Ch. 12.
9 T. L. JARMAN: op. cit., Ch. XVII.
10 G. S. KRAVCHENKO: 'Stalin's War Machine', in *Purnell's History of the Second World War*, p. 1060.

CHAPTER 31

1 C. SETON-WATSON: 'The Cold War – its origins' in J. L. HENDERSON (ed.): *Since 1945 – Aspects of Contemporary World History*.
2 A. FONTAINE: *History of the Cold War from the October Revolution to the Korean War, 1917–1950* trans. by D. D. PAIGE, Ch. 1.
3 Ibid., Ch. 3.
4 Ibid., Ch. 5.
5 G. F. KENNAN: *Soviet Foreign Policy 1917–1941*, Document 29.
6 A. FONTAINE: op. cit., Ch. 8.
7 G. F. KENNAN: 'The Sources of Soviet Conduct', in *Foreign Affairs XXV* (July 1947).
8 D. S. MCLELLAN: *The Cold War in Transition*, Ch. 1.
9 N. V. SIVACHEV and N. N. YAKOVLEV: *Russia and the United States*, Ch. 5
10 *Keesings Contemporary Archives*: 9869A.
11 Ibid., 14249A.
12 Ibid., 19057A.
13 Ibid., 4739A.
14 Ibid., 7770A.
15 Ibid., 22993A.
16 Ibid., 15221A.
17 Ibid., 23025A.
18 Ibid., 8579A.
19 C. BOWN and P. MOONEY: *Cold War to Détente*, Ch. 18.

Aspects of European History 1789–1980

CHAPTER 32

1 A. SPINELLI: 'European Union and the Resistance', in *Government and Opposition* (1967).
2 D. DE ROUGEMENT: 'The Campaign of the European Congresses', in *Government and Opposition* (1967).
3 A. WATSON: *Europe at Risk*, Ch. 6.
4 G. LICHTHEIM: *Europe in the Twentieth Century*, Ch. 14.
5 F. VON KROSIG: 'A Reconsideration of Federalism in the Scope of the Present Discussion on European Integration', in *Journal of Common Market Studies* (1970).
6 M. A. WHEATON: 'The Labour Party and Europe 1950–71', in *Government and Opposition* (1971).
7 R. VAUGHAN: *Post-War Integration in Europe*, Document 15.
8 *Keesings Contemporary Archives*, 22246A.
9 F. VON KROSIG: op. cit.
10 D. JOHNSON: 'The Political Principles of General de Gaulle', in *International Affairs* (1965).
11 *Keesings Contemporary Archives*, 19015.
12 Ibid., 19197A.
13 See G. LICHTHEIM: op. cit.
14 U. KITZINGER: 'Britain's Crisis of Identity', in *JCMS*, Vol. 6.
15 S. HOLT: 'British Attitudes to Membership', in G. IONESCU (ed.): *The New Politics of European Integration*.

CHAPTER 33

1 See A. COBBAN: *The Nation State and National Self-Determination*, Ch. II.
2 E. H. CARR: *Nationalism and After*, Ch. I.
3 A. COBBAN: *Rousseau and the Modern State*, Ch. IV.
4 H. KOHN: *Nationalism*, Reading No. 9.
5 H. KOHN: *The Mind of Germany*, Ch. 4.
6 H. KOHN: *Nationalism*, Reading No. 4.
7 H. KOHN: *Prophets and Peoples. Studies in Nineteenth Century Nationalism*, Ch. 3.
8 H. KOHN: *The Mind of Germany*, Ch. 7.
9 H. KOHN: *Prophets and Peoples*, Ch. 2.
10 'Thus Spoke Zarathustra', First Part, in W. KAUFMANN (ed. and trans.): *The Portable Nietzsche*.
11 H. KOHN: *Nationalism*, Reading No. 3.
12 'President Wilson's Fourteen Points, 8 January 1918', in J. A. S. GRENVILLE (ed.): *The Major International Treaties 1914–1973*, p. 59.
13 H. KOHN: *Political Ideologies of the Twentieth Century*, Ch. XI.
14 See J. DULFFER: 'Bonapartism, Fascism and National Socialism', in *Journal of Contemporary History* (1976).
15 See Ch. 32.

Notes

16   A. HUGHES: 'The Nation State in Black Africa', in L. J. TIVEY (ed.): *The Nation State*.
17   A. D. SMITH: *Nationalism in the 20th Century*, p. 115.
18   K. R. MINOGUE: *Nationalism*, Conclusion.

CHAPTER 34

1   See also V. I. LENIN: *The Three Sources and Three Component Parts of Marxism* (1913).
2   F. ENGELS: *Anti-Dühring*, extract in C. WRIGHT MILLS: *The Marxists*.
3   V. I. LENIN: *Karl Marx* (written in 1914).
4   K. MARX and F. ENGELS: *Manifesto of the Communist Party* (1848), I.
5   Quoted by LIN PIAO: 'The International Significance of Comrade Mao Tse Tung's Theory of People's War, 1965', in F. SCHURMANN and O. SCHELL, (eds): *Communist China*, p. 343.
6   K. KAUTSKY: *The Social Revolution* (1902), extracts in C. WRIGHT MILLS: op. cit.
7   E. BERNSTEIN: *Evolutionary Socialism* (1911), extract in C. WRIGHT MILLS: op. cit.
8   V. I. LENIN:,*A Short Biography* (Moscow 1959), p. 34.
9   E. H. CARR: *The Bolshevik Revolution*, Vol. 1, Ch. 4.
10   V. I. LENIN: *A Short Biography*, p. 51.
11   L. TROTSKY: *The Permanent Revolution*, extract in C. WRIGHT MILLS: op. cit.
12   Some extracts from Stalin's 1950 writings on language, in T. H. RIGBY (ed.): *Stalin*.
13   J. V. STALIN: *Leninism*, extract in C. WRIGHT MILLS: op. cit.
14   J. V. STALIN: *The Tasks of Building Executives*, extract in T. H. RIGBY: op. cit.
15   N. KHRUSHCHEV: *Speech to the Twentieth Congress*, 25 February 1956, extract in C. WRIGHT MILLS: op. cit.
16   S. SCHRAM: *Mao Tse Tung*, Ch. 3.
17   *Quotations From Chairman Mao Tse Tung* (Peking 1966), p. 11.
18   Ibid., p. 18.
19   MAO TSE TUNG: *On Contradiction*, extract in F. SCHURMANN and O. SCHELL (eds): *Communist China*, Part 1.
20   S. SCHRAM: op. cit., p. 216.
21   MAO TSE TUNG: *On New Democracy* (1940), extract in V. SIMONE (ed.): *China in Revolution*, Part 4.
22   I. DEUTSCHER: *Russia, China, and the West 1953–1966*, Ch. 7.
23   C. P. FITZGERALD: *The Birth of Communist China*, Ch. 6.
24   LIN PIAO: op. cit.
25   *Quotations From Chairman Mao Tse Tung*, p. 68.
26   C. P. FITZGERALD: op. cit., Ch. 7.
27   'Eurocommunism. The long, long march away from Stalin', in *The Economist* (5 November 1977).
28   M. AZCÁRATE: 'What is Eurocommunism?', in G. R. URBAN (ed.): *Eurocommunism, its roots and future in Italy and elsewhere*.

29   J. ELLENSTEIN: 'The Skein of History Unrolled Backwards', in G. R. URBAN (ed.): op. cit.

CHAPTER 35

1   M. S. ANDERSON: *The Ascendancy of Europe 1815–1914*, Ch. 4.
2   J. A. HOBSON: *Imperialism; A Study.*
3   See M. E. TOWNSEND: 'Commercial and Colonial Policies of Imperial Germany', in G. H. NADEL and P. CURTIS (eds): *Imperialism and Colonialism.*
4   T. E. POWER: *Jules Ferry and the Renaissance of French Imperialism*; Ch. 8.
5   See W. L. LANGER: *The Diplomacy of Imperialism* and *European Alliances and Alignments 1871–1890*; also A. J. P. TAYLOR: *The Struggle for Mastery in Europe*, especially Ch. XIII.
6   D. K. FIELDHOUSE: 'Imperialism; an Historiographical Revision', *Economic History Review*, xiv.
7   D. THOMSON: *Europe Since Napoleon*, Ch. 20.
8   A. J. P. TAYLOR: op. cit., Ch. XIII.
9   W. L. LANGER: *European Alliances and Alignments*, Ch. IX.
10   H. BRUNSCHWIG: 'The Origins of the new French Empire', in G. H. NADEL and P. CURTIS (eds): op. cit.
11   J. JOLL: *Europe since 1870; An International History*, Ch. 4.
12   R. ROBINSON and J. GALLAGHER: *Africa and the Victorians*, Ch. XV.

CHAPTER 36

1   *The Listener* (10 December 1954).
2   K. J. TWITCHETT: 'The Colonial Powers and the United Nations', in *Journal of Contemporary History*, IV. 1. (1969).
3   R. EMERSON: 'Colonialism', in *Journal of Contemporary History*, IV. 1. (1969).
4   See Ch. 35.
5   F. BROCKWAY: *The Colonial Revolution*, Ch. 2.
6   C. E. CARRINGTON: *The Liquidation of the British Empire*, Ch. I.
7   Ibid., Ch. II.
8   D. AUSTIN: 'The Transfer of Power: Why and How', in W. H. MORRIS-JONES and D. AUSTIN: *Decolonisation and After.*
9   See H. BAUDET: 'The Netherlands After the Loss of Empire', in *Journal of Contemporary History*, IV. 1, (1969).

Bibliography

JOURNALS

English Historical Review
European Studies Review
The Historical Journal
History
History Today
Journal of Modern History
Past and Present
French Historical Studies
The Russian Review
Soviet Studies
Survey
Journal of Contemporary History
The World Today
World Politics
Foreign Affairs
International Affairs
Journal of International Affairs
The Economic History Review
Journal of Economic History
Journal of European Economic History
Journal of Common Market Studies

GENERAL

New Cambridge Modern History (Cambridge):
    VIII *The American and French Revolutions 1763–93* (1965)
    IX *War and Peace in an Age of Upheaval 1793–1830* (1965)
    X *The Zenith of European Power 1830–70* (1960)
    XI *Material Progress and World Wide Problems* (1962)

363

Aspects of European History 1789–1980

XII *The Shifting Balance of World Forces 1898–1945* (1968)
XIII *Companion Volume* (1979)
XIV *Atlas* (1970).

Problems in European Civilization (Lexington, Mass.):

R. W. GREENLAW (ed.): *The Economic Origins of the French Revolution*
D. H. PINKNEY (ed.): *Napoleon*
H. F. SCHWARTZ (ed.): *Metternich, the 'Coachman of Europe'*
M. KRANZBERG (ed.): *1848 – A Turning Point?*
S. M. OSGOOD (ed.): *Napoleon III*
T. S. HAMEROW (ed.): *Otto von Bismarck*
A. E. ADAMS (ed.): *Imperial Russia after 1861*
H. M. WRIGHT (ed.): *The 'New Imperialism'*
R. F. BETTS (ed.): *The 'Scramble for Africa'*
L. DERFLER (ed.): *The Dreyfus Affair*
D. E. LEE (ed.): *The Outbreak of the First World War*
A. E. ADAMS (ed.): *The Russian Revolution and Bolshevik Victory*
S. W. PAGE (ed.): *Lenin*
I. J. LEDERER (ed.): *The Versailles Settlement*
R. N. HUNT (ed.): *The Creation of the Weimar Republic*
R. V. DANIELS (ed.): *The Stalin Revolution*
G. JACKSON (ed.): *The Spanish Civil War*
L. F. SCHAEFER (ed.): *The Ethiopian Crisis*
J. L. SNELL (ed.): *The Nazi Revolution*
J. L. SNELL (ed.): *The Outbreak of the Second World War*
D. E. LEE (ed.): *Munich*
S. M. OSGOOD (ed.): *The Fall of France, 1940*
N. A. GRAEBNER (ed.): *The Cold War*.

E. H. HOBSBAWM: *The Age of Revolution: Europe 1789–1848* (London, 1962).
R. F. LESLIE: *The Age of Transformation* (London, 1964).
K. R. PERRY: *The Bourgeois Century. A History of Europe 1780–1870* (London, 1972).
F. L. FORD: *Europe 1780–1830* (London, 1971).
J. ROBERTS: *Revolution and Improvement. The Western World 1775–1847* (London, 1976).
C. BRINTON: *A Decade of Revolution 1789–1799* (New York, 1943).
G. BRUUN: *Europe and the French Imperium 1799–1814* (New York, 1938).
N. HAMPSON: *The First European Revolution* (London, 1969).
R. R. PALMER: *The World of the French Revolution* (London, 1971).
G. RUDÉ: *Revolutionary Europe 1783–1815* (London, 1964).
J. GODECHOT, B. HYSLOP and D. DOWD: *The Napoleonic Era in Europe* (New York, 1971).
D. THOMSON: *Europe Since Napoleon* (London, 1957).
R. ALBRECHT-CARRIÉ (ed.): *The Concert of Europe* (London, 1968).
H. G. SCHENK: *The Aftermath of the Napoleonic Wars* (London, 1947).
F. B. ARTZ: *Reaction and Revolution 1814–1832* (New York, 1932).
J. DROZ: *Europe Between Revolutions 1815–1848* (London, 1967).
M. S. ANDERSON: *The Ascendancy of Europe 1815–1914* (London, 1972).
M. WALKER (ed.): *Metternich's Europe* (London, 1968).

Bibliography

W. N. MEDLICOTT: *From Metternich to Hitler* (London, 1963).

L. C. B. SEAMAN: *Vienna to Versailles* (London, 1955).

E. H. CARR: *From Napoleon to Stalin and Other Essays* (London, 1980).

J. WEISS: *Conservatism in Europe 1770–1945* (London, 1977).

E. L. WOODWARD: *Three Studies in European Conservatism* (London, 1963).

R. ALBRECHT-CARRIÉ: *A Diplomatic History of Europe Since the Congress of Vienna* (London, 1958).

J. L. TALMON: *Romanticism and Revolt. Europe 1815–1848* (London, 1967).

W. L. LANGER: *Political and Social Upheaval 1832–1852* (New York, 1969).

F. FEJTÖ (ed.): *The Opening of an Era: 1848* (New York, 1966).

D. WARD: *1848. The Fall of Metternich and the Year of Revolution* (London, 1970).

J. SIGMAN: *1848. The Romantic and Democratic Revolutions in Europe*, trans. (London, 1973).

P. N. STEARNS: *The Revolutions of 1848* (London, 1974).

F. EYCK (ed.): *The Revolutions of 1848–49* (Edinburgh, 1972).

E. J. HOBSBAWM: *The Age of Capital 1848–1875* (London, 1975).

L. L. SNYDER (ed.): *Fifty Major Documents of the Nineteenth Century* (Princeton, N.J., 1955).

G. A. KERTESZ (ed.): *Documents in the Political History of the European Continent 1815–1939* (Oxford, 1968).

N. RICH: *The Age of Nationalism and Reform 1850–1890* (London, 1971).

H. GOLLWITZER: *Europe in the Age of Imperialism 1880–1914* (London, 1969).

A. J. P. TAYLOR: *The Struggle for Mastery in Europe 1848–1918* (Oxford, 1954).

M. S. ANDERSON: *The Eastern Question 1774–1923* (London, 1966).

W. N. MEDLICOTT: *The Congress of Berlin and After* (London, 1963).

W. L. LANGER: *European Alliances and Alignments 1871–1890* (New York, 1931).

W. L. LANGER: *The Diplomacy of Imperialism* (New York and London, 1935).

D. K. DERRY and T. L. JARMAN: *The European World 1870–1945* (London, 1951).

C. J. H. HAYES: *A Generation of Materialism 1871–1900* (New York, 1941).

J. JOLL: *Europe Since 1870* (London, 1973).

J. M. ROBERTS: *Europe 1880–1945* (London, 1967).

J. R. WESTERN: *The End of European Primacy* (London, 1965).

G. LICHTHEIM: *Europe in the Twentieth Century* (London, 1972).

R. O. PAXTON: *Europe in the Twentieth Century* (New York, 1975).

H. W. KOCH (ed.): *The Origins of the First World War* (London, 1972).

J. RÖHL: *1914: Delusion or Design?* (London, 1973).

P. KENNEDY (ed.): *The War Plans of the Great Powers 1880–1914* (London, 1979).

F. FISCHER: *Germany's Aims in the First World War*, trans. (London, 1967).

F. FISCHER: *World Power or Decline. The Controversy over Germany's Aims in the First World War*, trans. (London, 1974).

J. C. KING (ed.): *The First World War* (London, 1972).

D. F. FLEMING: *The Origins and Legacies of World War I* (London, 1969).

M. FERRO: *The Great War 1914–1918*, trans. (London, 1973).

Aspects of European History 1789–1980

A. J. P. TAYLOR: *War by Timetable* (London, 1969).

A. J. P. TAYLOR: *The First World War* (London, 1963).

M. GILBERT: *The European Powers 1900–45* (London, 1965).

S. MARKS: *The Illusion of Peace, International Relations in Europe 1918–1933* (London, 1976).

M. TRACHTENBERG: *Reparation in World Politics* (London, 1980).

H. W. GATZKE: *European Diplomacy Between Two Wars, 1919–1939* (Chicago, 1972).

E. H. CARR: *The Twenty Years' Crisis 1919–1939* (London, 1939).

A. ADAMTHWAITE (ed.): *The Lost Peace* (London, 1980).

M. GILBERT and R. SCOTT: *The Appeasers* (London, 1963).

E. WISKEMANN: *Europe of the Dictators* (London, 1966).

F. P. WALTERS: *A History of the League of Nations* (London and New York, 1960).

E. LUARD (ed.): *The Evolution of International Institutions* (London and New York, 1966).

G. SCOTT: *The Rise and Fall of the League of Nations* (London, 1973).

R. HENIG (ed.): *The League of Nations* (Edinburgh, 1973).

C. M. KIMMICH: *Germany and the League of Nations* (Chicago, 1976).

M. BEAUMONT: *The Origins of the Second World War* (London, 1961).

A. J. P. TAYLOR: *The Origins of the Second World War* (London, 1961).

E. M. ROBERTSON (ed.): *The Origins of the Second World War* (London, 1971).

P. CALVOCORESSI and G. WINT: *Total War* (London, 1972).

B. H. LIDDELL HART: *History of the Second World War* (London, 1970).

W. LAQUEUR: *Europe Since Hitler* (London, 1970).

P. CALVOCORESSI: *World Politics Since 1945* (London, 1968).

S. C. EASTON: *A World History Since 1945* (San Francisco, 1968).

J. WATSON: *Success in Twentieth Century World Affairs* (London, 1974).

A. FONTAINE: *History of the Cold War*, trans. (London, 1969–70).

E. LUARD (ed.): *The Cold War: A Re-appraisal* (London, 1964).

L. J. HALLE: *The Cold War as History* (London, 1967).

D. HOROWITZ: *From Yalta to Vietnam* (rev. London, 1967).

C. BOWN and P. MOONEY: *Cold War to Détente* (London, 1976).

F. S. NORTHEDGE (ed.): *The Foreign Policies of the Powers* (London, 1968).

H. G. NICHOLAS: *The United Nations as a Political Institution* (London and New York, 1975).

M. HILL: *The United Nations System* (Cambridge, 1978).

The Fontana Economic History of Europe (London):

    3 *The Industrial Revolution*

    4 *The Emergence of Industrial Societies*, 2 vols

    5 *The Twentieth Century*, 2 vols

    6 *Contemporary Economics*, 2 vols.

D. H. ALDCROFT: *The European Economy 1914–1980* (London, 1978).

S. B. CLOUGH, T. MOODIE and C. MOODIE (eds): *Economic History of Europe: Twentieth Century* (London, 1969).

S. POLLARD: *European Economic Integration 1815–1970* (London, 1974).

A. WATSON: *Europe at Risk* (London, 1977).

H. ARBUTHNOTT and G. EDWARDS (eds.): *A Common Man's Guide to the*

Bibliography

Common Market (London, 1979).

P. COFFEY: *Economic Policies of the Common Market* (London, 1979).

G. IONESCU: *The New Politics of European Integration* (London, 1972).

J. M. VAN BRABANT: *Socialist Economic Integration* (Cambridge, 1980).

M. B. BROWN: *The Economics of Imperialism* (Harmondsworth, Middx, 1974).

G. LICHTHEIM: *Imperialism* (Harmondsworth, Middx, 1971).

D. K. FIELDHOUSE: *The Colonial Empires. A Comparative Survey* (London, 1966).

D. K. FIELDHOUSE: *Colonialism 1870–1945* (London, 1981).

P. D. CURTIN (ed.): *Imperialism* (London, 1971).

W. J. MOMMSEN: *Theories of Imperialism* (London, 1980).

R. ROBINSON and J. GALLAGHER: *Africa and the Victorians* (London, 1961).

F. BROCKWAY: *The Colonial Revolution* (Hart-Davis, St Albans, Herts., 1973).

A. D. SMITH (ed.): *Nationalist Movements* (London, 1976).

R. EMERSON: *From Empire to Nation* (Cambridge, Mass., 1960).

H. KOHN and W. SOKOLSKY (eds): *African Nationalism in the Twentieth Century* (Princeton, N.J., 1965).

E. H. CARR: *Nationalism and After* (1945).

H. KOHN: *Prophets and Peoples. Studies in Nineteenth Century Nationalism* (1946).

H. SETON-WATSON: *Nations and States* (London, 1977).

K. W. DEUTSCH: *Nationalism and its Alternatives* (New York, 1969).

H. LUBASZ: *Fascism: Three Major Regimes* (New York and Toronto, 1973).

G. L. MOSSE (ed.): *International Fascism* (London and Beverly Hills, 1979).

E. NOLTE: *Three Faces of Fascism* (New York, 1963).

M. KITCHEN: *Fascism* (London, 1976).

F. CARSTEN: *The Rise of Fascism* (London, 1967).

M. VAJDA: *Fascism as a Mass Movement* (London and New York, 1976).

S. J. WOOLF (ed.): *The Nature of Fascism* (London, 1968).

P. HAYES: *Fascism* (London, 1973).

R. N. CAREW HUNT: *Theory and Practice of Communism* (Harmondsworth, Middx, 1963).

C. WRIGHT MILLS: *The Marxists* (Harmondsworth, Middx, 1963).

I. DEUTSCHER: *Marxism in Outline* (London, 1972).

D. MCLELLAN: *Marx* (London, 1975).

D. MCLELLAN: *Engels* (London, 1975).

N. MCINNES: *The Western Marxists* (London, 1972).

G. R. URBAN (ed.): *Eurocommunism, its Roots and Future in Italy and Elsewhere* (London, 1978).

FRANCE

J. P. T. BURY: *France 1815–1940* (London, 1949).

D. W. BROGAN: *The French Nation from Napoleon to Pétain 1814–1940* (London, 1957).

A. COBBAN: *France Since the Revolution* (London, 1970).

Aspects of European History 1789–1980

A. COBBAN: *A History of Modern France*, 3 Vols (Harmondsworth, Middx, 1969–70).

T. ZELDIN: *France 1848–1945*, 2 Vols (Oxford, 1973).

D. JOHNSON (ed.): *French Society and the Revolution* (Cambridge, 1976).

W. DOYLE: *Origins of the French Revolution* (Oxford, 1980).

J. GODECHOT: *France and the Atlantic Revolution of the Eighteenth Century, 1770–1799* (New York, 1965).

J. KAPLOW (ed.): *France on the Eve of Revolution* (New York, 1965).

P. H. BEIK (ed.): *The French Revolution* (London, 1970).

A. COBBAN: *The Social Interpretation of the French Revolution* (Cambridge, 1964).

A. COBBAN: *Aspects of the French Revolution* (London, 1968).

A. COBBAN: *The Debate on the French Revolution* (London, 1950).

O. CONNELLY: *French Revolution/Napoleonic Era* (New York, 1979).

N. HAMPSON: *A Social History of the French Revolution* (London and Toronto, 1963).

L. MADELIN: *The French Revolution*, trans. (London, 1916).

G. LEFEBVRE: *The French Revolution from 1793 to 1799*, trans. (London and New York, 1964).

J. M. ROBERTS: *The French Revolution* (Oxford, 1978).

A. SOBOUL: *The French Revolution 1787–1799*. 2 Vols, trans. (London, 1974).

M. J. SYDENHAM: *The French Revolution* (London, 1965).

M. J. SYDENHAM: *The First French Republic 1792–1804* (London, 1974).

J. M. THOMPSON: *The French Revolution* (Oxford, 1943).

A. GOODWIN: *The French Revolution* (London, 1953).

R. BEN JONES: *The French Revolution* (London, 1967).

J. M. THOMPSON: *Leaders of the French Revolution* (London, 1929).

M. J. SYDENHAM: *The Girondins* (London, 1961).

G. RUDÉ: *The Crowd in the French Revolution* (Oxford, 1959).

D. I. WRIGHT (ed.): *The French Revolution: Introductory Documents* (Queensland, 1975).

D. I. WRIGHT: *Revolution and Terror in France 1789–1795* (London, 1974).

C. HIBBERT: *The French Revolution* (London, 1980).

N. HAMPSON: *Danton* (London, 1978).

J. L. CARR: *Robespierre* (London, 1972).

N. HAMPSON: *The Life and Opinions of Maximilien Robespierre* (London, 1974).

G. RUDÉ: *Robespierre* (London, 1975).

J. M. THOMPSON: *Robespierre and the French Revolution* (London, 1952).

M. LYONS: *France Under the Directory* (Cambridge, 1975).

R. B. HOLTMAN: *The Napoleonic Revolution* (Philadelphia, PA., 1967).

J. BOWLE: *Napoleon* (London, 1973).

V. CRONIN: *Napoleon* (London, 1971).

P. GEYL: *Napoleon, For and Against* (London, 1949).

M. HUTT (ed.): *Napoleon* (Englewood Cliffs, N.J., 1972).

R. BEN JONES: *Napoleon: Man and Myth* (London, 1977).

F. MARKHAM: *Napoleon* (London, 1963).

J. M. THOMPSON: *Napoleon Bonaparte: His Rise and Fall* (Oxford, 1953).

Bibliography

E. TARLÉ: *Napoleon's Invasion of Russia* (London, 1942).

H. A. L. FISHER: *Bonapartism.*

J. GODECHOT, B. HYSLOP and D. DOWD: *The Napoleonic Era in Europe* (New York, 1971).

I. COLLINS (ed.): *Government and Society in France, 1814–1848* (London, 1970).

J. and M. LOUGH: *An Introduction to Nineteenth-Century France* (London, 1978).

J. M. MERRIMAN (ed.): *1830 in France* (New York and London, 1975).

P. H. BEIK: *Louis Philippe and the July Monarchy* (Princeton, N.J., 1965).

T. E. B. HOWARTH: *Citizen King* (London, 1961).

R. PRICE (ed.): *1848 in France* (London, 1975).

R. PRICE (ed.): *Revolution and Reaction. 1848 and the Second Republic* (London and New York, 1975).

P. GUEDALLA: *The Second Empire* (London, 1946).

J. M. THOMPSON: *Louis Napoleon and the Second Empire* (Oxford, 1954).

T. ZELDIN: *Émile Ollivier and the Liberal Empire of Napoleon III.*

T. ARONSON: *The Fall of the Third Napoleon.*

W. H. C. SMITH: *Napoleon III.*

G. P. GOOCH: *The Second Empire* (London, 1960).

M. HOWARD: *The Franco-Prussian War* (London, 1961).

A. HORNE: *The Fall of Paris* (London, 1965).

R. L. WILLIAMS: *The French Revolution of 1870–1871* (London, 1969).

J. P. T. BURY: *Gambetta and the Making of the Third Republic* (London, 1973).

R. D. ANDERSON: *France 1870–1914* (London, 1977).

D. W. BROGAN: *The Development of Modern France (1870–1939)* (London, 1940).

D. THOMSON: *Democracy in France since 1870* (Oxford, 1946).

M. CURTIS: *Three Against the Republic* (Princeton, N.J., 1959).

J. HAMPDEN JACKSON: *Clemenceau and the Third Republic* (London, 1946).

D. R. ROBSON: *Georges Clemenceau. A Political Biography* (London, 1974).

R. KEDWARD: *The Dreyfus Affair* (London, 1965).

D. JOHNSON: *France and the Dreyfus Affair* (London, 1966).

H. TINT: *France since 1918* (London, 1970).

P. OUSTON: *France in the Twentieth Century* (London, 1972).

J. NÉRÉ: *The Foreign Policy of France from 1914 to 1945*, trans. (London, 1975).

W. L. SHIRER: *The Collapse of the Third Republic* (London, 1970).

J. P. T. BURY: *France: The Insecure Peace* (London, 1972).

A. ADAMTHWAITE: *France and the Coming of the Second World War* (London, 1977).

W. KNAPP: *France: Partial Eclipse* (London, 1972).

S. HOFFMAN: *Decline or Renewal? France since the 1930s* (New York, 1960).

H. TINT: *French Foreign Policy Since the Second World War* (London, 1972).

S. SERFATY: *France, De Gaulle, and Europe* (Baltimore, 1968).

P. M. WILLIAMS and M. HARRISON: *Politics and Society in De Gaulle's Republic* (London, 1971).

P. AVRIL: *Politics in France* (London, 1969).

Aspects of European History 1789–1980

D. L. HANLEY, A. P. KERR, N. H. WAITES: *Contemporary France, Politics and Society since 1945* (London and Boston, 1979).

GERMANY

A. RAMM: *Germany 1789–1919* (London, 1967).

H. W. KOCH: *A History of Prussia* (London, 1978).

E. J. FEUCHTWANGER: *Prussia: Myth and Reality* (London, 1970).

A. J. P. TAYLOR: *The Course of German History* (London, 1945).

E. J. PASSANT: *A Short History of Germany 1815–1945* (Cambridge, 1959).

W. CARR: *A History of Germany 1815–1945* (London, 1969).

H. HOLBORN: *A History of Modern Germany*, Vol. 3, 1840–1945 (London, 1969).

G. A. CRAIG: *Germany 1866–1945* (Oxford, 1978).

G. L. MOSSE: *The Crisis of German Ideology* (London, 1964).

W. M. SIMON (ed.): *Germany in the Age of Bismarck* (London, 1968).

T. ARONSON: *The Kaisers* (London, 1971).

A. PALMER: *Bismarck* (London, 1976).

F. B. M. HOLLYDAY (ed.): *Bismarck* (Engelwood Cliffs, N.J., 1970).

A. J. P. TAYLOR: *Bismarck: The Man and the Statesman* (London, 1955).

O. PFLANZE: *Bismarck and the Development of Germany* (Princeton, N.J., 1963).

W. N. MEDLICOTT: *Bismarck and Modern Germany* (London, 1965).

W. N. MEDLICOTT and D. K. COVENEY: *Bismarck and Europe* (London, 1971).

D. CALLEO: *The German Problem Reconsidered* (Cambridge, 1978).

E. EYCK: *Bismarck and the German Empire* (London, 1950).

H. BÖHME (ed.): *The Foundation of the German Empire. Select Documents* (Oxford, 1971).

K. S. PINSON: *Modern Germany* (New York, 1954).

J. J. SHEEHAN (ed.): *Imperial Germany* (New York and London, 1976).

H. KURTZ: *The Second Reich* (London, 1970).

M. BALFOUR: *The Kaiser and His Times* (London, 1964).

A. PALMER: *The Kaiser* (London, 1978).

K. H. JARAUSCH: *The Enigmatic Chancellor. Bethmann Hollweg and the Hubris of Imperial Germany* (New Haven, Conn. and London, 1973).

J. RÖHL: *From Bismarck to Hitler* (Harlow, Essex, 1970).

V. R. BERGHAHN: *Germany and the Approach of War in 1914* (London, 1973).

H. C. MEYER (ed.): *Germany from Empire to Ruin 1913–1945* (London, 1973).

E. FEUCHTWANGER (ed.): *Upheaval and Continuity. A Century of German History* (London, 1977).

A. J. RYDER: *Twentieth-Century Germany: from Bismarck to Brandt* (London, 1973).

V. R. BERGHAHN and M. KITCHEN (eds): *Germany in the Age of Total War* (London and New Jersey, 1981).

E. EYCK: *A History of the Weimar Republic*, 2 Vols (London and Cambridge, Mass., 1962).

Bibliography

A. NICHOLLS and E. MATTHIAS (eds): *German Democracy and the Triumph of Hitler* (London, 1971).

J. HIDEN: *Germany and Europe 1919–1939* (London, 1977).

J. R. P. MCKENZIE: *Weimar Germany 1918–1933* (London, 1971).

A. J. NICHOLLS: *Weimar and the Rise of Hitler* (London, 1968).

M. GILBERT: *Britain and Germany between the Wars* (London, 1964).

S. DELMER: *Weimar Germany* (London, 1972).

A. ASHKENASI: *Modern German Nationalism* (Cambridge, Mass., 1976).

R. KNAUERHASE: *An Introduction to National Socialism 1920–1939* (Columbus, OH., 1972).

J. NOAKES (ed.): *Government Party and People in Nazi Germany* (Exeter, 1980).

K. D. BRACHER: *The German Dictatorship*, trans. (London, 1970).

A. BULLOCK: *Hitler: a Study in Tyranny* (London, 1952).

W. CARR: *Hitler: A Study in Personality and Politics* (London, 1978).

J. C. FEST: *Hitler*, trans. (London, 1974).

N. STONE: *Hitler* (London, 1980).

W. L. SHIRER: *The Rise and Fall of the Third Reich* (London, 1960).

E. B. WHEATON: *Prelude to Calamity: The Nazi Revolution 1933–35* (London, 1968).

P. D. STACHURA (ed.): *The Shaping of the Nazi State* (London, 1978).

K. D. BRACHER: op. cit.

D. ORLOW: *The History of the Nazi Party*, 2 Vols (Pittsburgh, 1969, 1973).

H. GLASER: *The Cultural Roots of National Socialism* (London, 1978).

J. C. FEST: *The Face of the Third Reich*, trans. (London, 1970).

K. HILDEBRAND: *The Foreign Policy of the Third Reich*, trans. (London, 1973).

E. M. ROBERTSON: *Hilter's Pre-War Policy* (London, 1963).

J. P. STERN: *Hitler. The Führer and the People* (London, 1975).

R. GRUNBERGER: *A Social History of the Third Reich* (London, 1971).

K. SONTHEIMER: *The Government and Politics of West Germany*, trans. (London, 1972).

M. BALFOUR: *West Germany* (London, 1968).

T. PRITTIE: *Konrad Adenauer 1876–1967* (London, 1972).

T. PRITTIE: *Willy Brandt. Portrait of a Statesman* (London, 1974).

G. SMITH: *Democracy in Western Germany* (London, 1979).

IMPERIAL RUSSIA/USSR

B. PARES: *A History of Russia* (London, 1926).

B. H. SUMNER: *Survey of Russian History* (London, 1944).

G. VERNADSKY: *A History of Russia* (New Haven, Conn., 1929).

L. KOCHAN: *The Making of Modern Russia* (London, 1962).

B. DMYTRYSHYN (ed.): *Imperial Russia. A Source Book*, 1700–1917 (Hinsdale, Ill., 1974).

M. T. FLORINSKY: *Russia: A History and Interpretation*, 2 Vols (London, 1953).

H. SETON-WATSON: *The Russian Empire 1801–1917* (London, 1967).

Aspects of European History 1789–1980

J. N. WESTWOOD: *Endurance and Endeavour. Russian History 1812–1971* (Oxford, 1973).

M. RAEFF: *Plans for Political Reform in Imperial Russia 1730–1905* (Englewood Cliffs, N.J., 1966).

W. LAQUEUR: *Russia and Germany. A Century of Conflict* (London, 1965).

A. PALMER: *Alexander I* (London, 1974).

W. BRUCE LINCOLN: *Nicholas I* (London, 1978).

W. E. MOSSE: *Alexander II and the Modernization of Russia* (London, 1958).

D. FIELD: *The End of Serfdom. Nobility and Bureaucracy in Russia 1855–1861* (Cambridge, Mass. and London, 1976).

R. F. BYRNES: *Pobedonostsev. His Life and Thought* (Bloomington, Indiana, 1968).

H. SETON-WATSON: *The Decline of Imperial Russia 1855–1914* (London, 1952).

T. G. STAVROU (ed.): *Russia under the Last Tsar* (University of Minnesota Press, Minneapolis, 1969).

B. PARES: *The Fall of the Russian Monarchy* (London, 1939).

M. T. FLORINSKY: *The End of the Russian Empire* (New York, 1931).

R. CHARQUES: *The Twilight of Imperial Russia* (London, 1965).

D. FLOYD: *Russia in Revolt* (London, 1969).

G. KATKOV: *Russia 1917. The February Revolution* (London, 1967).

E. WILSON: *To the Finland Station* (London, 1940).

A. ULAM: *Lenin and the Bolsheviks* (London, 1966).

L. KOCHAN: *Russia in Revolution 1890–1918* (London, 1967).

H. SHUKMAN: *Lenin and the Russian Revolution* (London, 1966).

G. KATKOV and H. SHUKMAN: *Lenin's Path to Power* (London, 1971).

M. C. MORGAN: *Lenin* (London, 1971).

P. DUKES: *October and the World* (London, 1979).

L. FISCHER: *The Life of Lenin* (London, 1965).

L. SCHAPIRO and P. REDDAWAY (eds): *Lenin, The Man, The Theorist, The Leader* (London, 1969).

A. RABINOWITCH: *The Bolsheviks Come to Power* (New York, 1976).

R. MEDVEDEV: *The October Revolution* (London, 1979).

J. L. H. KEEP: *The Russian Revolution. A Study of Mass Mobilization* (London, 1976).

E. H. CARR: *The Russian Revolution from Lenin to Stalin, 1917–1929* (London, 1979).

E. H. CARR: *The Bolshevik Revolution 1917–1923*, 3 Vols (London, 1950).

E. H. CARR: *The Interregnum 1923–1924* (London, 1954).

E. H. CARR: *Socialism in One Country 1924–1926*, 3 Vols (London, 1958).

E. H. CARR and R. W. DAVIES: *Foundations of a Planned Economy 1926–1929*, 3 Vols (London, 1969).

I. DEUTSCHER: *The Prophet Armed; Trotsky: 1879–1921* (Oxford, 1954).

I. DEUTSCHER: *The Prophet Unarmed; Trotsky: 1921–1929* (Oxford, 1959).

I. DEUTSCHER: *The Prophet Outcast; Trotsky: 1929–1940* (Oxford, 1963).

W. LAQUEUR: *The Fate of the Revolution. Interpretations of Soviet History* (London, 1967).

R. PIPES: *The Formation of the Soviet Union* (Cambridge, Mass., 1954).

Bibliography

J. BRADLEY: *Allied Intervention in Russia* (London, 1968).

J. NETTL: *The Soviet Achievement* (London, 1967).

I. DEUTSCHER: *The Unfinished Revolution 1917–1967* (Oxford, 1967).

A. ULAM: *A History of Soviet Russia* (New York, 1976).

G. F. KENNAN: *Soviet Foreign Policy 1917–1941* (Princeton, N.J., 1960).

G. F. KENNAN: *Russia and the West Under Lenin and Stalin* (New York, 1960).

T. H. RIGBY (ed.): *Stalin* (Englewood Cliffs, N.J., 1966).

I. DEUTSCHER: *Stalin. A Political Biography* (Oxford, 1949).

I. GREY: *Stalin. Man of History* (London, 1979).

R. HINGLEY: *Joseph Stalin: Man and Legend* (London, 1974).

R. PAYNE: *The Rise and Fall of Stalin* (London, 1966).

A. B. ULAM: *Stalin. The Man and his Era* (London, 1973).

R. V. DANIELS: *The Stalin Revolution. Fulfilment or Betrayal of Leninism?* (Lexington, Mass., 1965).

A. SEATON: *Stalin as Warlord* (London, 1976).

A. NOVE: *Stalinism and After* (London, 1975).

R. CONQUEST: *The Great Terror* (London, 1968).

E. CRANKSHAW: *Khrushchev* (London, 1966).

A. BRUMBERG (ed.): *Russia Under Kruschev* (London, 1962).

A. BROWN and M. KASER (eds): *The Soviet Union Since the Fall of Khrushchev* (New York, 1975).

A. DALLIN and T. B. LARSON (eds): *Soviet Politics Since Khrushchev* (Englewood Cliffs, N.J., 1968).

D. R. KELLY: *Soviet Politics in the Brezhnev Era* (New York, 1980).

L. PIETROMARCHI: *The Soviet World*, trans. (London, 1965).

G. M. CARTER: *The Government of the Soviet Union* (New York, 1949).

R. W. DAVIES: *The Soviet Union* (London, 1978).

A. Z. RUBINSTEIN: *Soviet Foreign Policy Since World War II* (Cambridge, Mass., 1981).

N. V. SIVACHEV and N. N. YAKOVLEV: *Russia and the United States* (Chicago, 1979).

A. G. MAZOUR (ed.): *Soviet Economic Development. Operation Outstrip 1921–1965.* (Princeton, N.J., 1967).

M. DOBB: *Soviet Economic Development since 1917* (London, 1966).

R. J. HILL and P. FRANK: *The Soviet Communist Party* (London, 1981).

THE HABSBURG EMPIRE, AUSTRIA, CZECHOSLOVAKIA, HUNGARY

A. KANN: *A History of the Habsburg Empire 1526–1918* (Los Angeles and London, 1974).

A. J. P. TAYLOR: *The Habsburg Monarchy 1809–1918* (London, 1948).

C. A. MACARTNEY: *The Habsburg Empire 1790–1918* (London, 1969).

C. A. MACARTNEY: *The House of Austria. The Later Phase 1790–1918* (Edinburgh, 1978).

A. PALMER: *Metternich* (London, 1972).

A. MILNE: *Metternich* (London, 1975).

E. F. KRAEHE (ed.): *The Metternich Controversy* (New York, 1971).

Aspects of European History 1789–1980

R. J. RATH: *The Viennese Revolution of 1848* (New York, 1957).

F. R. BRIDGE: *From Sadowa to Sarajevo* (London, 1972).

A. J. MAY: *The Passing of the Habsburg Monarchy 1914–1918*, 2 Vols (Philadelphia, PA, 1966).

Z. A. B. ZEMAN: *The Break-up of the Habsburg Empire 1914–1918* (London, 1961).

Z. A. B. ZEMAN: *Twilight of the Habsburgs* (London, 1971).

E. CRANKSHAW: *The Fall of the House of Habsburg* (London, 1963).

K. R. STADLER: *Austria* (London, 1971).

L. VALIANI: *The End of Austria-Hungary*, trans. (London, 1973).

E. BARBER: *Austria 1918–1972* (London, 1973).

M. KITCHEN: *The Coming of Austrian Fascism* (London, 1980).

J. W. BRUEGEL: *Czechoslovakia Before Munich* (Cambridge, 1973).

E. STEINER: *The Slovak Dilemma* (Cambridge, 1973).

S. H. THOMSON: *Czechoslovakia in European History* (Princeton, N.J., 1943).

R. W. SETON-WATSON: *A History of the Czechs and Slovaks* (London, 1943).

J. KORBEL: *Twentieth-Century Czechoslovakia* (New York, 1977).

W. V. WALLACE: *Czechoslovakia* (London, 1976).

C. A. MACARTNEY: *Hungary. A Short History* (Edinburgh, 1962).

D. SINOR: *A History of Hungary* (New York, 1959).

ITALY

D. MACK SMITH: *Italy. A Modern History* (Ann Arbor, Michigan, 1959).

D. MACK SMITH (ed.): *The Making of Italy 1796–1870* (London, 1968).

S. J. WOOLF: *The Italian Risorgimento* (London, 1969).

D. MACK SMITH: *Cavour and Garibaldi 1860* (Cambridge, 1954).

M. SALVADORI (ed.): *Cavour and the Unification of Italy* (Princeton, N.J., 1961).

D. BEALES (ed.): *The Risorgimento and the Unification of Italy* (London, 1971).

D. MACK SMITH (ed.): *Garibaldi* (Englewood Cliffs, N.J., 1969).

C. HIBBERT: *Garibaldi and his Enemies* (New York, 1965).

J. RIDLEY: *Garibaldi* (London, 1974).

SIR I. KIRKPATRICK: *Mussolini. Study of a Demagogue* (London, 1964).

M. GALLO: *Mussolini's Italy*, trans. (New York, 1973).

R. COLLIER: *Duce! The Rise and Fall of Mussolini* (London, 1971).

E. M. ROBERTSON: *Mussolini as Empire-Builder* (New York, 1977).

M. GALLO: *Mussolini and Italy*, trans. (London, 1973).

C. C. BAYNE-JARDINE: *Mussolini and Italy* (London, 1966).

C. HIBBERT: *Mussolini* (Harmondsworth, Middx, 1975).

D. MACK SMITH: *Mussolini's Roman Empire* (London, 1976).

J. WOOLF (ed.): *The Rebirth of Italy 1943–1950* (London, 1972).

SPAIN

S. G. PAYNE: *A History of Spain and Portugal*, 2 Vols (University of Wisconsin Press, Wisconsin, 1973).

Bibliography

W. C. ATKINSON: *A History of Spain and Portugal* (Harmondsworth, Middx, 1960).

H. LIVERMORE: *A History of Spain* (London, 1958).

R. M. SMITH: *Spain. A Modern History* (Michigan, 1965).

R. CARR: *Spain 1808–1939* (Oxford, 1966).

R. CARR: *Modern Spain 1875–1980* (Oxford, 1980).

R. CARR: *The Spanish Tragedy* (London, 1977).

R. FRASER: *Blood of Spain* (London, 1979).

G. HILLS: *Franco* (London, 1967).

D. A. PUZZO (ed.): *The Spanish Civil War* (New York, 1969).

R. PAYNE: *The Civil War in Spain 1936–1939* (London, 1962).

S. G. PAYNE: *The Spanish Revolution* (London, 1970).

R. A. H. ROBINSON: *The Origins of Franco's Spain* (London, 1970).

H. THOMAS: *The Spanish Civil War* (London, 1961).

R. CARR and J..P. F. AIZPURUA: *Spain: Dictatorship to Democracy* (London, 1979).

M. GALLO: *Spain Under Franco*, trans. (London, 1973).

OTHER STATES

O. HALECKI: *A History of Poland* (London, 1978).

R. F. LESLIE (ed.): *The History of Poland Since 1863* (Cambridge, 1980).

M. B. PETROVICH: *A History of Modern Serbia*, 2 Vols (New York and London, 1976).

S. K. PAVLOWITCH: *Yugoslavia* (London, 1971).

S. CLISSOLD (ed.): *A Short History of Yugoslavia* (Cambridge, 1966).

S. G. EVANS: *A Short History of Bulgaria* (London, 1960).

G. J. BOBANGO: *The Emergence of the Romanian National State* (New York, 1979).

E. H. CROSSMAN: *The Low Countries 1780–1940 (Oxford, 1978)*.

T. K. DERRY: *A History of Scandinavia* (London, 1970).

J. CAMPBELL and P. SHERRARD: *Modern Greece* (London, 1968).

S. J. SHAW and E. K. SHAW: *A History of the Ottoman Empire and Modern Turkey*. Vol. II: *Reform, Revolution, and Republic: The Rise of Modern Turkey, 1808–1975* (Cambridge, 1977).